Thomas Jefferson's Lives

JEFFERSONIAN AMERICA

Peter S. Onuf and Andrew O'Shaughnessy, Editors

THOMAS JEFFERSON'S LIVES

Biographers and the Battle for History

Edited by
Robert M. S. McDonald

UNIVERSITY OF VIRGINIA PRESS / Charlottesville and London

University of Virginia Press
© 2019 by the Rector and Visitors of the University of Virginia
All rights reserved
Printed in the United States of America on acid-free paper

First published 2019

ISBN 978-0-8139-4291-9 (cloth)
ISBN 978-0-8139-4292-6 (ebook)

9 8 7 6 5 4 3 2 1

Library of Congress Cataloging-in-Publication Data
is available from the Library of Congress.

Cover art: Composite of Thomas Jefferson drawn from (*clockwise from top*)
Rembrandt Peale, *Official Presidential Portrait of Jefferson* (1800; Wikimedia);
H. R. Robinson, "Thomas Jefferson—Third President of the United States,"
lithographed and published by H. Robinson, New York & Washington, DC
(1840 and 1851; Library of Congress); obverse of the 2012 Jefferson nickel
(maogg/iStock.com); and stamp printed by the United States to honor
Thomas Jefferson (circa 1960; Spiroview Inc./Shutterstock.com).

For Peter S. Onuf

Contents

Foreword

> But, in a sense, nothing in life is planned—or everything is—
> because in the dance every step is ultimately the corollary of the
> step before; the consequence of being the kind of person one
> chances to be.
> —ANTHONY POWELL, *A Dance to the Music of Time*, 1955

In the way of such things, I happened to read these lines from the first volume of Anthony Powell's panoramic novel of England on my way to Charlottesville in the early summer of 2012 for the conference chronicled in this book, a meeting on "Jefferson's Lives" sponsored by the Sons of the American Revolution and Monticello's Robert H. Smith International Center for Jefferson Studies. Held in honor of Peter S. Onuf, the Thomas Jefferson Foundation Professor of History, emeritus, at the University of Virginia, the conference featured papers (published in the following pages) on major nineteenth- and twentieth-century biographers of Jefferson, by major twentieth- and twenty-first-century scholars of Jefferson.

It was a formidable gathering of formidable people about a formidable topic. As a biographer then in the last stages of preparing a one-volume life of Thomas Jefferson, I thus arrived in Albemarle County with no small amount of trepidation. Although I had written books on Franklin D. Roosevelt, Winston Churchill, Andrew Jackson, and God (and, yes, the first three sometimes confused themselves with the fourth), I knew from experience that Jefferson was of a different order, a man who, with Abraham

Lincoln, contained multitudes that no writer could hope to chart fully. And I was coming to hear a terrific collection of scholars—men and women whose work I knew and admired—put not Jefferson but his biographers in the dock. Writers like to judge, not be judged. Here, then, was a fraught enterprise.

In the end, I found the conference—and I suspect you will find this book—surely humbling but also inspiring. Listening to historians dissect the most noted nineteenth- and twentieth-century biographers of the most noted American of the early republic was of course sobering. From biographies by Henry S. Randall to Dumas Malone and Merrill Peterson, the works under consideration may have seemed, for a time, the final word on their subject. Taken together, these books form an important part of any scholarly or popular library of American history.

Yet when you think about it, there is really no such thing as the last word on a life of consequence. The work of the scholars at the conference and in this book is living testament to the Jeffersonian truth that life should be about the pursuit of reason, and reason, like history, is not static but kinetic. Or, as Powell might put it, every book is a corollary of the ones that have come before.

It is an inevitable dance. Biographies and scholarly works of each age supply readers and, ultimately, writers with insights and angles of vision that inform the thinking and the writing of the next. Beyond the barest listing of encyclopedic facts—a birth date, a list of offices held, a death date—there is no such thing as a totally objective life. Biographies, one sees here, often belong to the ages in which they were written no matter how hard some historians may try to transcend the passions and action of the time of composition. It can be no other. What resonated to nineteenth-century readers failed to engage later generations; and the work of later generations will undoubtedly give way to still other voices and other views.

Scholars like Onuf and Gordon S. Wood (the latter pays tribute to the former in the following pages) are good about reminding us that we are bound to see the world as Jefferson saw it, not as we know it turned out or as we wish it had been. He cannot be ripped out of his time and plunked down in ours. Thus the central role of scholarship to the making of biographies.

And there are the papers—or perhaps I should say the *Papers*. The work of Julian P. Boyd, the first editor of the Jefferson papers, has recently been explored in *A Companion to Thomas Jefferson* (ed. Francis Cogliano) by

Barbara Oberg and James P. McClure, Boyd's wonderful successors at Princeton. Jefferson's own role as his own biographer is examined in this volume by Jefferson Looney, who edits the *Retirement Series* at Charlottesville. In my experience there are only two effective ways to absorb the Jeffersonian ethos: to spend time at Monticello and to read these fine documentary editors' work. Along with the scholarly expeditions of Onuf and his colleagues, Oberg, McClure, and Looney enable us to recover more of that lost world, and more of the lost Jefferson, than we ever could on our own.

Which is, after all, the point of biography: to recapture as responsibly as we can the pressures the protagonist faced, the anxieties he experienced, the fears he harbored, the hopes he nurtured, and the battles he won and lost. There are some figures in our national history about whom we shall see the making of the books without end—Lincoln, Theodore Roosevelt, Franklin D. Roosevelt, and Jefferson chief among them. That is because, I think, all of these men held ultimate power at perilous hours and each fits FDR's 1932 test of a "great" presidency: "All our great Presidents," Roosevelt told the *New York Times Magazine,* "were leaders of thought at times when certain historic ideas in the life of the nation had to be clarified." Biography is one means by which we can seek to discover how greatness was achieved—if it was in fact achieved—when we all know that the historical actors were as flawed and imperfect as we ourselves are.

"I like the dreams of the future better than the history of the past," said Jefferson, but the two—past and future—are, like the head and the heart, contiguous regions with porous borders. The conversation—or, to return to Powell's image, the dance—between what has been written and what shall be is the conversation of nothing less than a civilized people.

My own view of Jefferson, for instance, has undoubtedly been shaped by the two decades I spent in journalism, watching and writing about politicians struggling with real problems in real time. The more I thought about Jefferson, the more I realized that his many apparent contradictions could be largely explained—not excused, but explained—by a deeper appreciation of how he spent most of his days: as a public man seeking or holding public office, fighting to address particular situations amid conflicting opinions and countervailing forces.

Seen as a politician working his way through what George Eliot would call the "dim lights and tangled circumstance" of the world, Jefferson became, for me at least, less enigmatic and more accessible, even admirable, for he found the world one way and left it quite another. Born a subject of Great Britain, Jefferson died as the author of the American promise that all men were created equal—a promise that has taken too long to make fully real, but which Jefferson set in train. Before we judge him too harshly, we should remember Arthur Schlesinger Jr.'s observation that self-righteousness in retrospect is easy—also cheap. Schlesinger's hero, President John F. Kennedy, would have agreed. "No one has a right to grade a President—even poor James Buchanan—who has not sat in his chair, examined the mail and information that came across his desk, and learned why he made his decisions," Kennedy once remarked to the historian David Herbert Donald. A bit of presidential overstatement, to be sure, but the point remains valid: politicians live and work in imperfect worlds, where even imperfect results can represent progress.

One conclusion to be drawn from these essays is that biographies are perishable. One generation's landmark may be another's laughingstock. A conference like the one recorded here is kind of *memento mori:* a reminder that death comes to us all, late and soon.

Rather than a dispiriting thought, however, I found the statement and indeed restatement of that great truth to be liberating. If all of our worldly work is provisional, then the writing of a life is an affirmative vote in the possibility of progress, however limited and however conditional.

Yes, we're all going to die, and yes, at our luckiest our books will be picked apart, if they're not forgotten altogether. Yet the alternative—to assume that everything has been said that's worth saying—is worse, and decidedly un-Jeffersonian. John Adams once outraged Jefferson by suggesting that mankind had essentially learned what there was to learn. Incredulous, Jefferson wrote: "I am among those who think well of the human character generally. . . . It is impossible for a man who takes a survey of what is already known not see to what an immensity in every branch of science yet remains to be discovered." It was, he believed, "cowardly" to think "the human mind is incapable of further advances."

And so the dance goes on.

Jon Meacham

Preface

During Thomas Jefferson's lifetime, Americans united around the supposition that he possessed the potential to change the world. What divided them was whether he would make it better or worse. Although his friends would not have disputed Edmund Randolph's contention that "it constituted a part of Mr. Jefferson's pride to run before the times in which he lived," his critics believed he was running in the wrong direction. Some, who associated Jefferson's political philosophy with the mob rule and butchery of the French Revolution, thought he embodied the "Demon of Jacobinism." Others scorned his alleged "irreligion" and "atheistical creed." Virginia congressman John Nicholas went so far as to describe Jefferson as "one of the most artful, intriguing, . . . and double-faced politicians in all America." Yet Tadeusz Kosciuszko, who left his native Poland to join the Continental army, praised Jefferson's selflessness and termed him "a True American Patriot." On the Kentucky frontier, Elize Winn extolled him as "all thats good and god like," while Margaret Bayard Smith, the well-connected wife of the editor of Washington, D.C.'s *National Intelligencer,* "looked upon Mr. Jefferson as the corner stone on which the edifice of republican liberty was to rest."[1]

The fact that all these people—all of them contemporaries and some of them individuals who knew him personally—possessed different conceptions of Jefferson helps to explain why biographers of later eras did so as well. In 1803, Jefferson assured George Clinton, the New York governor elected a year later to serve as his vice president, that only "multiplied testimony" and "multiplied views" could render a clear estimation of a person's leadership and character: "Much is known to one which is not known to another, and no one knows everything. It is the sum of individual knowledge which is to make up the whole truth." The problem in Jefferson's case is that these divergent views and conflicting testimonials, considered as a whole, seem to scramble the pieces of the puzzle more than fit them together. Even the increasing availability of the 19,000 letters Jefferson sent and the many thousand others he received, made possible since 1950 by the publication, volume by meticulously edited volume, of *The Papers of Thomas Jefferson,* can seem to confuse rather than clarify. As Merrill D. Peterson noted in his 1970 biography, although the third president "left to posterity a vast corpus of papers, private and public, his personality remains elusive. Of all his great contemporaries Jefferson is perhaps the least self-revealing and the hardest to sound to the depths of being."[2]

This volume examines not who Thomas Jefferson was but instead what his biographers made him out to be. It focuses less on history than on historiography—the changing landscape of historical interpretation—to explore the evolution of portrayals of his life. As such, its most proximate predecessor is Peterson's 1960 *The Jefferson Image in the American Mind.* Described by its author as "not a book on the history Thomas Jefferson made but a book on what history made of Thomas Jefferson," it endures as a pioneering landmark in the still-emerging field of "History and Memory" or "Memory Studies." Peterson's analysis explains how interpretations of Jefferson changed over time not only in response to new evidence but also to new generations' interests and preoccupations. In different eras Americans presented Jefferson as "the state rights republican and the majoritarian democrat, the man of Monticello and the party leader, the American and the world citizen." Conscripted to serve Whigs and Democrats, abolitionists and slaveholders, unionists and secessionists, Populists and Progressives, and seemingly every side of just about every subsequent struggle, the only constant was that Jefferson's image remained "a sensitive reflector," as Peterson wrote, "of American's troubled search for the image of itself."[3]

Taken together, this volume's essays yield a similar conclusion as well as an additional insight made possible by the fact that it shares Peterson's purpose while employing a more narrow focus. Like *The Jefferson Image in the American Mind, Thomas Jefferson's Lives* traces the development of depictions of Jefferson in the many decades since the third president's death. Like Peterson's book, this one considers how changes in social, political, economic, and diplomatic environments helped cause views of Jefferson to evolve. But while

Peterson's study cast a wide net upon sources ranging from 1826 eulogies to the records of efforts during World War II to memorialize Jefferson alongside the Tidal Basin in Washington, D.C., the contributors to this volume scrutinize the most elemental of historical sources and genres.

It is probably not particularly controversial to assert that the human past amounts to the life stories of all who have ever lived. On one level history might be understood as the sum of all biography. Yet one of the problems that has made the genre of biography contentious among professional historians is that very few who have lived left records of their experiences, and far fewer had experiences that biographers considered worth recording. The result is that those whose life stories have been told—individuals notable because of their achievements in war, science, statecraft, business, or the arts—have tended to be remarkable rather than representative. Scott Casper's 1999 *Constructing American Lives* illuminates how biographers in the nineteenth century often aimed to bolster readers' patriotism, morality, or admiration of the rags-to-riches stories of self-made strivers. These agendas overshadowed the contributions of common men and women by making exceptional people the norm as biographers' subjects. Scottish writer Thomas Carlyle went so far as to express an extreme manifestation of this phenomenon. "The history of what man has accomplished in this world," he contended in 1840, "is at bottom the History of the Great Men who have worked here. They were the leaders of men, these great ones . . . all things that we see standing accomplished in the world are properly the outer material result, the great practical realisation and embodiment, of Thoughts that dwelt in the Great Men." This goes too far. The world, after all, churns from the bottom up as well as from the top down. Patterns of history, which from one perspective might seem self-evident, from another result from and shape the spontaneous order produced by the past. But even when stepping back from the Great Man theory of history, it remains possible to assert a truth that is difficult to dispute: individuals matter. Their lives can have great influence.[4]

Jefferson believed as much—and not just in the sense eventually understood by George Bailey, the ordinary yet extraordinary character brought to life by actor Jimmy Stewart in Frank Capra's 1946 cinema classic, *It's a Wonderful Life*. This drama, which offered viewers a glimpse of the world had Bailey never been born, spotlighted the ways in which contingency makes a difference. Bailey's acts of common decency influenced the lives of others in profound ways. Bailey made possible the goodness of

Bedford Falls; without him, there would have existed the dystopian Potters-ville. In the twentieth century, the Everyman could be the Great Man. Yet the heroic individualism of Carlyle's nineteenth century took root in the eighteenth, when Americans gradually replaced their deference to members of what Jefferson described as "an artificial aristocracy founded on wealth and birth" with their admiration for the men whose "virtue & talents" qual-ified them for inclusion in what he called the "natural aristocracy." Not all natural aristocrats are created equal, however. Any virtuous and industri-ous person can be great like Bailey. But Francis Bacon, John Locke, and Isaac Newton, whom Jefferson considered "the three greatest men that have ever lived, without any exception," should "not be confounded at all with the herd of other great men." Applying a similar standard as Carlyle, Jefferson insisted that the preeminence of his "trinity" resulted from how their exceptional genius "laid the foundation" for the innovations their dis-coveries made possible.[5]

There is little doubt that Jefferson passes his own litmus test for inclusion in this upper echelon of greatness. His persistent popularity as a subject of biographers and topic for readers has attested to his continuing relevance throughout the history of the United States. While James Thomas Flex-ner described George Washington, the subject of his own works of biogra-phy, as "the indispensable man" because of "his role in the creation of the United States," Thomas Jefferson is the individual indispensable not only to the American people's self-government but also to their education, reli-gious freedom, and territorial expansion. Maybe most important, Jefferson proved essential to Americans' efforts, decades and centuries after his death, to breathe life into the lofty aspirations of the Declaration of Independence. The "self-evident" "truths" that "all men are created equal" in that "they are endowed by their Creator with certain unalienable rights" inspired not only the Revolutionary generation but also the generations that followed. Emboldening abolitionists, suffragettes, civil rights leaders, and countless other champions of liberty, the words Jefferson set on parchment in 1776 contributed to the dynamic expansion of the American ideal. Meanwhile, the contributions of Washington seem set in stone, like the laws brought down by Moses from Mount Sinai. In biblical terms, Washington is Old Tes-tament and Jefferson is New Testament. Joseph Ellis, who has authored biog-raphies of both figures, notes that Washington "is just too patriarchal, too distant," to enjoy a personal connection with modern Americans. Jefferson is different. "Washington is Jehovah, aloof and alone in heaven," Ellis writes, but "Jefferson is Jesus, who came to live among us."[6]

Yet it is Jefferson's continuing relevance—his palpable presence in the here-and-now—that exposes him, a man born more than 275 years ago, to never-ending criticism in the ever-advancing present. Since his death he has been disparaged for everything from his foreign policy to his religious beliefs. His views on slavery and race have been a magnet for censure from all sides. In the Civil War era, proslavery secessionists, noting his Declaration's philosophy of individual rights, criticized his "powder-cask abstractions" and "unreasoning radicalism." A century and a half later, Jefferson had again become a target on the issue of slavery, but not because he opposed it in principle but because he maintained it in practice. During the course of his lifetime, he owned hundreds of men, women, and children. He was so deeply embroiled in the institution of slavery that his first real memory was being carried, as a two-year-old, on a pillow from which he looked up into the face of a man whom the members of his family claimed as their property.[7]

No other member of his generation, northern or southern, even came close to advancing as many measures designed to chip away at the seemingly impenetrable edifice of slavery. That said, the frequency of his acts of opposition to slavery diminished as he aged. Maybe this phenomenon reflected the frustration of a man whose proposals to curb America's dependence on forced labor often failed to win adoption. Maybe it resulted from the pragmatism of a public figure whose antislavery ideas proved increasingly problematic. How to stand against the institution while also holding together a political alliance, rooted in the South, that to him seemed most likely to protect the liberty of the white Americans for whom the Revolution had been fought? Unlike Washington, whose last will and testament provided for the emancipation of all his slaves after the death of his wife, Jefferson died deeply in debt, a fact complicating his efforts to free even a select group of men and women. All were relatives of Jefferson's late wife, who died when he was thirty-nine. Some, it seems likely, were also his own children. The probability that, after his wife's death, he fathered sons and daughters with Sally Hemings, her half-sister, adds to the conundrum of his controversial legacy. It is true that Jefferson stood as a proponent of multitudinous measures aiming to loosen slavery's stranglehold on America. But if the central theme of his life was liberty, there can be no denying the dissonant facts that he lived and died as a slaveholder. "Many of Jefferson's assumptions reveal him to be a man thoroughly of his own time," notes John Boles, one of his most recent biographers, "which sometimes surprises us because we imagine him as so ahead of it."[8]

Biographers accept that individuals can shape history. This volume explores how individual biographers have shaped history as well—or at least its interpretation. It brings together essays by scholars of Jefferson and his era, all of whom embraced the challenge to assess some of the most important accounts of Jefferson's life. We limited ourselves to works published by members of previous generations. To have included more recent contributions, no matter how worthy, might either have compromised our own attempts at objectivity or exposed the compromises of our friends and ourselves. We also focused on works possessing enduring influence. All continue to serve as sources for assessments of the third president; several, although products of their time, asked questions or made observations so timeless that they seem likely to shape the historiography on Jefferson in perpetuity. In addition, to tell a richer, fuller, and more accurate story of how, over the past two centuries, Americans came to know Jefferson, we embraced a broad conception of biography.[9]

Since the battle for history began when the past was still the present, in the first section of this book, "Memory," we begin with Jefferson's attempts to compile and convey his own life story. Through the careful preservation and curation of his correspondence as well as editorial projects such as his "Anas," a collection of firsthand accounts shedding light on the political struggle between his Republican alliance and the Federalist faction steered by his archrival, Alexander Hamilton, Jefferson endeavored to explain himself to posterity. One step removed as a chronicler of Jefferson's life, George Tucker knew his subject personally. Appointed by Jefferson to teach at the University of Virginia, Tucker's 1837 *Life of Thomas Jefferson* relied on letters to which Jefferson's family gave him special access as well as his own knowledge of Jefferson and other protagonists. Tucker's work emerged as one of the first full biographies to gain national renown and endure as a source for subsequent works, such as those assessed in chapter 3. One step removed from Tucker, Henry S. Randall and James Parton never met the man about whom they wrote, but their respective 1858 and 1874 biographies made use of his available papers and the testimony of those who did. Of the two, Randall's was much more of an "authorized" biography, with information provided by Jefferson's relations. But no nineteenth-century account of Jefferson's life not pieced together by Jefferson himself could rival Sarah N. Randolph's 1871 *Domestic Life of Thomas Jefferson* in terms of insider influence. Randolph's book, based almost entirely on letters by or about Randolph's great-grandfather, in the years after the Civil War softened the edges of Jefferson's image by focusing on him as a faithful friend and humble patriarch of a large and loving family. All these works, which muted Jefferson's status as both a slaveholder and critic of slavery, sought to reinforce Jefferson's reputation as a truly national character capable of uniting the affections of Americans in both the North and South.

Perhaps the greatest outlier in this initial section focusing on works by individuals with personal connections to Jefferson is the chapter that considers Henry Adams's 1889–91 *History of the United States during the Administrations of Thomas Jefferson and James Madison.* Although neither a relative nor an acquaintance, Adams had a grandfather and great-grandfather who knew Jefferson well, and both developed a decided ambivalence. What sets Henry Adams apart from his nineteenth-century peers in this collection is his capacity for criticism—which seems an inherited trait. Yet John Quincy Adams and John Adams, sometimes Jefferson's enemies and other times his allies, bequeathed not only their skepticism but also their willingness to feel appreciation, admiration, and even a sense of wonder. Although not a biography per se, Henry Adams's important account made clear that the early republic was, in many regards, an era that Jefferson not only inhabited but also helped shape. The history of its politics parallels the history of his life.

A consideration of Adams's *History* serves as an apt transition from this volume's first section, "Memory," to its more brief consideration of "Rivalry." The old adage that all biographers fall in love with their subjects can be given a corollary. As the essays evaluating Jefferson's portrayal in biographies of Aaron Burr and Alexander Hamilton suggest, the tendency of biographers to empathize with those about whom they write often leads them to share their subjects' antipathies. Although Henry Adams's forbearers had mixed feelings regarding Jefferson, both Burr and Hamilton developed nearly unwavering hostility to their common rival. It should probably not surprise that Burr and Hamilton biographers—all of whom spent many months or even many years viewing the world through the eyes of their protagonist—often present

Jefferson in starkly negative terms. More interesting is how their perceptions of some of Jefferson's alleged vulnerabilities have changed over time, especially given how critiques of other supposed shortcomings have not.

"Rivalry" provides an instructive contrast to the final section, "History," which contains essays examining Jefferson biographies of the twentieth century, when greater access to primary sources by Jefferson and the other inhabitants of his world, together with the professionalization of the practice of history, should have resulted in increasingly full, fair, and factually correct accounts of the third president's life. In many respects they did. Yet historians never surrendered their discipline to pretensions of social science and neither, as some demanded, did they ever succeed in devoting themselves to the pursuit of "the past for its own sake." Peter Novick's *That Noble Dream*, an imposing book imposed on a generation of first-year history graduate students, highlights historians' wavering commitment to "objectivity." Could anyone truly cast aside all bias? If it were possible to conjure all the facts (and it is not), how would a historian know which ones to weave together to tell a story worthy of the attention of the people of the present? Even Herbert Butterfield, the Cambridge historian who in 1931 insisted that "the study of the past with one eye . . . upon the present is the source of all sins and sophistries in history," by 1944 gave his blessing to the "marriage between the present and the past." It was just as well. To the extent that twentieth-century biographies of Jefferson provide a reliable indication, the present and past will never be put asunder.[10]

Of course, more than the times in which scholars live influence the questions they ask and the answers they provide. Jefferson's biographies make clear the importance of the lives of biographers themselves. In the cases of Claude Bowers and Albert Jay Nock, partisanship and ideology shaped the third president's portrayal. For Gilbert Chinard and Marie Kimball, personal background and circumstance piqued interests in culture and society explored through the lens of Jefferson's life. Dumas Malone and Merrill Peterson, history professors at the University of Virginia, did more than any of their predecessors to create enduring and definitive accounts by leveraging all the advantages of modern scholarship. Yet each possessed a blind spot on the issue of Jefferson's likely sexual relationship with Sally Hemings, the enslaved half-sister of his late wife, in no small part because they dismissed it as impossible and unthinkable as well as too damaging to the memory of the man to whom they had devoted much of their lives.

They mistreated not only the evidence of Jefferson's connection with Hemings but also biographer Fawn Brodie. "That woman"—as they sometimes condescended—asserted that Jefferson and Hemings had engaged in a long-term, monogamous relationship resulting in the birth of several children. A University of California at Los Angeles history professor with degrees in English literature but no Ph.D., Brodie might be excused for sometimes eschewing the history discipline's evidentiary standards, but this makes all the more impressive her apparent success as a historical detective. It was the bias of pedigreed professionals that led them to misread the evidence, as law professor Annette Gordon-Reed, one of this volume's contributors, pointed out in her important 1997 book, *Thomas Jefferson and Sally Hemings: An American Controversy*. A team of medical scientists' 1998 revelation that men descended from Hemings seem to share the same genetic marker as male Jeffersons made Brodie's interpretation all the more convincing. By the end of the century, the insights of a writer with a master's in English literature, a lawyer, and a group of scientists seemed to expose that professional historians' "noble dream" of objectivity remained elusive.[11]

In addition to reinforcing our awareness that historical interpretations often reflect the times from which they emerge as well as the interests and commitments of the interpreters, the essays in this volume illuminate a less expected and perhaps more profound phenomenon. The biographers on whose work this volume focuses, whether because of or despite their lives or times, all offered not only interpretations that seem erroneous or dated but also glimpses of what might be described as "the authentic" Thomas Jefferson. It is not surprising that their varying perspectives would lead to different points of view, but it is nonetheless reassuring that different men and women, writing under different circumstances and working from distinct vantage points, could nonetheless render insights that, to our own eyes, register as true. No wonder that Jefferson, despite the vicissitudes of historiography, has for nearly two centuries remained a figure who endures in both his relevance to readers and his ability to attract writers.

This book is in honor Peter Onuf. His distinguished career took him from a Ph.D. at Johns Hopkins to faculty positions at Columbia, Worcester Polytechnic Institute, Southern Methodist, and Oxford, where from 2008 to 2009 he taught as the Harmsworth visiting professor. He retired in 2012 from the University of Virginia after serving for nearly a quarter century as

Thomas Jefferson Foundation professor. His life as a historian continues as the Senior Research Fellow at Monticello's Robert H. Smith International Center for Jefferson Studies. Those who know Peter might question the degree to which it is appropriate to honor him with a volume on this topic. Although always open to all good scholarship, Peter has never been known as a lover of biography. He is well known, however, for his love of irony—a fact that might have figured in his decision to author, with Gordon-Reed, *"Most Blessed of the Patriarchs": Thomas Jefferson and the Empire of Imagination.* Although, as they assert, it is "hardly meant to be a conventional biography of Jefferson that runs chronologically from his birth to his death," it is a biography nonetheless. Their goal was to expose Jefferson as a man with a life so long, with interests so diverse and accomplishments so varied, that he could have rightly claimed, as Walt Whitman claimed for America itself: "Do I contradict myself? Very well, then. . . . I contradict myself; I am large. . . . I contain multitudes." As Peter wrote in his 2007 book, *The Mind of Thomas Jefferson,* "the proliferation of possible Jeffersons does not constitute the failure of the biographical enterprise" but, instead, "the opposite. The search for a single, definitive 'real' Jefferson is a fool's errand, setting us off on a hopeless search for the kind of 'knowledge' that even (especially?) eludes sophisticated moderns in their encounters with each other—and themselves."[12]

In 1992, the editor of this volume, in his fourth year as an undergraduate at the University of Virginia, went to see director Lawrence Kasden's *Grand Canyon*, a film starring Danny Glover, Kevin Kline, Steve Martin, and Mary McDonnell. So did Peter Onuf and his wife, Kristin. Their presence in the row behind me was not apparent until the film ended. By that point I had been won over by the movie, which featured an ensemble of characters who, brought together by choice and circumstance, reached out in small but important ways to improve each other's lives. If there was any doubt that each one had been scripted to reprise, in the context of the late twentieth century, the role of George Bailey, then the final scene settled the matter. All of them, awestruck, peered over the south rim of the Grand Canyon. From their vantage point the Colorado River seemed a mere trickle, but over the course of five million years, during which its waters contoured and carved out the earth, it had made a huge impact.

In much less time, as Gordon Wood's afterword makes clear, Peter has exerted almost as large an influence on the ways in which we understand Jefferson and his world. But of course Peter is too modest to admit as much—and also, apparently, unlikely to fall for cinematic sentimentality. As the theater lights came on, I turned and saw him. "What did you think?" I asked. His response: "It was okay. Maybe a little bit hokey." A week or two later, he allowed a friend and me to take him to lunch at Baja Bean, a Mexican restaurant just off the university's grounds. My friend, Mark Miles, shared my sense of awe. Here was Peter Onuf, the rock star professor—the man who to us and so many other undergrads combined "smart," "fun," and "cool" in pretty much the same proportions that, in our own imaginations, we did. We were attempting to show our appreciation for his willingness to serve as the faculty sponsor for a one-credit, pass-fail course we helped organize on the history of the University of Virginia. We peppered him with questions, one of which still sticks in my mind. "Why," I asked, "did you decide to become a history professor?" At first his response confused us. "Because," he answered, "as a historian I couldn't hurt anyone." He clarified that he was referring to Vietnam, the war that raged while he was in college and graduate school. Of this we had no memory. More to the point, the Mr. Onuf we knew helped everyone.

All of the contributors to this volume have stories about Peter Onuf, all of which illustrate the ways he has helped them, mentored them, encouraged them, collaborated with them, or otherwise contributed to their lives. Some of the contributors were once his students; others he has known only as a peer. Every single one of us, however, has learned from him and felt inspired by the way he has contributed to the study of Jeffersonian America. He has done this through not only his own scholarship but also his efforts to encourage the scholarship of others.

This second contribution—Peter's cultivation of the work of others— has manifested itself through his patient and selfless willingness to critique others' writing, his steadfast support of the steady stream of scholars in residence at Monticello's International Center for Jefferson Studies, and of course through his dedication to his students—which in 2012, as Gordon Wood notes, earned him the American Historical Association's Nancy Lyman Roelker Mentorship Award.[13] It is no exaggeration to point out that Peter's ever-expanding circle encompasses virtually the entire subfield of Jefferson studies. As its leading practitioner, the tone he has set and the spirit he has exemplified have had ripple effects enjoyed by all. The world of Jefferson studies is charitable, open-minded, tolerant, reasonable, collegial, welcoming, and full of good laughs. Every once in a while one hears of other communities of historians that are not so idyllic. These Pottersvilles remind us that, thanks to Peter, the men and women who study Thomas Jefferson inhabit an academic version of George Bailey's Bedford Falls.

But Peter Onuf is more than Bailey, the Everyman. His own scholarship makes him a candidate for Jefferson's upper echelon. As Jefferson informed artist John Trumbull, what set Bacon, Newton, and Locke apart from "the herd of other great men" was the fact that they "laid the foundation" of knowledge on which others would build. Certainly that is what Peter has done. He credits "an explosion of new information about slavery at Monticello" and the accumulated accomplishments of *The Papers of Thomas Jefferson* for having made possible a "potentially" "transformative time in Jefferson scholarship."[14] While there is no discounting the invaluable contributions of the Thomas Jefferson Foundation and *The Papers of Thomas Jefferson*—two different but similarly unrivaled institutions—Peter overlooks his own role as Jefferson scholarship's indispensable man. He has offered so many transformative insights about Jefferson that it would be almost impossible to list them all. But perhaps his most important contribution is his insistence on even-handedness. Not long after the beginning of his time as a professor at the University of Virginia, he gathered a group of scholars to mark Jefferson's 250th birthday. Their essays, published in the landmark *Jeffersonian Legacies* volume, amounted to a watershed in Jefferson scholarship. A few were positive, a few others were unabashedly negative, but most offered mixed and balanced assessments. Reporting on the conference, the *Washington Post* quoted Peter: "I'd like to get moving away from the old obsession with thumbs up, thumbs down, good man or bad."[15]

His greatest service is to bring the historical profession's elusive yet noble dream of objectivity closer to reality. What a departure from the old tradition of Jefferson scholarship. As in this polarizing president's own day, since his death most writers weighed in as *pro* or *con*. What Peter Onuf has accomplished is to underscore the point that the task of a historian is not to cheer or jeer. It is not to support or detract. It is not to justify or criticize. It is not even to judge. The most important battle for historians is an internal and sometimes deeply personal one. It is the struggle to understand and then explain.

This volume traces its origins to the 2012 conference "Thomas Jefferson's Lives: Biography as a Construction of History." For the new and improved subtitle ("Biographers and the Battle for History"), thanks go to Joanne

Freeman. For nearly everything else, thanks go to the conference cosponsors, Monticello's Robert H. Smith International Center for Jefferson Studies and the National Society of the Sons of the American Revolution.

Andrew Jackson O'Shaughnessy, Saunders Director of the International Center, provided us with the prime real estate of Montalto, the house–turned–conference center perched more than 400 feet above Monticello. What an optimal vantage point from which to survey the uneven terrain of Jefferson historiography. To complement Andrew's gracious hospitality was the organizational efficiency of Joseph W. Dooley, director of the Sons of the American Revolution (SAR) Annual Conference on the American Revolution (and president general of the SAR's National Society in 2013–14). Joe marshaled support from a large number of groups and individuals—including the Mount Vernon Ladies' Association; Arlington Blue Top Cabs; the WinSet Group, LLC; the California Society SAR Ladies Auxiliary; the Virginia Society SAR; J. Thomas Burch Jr.; John H. and Elizabeth W. Franklin; Joseph R. Godfrey, Ph.D.; S. John Massoud; Samuel C. Powell, Ph.D.; James C. Rees; J. David Sympson; Timothy E. Ward; Henry Phillips Williams III, Ph.D.; and the George Washington Chapter, George Mason Chapter, and Thomas Jefferson Chapter of the Virginia Society, SAR—to make possible a terrific conference.

Also deserving of gratitude are those who helped transform a collection of conference papers into the chapters of a coherent and cohesive book. The wonderful professionals associated with the University of Virginia Press never fail to impress. This volume's anonymous peer reviewers gave the manuscript careful reads and offered smart suggestions. Dick Holway, senior executive editor, dazzles minds with his sagacity and wins hearts with his patience. Then he turns things over to Helen Chandler, assistant acquisitions editor, and Mark Mones, assistant managing editor, who combine good cheer with almost ruthless efficiency. The careful work of Robert Burchfield, our copyeditor, and Galen Schroeder, who prepared the index, helped to ensure the manuscript was worthy of inclusion in the press's venerable "Jeffersonian America" series, launched two decades ago by Peter Onuf and the late Jan Ellen Lewis, a contributor to this volume whose friendship, scholarship, and example continue to inspire those who enjoyed the good fortune to know her.

Quoted material is reproduced exactly as it appears in the cited sources, including variant spelling and misspellings. We have, however, used "*sic*" to note the misspelling of proper names, and we have supplied missing letters within square brackets when necessary for clarity. Abbreviations for sources used throughout the volume are identified in the list of abbreviations that follows this preface.

Notes

1. Edmund Randolph, "Edmund Randolph's Essay on the Revolutionary History of Virginia (1774–1782)," *Virginia Magazine of History and Biography* 43 (1935): 122; George Cabot to Alexander Hamilton, 11 October 1800, in *The Papers of Alexander Hamilton,* ed. Harold C. Syrett and Jacob E. Cooke, 27 vols. (New York, 1961–87), 25:149; Fisher Ames to Rufus King, 24 September 1800, in *The Life and Correspondence of Rufus King,* ed. Charles R. King, 6 vols. (New York, 1894–1900), 3:304; Chauncey Goodrich to Oliver Wolcott Jr., 26 August 1800, in *Memoirs of the Administrations of Washington and John Adams: Edited from the Papers of Oliver Wolcott, Secretary of the Treasury,* ed. George Gibbs, 2 vols. (New York, 1846), 2:411; John Nicholas to George Washington, 22 February 1798, in *The Papers of George Washington: Retirement Series,* ed. W.W. Abbot et al. (Charlottesville, Va., 1998–99), 2:99; Tadeusz Kosciuszko to TJ, [15 July–5 August 1798,] *TJP,* 30:453; Elize Winn to TJ, 20 February 1803, *TJP,* 39:558; Margaret Bayard Smith, *The First Forty Years of Washington Society,* ed. Gaillard Hunt (New York, 1906), 7. On Jefferson's reputation during his lifetime, see Robert M. S. McDonald, *Confounding Father: Thomas Jefferson's Image in His Own Time* (Charlottesville, Va., 2016).

2. Thomas Jefferson to George Clinton, 31 December 1803, as cited in *The Founders on the Founders: Word Portraits from the American Revolutionary Era,* ed. John P. Kaminski (Charlottesville, Va., 2008), xxiv–xxv; "General View of the Work," *TJP,* 1:xv; Merrill D. Peterson, *Thomas Jefferson and the New Nation* (New York, 1970), viii.

3. *Jefferson Image,* vii, 442.

4. Scott E. Casper, *Constructing American Lives: Biography and Culture in Nineteenth-Century America* (Chapel Hill, N.C., 1999); Thomas Carlyle, *On Heroes, Hero-Worship, and the Heroic in History* (London, 1840), 3.

5. Stephen Jay Gould, *Wonderful Life: The Burgess Shale and the Nature of History* (New York, 1989), 277–91; Don Higginbotham, *Revolution in America: Considerations and Comparisons* (Charlottesville, Va., 2005), 13–18, 22–25, 26–27; TJ to John Adams, 28 October 1813, *TJP:RS,* 6:564; TJ to John Trumbull, 15 February 1789, *TJP,* 14:561; TJ to Benjamin Rush, 16 January 1811, *TJP:RS,* 3:305.

6. James Thomas Flexner, *Washington: The Indispensable Man* (Boston, 1974), ix; Joseph J. Ellis, "American Sphinx: The Character of Thomas Jefferson," *Civilization* 1 (November–December 1994): 37.

7. *Jefferson Image,* 212–14; Henry S. Randall, *The Life of Thomas Jefferson,* 3 vols. (New York, 1858), 1:11.

8. Joseph J. Ellis, *His Excellency: George Washington* (New York, 2004), 261–65; John B. Boles, *Jefferson: Architect of Liberty* (New York, 2017), 2.

9. A few studies have considered the evolution of biographical interpretations of other major American historical figures. See, for example, Edward G. Lengel, *Inventing George Washington: America's Founder, in Myth and Memory* (New York, 2011); Barry Schwartz, *Abraham Lincoln and the Forge of National Memory* (Chicago, 2008); Barry Schwartz, *Abraham Lincoln in the Post-Heroic Era: History and Memory in Late Twentieth-Century America* (Chicago, 2008); Robert D. Habich, *Building Their Own Waldos: Emerson's First Biographers and the Politics of Life-Writing in the Gilded Age* (Iowa City, Iowa, 2011).

10. Peter Novick, *That Noble Dream: The "Objectivity Question" and the American Historical Profession* (New York, 1988), 272–78; Edward Hallett Carr, *What Is History?* (New York, 1961), 50–51 (Butterfield quotations).

11. Fawn M. Brodie, *Thomas Jefferson: An Intimate History* (New York, 1974); Annette Gordon-Reed, *Thomas Jefferson and Sally Hemings: An American Controversy* (Charlottesville, Va., 1997); Eugene A. Foster et al., "Jefferson Fathered Slave's Last Child," *Nature* 196 (5 November 1998): 27–28.

12. Annette Gordon-Reed and Peter S. Onuf, *"Most Blessed of the Patriarchs": Thomas Jefferson and the Empire of the Imagination* (New York, 2016), xxiii–xxiv; Peter S. Onuf, *The Mind of Thomas Jefferson* (Charlottesville, Va., 2007), 58–59.

13. For information on the Roelker Mentorship Award and its recipients, see https://www.historians.org/awards-and-grants/past-recipients/nancy-lyman-roelker -mentorship-award-recipients.

14. TJ to Trumbull, 15 February 1789, *TJP,* 14:561; Gordon-Reed and Onuf, *"Most Blessed of the Patriarchs,"* xxii–xxiii.

15. Peter S. Onuf, ed., *Jeffersonian Legacies* (Charlottesville, Va., 1993); Joel Achenbach, "Thomas Jefferson, Tarnished Icon?", *Washington Post* (17 October 1992), D-1.

Abbreviations

AHR	*American Historical Review*
Ford	Paul Leicester Ford, ed. *The Writings of Thomas Jefferson.* 10 vols. New York, 1892–99.
JAH	*Journal of American History*
Jefferson Image	Merrill D. Peterson. *The Jefferson Image in the American Mind.* New York, 1960.
JER	*Journal of the Early Republic*
JSH	*Journal of Southern History*
L&B	Andrew A. Lipscomb and Albert Ellery Bergh, eds. *The Writings of Thomas Jefferson.* 20 vols. Washington, D.C., 1903–4.
Lib. Cong.	Library of Congress, Washington, D.C.
TJ	Thomas Jefferson
TJP	Julian P. Boyd et al., eds. *The Papers of Thomas Jefferson.* 43 vols. to date. Princeton, N.J., 1950– .
TJP:RS	J. Jefferson Looney, ed. *The Papers of Thomas Jefferson: Retirement Series.* 15 vols. to date. Princeton, N.J., 2004– .
TJW	Merrill D. Peterson, ed. *Thomas Jefferson: Writings.* New York, 1984.
VQR	*Virginia Quarterly Review*
WMQ	*William and Mary Quarterly,* 3rd Series.

Thomas Jefferson's Lives

Introduction

The Many Lives of Thomas Jefferson

BARBARA OBERG

What is a biography? Simply defined, it is "the story of a person told by someone else."[1] No longer is biography the stepchild of history or literary criticism; it is a genre that stands on its own. Despite its popularity now— akin to the "biographical mania" of the late nineteenth century—we still do not quite know how to define it. Historians, literary critics, and others have expressed dismay at new ways of writing life stories. "Something horrid has recently befallen the craft of biography," Arthur M. Schlesinger Jr. lamented. Joyce Carol Oates defined biography as only "pathography." Freud dismissed the biographer as merely a writer of "lies, concealments, hypocrisy, flattery." Biographical truth, he insisted, "does not exist." The literary critic Stanley Fish accused biographers of substituting their own life story for that of the supposed subject and dismissed the whole enterprise as "only a bad game."[2]

Whether fiction, a life narrative embellished by imagination, or nonfiction, biographical narratives as far back as Plutarch's *Lives of the Greeks and Romans* continue to be of use to us. The lives of "great" men and women can warn or inspire, dazzle or dismay. Perhaps because we are unsure how to lead our own lives, we search for clues from the past and then offer them as lessons to our children.[3] Among the most revered and long-lived stories are those of men and women who rose from humble origins to achieve success and fame. Benjamin Franklin, the son of a lowly candle-maker, became a world-renowned scientist and champion of America in London and Paris during the American Revolution. As Mark Twain later complained, Franklin's words "brought affliction to millions of boys" whose fathers had read his "pernicious" autobiography and wanted them, like the young Franklin, to learn "algebra by the light of a smoldering fire" and study astronomy at mealtimes.[4] George Washington, who could not "tell a lie," became a famous general and the "father of his country." Abraham Lincoln grew up in a log cabin and ended up in the president's house.

What are we to do with Thomas Jefferson? He defies easy explanation and, although the attempts to write his life over the centuries have brought forth what Joseph Ellis called a "flood of ink," he remains a mystery. To Ellis, Jefferson is a "Great Sphinx of American history," half-man, half-lion. His National Book Award–winning biography, which appeared in 1997, described Jefferson as "the enigmatic and elusive touchstone for the most cherished convictions and contested truths in American culture."[5] In the summer of 2012, under the auspices of the Sons of the American Revolution and the International Center for Jefferson Studies, scholars met to discuss the nature and history of Jefferson biographies from George Tucker in 1837 through Dumas Malone, Merrill Peterson, and Fawn Brodie in the second half of the twentieth century. To counter the accounts by Jefferson's biographers, scholars of Aaron Burr and Alexander Hamilton presented their case.

Thomas Jefferson insisted that offering an account of his life was "the last thing in the world" he would undertake, as J. Jefferson Looney explains in his essay. Jefferson, who claimed reluctance to impose "merely personal or private" details on the public, would not write what we now call an "autobiography." He sensed the importance of what might be written *about* him, however, and left behind ample materials for someone else to tell his story. Because he wanted accounts of his life to be based not only on documents, official records, and the recollections of others but also on the "private record" of his life, he preserved scattered jottings, notes and memoranda, a record of his incoming and outgoing correspondence, letters, and fragments of autobiographical writings.[6] He hoped his biographers would replace the falsehoods his political opponents circulated in newspapers with the true narrative of the gaining of independence, the establishment of a new government, and the peaceful transfer of power from one political party to another in 1800–1801, which marked the triumph of republican values. Jefferson's biography was embedded in the nation's history.[7]

In the spring of 1802, other versions of that history began to appear. Jefferson wrote James Madison that John Marshall was preparing his *Life of George Washington,* which was scheduled for publication "just in time to influence the next presidential elections." To Jefferson, Marshall's work was not only a biography but a history of the nation with a Federalist bias.

Jefferson and Madison responded by asking Joel Barlow, a poet and diplomat whom Jefferson had met while in France as minister plenipotentiary, to write a history that would rectify Marshall's "perversions" and leave the "correct" history for posterity. To assist Barlow, they offered to supply confidential information that was "not on paper but only within ourselves, for verbal communication."[8] In the end, Barlow did not write the history, but Jefferson's desire for it made clear that his future reputation mattered to him and he would play a part in crafting it.

While all "heroes" of the founding generation have "feet of clay," Jefferson is a particularly glaring example of the flawed hero. His reputation was highly contested during his lifetime. His hostility to the conjunction of church and state in Virginia, for example, was misunderstood as hostility to religion in general, making him anathema to New England Federalists and many practicing Christians. Disagreements over his place in the American pantheon continued long after his death, and disputes over his legacy are as intense in the twentieth and twenty-first centuries as they were earlier. As John Milton Cooper wrote, Jefferson's ideas formed "an ideological battleground in the nineteenth century and beyond."[9]

Biographies are shaped by the times in which they are written. As political, economic, cultural, and intellectual circumstances change, biographers pose different questions and assign centrality to different issues. Each age creates its own Thomas Jefferson and adopts its own mythology about the "founding of the nation." Today's Jefferson is often the personification of the errors, inconsistencies, and hypocrisies that America displayed and displays. Was he an aristocrat or a republican? Was the nation to be aristocratic or republican? Could Americans live up to the spirit of July 4, 1776? Most troubling to us is how the reality of Jefferson the slave owner squares with the eloquent and idealistic language of the Declaration of Independence, his first inaugural address, and countless letters on politics, philosophy, literature, and natural history. These questions haunt us, and the battleground remains.

Given the complexities of Jefferson's life, the ambiguity of his reputation, and the ongoing revisions to our understanding of the early republic, the prospect of writing his biography can be daunting. Yet many have been willing, or even eager, to undertake the task. Some set out to tear him down, some to create a Jefferson worthy of a pedestal, and others, as they say, to "correct the record." Admirers and critics, hagiographers and haters, scholars, journalists, and popular historians seek to craft a biographical narrative that will substantiate their own point of view. When they recount Jefferson's story, they establish a place for themselves in the community of Jefferson scholars that began in the middle of the nineteenth century. The prestige of Jefferson biographers increases when their names are linked with his. We speak of "Randall's Jefferson," "Chinard's," "Peterson's," "Malone's," or "Brodie's," as if each of them has part ownership in Jefferson's life story. In a certain sense it *is* ownership. By the time authors have crafted an account of Jefferson's life, they have lived with him, as Brodie observed, for an "inordinate number of years" (four, seven, or, in the case of Dumas Malone, thirty) and formed an intimate, almost symbiotic, relationship.[10]

The first generation of Jefferson's biographers, those who wrote in the fifty years immediately following his death, had a direct personal connection with or an emotional tie to someone who had known him well. George Tucker (1775–1861), Henry S. Randall (1811–1876), and Jefferson's great-granddaughter Sarah N. Randolph (1839–1892) knew Jefferson or a member of his family or received stories and memorabilia from someone who had known him. All of them had access to the family papers. Tucker built upon an acquaintance of several years. Randall, who was fifteen years old when Jefferson died, interviewed members of the Jefferson family and passed on their tales. Sarah Randolph was the daughter of Jefferson's beloved grandson Thomas Jefferson Randolph, the "greatest of Godsends" that "heaven had granted." At T. J. Randolph's death, Jefferson's private papers passed to her.[11]

Tucker's friendship with Jefferson made him the natural person to undertake a biography. A year before Jefferson's death Tucker was named to the professorship in moral philosophy at the University of Virginia, where he also served as chair of the faculty. In addition to being colleagues, the two men lived in proximity to one another for just over a year. Their friendship was "cordial and constructive but neither especially close nor especially warm," as Christine Coalwell McDonald and Robert M. S. McDonald note. Along with unpublished correspondence and papers from the Jefferson family, Tucker used reminiscences of Jefferson's personal and public life supplied by James Madison, to whom he dedicated his biography. While Tucker had the materials for an intimate, personal account laced with anecdotes about the Jefferson he had known, he chose instead to abide by the norms of early nineteenth-century biography, presenting Jefferson's public life but shielding the personal. Tucker went out of his way to praise Jefferson's service to the nation because, of all the country's public figures, "the greatest injustice had been done to Mr. Jefferson." The "maledictions of his enemies" could seem louder than the praise of his friends.[12] He presented Jefferson's story and at the same time chronicled the early political history of the country. Both the biography and the history were located firmly in the intensely partisan politics of the early nineteenth century. In important ways, Tucker's "distinguished work," as Merrill Peterson described it, established a pattern for future biographers.[13]

Tucker, like other Jefferson biographers, had to confront two facts of Jefferson's life: his relationship with Sally Hemings and his unorthodox religious opinions, both of which remain difficult to unravel. To protect the private Jefferson, Tucker drew "a veil" over what he considered Jefferson's errors and defects. He dealt obliquely with the Hemings affair, minimizing its importance and doubting James Callender's credibility. He found the question of Jefferson's religious faith to be "uninteresting or irrelevant" to the story of his life, and he refrained from discussing in detail Jefferson's unorthodox—and incorrect in Tucker's opinion—religious views. The important point was that Jefferson insisted that an individual's religious beliefs were a private matter. When Tucker did raise the subject, he offered scanty, sometimes even incorrect, information and, as the McDonalds note, rewrote Jefferson's opinions to more closely resemble his own.

Meanwhile, Andrew Burstein considers two midcentury works, Henry S. Randall's "adulatory" three-volume Life of Thomas Jefferson (1858) and James Parton's identically titled and "breathless" single volume (1874). They described an individual who was "overwhelmingly decent, and unrivaled by any other career politician in natural grace and moral fitness." In political ideology Randall and Parton were "difficult to tell apart," and they treated a number of issues in a similar way. Both described Jefferson's father, Peter Jefferson, as a strong, manly figure and wrote little about his mother, Jane Randolph Jefferson. Neither writer paid much attention to Jefferson's presidency.

On the subject of slavery, however, Randall and Parton differed. Randall avoided any discussion and, when mentioning it, shifted to the passive voice and explained, as Burstein notes, that "it was not decided ultimately to pursue" the "topic of slavery."[14] Parton did not shy away from the topic and noted that Jefferson came to hate the system of slavery early on and "foretold the ruin" of it. Had Jefferson lived longer, Parton was sure, he would have eventually ended up on the right side of the issue. By creating an image of

Jefferson walking hand in hand with his daughters, trailed by their slaves "marching behind with their bundles and their children," Parton romanticized the life of a Monticello slave and obscured the reality of Jefferson the slave owner.[15]

Neither Randall nor Parton avoided Sally Hemings completely. Randall drew upon the recollections of Jefferson's grandson T. J. Randolph, who spoke about the matter when he and Randall were out on a walk together. In 1868, Randall relayed to Parton what Randolph had said, and Parton incorporated it into his biography. Randall blamed Peter and Samuel Carr, Jefferson's "perfectly notorious nephews," for the treatment of enslaved females that brought shame to the mountaintop. He linked the Carrs, and not the Jeffersons, to the story of a Hemings-Jefferson affair. In a footnote he pointed a finger at Federalist newspaper stories that described Jefferson's daughters as "weeping to see a *negress* installed in the place of their mother."[16] The stories, Parton suggested, were concocted by "the Campaign Liar" James Callender. That lie, which was introduced in 1796 to prevent Jefferson's election, was "clearly developed into a distinct species of falsehood" in 1800. A story that had been around for seventy-four years would doubtless circulate for a long time to come. Parton's index entries buried Sally Hemings (which he spells as "Henings") and ignored any mention of a connection with Jefferson. Her entry reads simply "Henings, mistake respecting."[17]

Randall went far beyond the Jefferson of official records or even the Jefferson revealed in personal correspondence. His account was filled with anecdotes from Jefferson's grandchildren, and, as Burstein indicates, he wrote in "the style of literary romance" with language at times "quite purple." He worked surrounded by an eclectic assembly of Jeffersoniana that included books, papers, plans for the garden, a drawing of the moldboard plow, a locket containing Jefferson's hair, and the journal of Dr. Robley Dunglison, the physician who attended Jefferson just before his death. Burstein observes that Randall's Jefferson was likable and, because he had been both mother and father to his daughters, had a "feminine softness."

Randall did not ignore Jefferson's public life. Brushing aside the vicious attacks on Jefferson's rocky tenure as governor of Virginia that Patrick Henry and the "Dictator Party" leveled, he emphasized not Jefferson's flight from British troops approaching Monticello in June 1781 or the Virginia legislature's inquiry into his conduct, but the resolution of thanks that the legislature passed on December 19, 1781. Never, gloated Randall, "did an official accusation end more abortively . . . and never was a vindication more triumphantly complete."[18] Writing in the heyday of "openly glorifying national biography," Randall lavished praise on the purchase of Louisiana, through which Jefferson "acquired peaceably and permanently for his country, more extensive and fertile domains than ever for a moment owned the sway of Napoleon."[19] Jefferson's religious views were a challenge for both Randall and Parton.

To recover Jefferson as a Christian, Randall dismissed completely the charges of the New England clergy who labeled him an "infidel" under the spell of France and rather heavy-handedly turned to stories from his grandchildren, who remembered hearing their grandfather "habitually speak reverently of God, the Savior, and the great truths of Christianity." Jefferson's weakness might be seen as his "tolerance of other people's sentiments to a point beyond what courtesy demanded."[20] During the battle for disestablishment of the Anglican Church in Virginia, Jefferson's words provided the opponents of the established church the weapons with which to fight.

Parton, the first American to call himself a journalist, was discouraged by the decline of political discourse and the rejection of American ideals that he saw around him in post–Civil War America. His biography of Jefferson appeared first in serial form in the *Atlantic Monthly,* but when it appeared as a book Parton had removed the criticisms of Thomas Mann Randolph to which his son, T. J. Randolph, had objected. Parton's preface bound America and Jefferson together in a way that future generations have seized upon to connect the man and the nation: "If Jefferson was wrong, America is wrong. If Jefferson was right, America is right."[21]

Sarah N. Randolph, whose work complemented Randall's, constructed from unpublished letters and reminiscences a "life and letters" biography. While he concentrated on Jefferson's life in politics, she, as Jan Ellen Lewis writes, put into "bold relief the beauties and charms of his domestic character." She kept Jefferson aloof from the partisan battles of the time, choosing instead to emphasize his intense dislike of public life. While the outside world constructed an "imaginary Jefferson," his family knew the "real Jefferson." According to family lore, Jefferson remained in politics only because he wanted to leave his children the legacy of his reputation. Randolph's work implicitly rebuts any story of a relationship with Sally Hemings because, as she insists, Jefferson simply would not have done such a thing to his daughters. Sarah Randolph's work, as Lewis points out, was "an act of recovery" from the damage that Jefferson's enemies had inflicted on him. They had also ruined his graveyard. The gates to it had been "entered, and the tombs desecrated." The granite obelisk over his tomb had been chipped away, leaving it "a misshapen column."[22] In 1871, when her work was published, Jefferson's reputation, like his grave, lay in ruins.

Tucker, Randall, Parton, and Sarah Randolph offered a praiseworthy Jefferson, while biographers of Aaron Burr and Alexander Hamilton vigorously challenged the positive interpretation. Their biographers believed that Parton's "wrong" and "right" were anchored in the Jeffersonian myth and therefore offered a false description of America. Advocates of Burr and Hamilton turned Parton's words upside down, arguing instead that if Jefferson was wrong, America was right, and if Jefferson was right, America was wrong. Like Jefferson's biographers, Burr's and Hamilton's claimed to study the evidence, uncover the flaws, and correct the history as told by Jefferson's friends, family, and admiring chroniclers of his life. What the "opposing biographers" wrote about him offers a radically different perspective, but one that can contribute to a fuller and more complex understanding and assessment.

Like Jefferson, the enigmatic Burr has puzzled Americans across the ages. Matthew Livingston Davis, the most influential of his biographers, wrote that to accord Burr the honor he deserved, Jefferson must first be reburied in "a new, less glorifying, literary coffin." Nancy Isenberg's essay looks at three Burr biographers who destroyed and then sought to rebury him: Burr's trusted political associate Matthew Davis, Boston attorney Samuel Knapp, and journalist and biographer James Parton. In preparation for his two-volume *Memoirs of Aaron Burr* (1836–37), Davis read T. J. Randolph's collection of Jefferson's memoirs and correspondence, in which Burr had even marked the passages to which Davis should pay particular attention. Davis was shocked by the "Jesuitical" Jefferson who was "jealous and distrustful" of Burr and whose behavior during the election of 1800 was unscrupulous. Burr's treason trial in 1807 only deepened his conviction that Jefferson possessed a "pathological hatred" of him. Davis would expose what really happened in the secret negotiations to break the tie votes in 1800–1801, clear Burr's name, and provide a correct and full account of two significant events in the nation's history. Knapp, whose *Memoir of the Life of Aaron Burr* appeared a year before Davis's *Memoirs,* claimed a personal acquaintance with Burr. Like Davis, Knapp made the election and the treason trial touchstones for building the case that Jefferson was a "deranged democrat" who was out to destroy what he could not control. Isenberg proposes that Knapp thought, mistakenly as it turned out, that prospects for Burr's reputation in the future "looked brighter," that a new generation would reverse the "erroneous" verdict of the Revolutionary generation, and that the time was right for his biography.

Two decades after Davis's and Knapp's works and seventeen years after he wrote a biography of Jefferson, Parton published the *Life and Times of Aaron Burr* (1858). Although he never met Burr, he spent three years talking with those who had known him. Despite what he might have learned from those conversations, Parton added little to what Davis and Knapp had written. He echoed their outrage and found in Jefferson an "absurdly excited" figure who imagined conspiracies everywhere. Parton reformulated the description of American democracy as a blend of "Jefferson's ideas and Burr's tactics" in a way that nicely captured the dynamic push and pull of politics and politicians in the early nineteenth century. He revised the historiography of the period between the Constitution and the annexation of Texas in 1845 by naming it "the age of Jefferson *and* Burr."

As Joanne Freeman tells us, Alexander Hamilton was "the aristocratic yin to Thomas Jefferson's democratic yang." They were opposites, but complementary to one another. Like Burr, Hamilton was the "chronic historical underdog." He had a cadre of family supporters, which Burr did not. Hamilton's widow engaged in a "non-stop" campaign to collect his papers and find a biographer. Her sons supported her efforts with "fist-clenched belligerence." Brushing aside his politics and "democracy problem," biographers contrasted Hamilton with Jefferson, "the scheming demagogue." To Hamilton's defenders, Jefferson's democratic excesses transformed Hamilton's supposed weaknesses into virtues. Hamilton was simply a "democratic champion with the best of intentions who lost his way." What was important for America was his clear national vision and, above all, that he "was *right*." John Church Hamilton, the most prolific of his father's defenders, countered the spate of pro-Jefferson books with a shower of insults and provided future biographers with a rich source of material upon which to draw. The last two decades of the nineteenth century saw a dramatic surge in biographies favorable to Hamilton, as the Civil War seemed to prove the necessity of a strong central government and the validity of Hamilton's beliefs. Future Massachusetts senator Henry Cabot Lodge, as well as John Torrey

Morse, editor of the "American Statesman" series, and Frederick Scott Oliver, a British businessman who wrote, as Joanne Freeman notes, "the most widely influential Hamilton biography of the early twentieth century," followed in John Church Hamilton's footsteps.

Henry Adams was a transitional figure in the universe of Jefferson biographers. The great-grandson of John Adams, Henry spent fifteen years researching and writing his nine-volume *History of the United States under the Administrations of Thomas Jefferson and James Madison* (1889–91). He fashioned a history, parts of which were so deeply entwined with Jefferson's life and politics that it was also a biography. The purpose of Adams's undertaking, as Richard Samuelson explains, was to compare, although not explicitly, Jefferson and John Adams. Understanding America and the American character in the late eighteenth and early nineteenth centuries meant first locating Jefferson and Adams in that world. Henry Adams grew up surrounded by Jefferson lore, and, like an impressionist painter, he worked delicately, creating Jefferson "touch by touch." He went out of his way to write as a judicious historian and biographer, not as a spokesman for his great-grandfather. Henry Adams's judgment was grounded in "ambivalence and irony," comments Peterson.[23] As Samuelson points out, when Adams gave Jefferson a "mixed review," he was also giving nineteenth-century America a mixed review. The problem with America, Adams concluded, was that there was too much Jefferson and not enough John Adams. The overly optimistic and visionary Jefferson aimed not only to establish a new nation but to create a better and stronger one than any before. Yet his strict constructionism in domestic policy and uncritical devotion to peace in foreign affairs were failures, Henry Adams believed, and left America weaker, not stronger. His great-grandfather and Alexander Hamilton had the more realistic approach to framing a strong and successful national government.

Jefferson's nineteenth-century biographers, from Tucker through Adams, reflected "the ebb and flow of American history" that Arthur Schlesinger Jr. posited. Political ideologies are cyclical, with traditional or conservative beliefs holding sway in some periods and progressive or liberal ideas in others. Americans are "reformers spring and summer"; in the fall and winter they "stand by the old." They are "reformers in the morning, conservers at night."[24] Jefferson was a man of the morning and of the spring and summer. His reputation rose and fell in a way that could meet the needs of whatever political ideology reigned at the time. From his death in 1826 until the end of the Civil War, both opponents and proponents of slavery and states' rights claimed him. His correspondence, writings, and public statements were ripe for picking by southern slaveholders as well as by those who still hoped the idealism of his rhetoric could become a reality. All sides made use of him to validate their opinions.

Jefferson's reputation barely survived the Civil War, while Hamilton's, because he presumably understood what it took to build an economy and government strong enough to carry on a war, received a boost. The "fame of Jefferson is waning, and the fame of Hamilton is waxing," James A. Garfield announced to Congress in 1865.[25] In the aftermath of Reconstruction, it was easy to hold Jefferson's politics responsible for the bloody conflict that had torn the nation apart. The Kentucky and Virginia Resolutions were early steps toward the undoing of the Union. The plantation economy of the South was outmoded and inefficient in the new industrial age. Jefferson, romanticizing the western farmer, was ambivalent about manufacturing and the new age. Herbert Croly, philosopher of the Progressive era and cofounder of the *New Republic,* observed bluntly in 1909 that the old Jeffersonians "would only bring chaos to the new industrial America." Vernon L. Parrington lamented in 1927 that Jefferson's vision of a nation of freeholding farmers was "thrust aside in the scramble for wealth" and that the old values and philosophies had been "swept out on the rubbish heap."[26] Jefferson was simply out of date.

While Croly and Parrington found Jefferson's ideas out of date, Frederick Jackson Turner laid the groundwork for a different approach to them. His 1893 address to the American Historical Association, titled "The Significance of the Frontier in American History," identified Jefferson's western farmers as the source of democracy. The independent American democrat hailed from the frontier, and, to many, Jefferson *was* the West. Andrew Jackson, Abraham Lincoln, and William Jennings Bryan, westerners and eager devotees of Jefferson, were the exponents of democracy in America for their generation. They were part of a tradition of ordinary Americans who fought to achieve democracy in an era that Beard traced back to Jefferson. It was Jeffersonian values that laid the groundwork for a new generation of reform Democrats and Republican Progressives who would refurbish his image as a political hero. His championing of democratic government gave leaders of the Progressive era the eloquent language with which to express their ideas and a platform from which to speak.

Woodrow Wilson was among these leaders. Although he attended the University of Virginia Law School, he was no fan of the university's founder. He thought Jefferson's commitment to a small government with limited powers was wrong and Hamilton's belief in a strong national government was right. Jefferson's ideas led to division and Hamilton's to unity. While preparing an address for the annual Jefferson Day dinner at the Waldorf Astoria in New York on April 16, 1906, Wilson was led to reconsider his view of Jefferson. He concluded that Americans too often thought of Jefferson as a politician with an "uncanny gift of contriving popular issues, organizing parties, and directing campaigns." They failed to see that in some ways he was simply a typical American of his region and generation. Born on the frontier, he was "familiar throughout his life with the simpler, plainer sides of American life."[27] His belief in democracy was as relevant in the twentieth century as it had been in the nineteenth, but Wilson also came to appreciate that democratic ends could only be achieved by Hamiltonian means. Protecting democracy in an industrial age required a government strong enough to address the emergence of big "trusts."

In the same way that practitioners of the "New History" such as James Harvey Robinson and Charles Beard wanted to reclaim the American past from conservatives and connect the writing of history to social change, Jefferson biographer Claude Bowers sought to rescue the Jefferson whose ideals of liberty and equality ought to be the basis and legitimacy of the nation from the post–Civil War conservatives. Brian Steele explores the work of Claude Bowers, whose *Jefferson and Hamilton: The Struggle for Democracy in America* appeared in 1925, just before the 1926 sesquicentennial of the Declaration of Independence.

Jefferson's admirers welcomed the book as a corrective to the attention accorded Hamilton in preceding decades. A Progressive Democrat and political activist, Bowers characterized the United States as the product of a clash of economic forces throughout its history and a nation still deeply divided along economic and class lines. Disagreements in the 1790s between Jefferson and Hamilton, the "disheveled figures seen by their contemporaries on the battle-field," remained the fundamental struggle of American politics and thought in the 1920s.[28] Like Wilson, Bowers initially preferred Hamilton to Jefferson. As he read Henry Cabot Lodge's ten volumes of Hamilton's works for a high school speech contest, however, his "consternation" at Hamilton's views grew. He revised his opinion of the two men, and his *Jefferson and Hamilton,* published in 1925, changed the tide of American scholarship. Intellectuals and statesmen had at last been "converted to Jefferson," wrote Peterson.[29]

Bowers, who gave the keynote address at the 1928 Democratic Convention, was confident that history would declare victory for Jefferson and the Democratic Party. Steele credits him with teaching Franklin Roosevelt that politics should be thought of in terms of "historical continuities" and that the struggles of the 1920s were an up-to-date version of those of the 1790s. Within months of the appearance of Bowers's volume Albert Nock, a libertarian who in the 1930s would become a vocal critic of the New Deal, published *Jefferson.* His Jefferson was a heroic figure, but because of his individualism, not his commitment to democratic ideals. Like Bowers, Nock accepted the Beardian view of American history as the story of competing class interests and observed that while Jefferson recognized that the Federalists used government to serve the interests of financiers and speculators, he failed to see that Republicans wanted a government that represented the particular class interests of farmers, mechanics, and tradesmen. Jefferson, Nock observed, was "incredibly naïve about economics."[30]

The rehabilitation of Jeffersonianism mushroomed during the Great Depression and the New Deal. Admiration of Jefferson peaked in 1943 with the 200th anniversary of his birth and the dedication of the Jefferson Memorial on the banks of the Potomac. The erection of the monument was "the most important thing to happen to Jefferson since July Fourth 1826," wrote Peterson.[31] Roosevelt, swept up in the celebratory appreciation of Jefferson and searching for ways to justify leading the country into war, suggested that the words of the founders, beginning with Thomas Jefferson, could offer a strong rationale for entering the war that broke out in Europe in 1939.[32] In addition to its political importance, Jefferson's legacy was being recast as a broader intellectual and cultural one that was central to America's place in the world.

Gilbert Chinard, a student of French literature who earned a degree from the University of Poitiers and spent most of his career teaching in American universities, wrote about a Jefferson who was both American and French, as Herbert Sloan tells us. Immersing himself in the vast collections of manuscripts at the Library of Congress as no scholar had done before, Chinard acquired a commanding knowledge of Jefferson and his world. He explored

Jefferson's years in France and the lifetime of correspondence that followed. As Chinard discovered, the letters that Jefferson exchanged with the men and women he met in Paris revealed the development of his political philosophy. Chinard also understood that this correspondence did not, as the most extreme Federalists charged, make Jefferson an atheist or a Jacobin. Instead, Jefferson's stay in France strengthened his attachment to his own country. To Chinard, Jefferson was "first, last and always" an American. He was the "apostle of Americanism." Roosevelt took hold of the phrase, retaining the word "apostle" but replacing "Americanism" with "freedom." Jefferson became the "Apostle of Freedom" to the world. While Chinard's biography was not exhaustive, it offered a new and important perspective on Jefferson and was, in Richard Hofstadter's words, "outstanding among modern studies of Jefferson."[33]

Sloan's essay also considers Marie Goebel Kimball, a Jefferson scholar, the first curator of Monticello, and the wife of Sidney Fiske Kimball, a member of the faculty at the University of Virginia. She envisioned a multivolume, large-scale biography that would do justice to the full range of Jefferson's interests. At the time of her death in 1955 she had published just three volumes, which carried Jefferson up to 1789. The first of these, which appeared in time for the centennial of Jefferson's birth, was well reviewed by Verner Crane and Carl Becker. But to Peterson, Kimball's interest was "essentially antiquarian," and she displayed "an uncritical devotion to the man and to all he had touched." Her main contribution to Jefferson scholarship was the large quantity of detailed information that she gathered, which enriched our understanding of the Jefferson family.[34] In a sense she was a social historian ahead of her time, notes Sloan. Neither Chinard nor Kimball dealt with slavery or Sally Hemings. Chinard referred to slavery only a handful of times, and Kimball quickly dismissed the "scurrilous charge of miscegenation." They mark the end of one era in Jefferson scholarship and an introduction to the next.

R. B. Bernstein places Dumas Malone, a central figure in the new era of Jefferson biographers, in the continuum of Jefferson biographers by linking his admiration of Jefferson to Kimball's and Chinard's. Peterson described Malone's work as the "capstone of the most fruitful eras of Jefferson historiography."[35] While scholars, reviewers, and general readers often attached "definitive" to Malone's work, he rejected that word and instead described his approach as "comprehensive." Only a comprehensive biography could do justice to a man with such broad-ranging interests and talents, but no Jefferson biography could be "definitive" because every generation would pose new questions. He used the introduction to each volume to define where he thought Jefferson scholarship should go and what questions it would face. Over the more than three decades he devoted to researching and writing his biography, both popular and scholarly attitudes toward Jefferson became increasingly ambivalent, and the nation's estimation of him rose and fell. Influenced by the fluctuations in how Americans defined and judged Jefferson, Malone began to reconsider his views. The public asked probing—sometimes troublesome—questions that differed significantly from those he had raised. The first volume appeared in 1948, only five years after a high point in Jefferson's reputation. By the time the sixth and final volume appeared in 1981, Jefferson had tumbled from his pedestal, and the premises on which Malone's magnum opus were based were called into question. His conception of what a Jefferson biography ought to be was thoroughly shaken when Fawn Brodie's *Intimate History* appeared in 1974.

Peterson's one-volume biography appeared in 1970, about halfway through the publication of Malone's six volumes. Although Peterson was twenty-nine years younger than Malone, the two were writing at the same time. Francis Cogliano identifies four stages in the trajectory of Jefferson's reputation and locates Peterson in the third, as one of a cadre of historians who came of age in the shadow of World War II, when Jefferson was becoming the embodiment of America's founding principles and aspirations. Roosevelt revered Jefferson and in his dedication of the Jefferson Memorial designated him the "Apostle of Freedom." This identification permeated Peterson's scholarship. Working at Harvard with the intellectual historian Perry Miller, in whose class Peterson read Parrington's work, he seized upon the word "image" as a way to describe Jefferson's contributions to our understanding of "the American Mind." One of the fruits of his efforts was *The Jefferson Image in the American Mind* (1960). The irony was that his enthusiasm for Jefferson came just as Jefferson's reputation was on the decline. Peterson saw how difficult it was for biographers to see Jefferson "clearly and objectively in his own life" because he was so deeply interwoven with "the whole epic" of American democracy. Instead of remaining part of the background to an American narrative, he deserved a prominent place out front. After two decades of study, Peterson still found him "an impenetrable man." Jefferson, it seemed, left a wealth of ideals and institutions to the nation, but the price he "exacted from posterity was to compel it to understand him." He looms over us still, challenging biographers.[36]

Brodie's work not only reshaped our understanding of Jefferson but revolutionized the definition of a Jefferson biography. She dared to ask, what *is* a subject's family? She turned the phrase "Jefferson's family life" inside out by insisting that his black family was as central to life at Monticello as his white family. Brodie's work, as Annette Gordon-Reed shows us, "demolished" the accepted template for his private life that Henry Randall had created almost a century earlier. She drew back the veil over Jefferson's life, and it would never again be fully drawn. "Her Jefferson" may have been worshipped by many, but in reality he was more deeply flawed than Americans realized, or would accept. In the years after her work appeared, historians and others vigorously challenged Brodie's motive, her use of evidence, her interpretation, and even her intellectual honesty. By insisting upon the validity of oral evidence, she expanded forever the definition of a legitimate "source." Stories that were passed down by word of mouth from members of Jefferson's black family generation after generation offered a deep, personal history radically different from the accepted view but crucial to a full understanding of the man. A good "Freudian," as Gordon-Reed writes, Brodie adapted the tools of the psychoanalyst to examine how Jefferson's early life on a plantation beside the Rivanna River shaped his personality and the course of his life.

To the community of traditional Jefferson scholars the interpretation offered by "that woman" was deeply flawed and irresponsible. Malone insisted that it was not history as he understood the word but "psychological speculation to the point of absurdity." Peterson compared Brodie to "a hound in pursuit of game," leaving us as "remote from the truth as when we began." Julian P. Boyd, the first editor of *The Papers of Thomas Jefferson*, accused her of "manipulation of evidence, the failure to give due weight to the overwhelming considerations of fact and plausibility which conflict with her preconceptions."[37]

Brodie's writing, as well as a number of other scholarly works that appeared in the four decades after hers, would have been unrecognizable to Tucker, Randall, Sarah N. Randolph, and Parton. No biographer can ignore her now. As each generation seeks to better understand Jefferson it recasts the narrative of his life. Biographers explore the history that Jefferson made and what history has made of him. Which biographer was "right"? Who was the "real" Thomas Jefferson? Or were there multiple "real" Jeffersons?

The search goes on. Each generation learns from the preceding and contributes to the ones to come. Brodie complicated what had been the accepted paradigm for a biography by adding a third element to the conventional definition. To the subject and the biographer she added the audience. Before the "power" of a biography can be complete, she wrote, a "life must first be lived, and then it must be written, and then it must be read."[38] Once a life is lived, it is over. Once a biography is written and published, it is finished. But because there will always be a new readership, the "audience" lives on.

The impulse to make sense of Jefferson will tempt new biographers to grapple with Ellis's "American Sphinx" and encourage us once again to reconsider his place in American history. Historians of the twenty-first century are no less interested than their forebears were. Among these are Jon Meacham, Annette Gordon-Reed and Peter Onuf, and John B. Boles. Their thorough research and insightful thinking about the work of the nineteenth- and twentieth-century biographers offer us a new foundation from which to explore Jefferson and his world. They took on that task because, as Meacham writes, the "story of Jefferson's life fascinates still."[39] None of these books will have the final say on Thomas Jefferson, but the words that each author has chosen to help us understand and evaluate him are based upon years of research, thought, and getting to know Jefferson.

Jefferson's reputation rises and falls. In the early twenty-first century, he is a deeply flawed man, knocked off the pedestal on which Americans had placed him. Meacham, Gordon-Reed and Onuf, and Boles have not joined the chorus of those who unrelievedly criticize Jefferson. Nor do their works resemble the hagiography of Tucker, Randall, Parton, or Sarah Randolph. Meacham, Gordon-Reed and Onuf, and Boles do not overlook Jefferson's failings, but also want to recognize his strengths and achievements. For Meacham, the real Jefferson was "a bundle of contradictions, competing passions, flaws, sins and virtues that can never be neatly smoothed out into a tidy whole." Gordon-Reed and Onuf note that they do not "always endorse Jefferson's formulations of why he did things or what he thought about matters," and they admit "the problematic nature of some of his actions and thoughts and their consequences." Boles is emphatic that to "understand certainly does not mean to approve or even forgive; rather, it means to comprehend," even if at times Jefferson "acted in ways we now find abhorrent." These are the disclaimers with which they begin.[40]

Meacham uses the concept of power—"the art of power"—as the thread that runs through Jefferson's life and helps us make sense of him. Whether it was the power of the pen, the power of personal relationships, or the power of the intellect, Jefferson was masterful. Above all, it is the power of the presidency that captures Meacham's attention most fully. Jefferson was "eager to wield the power he had long sought," he observes, and the story of his two terms as president "is one of a lifelong student of control and power." On March 4, 1809, he gave "a Farewell to Ultimate Power," as chapter 39 is titled.[41]

Gordon-Reed and Onuf explore Jefferson's "Empire of Imagination." His empire was vast because his expansive mind was shaped by a lifetime of radically different experiences, from his birth on a Virginia plantation tended by enslaved labor, to the world of the Enlightenment, which he encountered at the College of William and Mary, to a five-year residence in Paris, where he could participate in the intellectual, political, scientific, and artistic life of that vibrant city. Through a lively and learned correspondence with intellectuals from Paris to London to Washington, D.C., to Braintree, Massachusetts, Jefferson kept that "Empire of Imagination" alive.

Boles gives us a "full-scale biography" of Jefferson, "architect of American liberty," that begins "years before his birth" and ends with the inscription on his tombstone. His Jefferson is an "architect" who designed and built not only Monticello but also the Declaration of Independence and institutions like the Library of Congress, West Point, and the University of Virginia. He understood the complexities of liberty. In early 1790, not long after Jefferson had returned from France and the turmoil that was bubbling there, he cautioned that "the ground of liberty is to be gained by inches, that we must be contented to secure what we can get from time to time, and eternally push forward for what is yet to get. It takes time to persuade men to do even what is for their own good."[42] Jefferson was wise and prescient.

As we seek to fulfill Jefferson's charge to Madison to "take care" of him we must come to terms with the ugliest parts of his life while finding a way to hold on to the positive and inspiring aspects of his legacy. We build on the scholarship of those who came before us in order to increase our knowledge of Jefferson for the future. Previously unknown manuscripts in an uncataloged archival collection, the holdings of a private collector, or an item from the proverbial "dusty attic" will surface to surprise us. Documents that may have been deemed of secondary importance to political historians in the 1950s came to life in the hands of social and cultural historians beginning in the 1960s. A laundry list, a calling card, or a scribble on the back of an envelope can significantly alter our view of Jefferson and other "founders" and call for a new biography or revision of an old one. Fuller answers to enduring questions posed by journalists, pundits, political scientists, and historians will always be demanded.

While Brodie turned to the insights of psychoanalysis for a solution to the mystery of Jefferson, Robert Frost suggested another way of considering the puzzle. He predicted that Jefferson "will trouble us a thousand years." What did Jefferson mean when he said that "all men are created free and equal? . . . That's a hard mystery of Jefferson's." Perhaps only he knew the answer. What is certain is that each age will have to reconsider and decide for itself.[43]

Notes

1. Hermione Lee, *Biography: A Very Short Introduction* (New York, 2009), 5. Lee continues: "Why 'story' rather than 'account'? Because biography is a form of narrative, not just a presentation of facts." For excellent general introductions to biography as a genre, see Scott E. Casper, *Constructing American Lives: Biography and Culture in Nineteenth-Century America* (Chapel Hill, N.C., 1999), and Nigel Hamilton, *Biography: A Brief History* (Cambridge, Mass., 2007).

2. James Atlas, in "The Biographer as Murderer," *New York Times,* Magazine Section, 12 December 1993, quotes Arthur Schlesinger Jr. from the *New Republic.* The other quotations are from Robert D. Richardson, "The Perils of Writing Biography," in *Lives Out of Letters: Essays on American Literary Biography and Documentation, in Honor of Robert N. Hudspeth,* ed. Robert D. Habich (Madison, N.J., 2004), 253–54.

3. Annette Gordon-Reed, "Writing Early American Lives as Biography," *WMQ* 71 (2014): 492–93.

4. "The Late Benjamin Franklin," in *The Complete Humorous Sketches and Tales of Mark Twain,* ed. Charles Neider (Garden City, N.Y., 1961), 138.

5. Joseph J. Ellis, *American Sphinx: The Character of Thomas Jefferson* (New York, 1997), 10. See also George M. Curtis III, "Sphinx without a Riddle: Joseph Ellis and the Art of Jefferson Biography," *Indiana Magazine of History* 95, no. 2 (1999): 178.

6. *Jefferson Image,* 31.

7. See Francis D. Cogliano, *Thomas Jefferson: Reputation and Legacy* (Charlottesville, Va., 2006), 77–105.

8. *TJP,* 37:401.

9. John Milton Cooper Jr., *Woodrow Wilson: A Biography* (New York, 2009), 599.

10. Fawn Brodie, "Jefferson Biographers and the Psychology of Canonization," *Journal of Interdisciplinary History* 1 (1971): 155.

11. Cogliano, *Thomas Jefferson*, 79.

12. George Tucker, *The Life of Thomas Jefferson, Third President of the United States; with Parts of his Correspondence Never Before Published, and Notices of his Opinions on Questions of Civil Government, National Policy, and Constitutional Law*, 2 vols. (London, 1837), 1:xii.

13. *Jefferson Image*, 36.

14. Henry S. Randall, *The Life of Thomas Jefferson*, 3 vols. (New York, 1858), 3:539n, 667–69. Randall wrote: "This reminds us that we have been repeatedly requested, while preparing these volumes, to furnish a connected view of Mr. Jefferson's opinions on the subject of slavery, slavery limitation, emancipation, etc. Originally believing that such a summary would necessarily fall within the plan of the work, we promised to furnish it in these pages. As it was not decided ultimately to pursue an analogous course in regard to other prominent topics of Mr. Jefferson's life and opinions, the promised explanation will be placed in the Appendix." The Appendix concluded with, "We leave the subject to the judgment of the reader."

15. James Parton, *Life of Thomas Jefferson* (Boston, 1874), 745.

16. The line was originally published in a Boston newspaper and then copied into a Philadelphia paper. Randall, *Life of Thomas Jefferson*, 3:19n.

17. Parton, *Life of Thomas Jefferson*, 570, 754.

18. Randall, *Life of Thomas Jefferson*, 1:360.

19. Ibid., 3:66.

20. Ibid., 3:561; Parton, *Life of Thomas Jefferson*, 744.

21. Parton, *Life of Thomas Jefferson*, iii.

22. Sara N. Randolph, *The Domestic Life of Thomas Jefferson* (New York, 1871), 432.

23. *Jefferson Image*, 139.

24. Arthur Schlesinger Jr., *The Cycles of American History* (Boston, 1986), x, 23.

25. *Jefferson Image*, 222–23.

26. Herbert Croly, *The Promise of American Life* (Princeton, N.J., 2014), x; Vernon L. Parrington, *The Romantic Revolution in American Thought*, 3 vols. (New York, 1927), 2:473.

27. Arthur S. Link, *The Papers of Woodrow Wilson* (Princeton, N.J., 1973), 16:359.

28. Claude G. Bowers, *Jefferson and Hamilton: The Struggle for Democracy in America* (Boston, 1925), v. Bowers writes movingly about being "shocked" to discover that Hamilton "scorned democracy" in *My Life: The Memoirs of Claude Bowers* (New York, 1962), 39.

29. *Jefferson Image*, 280.

30. Ibid., 413.

31. Ibid., 379.

32. Roosevelt's idea led to the birth of a number of endeavors to collect and publish the correspondence and the papers of five of the "founding fathers." Nock had pointed to the deplorable neglect of Jefferson's papers, which brought "the literary and social character of this country into contempt." See ibid., 439. The creation of a massive project to edit Jefferson's papers, *The Papers of Thomas Jefferson*, which commenced at

Princeton University in 1943 under the leadership of Julian P. Boyd, was designed to offer Americans the resources for understanding important events of their history. See Barbara B. Oberg and James P. McClure, "'For Generations to Come': Creating the 'Definitive' Jefferson Edition," in Francis D. Cogliano, *A Companion to Thomas Jefferson* (Malden, Mass., 2012), 491–509.

33. Hofstadter, *American Political Tradition,* 352. For a thoughtful discussion of Chinard and his "Americanness," see *Jefferson Image,* 414–17.

34. *Jefferson Image,* 417.

35. Ibid., 454. Peterson links Malone to Randall, whose *Life* was the capstone of an earlier era. Malone, in the introduction to his first volume, praised Randall's biography as one that had not been matched "in scope and impressiveness." See Dumas Malone, *Jefferson and His Time,* 6 vols. (Boston, 1948–81), 1:viii.

36. *Jefferson Image,* 277.

37. For all of these charges, see Newell G. Bringhurst, "Fawn Brodie's Thomas Jefferson: The Making of a Popular and Controversial Biography," *Pacific Historical Review* 62 (1993): 453.

38. Annette Gordon-Reed, "Writing Early American Lives as Biography," *WMQ,* 3rd ser., 71 (2014): 502.

39. Jon Meacham, *Thomas Jefferson: The Art of Power* (New York, 2012); Annette Gordon-Reed and Peter Onuf, *"Most Blessed of the Patriarchs": Thomas Jefferson and the Empire of the Imagination* (New York, 2016); John B. Boles, *Jefferson: Architect of American Liberty* (New York, 2017). Quotation from Meacham, *Thomas Jefferson,* xxiii.

40. Meacham, *Thomas Jefferson,* 500; Gordon-Reed and Onuf, *"Most Blessed of the Patriarchs,"* xx–xxi; Boles, *Jefferson,* 3.

41. Meacham, *Thomas Jefferson,* 350, 351.

42. TJ to Charles Clay, 27 January 1790, *TJP,* 16:129–30.

43. Robert Frost, "The Black Cottage," in *The Complete Poems of Robert Frost* (New York, 1939), 75–76.

I   Memory

"Merely Personal or Private, with Which We Have Nothing to Do"

Thomas Jefferson's Autobiographical Writings

J. Jefferson Looney

On February 9, 1816, Thomas Jefferson dismissed Joseph Delaplaine's request for biographical details as follows: "You request me, in your last letter, to give you 'the facts of my life, birth, parentage, profession, time of going to Europe, returning, offices E^tc.' I really have not time to do it, and still less inclination. To become my own biographer is the last thing in the world I would undertake. No. If there has been any thing in my course worth the public attention, they are better judges of it than I can be myself, and to them it is my duty to leave it."[1] Despite this emphatic assertion, Jefferson did indeed leave a significant body of autobiographical writing. Much, but not all of it, was composed in his last decade. Most of it presents such confusion in definition and presentation that the principal object of inquiry is unraveling what should be accepted as part of Jefferson's scattered memoirs, what has been done with them in the past, and what needs to be done with them hereafter. The material considered consists of Jefferson's short descriptions of his life, his so-called Autobiography, the "Anas," his final plans to continue his memoirs, and the pertinent material scattered elsewhere in his papers.

Jefferson wrote his first short memoir in 1800. A campaign biography pseudonymously published by John Beckley was reprinted in a Richmond newspaper on September 2 of that year. Jefferson reacted to gaps and errors with an undated, untitled memorandum that began with the provocative statement that "I have sometimes asked myself whether my country is the better for my having lived at all? I do not know that it is. I have been the instrument of doing the following things; but they would have been done by others; some of them perhaps a little later." Presumably because they had been adequately covered by Beckley, Jefferson said nothing of his services as governor, diplomat, secretary of state, and vice president, and he devoted a single line to the Declaration of Independence. He began with his first public act, a successful campaign to improve the navigation of the Rivanna River. Jefferson wrote of his contributions to reform of the Virginia legal code, with particular attention to the disestablishment of the Episcopal Church, the ending of primogeniture and entail, and the prohibition of the importation of slaves. He laid claim to introducing olive plants and upland African rice into America, proudly noting that "the greatest service which can be rendered any country is to add an useful plant to its culture." A final paragraph corrected several errors in Beckley's biography, but the longest and most strongly worded section came earlier, when Jefferson argued that he had been denied proper credit for the act for apportioning crimes and punishments. After observing that his bill had been narrowly defeated in 1785, he indignantly recalled that, in the Virginia House of Delegates eleven years later, George K. Taylor "made & printed a long speech from which any person would suppose . . . that the thing had never been ment[ione]d before: for he takes care not to glance at what had been done before and he drew his bill over again, carefully avoiding the adoption of any part of the diction of mine."[2] In creating his memorandum Jefferson was evidently writing for himself and for posterity, for he is not known to have circulated it. The most revealing aspect is undoubtedly its insecure opening.

Jefferson was drawn more publicly into crafting his own biography seven years after leaving the presidency. Joseph Delaplaine was preparing his *Repository of the Lives and Portraits of Distinguished Americans.* He devoted much time and money to this ambitious project, which combined biographies of great Americans with engraved likenesses based on the best available life portraits.[3] When he could not obtain access to Gilbert Stuart's portrait of Jefferson, Delaplaine went so far as to travel to Monticello with the painter Bass Otis to obtain a sitting from him there.[4]

In response to Delaplaine's request for a memoir, Jefferson refused in the words with which this chapter begins, but he eventually directed him to a biography that had appeared in the British journal *Public Characters* in 1801, which he recalled as containing "tolerably exact and minute information." He had sold his copy to the nation with the rest of his library in 1815, and so he could no longer enumerate any errors. Delaplaine accordingly sent Jefferson a copy of the pertinent volume of *Public Characters* and asked him for any necessary corrections.[5] The retired statesman obliged with more than three pages of errata and addenda. When Delaplaine asked Jefferson for further facts the following year, he somewhat grudgingly replied on April 12, 1817, excusing his slow response because "my repugnance is so invincible to be saying any thing of my own history, as if worthy to occupy the public attention."

In his list of 1816 and letter of the following year, Jefferson gave the dates of his birth, marriage, and wife's death; admitted to reading seven languages; named the same Virginia statutes that he had thought significant in 1800; and provided a full enumeration of his diplomatic appointments. He claimed that, while his draft Virginia constitution of 1776 reached Williamsburg so late that it was used only to supply a belated preface, he believed it to be "the very first" state constitution "made by any person in America." As before, Jefferson wrote nothing of his term as governor. When asked to name his siblings and descendants and the scientific societies to which he belonged, he dug in his heels, remarking in the former instance that "I still think that many of the objects of your enquiry are too minute for public notice. The number, names, and ages of my children, grandchildren, great grandchildren E[t]c would produce fatigue and disgust to your readers, of which I would be an unwilling instrument." As to his society memberships, he advised Delaplaine that "they are many and would be long to enumerate, and would savour too much of vanity and pedantry. Would it not be better to say merely that I am a member of many literary societies in Europe and America?"[6]

Thus, in such directly autobiographical writing as he undertook through 1820, Jefferson reacted to the work of others, providing some corrections and filling some gaps but supplying very little in the way of personal information or introspection.

Early in 1821, Jefferson overcame his expressed aversion to writing about himself and produced his longest description of his life. In his opening on January 6 he stated his intention "to make some memoranda and state some recollections of dates & facts concerning myself, for my own more ready reference & for the information of my family." Before he laid his pen down for the last time on July 29 of the same year, Jefferson covered the period from his birth to his arrival in New York to take up his duties as secretary of state. In something like 32,000 words on ninety-three manuscript pages, Jefferson provided a very brief description of his parentage, education, and marriage.[7] He devoted the vast majority of the piece to his public life, especially his contributions to the revolutionary movement, his time in the Continental Congress, his legislative contributions in the Virginia House of Delegates, and his years in France. He again omitted his governorship, remarking that he had contributed materials to Louis H. Girardin for his history of Virginia and that Girardin had told the story well.[8]

Although historians and biographers quite properly mine it for specific statements of fact and descriptions of events, they have devoted surprisingly little attention to the creation or evaluation of this memoir. In his weighty one-volume biography, Merrill D. Peterson alluded to the work on page 4 as an "unvarnished chronicle" of Jefferson's "life to mid-passage," remarking that despite its value, it "sheds little light on the child who became the man." He did not mention it again in his remaining 1,000 pages. Even Dumas Malone cited it as needed but mentioned it only twice in the concluding volume covering the year it was written. He first alluded to its composition in a single sentence so that he could quote its stirring language on the eventual but possibly violent elimination of slavery, and he subsequently described it as "not an especially self-revealing document."[9]

Historians have generally reacted to the memoir with disappointment, because it contains little introspection and few personally revealing anecdotes. Comparisons with Benjamin Franklin's autobiography are common and set Jefferson up for failure, given the charm, candor, and literary quality of Franklin's effort. Two of the better analyses of Jefferson's memoir, an essay by James Cox and an introduction to an edition by Michael Zuckerman, point out that this negative reaction is largely unfair, in that it expects of Jefferson what he never claimed or wanted to be doing. His stated intention was to create memoranda to aid his own memory and inform his descendants, not to bare his soul. The failure to go into much detail about his private life is completely in keeping with his unwillingness to supply similar information to Delaplaine.[10]

Jefferson's memoir is nonetheless an exceedingly valuable work. It contains immensely useful and important descriptions of his activities in and reflections on the years leading up to and immediately following American independence, many of which are to be found nowhere else. Portions of the work are dry, but it is interlaced with flashes of eloquence and insight, such as his comment that France was the second choice, after their own land, of all civilized men; his shrewd word portraits of Edmund Pendleton and James Madison; and his penetrating discussions of the debates over the disestablishment of the Virginia Episcopal Church and the events leading up to the French Revolution.

Confusion about the memoir has flourished because its textual history has been insufficiently studied. It was published in each of the four earlier collected editions of Jefferson's works, starting with that of Thomas Jefferson Randolph in 1829. It has also appeared in innumerable selections of his writings, most importantly those of Adrienne Koch and William Peden (1944) and Merrill Peterson (1984), and a few stand-alone editions, with one introduced by Malone in 1959 and another introduced by Michael Zuckerman in 2005.[11] Over the years full or partial translations have appeared in many foreign languages, including Spanish, Russian, Italian, Hungarian, and Chinese.[12]

Despite this proliferation of versions, there is no reliable published text, and the available editions pose many pitfalls to the reader. Even the title requires rethinking. The work is generally called the Autobiography, but Jefferson himself gave it no title. Randolph called it a "Memoir." Henry A. Washington was the first to refer to it as the "Autobiography," and all subsequent editors followed his lead.[13] But the word itself promises too much and has influenced the critical reaction. Something like "Jefferson's Notes on His Early Career" would be more accurate and less open to misconstruction.

Only two editors seem to have based their work on Jefferson's original manuscript: Thomas Jefferson Randolph in 1829 and Paul Leicester Ford in 1892. With or without full attribution, every other edition has simply copied these early transcriptions with greater or lesser care. The collected editions of Washington (1853–54) and of Andrew A. Lipscomb and Albert E. Bergh (1903–4) are based on Randolph. So is the edition of 1959, to which Malone apparently contributed only a general introduction cobbled together from the first volume of his Jefferson biography.[14]

The Zuckerman edition is a photofacsimile of a 1914 reprint of Ford, with Zuckerman's introduction attached to the front. Setting aside broader issues about Ford's work to be considered below, this approach creates confusion when footnotes direct the reader to documents "Printed in this edition" under specific dates, but not included in the Zuckerman reprint, or when folio-gathering numbers at the foot of pages refer not to the volume in hand but to the original Ford volume.[15]

The Randolph and Ford editions met the needs of their time and satisfied generations of scholars, but comparison with Jefferson's manuscript suggests the need for a reliable modern edition. Randolph does not preserve Jefferson's punctuation, capitalization, spelling, superscripting, or abbreviations. Ford is much more scrupulous on some of these points, as indeed on all points of accuracy, but he is sometimes inconsistent in puzzling ways. A prime example is Jefferson's record of the dates he worked on the document. He gave the date he began, the subsequent dates on which he returned to the manuscript, and the date he laid down his pen for the final time, giving a total of eighteen days of composition.[16] Randolph gave only the opening date, silently dropping all the others. Ford recorded the first and last date but omitted almost half of those in between. The version in Peterson's Library of America collection of 1984 is based on the 1892 Ford edition and duly relied on that work in drawing the incorrect but understandable conclusion that Jefferson did not work on the memoir between January 6 and February 6, when he in fact recorded working on it on five days between those dates.[17]

Both early editions also left ample scope for confusion about the contents of the original manuscript. Randolph included a fifty-six-page "Appendix" of related documents in notes that he lettered from A to H. Many of them are documents that Jefferson referred to specifically in the Autobiography, sometimes with actual citations (for example, "see my letter of Aug. 31. 20. to mr John Saunderson"), sometimes without. Randolph's appendix also contains Jefferson's memorandum on his public service of 1800, which is not mentioned in the Autobiography but may have been filed with it by Jefferson.[18]

Ford omitted the Appendix but provided cross references in his footnotes to many pertinent documents included elsewhere in his edition. The net effect of the approach in both editions is that the reader has no way of telling which documents Jefferson physically included with or near the Autobiography.

Jefferson's Notes of Proceedings in the Continental Congress, June 7 to August 1, 1776, provides a particularly important and murky example. This twenty-page description of the events during these crucial months, which includes a text of the Declaration of Independence showing all of the congressional changes to Jefferson's draft, is included by Ford and Randolph incorporated at its proper place as part of the Autobiography. Both editors indicate in footnotes that these notes were written earlier on different paper and ink and then incorporated into the Autobiography. Julian P. Boyd went on to show in the first volume of the *Papers of Thomas Jefferson* that this particular text was prepared no later than 1783, with a few further additions and emendations dating to the years 1819–25, and he printed them as a distinct document at the date of the events they described in 1776.[19]

Because all published versions of the Autobiography incorporate these earlier notes, some historians have loosely stated that Jefferson's annoyance or disappointment at the alterations and abridgements that Congress made to the Declaration of Independence still rankled so much in 1821 that he included both versions in the Autobiography.[20] In fact, he merely interleaved with the Autobiography a much older text that gave both versions, and this older text was part of a much longer narrative of events from 1776.

Greater attention to the manuscript may yield information on Jefferson's working method and probable intentions. Although Boyd did not create an edition of the Autobiography, he provided the most detailed physical description of it to date as part of his editorial note on the 1776 congressional proceedings.[21] Boyd observed that Jefferson numbered the pages of the Autobiography before the proceedings were interleaved with it, and also that he evidently replaced one page with a shorter version that made the congressional proceedings fit better at the point of their insertion, which probably occurred well after the July 1821 date on which Jefferson ostensibly ceased work on the Autobiography. The proceedings were most likely moved in connection with one of the late inquiries about his role in authoring the Declaration.

Boyd's observation strongly suggests that Jefferson returned to the Autobiography after July 1821. The manuscript provides other clues. Jefferson claimed that he was dashing off these notes in haste and without much enthusiasm, concluding his entry for February 7 with the admission that "I am already tired of talking about myself." But Jefferson evidently made a fair copy of the manuscript at least once. With three exceptions, the ninety sheets on which it is written have blank versos. Most of the pages are quite clean, with only a handful of the cross-outs and interlineations typical of Jefferson's drafts. Furthermore, Jefferson habitually wrote his drafts with wide margins to allow plenty of space for emendations as he revised. Yet only two pages of the manuscript, the first and the one he rewrote or reverted to in order to accommodate the congressional notes, are in this typical draft format. The rest have narrow margins and generally fill up the page. At certain points Jefferson lets a page run short and explicitly states that a specific document is to follow.[22] In sum, the manuscript was evidently revised carefully and copied with an eye to eventual publication. Whether Jefferson decided against contemporary publication or always intended it as a legacy for posthumous editors is unclear. A scholarly edition is needed to consider just such questions and make this memoir more understandable.[23]

The late Frank Shuffelton suggested that Jefferson's "Anas"—the documents he wrote and collected during his term as the nation's first secretary of state—should be regarded as in some sense a continuation of the Autobiography. He argued that, despite their many differences, the two can fruitfully be examined together as Jefferson's one extended exercise in writing and arranging the account of his own life. This insight has greatly benefited subsequent research on the subject.[24] Properly defining one's terms and further documentary scholarship are needed, however, to understand fully the documents constituting the "Anas" and their crucial place in the history of the emerging American political party system.

Jefferson was always meticulous about keeping records and preserving his correspondence, and his years as secretary of state were no exception. During this period he continued the epistolary record, the Summary Journal of Letters, in which he listed what he sent and received.[25] Although he enumerated a great deal of public correspondence, Jefferson did not routinely include his communications with George Washington or fellow cabinet members, evidently thinking of them more as interoffice memos than letters. Jefferson chose instead to preserve a separate grouping of official and unofficial records of his tenure in office. To his correspondence with other members of the executive, Jefferson added drafts of letters composed for President Washington, state papers prepared for Congress, bills and resolutions drafted for individual congressmen, translations of French and Spanish documents for Washington's use, cabinet opinions, and other official documents.

Jefferson also began to jot down his reactions to the emerging political situation and record what can only be described as gossip about his enemies.[26] Alarmed by what he increasingly came to see as an attempt by a faction led by Treasury Secretary Alexander Hamilton to hijack the American experiment in republicanism and steer it toward an authoritarian central government, Jefferson began to document his suspicions. The first such memorandum, describing a conversation with Hamilton, was dated August 13, 1791. It may be no coincidence that Jefferson began taking notes on the inner workings of the national government at the same time that he was exposed to James Madison's daily notes on the Federal Convention of 1787. With the stakes so high, it made sense to capture correctly the words and deeds of foes as well as friends.[27]

Jefferson left extraordinarily candid and lively accounts of cabinet meetings. He detailed his growing suspicions about Hamilton as well as his continuing respect for Washington. He vented his frustration that the first president did not share his doubts about the treasury secretary. Jefferson recorded his scorn for Henry Knox, whom he roundly dismissed as a fool, as well as his account of one memorable meeting in which Washington was goaded into losing his temper. He also registered his annoyance that Edmund Randolph could not be counted on to side with him in cabinet votes.[28] From friends like House clerk John Beckley, Jefferson heard and preserved descriptions of attempts to give royalist trappings to levees and balls for a reluctant president, of allegedly corrupt financial transactions by Hamilton and a monarchical proposal he had supposedly circulated in about 1787, of conversations in which Federalists were overheard disparaging trial by jury and supporting a hereditary Senate, and of an allegation that Hamilton and others had been promised British pensions if their efforts to subvert the American experiment in self-government were exposed and they had to flee.[29]

Jefferson's original method in filing and grouping these documents has not been discovered, but at some point after leaving office he had them bound into three volumes. Recognizing their explosive nature, he took care to have the binding done under his own eye and without permitting the artisan doing the work to read any of the documents therein. Jefferson subsequently turned again to these volumes and in 1818 prefaced them with "Explanations of the 3. volumes bound in Marbled paper." There he stated that the collection began as his "official opinions given in writing by me to Gen¹ Washington . . . with sometimes the documents belonging to the case." Jefferson initially took "no other note of the passing transactions: but, after awhile, I saw the importance of doing it, in aid of my memory." Thereafter he often "made memorandums on loose scraps of paper, taken out of my pocket in the moment, and laid by to be copied fair at leisure, which however they hardly ever were." Despite being "ragged, rubbed, & scribbled," he had added these "scraps" to the volumes being bound.[30]

In the 1818 preface Jefferson claimed that at that time he had given the entire collection a "calm revisal, when the passions of the time" had receded, and had removed everything "incorrect, or doubtful, or merely personal or private, with which we have nothing to do." He argued at considerable length that preservation of the rest had become necessary to counteract the negative picture of the Republican party given in 1807 in the final volume of John Marshall's biography of Washington. Asserting that Republicans united purely on questions of principle and especially "to keep the government within the line of the constitution, and prevent it's being monarchised in practice," Jefferson angrily summarized Marshall's depiction of the Republican party as "a mere set of grumblers, and disorganisers, satisfied with no government, without fixed principles," and motivated primarily by a lust for public money and offices. Jefferson felt confident that his collection of documents would correct the historical record on this point.[31]

This preface was not Jefferson's first attempt to challenge what he regarded as Marshall's bold and outrageous attempt to appropriate the legacy of the American Revolution for the Federalist party. He knew that Marshall was writing such a history by 1802, when Jefferson began offering his own collection of documents to Joel Barlow, urging him to write a competing account. After leaving office in 1809 Jefferson began, but did not finish, a memorandum detailing errors in Marshall's final volume and again promised to make all of his papers available to Barlow, who died without taking up this task.[32] Jefferson's later efforts to enlist Supreme Court justice William Johnson were also unavailing.[33] Forced to leave the job and his own archive to posterity, Jefferson evidently instructed his son-in-law and grandson to publish this material, or at least the preface. Concerned that it not be lost, he also showed the preface to Joseph C. Cabell and James Madison, whom he alerted to his intentions.[34]

As it turns out, posterity has been unable to experience the three volumes in the cohesive form that Jefferson intended. His grandson Thomas Jefferson Randolph ended the first collected edition of Jefferson's works in 1829 with a selection of the private memoranda and notes that he entitled the "Anas," an invented word not used by Jefferson. It derives from the same root as the suffix "ana" and means something like "notable sayings" or "miscellany." Randolph began with Jefferson's 1818 preface and explained that, because the "official opinions and documents" referred to therein were "very voluminous," they had been omitted for the most part, "to make room for the conversations which the same volumes comprise." Randolph's note also referred to these volumes as "containing the ANAS to the time that the Author retired from the office of Secretary of State." This would appear to suggest that Jefferson had left some other memoranda that could be seen as a continuation of this material, and Randolph did indeed add documents dating from 1797 to 1806.[35]

The publication of the "Anas" in 1829 had an immediate impact on the historical literature of its day, and its documents have remained essential sources ever since. Condemned by some for airing the Washington administration's dirty linen and its liberal inclusion of unsubstantiated allegations, Jefferson would have been pleased by its success in showing the ideological fault lines dividing the cabinet.[36] It was reprinted in the same form in Henry A. Washington's edition in 1853–54. Ford's new and much more accurate 1892 version was transcribed from the original, restoring text that Randolph had excised and adding more "Anas"-like documents dated as late as February 1809. The 1903 edition of Jefferson's works by Andrew A. Lipscomb and Albert Ellery Bergh included a version of the "Anas" copied directly from the Randolph/Washington versions but supplemented with the documents added by Ford. Also in 1903, Franklin B. Sawvel published what is still the only single-volume version of this material, entitled *The Complete Anas of Thomas Jefferson*. It made a number of confused claims to originality but is largely based on Ford's work.[37]

Ford and Sawvel both asserted that the papers had been rearranged in such a way that Jefferson's original sequence could not be recovered, but as the editors of the Jefferson Papers at Princeton demonstrated in 1986 in an exhaustive discussion of the publication history of the "Anas," this does not seem to be true. The three volumes as described by Jefferson in the 1818 preface remained intact until after they were transferred from the State Department to the Library of Congress in 1904. It is possible but by no means certain that Jefferson left one or more additional volumes of political miscellany from which was taken the vice-presidential and presidential material included in various combinations in all editions of the "Anas."[38] What is clear is that Jefferson intended for the three volumes of official and unofficial material from his years as secretary of state to be kept together and treated as a unit.

Unfortunately, at some point after 1904 and probably before 1920, the Library of Congress removed the bindings of the three volumes and dispersed their contents chronologically within the first series of its Jefferson Papers collection. Had there been no other evidence, this act of archival vandalism would have been irreversible. Fortunately, in the 1980s the editors of the Jefferson Papers reported that a six-page list of documents in Jefferson's hand and filed with his Summary Journal of Letters was almost certainly a table of contents for these volumes, most probably prepared when they were bound. The list, currently referred to as the Summary Journal of Public Letters, was written on paper bearing a watermark of 1800 and of a type that Jefferson used as late as 1802.[39] He most likely rearranged the documents thus listed, had them bound, and prepared the table of contents in the spring of 1802 as he began considering ways to counteract Marshall's upcoming biography of Washington.[40]

Under the successive editorships of Boyd, Charles T. Cullen, and John Catanzariti, all of the extant documents listed in Jefferson's Summary Journal of Public Letters, both the official material and the notes and memoranda through the end of 1793 hitherto printed as the "Anas," have been published with appropriate scholarly apparatus in the definitive edition of *The Papers of Thomas Jefferson*. Each document appears at its appropriate chronological point, which is fine for many purposes. However, a strong case can be made for the feasibility and utility of a new edition of the surviving documents referenced by Jefferson's Summary Journal of Public Letters and accounting for those listed there and not found. It would be most instructive to see the collection as Jefferson arranged it without the need to sort through a dozen volumes of the Jefferson Papers to reconstruct his own selection of material documenting a crucial period of his life.[41] Only then would scholars be able to experience this idiosyncratic history of these years as Jefferson intended.

A new edition of the material from Jefferson's three-volume collection would have a number of additional benefits. The documents could be presented using the new, more literal transcription policy subsequently adopted by the Jefferson Papers. By preserving Jefferson's very liberal use of abbreviations in this material, it would be possible to grasp the haste and immediacy with which he recorded conversations and transactions, recordkeeping that has been harder to appreciate as smoothed out and modernized in earlier volumes. Further work on this material might also provide better understanding of the dating problem. In his Summary Journal of Public Letters, Jefferson provided exact dates for a number of undated documents, some of which can be shown to be incorrect. More needs to be done to determine whether he was providing his best guess as to the correct dates, with understandable errors some years after the fact, or whether he was drawing on some as-yet-undiscovered source to arrive at these conjectural dates. It is also at least possible that Jefferson misdated some items intentionally. For example, by moving the date for his draft of the American Philosophical Society's Instructions to André Michaux from April 1793 to January 23 of that year, he placed them safely well before the arrival in America of French minister plenipotentiary Edmond Charles Genet, whose undiplomatic behavior greatly embarrassed Jefferson and whose recruitment of Michaux to his revolutionary schemes led to the premature end of the latter's scientific expedition to the West.[42]

Such an edition would also make it far easier to locate and assess the places where Jefferson eliminated or edited earlier entries. In 1818, he claimed to have cut substantially while revising the "Anas." His changes were in fact probably quite modest. A quick survey of his Summary Journal of Public Letters turns up only a few documents not now extant, albeit with such fascinating titles as "Notes. Hamilton" of October 6 and 11, 1792, and "Clymer's adventures," dated October 22, 1792, all three of which apparently related to the early stages of the Whiskey Rebellion. In addition, a single edition would facilitate finding and analyzing the places where Jefferson retained a document in 1818 but edited it to eliminate or soften some of the contents. This too seems to have been infrequent, but some of the known instances are very revealing.

Jefferson, for example, canceled most of a 1792 entry relating to Hamilton's affair with Maria Reynolds. Hamilton admitted this transgression five years later to counter accusations by James Callender of financial impropriety. Inasmuch as Callender was the same scandalmongering journalist who in 1802 alleged Jefferson's sexual relationship with Sally Hemings, Jefferson may have been less inclined to spotlight the Reynolds story in 1818 than he had been in 1792. Jefferson also included a 1793 rumor that Hamilton, Rufus King, and William Loughton Smith had pensions waiting for them in England, but he later added as a footnote that the story was "impossible as to Hamilton. He was far above that." By 1818, Jefferson may have developed a more positive view of Hamilton's character, but he could also have realized that impugning the honor of Hamilton, slain in an 1804 duel with Aaron Burr, might backfire and undermine his own reputation.[43]

A new edition would enable readers to draw their own boundary between "public" and "private" in Jefferson's collection of documents. Since

Randolph's time, the notion of a reasonably cohesive collection of private memoranda and notes that historians cite as the "Anas" has been at least tacitly accepted. However, quite a few items listed in Jefferson's Summary Journal of Public Letters but not hitherto included in the "Anas" do not readily qualify as public documents, such as the 1792 "Agenda to Reduce the Government to True Principles" and "Extempore thoughts and doubts on very superficially running over the bankrupt bill," as well as the 1793 Report on Edmond Charles Genet and Gouverneur Morris, in which Jefferson describes to the president in minute and fascinating detail his thought processes during negotiations with the obstreperous French minister.[44] Here and in many other cases the value of seeing the full three-volume collection as Jefferson intended it would provide new insights into the ways in which, as compiler and editor of his own writings, he sought to shape readers' understanding of his life and political goals.[45]

Influenced by the pioneering work of Shuffelton, historians now often discuss the Autobiography and the "Anas" as a single unit, albeit with great differences one from the other, which collectively bring his story from birth to the end of 1793. The 1821 memoir having been written after Jefferson prepared his preface to the corpus detailing his service as secretary of state, and with the memoir ending where the latter begins, this conceptual strategy is reasonable and useful. However, Jefferson did not necessarily think of the "Anas" as part two of the Autobiography. He certainly considered continuing his memoir.

Jefferson left one such clue in the Autobiography itself, hinting on February 7, 1821, that he would "recur again" to his efforts to promote education "towards the close of my story, if I should have life and resolution enough to reach that term." In July, he ceased work on the memoir, long before it reached his ongoing efforts to found the University of Virginia, presumably thus referenced.[46]

But Jefferson did consider taking up his pen again after July 1821. Later that year John Wayles Eppes urged him to prepare a "view of your administration." Arguing that this could be Jefferson's "most valuable legacy" to posterity, Eppes offered to loan Jefferson his own set of state papers and newspapers. Jefferson replied in October that "I am too old to begin any serious work. It had always been my intention to commit to writing some notes and explanations of particular and leading transactions which history should know. But in parting with my library to Congress, I parted with my whole collection of newspapers, journals, state papers, documents E'c without the aid of which I have been afraid to trust my memory. If you can lend me the collection mentioned in your letter for a winter or two, I will immediately proceed to do what I think most material." Jefferson asked Eppes to keep this plan a secret.[47]

In 1822, Jefferson sent a cart for Eppes's collection, stating that "the information I need is generally" from 1789 forward. After the final year of his presidency, he needed "nothing at all." He listed the items he particularly wanted, including congressional journals, state papers, and all newspapers published within the same twenty-year period. Jefferson observed that advancing age and especially the burden of keeping up with unwanted correspondence left him only "the mere offal of my time" for the project, but "still I will try to do what these will admit." Eppes quickly sent the desired material and urged Jefferson to drop his correspondence "in mass & devote the remainder of your life to completing a work which may at some future day become a school book in which our young men may learn the value of principles which terminated only with life—I think too that such a work you owe in some degree to your future fame." After all, Marshall had written with the "express purpose of casting a cloud over some of the most important events of your life."[48] Jefferson seems to have progressed no further. Nonetheless, his interest in obtaining from Eppes everything dating between 1789 and 1809 suggests that he did not regard the "Anas" as a formal continuation of his memoir.

Jefferson's final exercise in autobiography came early in 1826 as part of his "Thoughts on Lotteries," prepared to assist his grandson Thomas Jefferson Randolph in lobbying the Virginia General Assembly for a bill to raffle Monticello after Jefferson's financial situation became desperate. An essay tinged with pathos listed each of his offices from election to the House of Burgesses through service as rector of the University of Virginia. Jefferson singled out for the last time his authorship of state laws promoting democracy and liberty, but he also emphasized his leadership as vice president, arguing that "nothing on earth is more certain than" that, if Jefferson had "withdrawn from my post, the republicans thro'out the Union would have given up in despair and the cause would have been lost for ever." While acknowledging many coadjutors, Jefferson ended his list of achievements with his creation of the University of Virginia, proudly concluding that his native state would soon "fill all it's offices with men of superior qualifications and raise it from it's humbled state to an eminence among it's associates which it has never yet known."[49]

In his 1826 summary, as in each earlier one, Jefferson focused almost exclusively on his public actions, service, goals, and achievements. The insights and memories in his autobiographical writings considered thus far are valuable and sometimes eloquent, but one must seek elsewhere for his own descriptions of his trip to the middle colonies in 1766, of the decades-long process by which he built up his library, of his battles as president to relax the rules of social hierarchy in interactions with diplomats, and of his temperance in eating and drinking as well as his daily schedule and the general state of his health.[50] The works described above do not give Jefferson's reactions to the destruction by fire in 1770 of his Shadwell birthplace, the devastation of his property by the British general Cornwallis and the far more genteel treatment he received from Tarleton, the death of Jefferson's wife in 1782 and his trusted enslaved servant Jupiter in 1800, or the antisocial tendencies he began to observe in himself during his first retirement.[51] They do not include personal expressions of his views on religion, the cultivation of good humor, the study of mathematics, or the philosophy of Plato.[52]

Jefferson did provide essential autobiographical material on all of these subjects and many more, and he indicated where it could be found. Yet just as Jefferson refused to complete a memoir, he also opposed the writing of a biography during a subject's lifetime. In 1823, Jefferson wrote to Robert Walsh that

> I do not think a biography should be written, or at least not published, during the life of the person the subject of it. It is impossible that the writer's delicacy should permit him to speak as freely of the faults or errors of a living, as of a dead character. There is still however a better reason. The letters of a person, especially of one whose business has been chiefly transacted by letters, form the only full and genuine journal of his life; and few can let them go out of their own hands while they live. A life written after these hoards become opened to investigation must supercede any previous one.[53]

Jefferson himself thus attested to the superior validity of the biographies discussed in this book. And he rightly concluded that he penned his truest autobiography in his vast correspondence.

In 1942, Bernard Mayo produced a complete autobiography for Jefferson with his much-reprinted *Jefferson Himself*.[54] However, with choices and commentary that present Jefferson in an especially favorable light, as well as the use of unreliable transcriptions, that particular collection is now dated. The year after Mayo published it, Boyd was appointed the founding editor of *The Papers of Thomas Jefferson*, an ambitious and pioneering project to collect and publish accurate transcriptions of the entire body of Jefferson's words, as well as incoming correspondence. With Malone and Peterson, Boyd formed part of a mid-twentieth-century triumvirate of scholars that had an immense and enduring impact on the interpretation and documentation of Jefferson's life. Although he neither completed the *Papers* nor published a separate biography, in a myriad of ways and venues Boyd fashioned and passionately defended an extremely influential interpretation of Jefferson. He is by far the most important chronicler of Jefferson's life *not* considered in this volume.

With the definitive edition of Jefferson's correspondence and other papers now well past the halfway point, the "hoards" of writing that constitute Jefferson's broadly defined autobiography are increasingly and belatedly enabling him to tell his story in his own words. That it will make its way in a new and boisterous sea of varying interpretations, conflicting evidence, changing values, and competing stories would have neither surprised nor displeased him.

Notes

1. TJ to Joseph Delaplaine, February 9, 1816, *TJP:RS,* 9:459.

2. TJ, Summary of Public Service, [after 2 September 1800,] *TJP,* 32:122–25.

3. Delaplaine to TJ, 23 May 1813, *TJP:RS,* 6:125–26; Delaplaine to TJ, 16 April 1814, ibid., 7:295–96.

4. Alfred L. Bush, *The Life Portraits of Thomas Jefferson,* rev. ed. (Charlottesville, Va., 1987), 64–67.

5. TJ to Delaplaine, 9 February 1816, *TJP:RS,* 9:459; Delaplaine to TJ, 11 May 1816, ibid., 10:38–39.

6. TJ's Corrections to his Biography in *Public Characters,* [ca. 3 June 1816,] *TJP:RS,* 10:114–17; Delaplaine to TJ, 17 March 1817, ibid., 11:202–3; TJ to Delaplaine, 12 April

1817, ibid., 251–52. In TJ's Corrections, he gave his birthday as 2 April 1743, the date as it stood in the Julian calendar. With the eleven-day shift caused by adoption of the Gregorian calendar in 1752, Jefferson's birthday is now generally celebrated on 13 April.

7. TJ, "Autobiography," [6 January–29 July 1821,] *TJW,* 3. The manuscript is in TJ Papers, folio nos. 39061–70, 39081–160, Lib. Cong.

8. In 1816, Girardin had finished work begun by the deceased Skelton Jones and published a fourth volume, covering the American Revolution, to supplement John Daly Burk, *The History of Virginia, from its First Settlement to the Present Day,* 3 vols. (Petersburg, Va., 1804–5).

9. Merrill D. Peterson, *Thomas Jefferson & the New Nation: A Biography* (New York, 1970), 4; Dumas Malone, *Jefferson and His Time,* 6 vols. (Boston, 1948–81), 6: 341–42, 489.

10. James M. Cox, "Recovering Literature's Lost Ground through Autobiography," in *Recovering Literature's Lost Ground: Essays in American Autobiography* (Baton Rouge, La., 1989), 33–54; Michael Zuckerman, introduction to *The Autobiography of Thomas Jefferson, 1743–1790,* ed. Paul Leicester Ford (Philadelphia, 2005), vii–xxx.

11. Thomas Jefferson Randolph, ed., *Memoir, Correspondence, and Miscellanies from the Papers of Thomas Jefferson* (Charlottesville, Va., 1829), 1:1–89, with appendix, 91–146; Adrienne Koch and William Peden, eds., *The Life and Selected Writings of Thomas Jefferson* (New York, 1944), 3–114; *TJW,* 1–101; *Autobiography of Thos. Jefferson. With an Introduction by Dumas Malone* (New York, 1959).

12. *Autobiografía de Tomás Jefferson* (Mexico City, 1963); *Avtobiografiia: Zametki o shtate Virginiia* (Leningrad, 1990); *Thomas Jefferson, o Della felicità,* trans. Maurizio Barbato (Palermo, Italy, 1999), 95–232; *Új rend egy új vilagban: dokumentumok az amerikai politikai gondolkodás korai történetéhez,* trans. Csaba Lévai (Debrecen, Hungary, 1997), 124–30; *Jiefeixun ji* (Beijing, 1993).

13. Henry A. Washington, ed., *The Writings of Thomas Jefferson,* 9 vols. (New York, 1853–54), 1:1–110, with appendix, 111–78.

14. Ford, 1:1–153; L&B, 1:1–164, with appendix, 165–262; *Autobiography of Thos. Jefferson. With an Introduction by Dumas Malone.*

15. See Ford, 1:33n.

16. This may be an undercount. Jefferson did not record dates between 25 May and 29 July, but he probably did not compose the forty intervening manuscript pages in just one day.

17. Randolph, *Memoir, Correspondence, and Miscellanies,* 1:1; *TJW,* 1549n. Jefferson recorded composition dates of 6, 10, 11, 12, 16, 17 January, 6, 7, 8, 9, 10, 11 February, 16 March, 17, 18, 24, 25 May, and 29 July 1821. Of these, Ford only included those of 6 January, 6, 7 February, 16 March, 17, 18, 24 May, and 29 July 1821 (Ford, 1:1, 60, 66, 84, 94, 96, 100, 153).

18. The folio number 39161 stamped on the memorandum by Lib. Cong. places it immediately after the autobiography, and Randolph's inclusion of it in the appendix suggests that he may have found it there.

19. Notes of Proceedings in the Continental Congress, [7 June–1 August 1776,] *TJP,* 1:299–329.

20. See, for example, Matthew E. Crow, "History, Politics, and the Self: Jefferson 'Anas' and Autobiography," in *A Companion to Thomas Jefferson, ed.* Francis D. Cogliano (Oxford, 2012), 486.

21. Notes of Proceedings in the Continental Congress, [7 June–1 August 1776,] *TJP,* 1:299–300.

22. The substituted page 23 is somewhat mysterious. Boyd argues that Jefferson wrote it after completing this section in order to provide the proper link for insertion of the congressional notes. But the page is dated as having been composed 11 and 12 January, which suggests instead that it is the original draft for this page. Furthermore, it is in the narrow-margin format typical of Jefferson's drafts, and it runs to the foot of the page. See TJP, 1:299–300; TJ Papers, folio no. 39082, Lib. Cong.

23. Since this chapter was written, it has tentatively been decided that the Autobiography will be included in *TJP:RS.*

24. Shuffelton unfortunately did not live to publish his own findings on this point. An excellent example of the value of considering the two works in tandem is Crow, "History, Politics, and the Self," 477–90.

25. The Summary Journal of Letters is filed at the end of TJ Papers, ser. 1, Lib. Cong.

26. The best discussion of this aspect of the "Anas" and indeed of the political culture of these years is Joanne B. Freeman, *Affairs of Honor: National Politics in the New Republic* (New Haven, Conn., 2001), esp. 62–104.

27. In the summer of 1791 Jefferson had John Wayles Eppes, his nephew and future son-in-law, prepare a handwritten copy of Madison's notes, thus backing up this priceless record. The work was done under strict injunctions of secrecy, and Jefferson and Eppes may be the only ones not living with Madison who had the chance to read his notes during his lifetime (William T. Hutchinson, William M. E. Rachal, Robert A. Rutland, John C. A. Stagg, et al., eds., *The Papers of James Madison,* 17 vols. [Chicago and Charlottesville, 1962–91,] 10:7; Robert A. Rutland, John C. A. Stagg, et al., eds., *The Papers of James Madison, Presidential Series,* 9 vols. [Charlottesville, 1984– ,] 2:609–11).

28. TJ, Notes of Cabinet Meeting on Edmond Charles Genet, 23 July 1793, *TJP,* 26:554–55; TJ, Notes of Cabinet Meeting on Neutrality, 3 August 1793, ibid., 608; TJ, Notes of Cabinet Meeting on Edmond Charles Genet, 2 August 1793, ibid., 602–3; TJ, Notes of Cabinet Meeting on Neutrality, 30 July 1793, ibid., 588; TJ, Notes of Cabinet Meeting on a Commercial Treaty with France, 23 August 1793, ibid., 750.

29. TJ, Memorandum of Conference with the President on Treaty with Algiers, 11 March 1792, ibid., 23:257; TJ, Notes on Alexander Hamilton and the Bank of the United States, 31 March 1793, ibid., 25:474; TJ, Notes on Alexander Hamilton and "Veritas," 12 June 1793, ibid., 26:267; TJ, Notes on Conversations with John Beckley and George Washington, 7 June 1793, ibid., 219–20; TJ, Notes on Levees and Assumption, 16 February 1793, ibid., 25:208; TJ, Notes on Ceremonial at New York, 10 June

1793, ibid., 26:248–49; TJ, Notes of a Conversation with John Beckley, 1 December 1793, ibid., 27:467.

30. TJ, Explanations of the Three Volumes Bound in Marbled Paper (the so-called "Anas"), 4 February 1818, *TJP:RS,* 12:417–29 (quote on 417).

31. Ibid., 417, 418–19; John Marshall, *The Life of George Washington,* 5 vols. (Philadelphia, 1804–7).

32. TJ to Joel Barlow, 3 May 1802, *TJP,* 37:400–402; TJ to Barlow, 8 October 1809, *TJP:RS,* 1:589; TJ, Notes on the Fifth Volume of John Marshall's *Life of George Washington,* [ca. 4 February 1818,] ibid., 12:429–31.

33. TJ to William Johnson, 4 March 1823, TJ Papers, Lib. Cong.; TJ to Johnson, 12 June 1823, ibid.

34. Joseph C. Cabell's Memorandum on the Introduction to the "Anas," 9 April 1818, *TJP:RS,* 12:431–32.

35. Randolph, *Memoir, Correspondence, and Miscellanies,* gives his version of the "Anas" at 4:443–523, with his note at 443n and the post-1793 material at 501–23. In describing the editing work done by the family prior to publication, Martha Jefferson Randolph referred to "the *Ana* of which there are three volumes" (Randolph to Ellen W. Randolph Coolidge, [ca. 28 May 1829,] Coolidge Correspondence, Special Collections, University of Virginia Library).

36. *Jefferson Image,* 34–36, 76–77; Freeman, *Affairs of Honor,* 277–78.

37. Washington, *Writings of Thomas Jefferson,* 9:87–211; Ford, 1:154–339; L&B, 1:263–492; Franklin B. Sawvel, ed., *The Complete Anas of Thomas Jefferson* (New York, 1903).

38. See The "Anas," [Editorial Note,] *TJP,* 22:36.

39. The Summary Journal of Public Letters, or SJPL, is in TJ Papers, 20:209–11, Lib. Cong., interfiled with the Summary Journal of Letters before the sheet beginning with entries for letters written 30 September and received 26 September 1789. It is not to be confused with a second list of documents from this period also known as the SJPL, which is in a clerk's hand and is unrelated to the "Anas." For the finding that the SJPL in TJ's hand was written on paper watermarked 1800 and used as late as 1802, and that it was a list of the contents of the "Anas," see Foreword, *TJP,* 22:ix–xi; The "Anas," [Editorial Note,] ibid., 33. This volume was edited by Charles T. Cullen, Eugene R. Sheridan, and Ruth W. Lester. Sheridan repeated the finding that SJPL was the table of contents of the "Anas" in his "Thomas Jefferson and the Giles Resolutions," *WMQ* 49 (1992): 607n.

40. On 25 December 1809, Jefferson refused to send Eppes his 15 February 1791 Opinion on the Constitutionality of the Bill for Establishing a National Bank, stating that it was "bound up in a Huge Quarto volume, which cannot be trusted by post. Indeed it contains all my most secret communications, while in the office of state, & never was in the hands of any person but myself" (*TJP:RS,* 2:92). On the strength of this reference to a single, large quarto volume, the Jefferson Papers editors concluded that at some point after 1809 and before he wrote his 1818 preface, Jefferson rearranged the papers and had them rebound in three volumes (The "Anas," [Editorial Note,] *TJP,* 22:33). No other evidence supports this conclusion. It seems likelier that there was only

one binding job, of three volumes, done about 1802 at roughly the same time that Jefferson compiled his table of contents, and that in his 1809 letter to Eppes, Jefferson was simply referring to the specific volume of these three that contained the bank opinion.

41. The earliest document printed in the various editions of the "Anas" is dated 13 August 1791, but the SJPL lists material as early as October 1789.

42. TJ, American Philosophical Society's Instructions to André Michaux, [ca. 30 April 1793,] *TJP*, 25:624–26. See also Editorial Note on Jefferson and André Michaux's Proposed Western Expedition, ibid., 75–81. For other examples of dating discrepancies, see TJ, Cabinet Memorandum on French Privateers, [1 June 1793,] ibid., 26:155–56; Edmund Randolph to TJ, [ca. 24 July 1793,] ibid., 561–62.

43. TJ, Notes on the Reynolds Affair, 17 December 1792, ibid., 24:751; TJ, Notes on Conversations with John Beckley and George Washington, 7 June 1793, ibid., 26:219.

44. TJ, Note of Agenda to Reduce the Government to True Principles, [ca. 11 July 1792,] ibid., 24:215–16; TJ, Thoughts on the Bankruptcy Bill, [ca. 10 December 1792,] ibid., 722–23; TJ, Report on Edmond Charles Genet and Gouverneur Morris, 11 December 1793, ibid., 27:504–6.

45. In the years since this chapter was presented at the "Jefferson's Lives" conference, many of the goals for a new edition of Jefferson's three-volume collection described here have been realized with online publication in April 2018 of a website on the "3. volumes bound in Marbled paper" (http://jefferson3volumes.princeton.edu/). Inspired by conversations with the author and by perusal of this chapter, John C. Van Horne has done a masterful job creating a database that provides access to each of the approximately 800 documents listed in the Summary Journal of Public Letters. Created in collaboration with the Jefferson Papers project at Princeton and the Center for Digital Editing at the University of Virginia, the website copies the transcriptions, with source and textual notes, for each document as originally printed in *The Papers of Thomas Jefferson* or, when not printed there, from other sources such as *The Papers of George Washington*. The database also gives the location and description of each document in the Summary Journal of Public Letters; links to their online publication in the Founders Online and American Founding Era websites, which reproduce all of the *Jefferson Papers;* indicates which documents appeared in previous published versions of the "Anas"; and lists those no longer extant. The reader can thus easily experience Jefferson's collection in its original sequence. Remaining desiderata would be a new transcription of each document using the more literal transcription methods now in use at the *Jefferson Papers* and based on the versions retained by Jefferson (the master texts printed in *The Papers of Thomas Jefferson* were sometimes later versions copied by clerks from his drafts), and with annotation tailored to this collection rather than the broader corpus in which they were published by the *Jefferson Papers*. But this massive job awaits its own editor, and when it is undertaken it will be greatly aided by Van Horne's efforts.

46. TJ Papers, folio nos. 39095–96, 39160, Lib. Cong.

47. Eppes to TJ, 15 October 1821, Massachusetts Historical Society; TJ to Eppes, 23 October 1821, TJ Papers, Lib. Cong.

48. Eppes to TJ, 27 November 1821, Massachusetts Historical Society; Eppes to TJ,

22 January 1822, ibid.; TJ to Eppes, 17 January 1822, Special Collections, University of Virginia Library.

49. TJ, "Thoughts on Lotteries," TJ Papers, folio nos. 41744–46, 39346–47, Lib. Cong., was not published during his lifetime. The extant draft is undated but was probably prepared before 20 January 1826 (Malone, *Jefferson and His Time,* 6:473–74).

50. TJ to John Page, 25 May 1766, *TJP,* 1:18–20; TJ to Francis Willis, 23 July 1766, ibid., 21; TJ to Samuel H. Smith, 21 September 1814, *TJP:RS,* 7:682; TJ to James Monroe, 8 January 1804, *TJP,* 42:249; TJ to Vine Utley, 21 March 1819, *TJP:RS,* 14:156–58.

51. TJ to John Page, 21 February 1770, *TJP,* 1:34–35; TJ to William Gordon, 16 July 1788, ibid., 13:362–63; TJ to Chastellux, 26 November 1782, ibid., 6:203; TJ to Thomas Mann Randolph, 4 February 1800, ibid., 31:360; TJ to Mary Jefferson Eppes, 3 March 1802, ibid., 36:676–77.

52. TJ to Peter Carr, 10 August 1787, ibid., 12:15–17; TJ to Benjamin Rush, 21 April 1803, ibid., 40:251–55; TJ to Thomas Jefferson Randolph, 24 November 1808, TJ Papers, Lib. Cong.; TJ to Benjamin Rush, 17 August 1811, *TJP:RS,* 4:87; TJ to John Adams, 5 July 1814, ibid., 7:453–54.

53. TJ to Robert Walsh, 5 April 1823, Special Collections, University of Virginia Library.

54. Bernard Mayo, ed., *Jefferson Himself: The Personal Narrative of a Many-Sided American* (Boston, 1942; reprinted by the University Press of Virginia ten times between 1970 and 1998).

2 "More Loved . . . and More Hated"

George Tucker on Thomas Jefferson

CHRISTINE COALWELL MCDONALD AND ROBERT M. S. MCDONALD

George Tucker's 1837 *Life of Thomas Jefferson* occupies an almost singular place among Jefferson biographies. It is a secondary source written by a primary source—a man who had known Jefferson personally and, as professor of moral philosophy at the University of Virginia, had worked with and for him. Sometimes described as the first Jefferson biography, in fact it is merely the first major one, for earlier, more brief and less authoritative accounts of the third president's life had already been penned by John Beckley, B. L. Rayner, and William Linn. These, like Tucker's, had clear interpretive slants. Beckley, a key political operative, described Jefferson as "the friend and benefactor of the whole human race," while Rayner praised his "firmness" of resolve and reported that, even after two terms as president, his mind remained "unshaken in its principles." Linn, in words that would have pained his namesake, Jefferson-hating father, noted that, in Jefferson's own day, his reputation had been "furiously assailed by political opponents" but had lately been buoyed by "candid" Americans' appreciation of "the excellencies of his character."[1] Tucker, for his part, announced in his preface the goal of "vindicating" the "purity," "justness," and "wisdom" of Jefferson and his party. Yet he also sought to offer a "dispassionate narrative" of Jefferson's political life. Unlike his predecessors, his goal was not so much to outdo Jefferson's critics in their partisanship but rather to present a more impartial and correct account. In this he largely succeeded, in part, perhaps, because his political, personal, and professional connections to Jefferson were not as close as at first glance they appear.[2]

Like his subject, Tucker enjoyed a long, varied, and consequential life.

Born four months after the first scenes of the War for Independence at Lexington and Concord, he died two days prior to the start of the Civil War at Fort Sumter. A native Bermudan, his parents were cousins (although distant ones, as he pointed out) who led a prosperous merchant family. As a child, he later confessed, he was much indulged. Prone to pranks and mishaps, for no real reason he fed his first teacher a shard of glass. He tricked his cousin to walk blind into a pit and threatened to set fire to his family's housekeeper's dress. He suffered greatly when he stabbed himself through the foot with a sword and knowingly ate a poison fruit. Somehow he managed to insert three- or four-inch pencils up his nose with impunity. Having survived his youth, he traveled to Williamsburg, where he studied law under his older cousin, St. George Tucker, a professor at the College of William and Mary. The younger Tucker went on to serve as an attorney, author novels, and pen numerous essays on economics, slavery, morality, metaphysics, and aesthetics. He represented Pittsylvania County in the Virginia House of Delegates before holding office, from 1819 to 1825, as a Republican member of Congress.[3]

If by his teenage years, as he remembered, he "had become a decided republican in my politics," by the time he joined the House of Representatives he had decided to become less decided. Given his party and region, his votes seemed conventional enough: "yes" to the unconditional admission of Missouri, "no" to tariffs, and "no" to internal improvements bankrolled by the national government. But his writings tell a different story. Here he said "yes" to tariffs, as well as to central banking, government promotion of manufacturing, and other interventions that seem decidedly Hamiltonian. Was he the original "RINO"—a Republican in name only? If so, he tried hard to hide it, and certainly he did his best to present his views in palatable terms. A few years later, he penned for the university's *Virginia Literary Museum* a series of six articles on the promotion of manufacturing. At the start of each he quoted Jefferson: "We must now place the manufacturer by the side of the agriculturist."[4]

It seems likely that Jefferson, who in 1825 invited Tucker to assume at his new university the chair in moral philosophy, remained unaware of at least some of his views, many of which had been published anonymously. Adrienne Koch, the prolific mid-twentieth-century historian, considered it an enduring "mystery" why Jefferson appointed to such an important post a man "whose views on government were widely different" from his own. One theory is that Tucker's moderate politics actually worked in his favor. Few wished to inflict on the university an ordeal such as the one it had endured when the controversial Thomas Cooper, vilified as a radical in religion and politics, accepted but then withdrew from an appointment to the faculty. In addition to Tucker's intelligence and intellectual versatility, his greatest qualification might have been his ability to mollify the school's critics. Plans for the university drew censure from proponents of the College of William and Mary, from which he had graduated; Virginians in the southwest part of the state, whom he represented in Congress; and members of established faiths such as Episcopalians, to whose religion he subscribed. Federalists, fearing that Jefferson aimed to indoctrinate the rising generation, also opposed the university. They made no effort to oppose Tucker, however, whose friend John Marshall was also Jefferson's enemy. Tucker later reported that Marshall "had always shewn me kindness, seeing doubtless my high respect for him."[5]

What a shame that Tucker's *Life of Jefferson* recorded so few similar insights about his relationship with the third president, who had shown him the kindness of making possible a profession that Tucker apparently considered more attractive than the continuance of his (undistinguished, by his own account) congressional career.[6] Tucker, the first chairman of the University of Virginia's faculty, interacted often with Jefferson, the school's founder and first rector of its Board of Visitors. Yet his biography is largely devoid of the colorful anecdotes that punctuate his own autobiography, written more than two decades later. Jefferson's personality—his manner and motivations— apparently mattered little to Tucker. The same held true for Jefferson's private life, which beyond basic details merited only scant attention.

Tucker's preference for the public aspects of Jefferson's life not only reflected the norms of his genre in the first part of the nineteenth century. It also reinforced Jefferson's own almost obsessive efforts to shield his private life from the public's gaze. When in 1817 Joseph Delaplaine, author of a *Repository of the Lives and Portraits of Distinguished American Characters*, asked Jefferson to supply the names of his grandchildren, he refused. Such details, "too minute for public notice," could only "fatigue" readers.[7] Yet it also seems possible that Tucker's focus on the professional over the personal resulted from the nature of his relationship with the former president, which appears to have been cordial and constructive but neither especially close nor especially warm. One of the goals of the biography, Tucker later wrote, was to place Jefferson's "virtues and services in a true light before his countrymen" while also "drawing a veil over his errors and defects to which I was not blind."[8]

Tucker possessed a capacity to find fault not only with Jefferson but also with his grandson Thomas Jefferson Randolph, whose 1829 edition of some of the third president's writings, the professor wrote in his biography's preface, demonstrated "a want of caution." Containing Jefferson's "unreserved communications to confidential friends," Randolph's indiscreet publication opened old wounds and made for his late grandfather new enemies among those who regarded Jefferson's private letters "as if they had been deliberately written by him for the press." In addition, Tucker thought, the volumes contained statements "uttered when the fever of party excitement was at its height, and when he was goaded by every species of provocation." These poorly represented the *real* Jefferson, Tucker believed; Randolph's publication of them led people to view his most impassioned pronouncements "as the settled convictions of his mind."[9]

It seems odd that Tucker, who lived in general proximity to Jefferson for little more than a year, would claim to have a firmer grasp on his views than his grandson, who was thirty-three when Jefferson died. It seems odder still that Tucker, in a venue as enduring and public as the biography of Randolph's grandfather, would chastise Randolph for poor judgment. Yet signs of strain in his relationship with Jefferson's family stretched back to his arrival in Charlottesville, when it seems clear that at least some of the members of the Tucker and Jefferson families failed to hit it off. In July 1825, after Jefferson's granddaughter Cornelia paid the Tuckers a visit at Pavilion IX, she reported to her sister, Ellen, that the professor's daughters were the most "silent stupes . . . I ever saw." Tucker's niece was also present. Another silent stupe, she, at least, was "pretty." A few months later, Mary Randolph—sister of Cornelia, Ellen, and "Jeff"—gossiped about Tucker's failed attempts to marry his daughters to Professors Charles Bonnycastle and John Emmet. (In 1827, Emmet finally married Mary Byrd Farley Tucker—the pretty niece. Daughter Eliza wed Professor Gessner Harrison in 1830, while Maria Tucker waited until 1840 to marry Albemarle County planter George Rives.) Meanwhile, Cornelia observed that "Mr. Tucker is not much liked . . . his eccentricity of character does not please and in his capacity of professor he is still less thought of, at least by the students." Robert Lewis Dabney, a cousin, about fifteen years later echoed this early assessment, denouncing Tucker's "pestilent examinations" and "dull and uninteresting" lectures. The biggest change was that Tucker, "the old granny," had gained a nickname.[10]

The point is not to portray the Jeffersons and Tuckers as the Hatfields and McCoys. Their relationship was too ambivalent and too interdependent for an outright family feud, which neither side could hazard. Nevertheless, they sometimes snarked and sparred, using each other for maximum gain while abusing each other at minimum risk. Tucker, for example, imposed on Joseph Coolidge, Jefferson's grandson-in-law, the task of seeking a Boston press for his science fiction novel, *A Voyage to the Moon*. Coolidge "made an effort" and "went to every publisher." He eventually "procured an offer from *one*, (only)." He wrote back to Tucker, urging quick action. He received no response. Coolidge complained that Tucker, who settled on a New York printing house, "took no notice in any way" of "the trouble he had given, or of the invitation he had rec[eive]d." Disgusted, Coolidge "thought at least if there was no other answer there would have been one in the shape of a presentation copy—wh[ich] would not have cost him 50 c[en]ts!"[11]

Minor tensions and resentments neither discouraged Jefferson's family from sharing with Tucker their opinions regarding the third president's character nor prevented them from making available to Tucker their collection of unpublished correspondence and other documents. Nicholas Trist, Jefferson's grandson-in-law, even did him the favor of selecting from the thousands of items letters meriting particular attention. Certainly Tucker did not lack for materials. The project commenced in 1830, and two years later he publicized his intentions to author "a single volume, of five or six hundred pages." When published in 1837, the two-volume tome exceeded 1,200 pages. "The work has been far longer in preparation than . . . expected," Tucker wrote, in part because of "the labour of winnowing what was useful and pertinent from the heterogeneous mass" of sources.[12]

In many respects Tucker's most influential source was James Madison, to whom Tucker dedicated his *Life of Thomas Jefferson*. Madison read parts of Tucker's manuscript, offering suggestions and making corrections. Printed in the front matter of Tucker's biography is Madison's last letter, which was written to him. Jefferson had asked Madison to take care of him when dead, and Madison did so until the day before his own death. Writing on June 27, 1836, Madison expressed "confidence" in Tucker's "capacity to do justice to a character so interesting to this country, and to the world; and I may be permitted to add, with whose principles of liberty and political career mine have been so extensively congenial." If Madison had felt great affection for Jefferson, Tucker, in his autobiography, revealed that Madison "has always been a great favorite with me"—indeed "an especial favorite with me ever since I had known him, for independent of his profound and far-reaching views in the science of government and legislation, he had unwonted gentleness and suavity of manner, which joined to a large fund of anecdote which he told very well, made him one of the most companionable men in existence. His habitual cheerfulness was the more remarkable" given that Madison's physician had told Tucker that Madison had for twenty years been "afflicted by three diseases any one of which might at any moment have carried him off." Meanwhile, "Mr. Jefferson too had most winning manners when he chose to exert them, but he was occasionally somewhat dictatorial and impatient of contradiction, which Mr. Madison never appeared to be."[13]

In some respects Tucker deserves accolades for a remarkably evenhanded account of Jefferson's career. His coverage of the rivalry between Jefferson and Hamilton in the early 1790s, for example, recognizes in both men good motives and great talents. Unlike many of his successors, Tucker refused to demonize his subject's rival. To some this seemed a defect of the study. Hugh Blair Grigsby, one of Virginia's leading nineteenth-century historians, observed that Tucker "may be supposed to have regarded the republican leaders with the kindest of feelings," but "in comparing Hamilton and Jefferson . . . awards the palm of genius to Hamilton."[14]

Tucker also rendered dispassionate accounts of Jefferson's "mildness" and "moderation" as a slaveholder as well as his many efforts to curb slavery as an institution. The former congressman, who among Virginians of the 1830s increasingly stood out given his acknowledgment of the "mischief" of the South's system of labor, admired how Jefferson "braved popular feeling" by revealing his negative "opinions on domestic slavery." But while Tucker provided matter-of-fact accounts of Jefferson's efforts to allow voluntary emancipation, leverage the Declaration of Independence to condemn the Atlantic slave trade, hamper slavery first by restricting and then by promoting its diffusion, and prohibit the importation of enslaved Africans into the United States, he made clear his belief that Jefferson had gone too far by supporting gradual emancipation. Although Jefferson believed it "practicable" to liberate and then resettle people enslaved in Virginia, Tucker maintained that the "difficulties" of such a plan "must be admitted to be great . . . by every one who gives to the subject an attentive examination."[15]

Despite the general impartiality of his narrative, at certain junctures Tucker's equanimity melted away. The specific issue of Jefferson's reportedly sexual relationship with Sally Hemings, an enslaved woman at Monticello, furnishes the first of two examples. Tucker offered an oblique denial that came in the form of an attack on the credibility of James Callender, a "mercenary writer" who assailed Jefferson with "a torrent of scurrility and slander, of which no example had been previously afforded in the United States, not even by himself." Leaving unspecified the "calumnies" at issue, Tucker focused instead on Callender, who in the 1790s had left his native Scotland for "asylum in this country either from poverty or prosecution. He soon found employment in Philadelphia, as a political writer, on the side of the republican party." Jefferson and others, "learning of Callender's indigence, made him donations of small sums of money from time to time." If offered as mere charity, Callender appeared to understand these payments as remuneration, for he "redoubled his efforts" to attack President John Adams and other Federalists "with all his powers of argument and vituperation." His writings, according to Tucker, "were in such a style of exaggeration, and expressed in a strain of ribaldry and vulgarity so unusual, that he was likely to injure the cause he espoused . . . more than to serve it." Even so, Callender believed himself to have contributed to Jefferson's election, which he learned of while incarcerated under the Adams administration's Sedition Act. Jefferson, once inaugurated, pardoned him and all other victims of this measure, but Callender believed he deserved even more. Denied a political appointment as Richmond's postmaster, not even an additional $50 "gratuity" could cure Callender of his "ingratitude" toward Jefferson, whose supposed "ill-treatment" of him, he thought, "justified his desertion" to the Federalist *Richmond Recorder*. While employed by this "obscure journal" he not only generated "slanders and ribaldry with untiring virulence" but also became "a habitual sot." His body was discovered one morning in the James River, "where he was bathing, it was supposed, in a state of intoxication."[16]

Although Tucker intended to undermine the credibility of Callender, his curious defense of Jefferson also undermines his own claim to have authored an "honest and dispassionate" narrative. Although there is no reason to dispute his implied skepticism of Callender's portrayal of the Jefferson-Hemings relationship, and although there is no reason to suspect that, up to this point, his account contained any information he believed false, Tucker's rhetoric nevertheless stacked the deck in Jefferson's favor. His attempt to make Callender the issue was, if not particularly fair, at least fairly powerful as an argumentative technique. Few men were less appealing. Then there was the fact that Tucker never mentioned Callender's actual charges against Jefferson. By eliding these, he avoided repeating and disseminating them while also relieving himself of the burden of substantiating his assertion that they were "improbable" and "unsupported by evidence." All the while, Tucker maintained the pretense of evenhandedness, balancing his inventory of Callender's flaws with praise for his "good genius, improved by education," and "the coarse vigour of his style"—characteristics that also helped to excuse Jefferson for ever noticing him. Finally, Tucker minimized the charges' importance, and therefore any reason for giving them much coverage. They amounted to "minor vexations which Mr. Jefferson experienced in the early part of his administration."[17]

Even so, Tucker admitted, no one could deny "that Mr. Jefferson was annoyed by the libels," a fact made clear "by a long letter which he wrote to Mr. Monroe . . . on the 15th of July, 1802, in which he gives a detail of his first acquaintance with Callender, and of all the dealings or communications he ever had with him." Yet this was not entirely true, as Tucker possibly knew and certainly should have known. Although Jefferson wrote this letter to Monroe in July, Callender's accusations would not appear on the pages of the *Recorder* until September. Maybe Tucker stands guilty of only an oversight. His mention of the letter to Monroe, an oddly placed short paragraph in an oddly placed brief discussion of Callender interceding almost inexplicably in an extended analysis of foreign policy, at first glance seems little more than a gratuitous attempt to direct readers toward a letter, already published in T. J. Randolph's edition of Jefferson's writings, that provided the bulk of information for the preceding two pages. Here, however, Jefferson not only detailed how he came to consider Callender "as a proper object of benevolence" and make him a recipient of "my own charities" until he found it necessary to make clear to the writer that public offices were not his personal property to "give away" to those "totally unfit" for such posts. He also informed Monroe that he had no idea "what use the tories will endeavour to make of their new friend." This, of course, is what made Jefferson's letter seem such an effective defense. It had nothing specific against which to defend. It impugned Callender's credibility with no apparent foreknowledge of his still-to-be-levied charges. But Tucker's misrepresentation of Jefferson's missive weakened its rhetorical punch only with readers who had access to the letter's text and bothered to consult it. In the eyes of everyone else, Tucker's reference to the letter as Jefferson's "annoyed" response to Callender's "libels" had the effect of providing the third president with something he himself never supplied: a written refutation of them. Tucker's readers, assured of its existence if not provided its substance, could choose between believing the man whose biography they had purchased or trusting Callender, his Judas, a "mercenary" "sot" portrayed as both pathological and pathetic.[18]

Tucker did not always go to such great lengths in Jefferson's defense. At the University of Virginia, his preference for a more realistic, more Madisonian order of things manifested itself much as expected—especially if one expected what Jefferson did not. When offered the professorship, Tucker remembered in his autobiography, he found that "Mr. Jefferson, whose address and powers of pleasing were very great, so favorably represented the life I should lead, that I no longer hesitated." Yet the environment that took shape in Charlottesville proved far from idyllic. In the first two decades of the university's life, Tucker had good reason to fear for his own. Bad enough that the students, unruly and impatient with authority, drank, brawled, vandalized property, harbored prostitutes, hurled bottles of urine through professors' windows, and sank a cadaver from the medical school in the pond that served as the water supply. Worse yet, they threatened, punched, and horsewhipped members of the faculty, one of whom in 1840 would be shot and killed by a student. It is difficult to reconcile these facts with Tucker's later claim, in his autobiography, that he and his colleagues viewed their time at the fledgling institution as "one of the happiest portions of our lives." It is even more difficult to reconcile them with his account of the history of student discipline in his biography of the university's founder.[19]

Here, his narrative lays blame for these acts of rebellion at the feet of Jefferson, whose "little code" for student self-government applied to the university "some of his political doctrines. Thus, believing that the authority of government is often needlessly exerted, and the restraints of law are too much multiplied, he allowed more latitude and indulgence to students than was usual." Jefferson's "liberal and indulgent views" about governance "well accorded both with the temper of the professors, and their inexperience, and they undertook to conduct a body of youths, by appeals to their reason, their hopes, and to every generous feeling, rather than to the fear of punishment, or dread of disgrace. The imperfection of this system was not long in manifesting itself." Tucker pointed to the "habitual" "nightly disorders," which soon "reached a point of riot and excess" as the students "openly resisted the authority of the faculty." Among the worst offenders was Jefferson's own grandnephew, Wilson Miles Cary, whose expulsion helped to announce a new system of discipline. This one, "liberal without being lax," brought about "a degree of order and regularity" that Tucker described as both "progressively increasing" and "supposed to be now nowhere exceeded."[20]

Less history than fiction, no one stood more aware of this narrative's obvious falsehood than Tucker, who experienced firsthand the reality that Cary's 1825 removal served less as a turning point than the first of many low points. In addition to the drinking, whoring, fighting, and flogging that marked student misbehavior in the school's first fifteen years, Tucker in 1834 twice discovered on his Pavilion IX windowsills makeshift bombs loaded with gunpowder that, had they exploded, would have caused "serious injury." Jefferson's "little code" with little government may have had its flaws, but it is not as if the new regime of new rules regulated behavior with any great degree of newfound success. Why did Tucker suppress these later examples of serious misbehavior while singling out for blame Jefferson's earlier code of conduct? Maybe what motivated him was a desire to bolster the reputation of the university or—given his roles as longtime professor and three-time chairman of the faculty—of himself. Maybe Tucker, in some fundamental way, shared the reckless mischievousness of the students, and once again took delight in feeding an authority figure, this time the late president, a shard of glass. But maybe, in addition to these inducements, he could hardly resist the opportunity to set up for failure the "political doctrines" to which Jefferson's original code conformed.[21]

Tucker began his account by noting that, more than any other member of the founding generation, "it was the fate of Thomas Jefferson to be at once more loved and praised by his friends, and more hated and reviled by his adversaries." He understood that "to write the life of one, who was the object of such lively and opposite sentiments," constituted nothing short of a "hazardous task" since, "with one portion of the public, any praise would be distasteful," while, "with another portion, nothing less than one unvarying strain of eulogy would prove satisfactory." His prophecy proved accurate.[22]

Reviewers with Federalist sympathies panned his generally favorable biography of Jefferson. Yet one of Tucker's most vociferous critics, prominent Episcopal clergyman Francis Hawks, also provided some of the most interesting criticism. In an era that had largely moved beyond the traditional rivalry of Federalists and Republicans, Jefferson still possessed a potential to divide—and not only on matters of politics but also on questions of culture. "Of Mr. Jefferson's political career it is not our purpose to speak particularly; as a statesman, we leave him in the hands of those, who deem it of more importance to study the politician than the man," Hawks wrote in his *New-York Review and Quarterly Church Journal.* What mattered to him were not Jefferson's "public acts" but his "private virtue," which no one should doubt remained "one of the ingredients requisite to make the good statesman. Of the defects of moral character in the third president, the book before us says almost nothing, for it is little else, save decided eulogy or elaborate defense." At Tucker's hands, Jefferson's faults were "either entirely overlooked, or barely hinted at, or accompanied invariably by an apology."[23]

Hawks reminded his readers, however, that no one should forget that Jefferson, "avowedly," was no "believer in Christianity." It was his "fatal, practical mistake in discarding the aid of Christianity in the formation of his own moral character. He deliberately threw away the noblest element of true greatness, and he reaped the inevitable consequences." Yet Tucker provided only "scanty" information "on the subject of Mr. Jefferson's religious opinions," much of it wrong. Madison's description of his late friend's piety, highlighted by Tucker, clearly misrepresented Jefferson's views, Hawks alleged. So did Jefferson himself if, as Tucker asserted, he described himself as a Unitarian. Hawks knew of no Unitarian who "would permit himself to speak of Christ, in the terms which Mr. Jefferson has used." Among the many examples of Jefferson's heresies, Hawks informed readers, stood his claim that "Jesus did not mean to impose himself on mankind as the Son of God."[24]

Hawks's damning critique provoked a response from Tucker, who in 1838 penned a forty-six-page rebuttal that, as Merrill Peterson observed, "should be read as an appendix to the biography." Tucker began his response with the somewhat withering reflection that Reverend Hawks's indictment of Jefferson's character was itself not particularly Christian. One might expect, Tucker wrote, "a clergyman" such as Hawks, operating "far above the passions and prejudices of worldly men," to feel "distressed, if," when reviewing an account of another man's life, "he should be obliged to hold them up to public indignation." Yet Hawks, Tucker observed, clearly reveled in the task.

Turning from Hawks's motivations to the substance of his attack, Tucker offered a much fuller discussion than what had appeared in his biography of Jefferson's thoughts on religion. He admitted a limited ability, however, to describe with precision Jefferson's religious thoughts. While Hawks charged that Jefferson aimed to propagate infidelity, Tucker pointed out that the third president's belief in the intensely personal nature of faith made him reluctant not only to preach but also to profess. He did, however, attend church services and donate money to religious groups. His bill for religious freedom in Virginia aimed not to harm religion, as Hawks charged, but instead to ensure its free exercise. The same stood true for the university, which Hawks believed Jefferson intended as an incubator for infidels. To the contrary, Tucker attested, students could, and regularly did, practice their faiths freely in an environment of tolerance.[25]

Tucker's defense, although probably effective, nonetheless seems predictable. His argument constituted the antithesis of Hawks's thesis. There was little nuance in Tucker's characterization of Jefferson's faith, a topic that apparently struck him as either so uninteresting or irrelevant that only in response to Hawks's review did he pay much attention to it at all. Then again, maybe it was the nuanced nature of Jefferson's religious views that deterred him. With a few rare exceptions, when Tucker felt dissonance between his own views and those of his subject, his tendency was to revise Jefferson's opinions so that they more closely approximated his own.

In many respects it seems as if Tucker had wished he had written a biography of the man to whom his book was dedicated. He felt closer to Madison, both personally and politically. Yet the question is not where to situate Tucker in the narrow continuum between Jefferson's relative radicalism and Madison's relative conservatism but how far to place him outside of that continuum, for in his *Life of Thomas Jefferson* and other writings he seems more conservative than either Jefferson or Madison. In the four-volume history of the United States that he penned toward the end of his life, for example, he made the case that, properly understood, liberty was neither an absolute right nor anything more than a means to an end greater than itself. "It must be qualified by justice, order, and obedience to the laws," he argued, for it merely amounted to "the desire to do what we please; and it is this desire which animates the tyrant, the criminal, and, in short, every violator of the law." "We must not," he maintained, "fall into the error of the miser, who values money for its own sake, and not for its uses. Liberty is a means . . . of advancing human happiness, when placed under proper restraints. But, in the freest countries in existence, a very large majority of the community are subjected to the will of others, and have a very limited share of liberty." So what if they are "deprived of most civil rights"? An essential task of any government, he thought, was to divine the "distribution of civil rights and power which it thinks will best promote the public welfare and safety."[26]

No wonder Henry S. Randall, whose 1858 biography eclipsed Tucker's as the standard treatment of Jefferson's life, confided that Tucker fundamentally failed to understand the third president. In recounting Jefferson's life, Randall said, Tucker does "not *skim,* but he does not go to the *bottom.* He did not understand the great ethnic features (if I may so term them) of his subject.—He did not understand the inner history of parties; the *spirit & soul of the times.* . . . He did not go vastly beyond official records. He did not enter into Jefferson's *feelings* any more than he occupied his stand point in the colder matters of opinion." Tucker telling Jefferson's story, Randall said, "was ice trying to represent fire!"[27]

Notes

1. "Americanus," [John Beckley,] *Address to the People of the United States; with an Epitome and Vindication of the Public Life and Character of Thomas Jefferson* (Philadelphia, 1800), 24–32; B. L. Rayner, *Life of Thomas Jefferson: With Selections from the Most Valuable Portions of His Voluminous and Unrivalled Private Correspondence* (Boston, 1834), 305, 370; William Linn, *The Life of Thomas Jefferson: Author of the Declaration of Independence, and Third President of the United States* (Ithaca, N.Y., 1834), 2, 6. For information on William Linn and his father, see John Howard Brown, ed., *Lamb's Biographical Dictionary of the United States,* 7 vols. (Boston, 1900–1903), 5:77–78.

2. George Tucker, *The Life of Thomas Jefferson, Third President of the United States,* 2 vols. (Philadelphia, 1837), 1:xii.

3. George Tucker, "Autobiography of George Tucker," 1 January [– (?) March] 1858, *Bermuda Historical Quarterly* 18 (1961): 82–135. See also Robert Colin McLean, *George Tucker: Moral Philosopher and Man of Letters* (Chapel Hill, N.C., 1961), esp. 3–26; Tipton R. Snavely, *George Tucker as Political Economist* (Charlottesville, Va., 1964), esp. 1–6; Sarah Funderburke, "George Tucker (1775–1861)," in *Encyclopedia Virginia,* ed. Brendan Wolfe, http://www.EncyclopediaVirginia.org/Tucker_George_1775-1861.

4. Tucker, "Autobiography of George Tucker," 92, 130–35; McLean, *George Tucker,* 23, 25; Snavely, *George Tucker,* 27–28, 83–87. For the use of Jefferson's name to advance

Tucker's arguments, see, for example, [George Tucker,] "The Policy of Encouraging Manufactures," *Virginia Literary Museum and Journal of Belles Lettres, Arts, Sciences, &c.*, 1 (24 June 1829): 17. For the text of the letter from which Tucker quoted, see TJ to Benjamin Austin, 9 January 1816, *TJW*, 1369–74.

5. Adrienne Koch, "The Versatile George Tucker," *Journal of Southern History* 29 (1963): 506; Dumas Malone, *Jefferson and His Time*, 6 vols. (Boston, 1948–81), 6:366, 368, 376–80, 384, 397; McLean, *George Tucker*, 24–25; Tucker, "Autobiography of George Tucker," 119.

6. "I had then a livelier ambition to be a great chess player than to be a distinguished member of Congress," Tucker admitted. See Tucker, "Autobiography of George Tucker," 132.

7. Scott E. Casper, *Constructing American Lives: Biography and Culture in Nineteenth-Century America* (Chapel Hill, N.C., 1999), 39–40, 52, 61–62; Joseph Delaplaine to TJ, 17 March 1817, TJ Papers, Lib. Cong.; TJ to Delaplaine, 12 April 1817, ibid. Delaplaine's 1815 sketch of Jefferson's life focused on his public contributions, offering a few sentences on his marriage and family in its final paragraph; see Joseph Delaplaine, *Delaplaine's Repository of the Lives and Portraits of Distinguished American Characters*, parts 1 and 2 (Philadelphia, 1815), 125–55, esp. 154–55.

8. Tucker, "Autobiography of George Tucker," 141.

9. Tucker, *Life of Thomas Jefferson*, 1:xiii.

10. Cornelia J. Randolph to Ellen W. Randolph Coolidge, 13 July 1825, Ellen Wayles Randolph Coolidge Correspondence, University of Virginia Library; Mary J. Randolph to E. W. R. Coolidge, 23 October 1825, ibid.; McLean, *George Tucker*, 30, 34; C. J. Randolph to E. W. R. Coolidge, 3 August 1825, Ellen Wayles Randolph Coolidge Correspondence, University of Virginia Library.

11. Joseph Coolidge to Nicholas P. Trist, 4 December [1827], Nicholas Phillip Trist Collection, Lib. Cong.

12. Extract from Ellen W. Randolph Coolidge [to George Tucker], 27 January [1833 or 1834], Ellen Wayles Randolph Coolidge Correspondence, University of Virginia Library; *Jefferson Image*, 122; *National Gazette* (Philadelphia), 24 January 1832; Tucker, *Life of Thomas Jefferson*, 1:xvii.

13. Tucker, *Life of Thomas Jefferson*, 1:[ix–xi]; Tucker, "Autobiography of George Tucker," 123, 141–42.

14. Review of Henry Randall's *The Life of Thomas Jefferson*, as cited in Frank J. Klingberg and Frank W. Klingberg, eds., *The Correspondence between Henry Stephens Randall and Hugh Blair Grigsby, 1856–1861* (Berkeley, Calif., 1952), 13.

15. Tucker, *Life of Thomas Jefferson*, 1:11, 120, 2:502, 1:123.

16. Ibid., 2:119–20.

17. Ibid., 1:xii, 2:119–20.

18. Ibid., 2:120–21; TJ to James Monroe, 15 July 1802, in *Memoirs, Correspondence, and Private Papers of Thomas Jefferson*, ed. Thomas Jefferson Randolph, 4 vols. (London, 1829), 3:502–4.

19. Tucker, "Autobiography of George Tucker," 135, 136; Cameron Addis, "The

Jefferson Gospel: A Religious Education in Peace, Reason, and Morality," in *Light & Liberty: Thomas Jefferson and the Power of Knowledge,* ed. Robert M. S. McDonald (Charlottesville, Va., 2012), 107–8; Rex Bowman and Carlos Santos, *Rot, Riot, and Rebellion: Mr. Jefferson's Struggle to Save the University That Changed America* (Charlottesville, Va., 2013), 35–37, 103–4, 107–8, 116–18, 121–26, 136–37, 141.

20. Tucker, *Life of Thomas Jefferson,* 2:479–81.

21. Bowman and Santos, *Rot, Riot, and Rebellion,* 2, 91 (quotation).

22. Tucker, *Life of Thomas Jefferson,* 1:xi.

23. F. L. Hawks, *The New-York Review and Quarterly Church Journal* (1 March 1837), 8.

24. Ibid., 8–9, 11, 14. The quote appears in TJ to William Short, 4 August 1820, in *Memoir, Correspondence, and Miscellanies, from the Papers of Thomas Jefferson,* ed. Thomas Jefferson Randolph, 4 vols. (Charlottesville, Va., 1829), 4:327: "That Jesus did not mean to impose himself on mankind as the son of God, physically speaking, I have been convinced by the writings of men more learned than myself in that lore." Perhaps to remove the ambiguity introduced by "physically speaking," Hawks does not quote the full sentence.

25. *Jefferson Image,* 127–29; "A Virginian" [George Tucker], *Defence of the Character of Thomas Jefferson, Against a Writer in the New-York Review and Quarterly Church Journal* (New York, 1838), 6.

26. George Tucker, *History of the United States from Their Colonization to the End of the Twenty-Sixth Congress, in 1841,* 4 vols. (Philadelphia, 1856–58), 4:429–31.

27. Henry S. Randall to Hugh Blair Grigsby, 4 December 1856, in Klingberg and Klingberg, *Correspondence Between Henry Stephens Randall and Hugh Blair Grigsby,* 71.

3   "Dexterity and Delicacy of Manipulation"

Biographers Henry S. Randall and James Parton

ANDREW BURSTEIN

It begins with the generally unrecognized influence of Martin Van Buren, who liked to think of himself as the political son of Thomas Jefferson. His *Inquiry into the Origin and Course of Political Parties in the United States,* posthumously published, testified to a life of partisan energy. Here, the scrappy, indefatigable eighth president advanced the Jeffersonian principle that the drift toward rule by a moneyed oligarchy could only be arrested by the spirit of democracy. Appended to the *Inquiry* was the long letter Jefferson had sent to Van Buren in 1824, defending his organized political activities in the greatly divisive 1790s. Lavishing praise on the third president, Van Buren insisted that beyond his "spirit-stirring pen," Jefferson was a "pure patriot," and his achievements "unequaled in the history of man."[1]

Both Henry Stephens Randall (1811–1876) and James Parton (1822–1891) launched their careers as presidential biographers in the 1850s, and both felt strong attachments to Van Buren. Randall was, like Van Buren, an upstate New Yorker, and also a personal friend and longtime supporter. As a teenager, the British-born Parton exulted on shaking hands with the sitting president, and much later, as Andrew Jackson's biographer, directly sought an interview with him. Randall's massive three-volume biography, *The Life of Thomas Jefferson,* was the New York Democrat's one major book, published in 1858. The prolific Parton, who hit the ground running with thorough treatments of three major figures, Horace Greeley, Aaron Burr, and Jackson, did not undertake his single-volume *Life of Thomas Jefferson* until a full decade after Randall's appeared, and it was not issued in full until 1874.[2]

Two themes preoccupied Randall as he wrote. The first was the world of Monticello: the author had decided early in the process to honor the late president's grandchildren, who entertained him in Virginia, in 1851, and supplied him with an abundance of anecdotes (both in writing and in person). For them, he would present Jefferson as a good-natured family man. The second of Randall's purposes was to distinguish Jefferson's defense of republicanism from Alexander Hamilton's undisguised preference for a strong, permanent alliance between the federal government and the wealthiest Americans. His treatment of Jefferson was thus designed to situate its subject at the crossroads of history, just as Martin Van Buren would have it.[3]

Randall's was the era of an openly glorifying national biography and unabashed sentimentalization of the American Revolution. In the 1830s, Jared Sparks had edited the writings of Benjamin Franklin and George Washington, principal heroes of a heroic age. In 1841, Charles Francis Adams followed with the letters of his grandparents, John and Abigail Adams. Washington Irving, graduating from satirist and storyteller to the popularizer of a George Washington–like Christopher Columbus, ended his writing career, in the 1850s, with a multivolume life of the man after whom he was named.

But the coming Civil War also brought with it a reactionary element. Had sacralization of the Revolution rendered an objective understanding of American history impossible? Debate ensued over which section could more legitimately claim the founding moment. Some in the late 1850s pointed to the gaudiness and bombast in Fourth of July oratory; others understood the Declaration of Independence as a metaphor for contradictory notions: the sanctity of the Union and the political right to separate.

Randall's three volumes, published in New York, were meant as a balm of sorts, an uplifting portrayal of an age of enlightened propositions; yet they were more favorably received in the South. Jefferson the Virginian was showcased as the most well-rounded, refined, and resilient of the founders. By showing Hamilton to be out of step politically, Randall's work served as justification for all future monuments to the Jefferson whose "spirit-stirring pen" enshrined a world-transformative humanism; this was the Jefferson whom President John F. Kennedy could wittily place above the combined genius of a group of Nobel laureates when, in 1962, he celebrated "the most extraordinary collection of talent" to gather at the White House "with the possible exception of when Thomas Jefferson dined alone."[4]

On the eve of its publication, Randall's *Life of Thomas Jefferson* was previewed in the *New York Commercial Advertiser,* and other newspapers reprinted the article. It featured a view of Randall in his private study. "Piles of books lay stacked up in every corner" of a room that had come to resemble a museum of Jeffersoniana: manuscripts, views of Monticello, ground plans of the gardens, the "pocket book" in which Jefferson first copied down the sublime speech of the Mingo Indian Logan, as featured in *Notes on Virginia.* Randall also had by his side "a neat drawing" of Jefferson's award-winning invention, the "plow of least resistance," as well as lockets of the founder's hair and copies of his favorite ballads. There could be no doubt that New York's former secretary of state and "Superintendent of Public Instruction" had in his possession a historical trove.

As he continued narrating, Randall's interviewer betrayed his utter awe: "To my wondering inquiry why none of these things had ever come to light, Mr. Randall informed me that nearly or quite all of these volumes and manuscripts . . . were found by Mr. Jefferson's family in 1851, in a dark and entirely forgotten receptacle, where they had lain since Mr. Jefferson's death." This supposedly secret cache included over 300 letters exchanged between Jefferson and his two daughters, none of which had been published in any form up to this point. To these were added "contemporaneous narratives and diaries" from Jefferson's several grandchildren and the journal of Robley Dunglison (the young doctor from England who attended to the ex-president at the end of his life) as well as "pretty minute recollections of Mr. Jefferson's most intimate personal friends." The author's principal benefactors, grandchildren Thomas Jefferson Randolph and Ellen Randolph Coolidge, informed him that they had nothing to hide. Jefferson would "pass muster" with posterity "exactly as he was," on the basis of his personal writings and the reminiscences of knowledgeable people, without the need to manufacture any more positive image. Or so the author explained to the writer of this puff piece.[5]

Not surprisingly, then, Randall's Jefferson was an eminently likable character, as unprepossessing as he was talented. He was industrious more than he was ambitious, proficient in all things he attempted. He was reasonable, too, and a good listener who never raised his voice in anger. He was uncommonly devoted to his wife, to his children and grandchildren, and to his countrymen. Over his long public career, he did not waver.

He had inherited strength of character from a father whom Randall describes heroically. Peter Jefferson "was no ordinary man." Unlike many of his wealthier Tidewater contemporaries, he did not owe his success to "ingratiating manners." Made of sterner materials than the James River planters, unfazed by physical challenge, he was "of gigantic stature and strength—plain and averse to display," a perfect symbol of self-reliance. An accomplished surveyor in the George Washington mold, the frontier colonel ranged about the "savage wilderness," where he was "regarded with peculiar respect and veneration by the Indians far and near." At times, he subsisted on the raw flesh of the game he killed and slept in the hollow of a tree.

An anecdote told by family members demonstrated his superiority over the people he owned: "He once directed three able-bodied slaves to pull down a ruinous shed by means of a rope. After they had again and again made the effort, he bade them stand aside, seized the rope, and dragged down the structure in an instant." These qualities of courage, added to his mathematical ability, explained why the proud Randolph family took a liking to Peter Jefferson and agreed to a family alliance. "His judgment was swift and solid," Randall wrote. "His mind once made up, no danger could turn him aside—no obstacles thwart his iron will, and calm, but resistless energy."

At this juncture, Randall reveals nothing about the mental capacity or personality of Thomas Jefferson's mother, Jane Randolph Jefferson. Although his father died when he was fourteen and his mother survived for nearly twenty more years, Peter left his total imprint; all Jane gave Thomas was "his slim form and delicate fibres"—the quality known as sensibility. In a strained effort not to slight the Randolph lineage, Randall adds here that the future president was "the auspicious combination of new strength with old courtly culture, of the solid with the showy, of robust sense with the glitter of talent!" Clearly, the character and values of one family are privileged over the other. Before exiting the subject, however, Randall states that Jane Jefferson was, in fact, "an agreeable, intelligent woman" and "a notable housekeeper," fond of letter writing. But he offers nothing more profound. Presumably, in overseeing the closest thing history has to an authorized life of Thomas Jefferson, the Randolph grandchildren conveyed to the dutiful biographer no portrait of the great man's mother.[6]

In setting forth Jefferson's ethical foundation, habits of study, and inherent preferences, Randall draws, as many interpreters have since, on the moralistic 1787 letter to nephew Peter Carr, in which Jefferson declared that ethics was not a science but a natural endowment, and therefore of secondary importance in a young man's education. The moral sense, he wrote, was "as much a part of man as his leg or arm," though, like those limbs, it could be "strengthened by exercise."

Randall's incisive Jefferson was a man of many parts—mathematician, linguist, and legal scholar—who knew the difference between the empirical demands of science and other forms of knowledge and social engagement. Possessing "little relish" for metaphysical explanations, he "studied the actual. . . . Though not destitute of imagination, and even fond of its higher objective creations, as for example in the Greek poets, he could not tolerate its intrusion in systems designed to influence the sober realities of life, or the solemn questions of the hereafter."

Conscientious in pursuing enlightenment, Jefferson did not lie to himself. Along the path to knowledge, he acquired a commitment to bettering the human condition, seeking the greatest good for the greatest number of people. He was "eminently perceptive," his biographer crooned, as he pored over Jefferson's favorite reading matter. "The stern practicalist looked through and spurned what was, to him, the abasement of self-delusion, or the criminality of intentional deceit." Jefferson contemptuously dismissed Plato, gradually warmed up to Plutarch (demonstrating an admirable intellectual flexibility), and impulsively rejected "the morbid taste for the mysterious" in suspense novels.[7]

Randall's language can be, at times, quite purple. As the narrative continues, effusions de-escalate but slowly. Jefferson knows how to cultivate his natural gifts. He is a good judge of character who chooses his lifelong teachers well. In Williamsburg, as a host of others succumbed to the popular vice of gambling, he "escaped the contamination." While single, he remained "rather a favorite with the other sex, and not without reason."

This is where Randall, despite his subject's lack of interest in modern fiction, indulges in the style of literary romance, painting Jefferson as a man of irresistible magnetism:

> His appearance was engaging. His face, though angular, and far
> from beautiful, beamed with an intelligence, with benevolence, and
> with the cheerful vivacity of a happy, hopeful spirit. His complexion
> was ruddy, and delicately fair; his reddish chestnut hair luxuriant
> and silken. His full, deep-set eyes, the prevailing color of which
> was a light hazel . . . were peculiarly expressive, and mirrored, as

the clear lake mirrors the cloud, every emotion which was passing through his mind.

The footnote contains a detailed description of Jefferson's hair color in the various stages of aging, disputing the common shortcut of those who said his hair was red. Randall designates it as auburn. "A locket, containing his hair at these periods, lies under our eye as we write," he explains, as if to justify the extravagant script.

Here, too, in order to certify Jefferson's attractiveness to women, his biographer casually discards the factual story of the young suitor's rejection by Rebecca Burwell (in later years the mother-in-law of Jefferson antagonist Chief Justice John Marshall) by affirming a tradition that speaks of her as "more distinguished for beauty than cleverness." In sum, even in his twenties, Jefferson "was not a young man to be lightly regarded by the young or old of either sex." Tall, erect, and graceful, "an expert musician, a fine dancer, a dashing rider," he was earnest, methodical, charming, "gentle and forgiving"—and, the reader is meant to infer, a magnificent presence.[8]

Arriving at the critical stage in Revolutionary deliberations in 1775–76, when Jefferson sat in the Continental Congress, he was known (Randall takes his cue from John Adams's autobiographical jottings) for his "masterly pen," and was received "with open arms" by his colleagues in Philadelphia. Although silent within large group deliberations, he was, as Adams himself affirmed, "so prompt, frank, explicit, and decisive" as a member of smaller committees and in one-on-one conversation that he could not be overlooked or undervalued.

Randall is cagey here. He is at once promoting Adams and setting him up as an unreliable witness to history. Cleverly inserting evidentiary statements by New Yorker John Jay, who was not one to fawn over Jefferson, and fortifying his interpretation with papers collected by the nineteenth-century archivist Peter Force, Randall "proves" that those who would become political adversaries of Jefferson's—the outspoken Adams and the charismatic Patrick Henry in particular—wavered or behaved carelessly at notable moments in the lead-up to independence.

No one's commitment to the cause appears as philosophically consistent as Jefferson's. If there was nothing insidious in Adams's flawed memory as an ex-president trying to put his imprint on the spirit of 1776, the same could not be said of William Wirt's Henry—that oft-reprinted biography of the great orator still had legs in the 1850s. Randall takes Wirt to task for assigning to the great orator a prophetic power over the course of human events that was unwarranted.[9]

Randall has seeded the ground. He dwells on personal and partisan differences among key members of Congress in 1775–76: Adams is loud and contentious; Jefferson is mild and opposed to faction—his hands are clean. A collective portrait of a Congress of fragile egos is a preview to Randall's drawn-out discussion of whether Adams or Jefferson remembered with greater precision just how the three-person committee to draft the Declaration of Independence operated. Were the two of them, as Adams insisted in 1822, equally tasked with responsibility for the draft? Or, as Jefferson informed James Madison (and communicated to posterity), was he alone given the charge? The third committee member, Benjamin Franklin, did not leave a record.

It mattered greatly to Randall that the contradiction should be resolved. With an erudite analogy to James Boswell's treatment of Samuel Johnson, he prepared to set the facts straight once and for all. Adams, as he had been documenting, was "careless, impetuous, and understudied in his statements." He made "honest" mistakes. Jefferson, by contrast, kept meticulous notes. Yet in the 1850s, confused by competing eulogistic tributes, interpreters of the Revolutionary record had diminished Jefferson's authorial performance, accepting Adams's version. Randall sought nothing less than a reversal of history's verdict, crediting Jefferson as the singular author of the revered Declaration. In this, we know, he succeeded.[10]

The next delicate episode in Jefferson's public life that Randall recast to protect his subject's reputation involves a long-standing charge of cowardice. The matter dates to Jefferson's wartime governorship of Virginia (1779–81), which ended ignominiously with invasion of the interior of the state by forces under Lord Charles Cornwallis and the traitor Benedict Arnold. Jefferson fretted, during his retirement years, about the damage done to his fame in histories authored by John Marshall (ostensibly a five-volume biography of Washington) and General Henry "Light-Horse Harry" Lee, whose Revolutionary memoir made Jefferson appear inept.

As Lee's two volumes were issued in 1812, the French-born Louis Girardin arrived in Jefferson's neighborhood, where he taught school. With Jefferson's encouragement, he got to work righting the wrongs done to the man who was now his patron, and in 1816 published a rejoinder, which, while useful, did not entirely undercut the unfriendly works by Marshall and Lee. For his part, Randall made good use of Girardin, but went well beyond it.[11]

At the heart of the issue were charges brought against Governor Jefferson, after he stepped down, as a result of "precipitate action" by George Nicholas, a member of the state legislature. Nicholas acted at the behest of Patrick Henry, Jefferson's predecessor as governor who remained his enemy for years to come. Randall listed the great Revolutionary names of Washington, Lafayette, and Steuben among those who either praised the governor for his steadiness or maintained an unhesitating friendship with him afterward. Early on, before the British invasion, Jefferson had announced his intention of leaving office, and could not be said to have feared leading Virginia through such difficult times. "But for his resignation," wrote Randall, "there is no question he would have been triumphantly reelected."

All that stood between him and a well-earned retirement from politics was Henry and those who thought the inspirational orator should be appointed "dictator" to see the state through the ongoing crisis. Theirs was, in Randall's unapologetic parlance, "the Dictator party," and it made no sense to Jefferson's adoring biographer that Henry should have been lavished with any kind of trust. Randall writes disparagingly: "If he had exhibited any particular military capacities, or indeed had any military experience, history has not very carefully preserved the fact." Henry was a man of "unbounded popularity" but minimal ability. Somehow, Jefferson was "blamed for not making preparations for invasion, which Governor Henry, the proposed Dictator, had never thought of making." The industrious one was temporarily overshadowed by the demagogue.

Panic had created the mad desire for a savior. Fortunately for Jefferson, as the British retreated and fear subsided, so did belief in the urgent need for Henry's guiding hand. The Virginia House of Delegates unanimously commended Jefferson for his "impartial, upright, and attentive administration," disavowing all suggestions that he was a coward or deserved censure. "George Nicholas did more than make a retraction," Randall concludes the chapter. "He became one of the staunchest and most efficient of that band of devoted personal and political friends" who stood by Jefferson as his star continued to rise.[12]

In narrating the September 1782 death of Martha Wayles Jefferson, devoted wife of ten years, Randall returns to elaborate language. He purports to feel Jefferson's pain as the delicate mother lay dying over the summer months, following a difficult childbirth: "A momentary hope for her might sometimes flutter in the bosom of her lonely husband, but in reality it was a hope against hope—a hope against reason—and he knew it to be so." She was meant to "shed mellow radiance over the retirement to which he was fondly looking forward." Instead, he sat at her bedside awaiting the inevitable—a unique opportunity for the biographer to establish the raw humanity of his subject.

Randall at length projects the future to which Jefferson has resigned himself, sketching out the memory of a marriage never to be marred or discounted by the appearance of a second wife. Knowing her fate, "Mrs. Jefferson had returned her husband's affection . . . with the idolatrous gratitude of a wife who knew how often her husband had cast away the most tempting honors without a sigh, when her own feeble health had solicited his presence and attention. And now as the dreadful hour of parting approached, her affection became painfully, almost wildly absorbing. . . . Her eyes ever rested on him, ever followed him." The nature of this scene, and Jefferson's broken-down wandering about his private mountain in the weeks following, helped to explain why the self-regulated widower had so much affectionate concern for the upbringing of his motherless daughters.

After his wife's death, Jefferson was pressed back into national service by his friends Madison and James Monroe, accepting appointment to France after a stint in the Confederation Congress. In both roles he would prove himself, once again, a dispassionate man of high ideals who avoided confrontation. Despite the wounds he had suffered as an underappreciated governor, Randall's Jefferson never developed a hostile or vindictive side—something no twenty-first-century interpreter of Jefferson would claim.[13]

As Thomas Jefferson Randolph was helping the friendly biographer prepare his work, he remarked of his grandfather generally: "Unreserved and candid himself, he was a listener, encouraging others to converse." Randall chose to insert the above statement in the context of rationalizing how one as naturally superior as Jefferson could have failed to dominate as a legislator once he returned to the political maelstrom in the mid-1780s. "Mr. Jefferson was a brilliant man," he explains, "guilty, sometimes, of making even legislative enactments readable, if not eloquent!" But in deliberative bodies, a different type, the "dull, plodding, slow-thinking man," will hammer policy into the shape of a law. Posing a straw man question, "Did Jefferson lead or follow?", the biographer combines the tactful statesman (and future party symbol) and indulgent father into one: he gave advice readily, but listened well and offered solace when needed.

In a curious way, Randall chose to separate Jefferson from standard politicians of his day by emphasizing his role as both father and mother to his growing daughters, Martha and Maria. He exhibited a "feminine softness and feminine general cast of his feelings in a few particulars—especially where his family was concerned." The early death of his wife had molded an already existing softness of disposition into a functioning quality. Attuned to the needs of the vulnerable, "he had the feminine dexterity and delicacy of manipulation; he had the feminine loving patience." He was sharp-eyed and attentive, said his family, but incapable of committing an injustice. He never spoke a word that he lived to regret.[14]

Having so neatly established the nonconfrontational temperament this fatherly-motherly Jefferson exuded, Randall used it to advantage in describing his role in the bitter and unsparing politics of the 1790s. Perhaps it means something more now when we consider that Jefferson's nemesis, Secretary of the Treasury Hamilton, belittled Secretary of State Jefferson, along with the slightly formed Congressman Madison, for their "womanish resentment" toward the unstoppable commercial might of Great Britain, and their "womanish attachment" to the self-destructive lesser power of France.[15]

The self-satisfied, hypermasculine Hamilton had served on General Washington's staff and saw combat at Yorktown. Jefferson, who never went to war, was temperamentally opposed to the Hamiltonian tactic of insult and affront. In a battle of pens in 1792, the two wrote separate long responses to Washington, when the president called on his cabinet officers to harmonize. In a chapter-long presentation, Randall once again comes to Jefferson's defense. He terms the Virginian "always a liberal compromiser," but in this instance finds he has to acknowledge that Jefferson's historical reputation suffers from the appearance that Hamilton's letter was the more "magnanimous" of the two and displayed "more liberality and less implacability of purpose." Yet, as he assesses the political systems of Jefferson and Hamilton, the directness of Jefferson becomes the proper, indeed the ethical, choice.

Hamilton believed that "men are weak and corrupt, and must be controlled by force," Jefferson that "an enlightened popular judgment" could decide most questions. These were irreconcilable principles. In Randall's exposition, Washington is swayed by Hamilton's economic programs, but as readily persuaded by Jefferson on moral questions, capable of understanding that the personal attacks leveled by Hamilton are as fraudulent as they are malicious. Jefferson is able to prove, for instance, by supplying documentary evidence, that the charge of his being opposed to the federal Constitution during the ratification process was a fabrication. Randall states of Jefferson: "He seems to have readily satisfied General Washington that he was not one of those who constantly lauded it in public . . . while denouncing it in secret as a frail and worthless fabric!" (The secret denunciation is an allusion to Hamilton's 1802 letter to friend and fellow New Yorker Gouverneur Morris, which Randall obviously regards as a "gotcha" moment, not the casual language of an out-of-office politician.)

In his discussion of the cabinet controversy, Randall describes the treasury secretary as a posturing hypocrite who, "with protestation on his lips of warm respect," appealed as an injured man of honor to President Washington and simultaneously, anonymously, composed nasty, whiny opinion pieces about his rival for the political newspapers. The "paternity" of these articles (which mock Jefferson's "quiet, modest, retiring" demeanor, and label him an "intriguing incendiary") was immediately obvious to all who read them. Hamilton would stop at nothing in scheming to "disable" his upright opponent. The self-aggrandizing treasury secretary had a fatal flaw: he had "made the system of the British Ministry the model of his conduct."[16]

Jefferson is taken at his word in honestly seeking release from the pressures of office at the end of 1793. During his two years of domesticity, the widower proved inseparable from his children, the now married Martha ("dignified and highly agreeable") and teenaged Maria ("a dazzling vision of beauty"). With Jefferson at Monticello, and Madison a force in Congress but remote from the president, Hamilton's "haughty will" overrode his less impressive remaining opponents in the Executive; an oversized army he recruited made a travesty of Washington's administration in the "Whisky War" of 1794. The course of human events had to be reversed.

President Washington conveyed a "noble" vision. But his "graceful" effort to create a nation free of organized political parties had proven to be a mere "day-dream." By the end of his administration, he heard no voice that was not Hamilton's, or Hamilton's men. Republicans refused to join his cabinet, because, in Randall's words, "Hamilton was a disagreeable antagonist to meet there." A bogeyman. Only a Jefferson or a Madison was equipped for this daunting challenge in 1796. At the latter's urging, responsibility fell to

Jefferson. A passion for farming notwithstanding, he was pressed back into service.[17]

Randall's interpretation of the Adams years and the transformative election of 1800 is almost muted in comparison to his consideration of Hamilton's ambitious plans of military action ("his great warlike scheme," "gorgeous South American visions") and subversion of the presidential contest. In whatever he tried, the egotistical Hamilton could brook no interference, and Adams's growing independence ruined his future plans. Randall explains that the death of Washington at the end of 1799 left Hamilton "without any adventitious protection."[18]

In his bid to end the "paroxysms" of Federalist policies, Jefferson found a new opponent of comparable means in the New England clergy, which attacked his moral and religious character at once. Supposing him an "infidel" on the strength of his support for the French, the clergy knew nothing whatsoever of his actual beliefs, Randall underscores, and were unmoved that Jefferson directed at them "not a particle of aggressive provocation." But they were "foes of science," and Jefferson "had ventured to offer scientific cosmic explanations and suggestions, and had questioned the Mosaic record." He was branded, therefore, an "atheist." With a deft, if dismissive, broad brush, Randall ridicules the narrow-minded religious complainants and puts them in their place.

The subject of Jefferson's religious views is so significant to Randall that he devotes the very last chapter of the third and final volume to a concentrated testimony. Speaking to his own generation, and heavy-handedly recovering Jefferson as a Christian, he insists that the third president clothed his most important public addresses "in the most explicit language," avowing God's revelatory guidance and declaring "his belief in the efficacy of prayer." Beyond that, out of a desire not to "injure" anyone's feelings, he remained circumspect; he feared that what he said would otherwise be construed as "propagandism." The Randolph clan stuck to this line of interpretation; and in what must now read as a less than authoritative final statement, Randall writes: "All of Mr. Jefferson's grandchildren" concurred that their grandfather had withheld his personal religious views, saying to them: "If I inform you of mine, they will influence yours—I will not take the responsibility of directing any one's judgment on this subject." Leaving nothing to chance, Randall ends determinedly: "They heard him habitually speak reverently of God, the Saviour, and the great truths of Christianity."[19]

In 1801, as Jefferson is swept into office, his biographer relaxes somewhat. One would suppose, he writes as volume 2 concludes, that "our narrative . . . would become more minute." But the opposite is in fact the case, as he states unabashedly: "the scale of recital will be abridged." The reason he gives takes barely a line: "the great struggle of the parties was substantially over." This seems an odd editorial decision, but Randall is quite literal: he gives short shrift to the presidency.[20]

His President Jefferson is an able, discreet, and determined executive, and the narrative of his two terms is a straightforward "Life and Letters" treatment, privileging dispatches and diplomacy (in particular, the Louisiana Purchase), with occasional reminders of "partisan recrimination" from frustrated Federalists whose sudden constitutional scruples are easy to expose for their hypocrisy: "The reputation acquired by the Administration from the Louisiana purchase would have been great under any circumstances. But the bitter opposition of its opponents added to the effect."

Unlike modern historians' less glowing verdict, the second term is cast as a commendable continuation of the first. Randall holds, for instance, that U.S. Navy successes in the War of 1812 redounded to Jefferson's credit. The small fleet's "weakness," he insists, "was one of its principal protections"; it was "absurd," the biographer avers, for any to have expected President Jefferson to "suffer our debt to increase" by competing with the Royal Navy. As to the Embargo, Randall further discredits New England Federalism by explaining that the farmers of the South were more affected than their northern counterparts—as with Louisiana, the "disingenuousness" of the opposition was striking. If Jefferson misread the mind and mood of his countrymen, it was only in expecting the Revolutionary consciousness to have reasserted itself; but "nerve was wanting" to "vindicate" the cause of the rights of neutrals without resort to war. If "cessation of commerce called forth grumblings on full stomachs," and people were loath to sacrifice for the greater good, it was not the president's fault.[21]

The first half of volume 3 is all it takes to deal with Jefferson's presidency, but reviewers did not seem to mind. While critical of the biographer's Jefferson-can-do-no-wrong bias, the reviewer for the *Southern Literary Messenger* said that the final volume was "the most entertaining of all," and that its charm lay in its portrait of "the eminent statesman at his own fireside . . . ever cheerful and considerate." Once done with the error-free presidency, the second half of this volume is wholly devoted to a man "beguiling the leisure of retirement" with his books, horseback riding, and correspondence. In obtaining a detailed picture of life at Monticello, we see how critical Randall's time in Virginia with the grandchildren was.[22]

Anecdotally rich, with complete transcriptions of letters Randall received from family members, these pages tell how Jefferson devoted himself to the rising generation and recoiled from his celebrity: "A female once punched through a window-pane of the house, with her parasol, to get a better view of him. He was waylaid in his rides and walks." Uninvited visitors to the mountaintop would gawk at him "as they would have gazed on a lion in a menagerie." As to Jefferson's spending habits, Randall is, not surprisingly, kind and sympathetic. "Mr. Jefferson could not know, when he left public life, either the general or special pecuniary disadvantages which awaited him. His temper, as in youth, was sunny and hopeful." He was obliged to spend on the "fashionable company" who came by, and he was unfailingly generous. He suffered for his gentility, not his indulgences.[23]

A composite portrait of the modest patriarch emerges in the story, which Randall had "from the lips of the good parson" whom it concerns, that addressed Jefferson's warmth and conversational skill as well as his unoffending religious persona. The story is set at a tavern on the road between Monticello and Jefferson's even more remote retreat of Poplar Forest, near 100 miles distant, outside Lynchburg. The two sat together in a room, strangers to each other, and began discussing a variety of topics. The parson was first led to believe than his new acquaintance was an engineer, then a farmer, then a clergyman like himself, but whose sectarian association was unclear. On waking the next morning, the parson asked the landlord about the mysterious stranger. "What," he replied, "don't you know the Squire?—that was Mr. Jefferson." And the parson had to admit that the ex-president's reputation for infidelity was mistaken: "I tell you that was neither an atheist nor irreligious man—one of juster sentiments I never met with."[24]

Randall's 2,000-page biography, although brought before the public on the eve of the Civil War, has surprisingly little to say about slavery. This was intentional. The author privately acknowledged that he had made an effort to soften Jefferson's antislavery credentials so as to mollify southern readers. In a footnote in volume 3, he explains awkwardly in passive voice that "it was not decided ultimately to pursue" slavery in the work. The most concentrated discussion comes in an appendix that superficially associates Jefferson with the colonization movement, acknowledging his feeling that no amount of education "would render it expedient" to confer citizenship on blacks.[25]

Finally, there is the matter of race and sex, and what Jefferson's fidelity to the memory of his long-dead wife might have consisted in. This was the subject of an exchange that took place in 1868 between Randall and a more celebrated national biographer, James Parton. What could Randall tell him about the scandalous rumor that Jefferson had fathered the children of his slave Sally Hemings?

In his reply to Parton, Randall recounted a walk he took through "mouldering Monticello" with Thomas Jefferson Randolph, when the latter raised the issue as they stood before the "smoke blackened and sooty room" that had once belonged to Hemings. Randolph acknowledged a relationship between Hemings's family and his own family, but explained that his grandfather was not its cause. The "connection" between the attractive enslaved females and Jefferson's nephews Peter and Samuel Carr was "perfectly notorious" on the mountaintop.

Parton reprinted a portion of Jeff Randolph's statement in the text of his *Life of Thomas Jefferson.* He did so to separate Jefferson from the charges of his political detractors, concluding in dramatic fashion: "So much for this poor Campaign Lie, which . . . will, doubtless, walk the earth as long as weak mortals need high examples of folly to keep them on endurable terms with themselves." And so the matter was to put to rest, although not for all time.[26]

Parton, as Scott E. Casper writes, was "the first American writer to be identified above all by the term biographer." Prior to his single-volume Jefferson biography of 1874, he published treatments of others whose lives intersected with Jefferson's: Aaron Burr (1858), Andrew Jackson (1860), and Benjamin Franklin (1864). He was, indeed, the first major Jefferson biographer to undertake a discussion of what Randall referred to in his 1868 letter as the "Dusky Sally Story." He was also, among his generation of biographers, the most committed to the masses of readers who wanted an easily accessible life story that read like a novel—a formula that annoyed erudite reviewers.[27]

Parton, trained as a journalist, was born in Canterbury, England. He came to New York with his widowed mother and siblings in 1827, when he was five, and had as his playground the swamps along the East River of Manhattan. He did not officially obtain U.S. citizenship until 1846. In his twenties, while teaching school, Parton began contributing to Nathaniel Parker Willis's *Home Journal.* After he authored a good many pieces without pay, the nationally prominent Willis took him on as an editorial assistant. In this capacity, Parton eventually came to meet and love the spirited writer, eleven years his elder, who published under the pseudonym Fanny Fern. Unbeknownst even to her family, before she acknowledged herself, Fanny was none other than Willis's sister, Sara. She, a women's rights advocate, and Parton, sympathetic to the cause, were married in 1856.

This was not long after the publication of his first biography. He took as his subject the popular (and very much alive) *New York Tribune* editor and publisher Horace Greeley, whose rise to prominence was a quintessential American success story. The book was a best seller and received critical praise. Greeley, it is worth mentioning, enjoyed Randall's *Life of Thomas Jefferson,* writing as much to its author. At the same time, he suggested that Federalist historiography no longer prevailed in the minds of most—which was to say that, in writing against an effete tradition, Randall had overplayed his hand.[28]

The Life of Horace Greeley changed the trajectory of Parton's career. Tackling Burr next, he showed his indefatigability by attempting an objective work about a reviled public figure. It, too, sold well (sixteen editions in five years), although the reviews were, predictably, mixed. By the time he embarked on his Jefferson biography, Parton was a popular lecturer, and on familiar terms with some of the nation's best-known essayists and fiction writers. He was even advising the political cartoonist Thomas Nast on ways to entertain the public.

Parton's Jefferson biography was serialized in the *Atlantic Monthly* from January 1872 through October 1873. The magazine's editor, no less a literary figure than William Dean Howells, proved an energetic cheerleader throughout the project. Thomas Jefferson Randolph, it should be noted, was less of a fan; now in his eighties, he protested Parton's characterization of his father, Thomas Mann Randolph, and brother-in-law Charles Bankhead (who had once stabbed him) as incorrigible alcoholics. To conciliate the proud Randolph family, when *The Life of Thomas Jefferson* was published in book form, Parton excised the offensive language.[29]

In the political ideology that infuses their biographies, Parton and Randall are difficult to tell apart. The first paragraph of Parton's preface wraps up with the oft-quoted assertion: "If Jefferson was wrong, America is wrong.

If America is right, Jefferson was right." He telegraphs his purpose of writing a book to show how Jefferson's first principle, the positive vitality of democracy, emanated from the founder's matchless belief in the educability of citizens, and in an infectious optimism extending from that one insatiable intellect to all future Americans.

At the outset of his tale, Parton renders Peter Jefferson much as Randall does, "a superb specimen" of manly independence, with "the strength of three strong men." But Parton speculates as Randall would not have dared, triangulating from naturalist John Bartram's incidental visit to the home of Jefferson's maternal grandfather that the future president had "derived his temper, his disposition, and his sympathy with living nature" from that side of the family. As Jane Randolph Jefferson was "the tenderest of women," Peter Jefferson equaled in strength his wife's tenderness. Such license instructs us that Parton was less interested in historical truth than he was in telling a breathless story.[30]

Unlike Randall, who shunned discussion of slavery, Parton asserts early on, in a chapter titled "Our Jefferson's Childhood," that his hero "came to hate slavery" and "foretold the ruin of the system." Under his father's tutelage, however, he witnessed how slavery could take a positive form: "He saw his father patiently drilling negroes, not long from their native Africa, into carpenters, millers, wheelrights, shoemakers, and farmers." Jefferson's was "a busy, healthy home," where the lad acquired his vaunted love for music and the arts.[31]

Of Jefferson's entry into national politics as a member of the Second Continental Congress, Parton builds on Adams's praise for Jefferson's "happy talent for composition." Congress, in the Virginian's first week as a delegate, was "extremely solicitous" of that talent amid "the alarm, the rapture, the apprehension" of eventful times. Jefferson was "naturally urged" to prepare the Declaration of Independence, and as naturally "touches the heart" with his determined style. As always, Parton fills in gaps with dramatic stylings of his own, painting a picture of the exalted signers concluding their momentous work briskly as "swarms of flies" descend on the room from the livery stable nearby. "French critics censure Shakespeare for mingling buffoonery with scenes of the deepest tragic interest," he writes digressively, but amid this most august of assemblies, flies are driving great men away, precisely as Shakespeare would have staged the scene.[32]

Parton accounts for Patrick Henry's vocal power: "artifice, management, extreme and sudden changes in tone, adroit repetition of telling phrases." Jefferson, by contrast, exhibited no artifice: "not once in his whole public career did he lose or weaken a point by needlessly wounding an opponent's self-love." Conceiving laws for his state in the midst of the Revolution, Jefferson conquered with reason. "Never, perhaps, since the earliest historic times," says Parton, fearless as to the cost of exaggeration, "has one mind so incorporated itself with a country's laws and institutions as Jefferson's with those of new-born Virginia." Once again, the author does not shy from the slavery issue, confident that Jefferson is on the right side of history. The "benevolent revisers" of Virginia's laws (Jefferson, Edmund Pendleton, and George Wythe) momentarily dwelled in "the shade of the noble, unpractical Plato," in attributing to Virginians "a degree of self-control, far-seeing wisdom, and executive genius" that no human community ever commanded. As such, they envisioned gradual emancipation, but ultimately shelved the overoptimistic idea.[33]

Parton applies the reason- and morality-filled 1787 letter to Peter Carr in its chronological place, much later in his text than Randall's, because he finds it of greatest use in advance of the confrontation with Hamilton. Here, Parton is led to gush that Jefferson "had more in him of that which makes the glory and hope of America than any other living creature known to us." On the altogether serious matter of party competition in the 1790s, Parton begins by directly comparing Hamilton's imperiousness to Jackson's: their self-confidence was "absolute and entire." Jefferson cannot but be disgusted by the coarseness of that brand of pride, in consequence of his virtuous self-cultivation.

"Hamilton was singularly incapable of Americanization," Parton pronounces, damning the West Indian–born social climber in a choice phrase. Then, in a sideways dig, he snickers that Hamilton, with "ludicrous gravity," proposed using slaves as soldiers in the Revolution, noting "that their stupidity and ignorance would be an advantage." Parton likes to pile on, especially when comparing Jefferson's alleged offenses with Hamilton's overt misdeeds. Of the hard-hearted militarist's spectacular affair with the married Maria Reynolds, he writes that Hamilton's actions were "a thousand times worse" than Jefferson's tame reference to the weakened "Samsons" and "Solomons" in the notoriously leaked letter to his Italian friend Philip Mazzei, which Federalists pounced on and exploited as an insult to the venerable Washington.[34]

Like Randall, Parton devotes surprisingly little space (barely one-eighth of the book) to Jefferson's presidency. In his sunny final "Summary," however, Parton is expansive. He allows that Jefferson "was a limited and defective person, like all the rest of our race." But this is a throwaway line, so as not to make the superlatives that follow sound outlandish. On the tender subject of slavery, the biographer offers a simple (to him rational) explanation for a lifelong failure to act. He pictures Jefferson, hand in hand with his two daughters, trailed by their many slaves ("with their bundles and their children"), marching to freedom. Amid the pathos of the scene, Parton imagines "a mob of white trash" entering the frame and murdering Jefferson for his noble intent: "contemporaries might have said it served him right." What reader, then, would ask Jefferson to be a "John Brown" abolitionist? For this founder to have pressed the cause would have resulted in meaningless sacrifice; thus he does not deserve history's censure.[35]

Parton's *Life of Thomas Jefferson* was a commercial disappointment, and the biographer stopped writing singular lives of earlier American leaders after this. He did, however, find happy employment in the fall of 1874, and for the next three years, writing a weekly column for the *New York Illustrated News*. He remained a fixture on the New York scene for decades, and as a freethinker went on to produce a life of the religious skeptic Voltaire. Parton continued to invoke Jefferson and Madison as small-government liberals who still had something to say to the modern world.[36]

Unlike the superproductive Parton, Henry S. Randall, his predecessor in Jefferson biography, was neither a colorful personality nor did he aim to distinguish himself further as a man of letters. In 1858, the influential *Atlantic Monthly* had called the three "huge octavos" unwieldy instruments, "diffuse and digressive," and overloaded with "tawdry tinsel"—and their author unknowingly incompetent. In an 1871 "Reviews of New Books," the *New York Herald* unflatteringly placed Randall's "magnum opus" alongside a forthcoming family memoir by Jefferson's great-granddaughter Sarah N. Randolph. The author of the review termed Randolph "a young lady of cultivated mind and a careful pen." Although she had seen fit to compliment Randall's work, the otherwise polite critic begged to differ: "We think his ambitious and frequently turgid rhetoric has not always adorned his subject so much as it has overwhelmed it."[37]

"Overwhelming" is an apt word. Together, Randall and Parton made Thomas Jefferson overwhelmingly decent and incomparably righteous—unrivaled by any other career politician in natural grace and moral fitness.

Notes

1. Martin Van Buren, *Inquiry into the Origin and Course of Political Parties in the United States* (New York, 1867), introduction, 163–69, 424, and appendix.

2. Milton E. Flower, *James Parton: The Father of Modern Biography* (Durham, N.C., 1951), 11, 57. Van Buren warned Randall that writing a "true" life of Jefferson was a "fearful responsibility." See Randall to Hugh Blair Grigsby, 4 December 1856, in *The Correspondence between Henry Stephens Randall and Hugh Blair Grigsby, 1856–1861*, ed. Frank J. Klingberg and Frank W. Klingberg (Berkeley, Calif., 1952), 71.

3. *Jefferson Image,* 149–52. Note that Van Buren ran for president in 1848 as the breakaway Free-Soil Party candidate, and while Randall supported his antislavery stand at the time, he remained a Democrat, sympathetic to southern concerns, in the crucial middle years of the next decade, as he was completing *The Life of Thomas Jefferson.*

4. Scott E. Casper, *Constructing American Lives: Biography and Culture in the Nineteenth Century* (Chapel Hill, N.C., 1999), 138–45; Andrew Burstein, *The Original Knickerbocker: The Life of Washington Irving* (New York, 2007), chaps. 9 and 14; Michael Kammen, *A Season of Youth: The American Revolution and the Historical Imagination* (Ithaca, N.Y., 1978).

5. "A Life of Thomas Jefferson," *New York Commercial Advertiser,* as reprinted in *the Georgia Telegraph,* 12 May 1857.

6. Henry S. Randall, *The Life of Thomas Jefferson,* 3 vols. (New York, 1858), 1: 12–17.

7. Ibid., 24–29.

8. Ibid., 30–35.

9. Ibid., 113–14, 123–28. Randall was writing largely to answer unresolved controversies generated in the early 1820s. Massachusetts and Virginia each assigned Revolutionary primacy to its sons. Jefferson's grandchildren were already adults at the time and lived with Jefferson or in close proximity to Monticello; they no doubt took a keen interest in how their grandfather's biographer would treat this subject. Randall incorporated into the discussion widespread rumors that John Adams was for a considerable time "hostile" to Washington. See ibid., 146–53.

10. Ibid., 164–70.

11. Andrew Burstein, *Jefferson's Secrets: Death and Desire at Monticello* (New York, 2005), 222–28.

12. Randall, *Life of Thomas Jefferson,* 1:346–60.

13. Ibid., 380–82.

14. Ibid., 402–3, 481.

15. Andrew Burstein and Nancy Isenberg, *Madison and Jefferson* (New York, 2010), 245–48.

16. Randall, *Life of Thomas Jefferson,* 2:69–92, 194.

17. Ibid., 223, 243, 247–48.

18. The South American scheme concerned a commitment to work with the filibustering operations of Francisco de Miranda, discussion of which begins on page 434

of vol. 2 and continues, off and on, for 100 pages. Randall reports, in an exclamatory phrase, that Hamilton intended to command the expeditionary forces that would "revolutionize" Mexico and South America. Ibid., 440.

19. Ibid., 516, 539–40, 650–52, 3:553–61.

20. Ibid., 2:654–55.

21. Ibid., 85, 129, 258–59.

22. *Southern Literary Messenger,* new series, 6 (August 1858): 159.

23. Randall, *Life of Thomas Jefferson,* 3:331–33.

24. Ibid., 345.

25. Ibid., 539, 667–69. To a sympathetic correspondent, former Virginia legislator and political historian Hugh Blair Grigsby, Randall explained that his strategy was to avoid aggravating the "intense sensibility in the public mind" by dealing at length with slavery. "I want to take a fair, manly course in my book, neither quixotic nor cowardly." Outlining what he would commit to the page, he asked Grigsby if setting forth facts without including commentary would satisfy southern readers; he was certain that his approach would offend northern abolitionists, whom he termed *"fanatics."* Randall identified himself as a nationalist who supported popular sovereignty in the western territories. Randall to Grigsby, 18 June 1856, in Klingberg and Klingberg, *Correspondence between Henry Stephens Randall and Hugh Blair Grigsby,* 58–60.

26. James Parton, *Life of Thomas Jefferson* (New York, 1874), 568–70; Flower, *James Parton,* 236–39. For more detail, see Annette Gordon-Reed, *Thomas Jefferson and Sally Hemings: An American Controversy* (Charlottesville, Va., 1997).

27. Casper, *Constructing American Lives,* 220–23, 229–31.

28. Flower, *James Parton,* chaps. 1–4; Casper, *Constructing American Lives,* 189. Flower observes that Parton's marriage to Fanny Fern was not made awkward by the partners' age difference, but by her hypersensitivity and his impetuosity (*James Parton,* 38). They remained together, living mainly in Manhattan, until her death in 1872.

29. Flower, *James Parton,* 130–33, 143–47.

30. Parton, *Life of Thomas Jefferson,* 1–9.

31. Ibid., 12.

32. Ibid., 164–69, 187–93.

33. Ibid., 204, 209, 213, 217–18.

34. Ibid., 340, 353, 355, 534.

35. Ibid., 743–45.

36. Flower, *James Parton,* 153–54, 172–73.

37. "Thomas Jefferson," *Atlantic Monthly* (November 1858): 706–17; "Reviews of New Books," *New York Herald,* 6 August 1871.

4 "A Beautiful Domestic Character"

Sarah N. Randolph's *The Domestic Life of Thomas Jefferson*

Sarah N. Randolph's biography of her great-grandfather Thomas Jefferson, *The Domestic Life of Thomas Jefferson: Compiled from Family Letters and Reminiscences by his Great-Granddaughter,* is not really a biography. Instead, it is a collection of letters, many never previously published, interspersed with brief introductory remarks and the occasional anecdote. Of course, as Bernard Mayo would later demonstrate, it is eminently possible to construct a readable, coherent biography of Jefferson out of his own writings, but Randolph's compilation coheres into a narrative only with some effort by the reader.[1] Without headnotes or other editorial interventions, it is often impossible for those not already familiar with Jefferson's life to understand the context for the letters or all the references within them. The book is organized chronologically for the most part, which means that even in a book whose focus is Jefferson's domestic life, there are awkward jumps from one topic or correspondent to the next. A letter to the Reverend Isaac Story about whether there is an afterlife is followed immediately by one to John Dickinson about "the delights of domestic . . . tranquillity." Likewise, Randolph moves immediately from an excerpt from Jefferson's first inaugural address to the observation that "the house at Monticello was still unfinished when Mr. Jefferson returned there on a visit in early April."[2]

The result of Randolph's seemingly artless method is to force the reader to focus on what she identifies as the subject of her work: "a faithful picture of him as he was in private life—to show that he was, as I have been taught to think of him by those who knew and loved him best, a beautiful domestic character." Randolph brings us back to Monticello and Jefferson's white family, returning him to his domestic setting.[3] Events important to national politics and Jefferson's public life serve as grace notes, ornaments that decorate Randolph's account of her great-grandfather.

Let us look more closely, for example, at the positioning of the excerpt from the first inaugural. Randolph describes succinctly the complications of the election of 1800, culminating in Jefferson's selection as president by the House of Representatives in its thirty-sixth ballot on February 17, 1801. Immediately thereafter, she excerpts a letter to Thomas Mann Randolph in which Jefferson explains to his son-in-law that he hopes he "may be able to leave this place by the middle of March." Next follows Randolph's description of Jefferson's "unostentatious" inauguration and the characterization of the address, "whose chaste and simple beauty" was widely familiar but whose "eloquent close" she could not resist reprinting. Thence Randolph returns her great-grandfather directly to Monticello for a "visit early in April," without explaining what business might have detained him in the capital longer than his predicted departure, in mid-March. She is interested only in the beauty of the inaugural address, as an illustration of her grandfather's character. The content concerns her not at all.[4]

In the way that it addresses Jefferson's public life, Randolph's biography is in some ways the obverse of Henry S. Randall's *The Life of Thomas Jefferson*. Together they are the opposite faces of the same coin. Both Randolph and Randall prefer to let Jefferson speak for himself. As Randall puts it, he prefers "in all cases to give Mr. Jefferson's words . . . instead of attempting to convey the substance in any briefer synopsis." Both, then, are largely the books Jefferson might have written about himself. Randall, however, tends to segregate Jefferson's family life by placing a group of letters to his daughters at the back of the first of his three volumes, explaining that "we . . . prefer it to scattering them in chronological order, amidst a recital of events with which they have so little connection as with politics and general history." In the subsequent volumes, Randall frequently places family letters, in particular those to and from Jefferson's daughters and granddaughters, at the end of chapters and in several of the appendixes at the end of the final volume. Here, domestic life provides the grace notes. Randolph herself considered her book a complement to Randall's rather than a replacement. "I am well aware," she wrote, "that the tale of Jefferson's life, both public and private, has been well told by the most faithful of biographers in 'Randall's Life of Jefferson,' and that much of what is contained in these pages will be found in that admirable work, which, from the author's zealous devotion to truth, and his indefatigable industry in collecting his materials, must ever stand chief among the most valuable contributions to American history."[5]

With a subject so amorphous as "domestic character," however, and with neither the signposts of political events nor an active authorial hand shaping the material, Randolph's biography can seem unshaped as well. Still, certain themes emerge. *The Domestic Life of Thomas Jefferson* is an act of recovery. Randolph brackets her account with descriptions of ruin. Her book concludes with a description of the monument that Jefferson instructed be placed upon his grave. It was to be made of "coarse stone . . . that no one might be tempted hereafter to destroy it for the value of the materials." His plans were for naught, however, Randolph explains. The gates enclosing the family graveyard "have been again and again broken open, the grave-yard entered, and the tombs desecrated. The edges of the granite obelisk over Jefferson's grave have been chipped away until it now stands a misshapen column. Of the slabs placed over the graves of Mrs. Jefferson and Mrs. Eppes not a vestige remains, while of the one over Mrs. Randolph only fragments are left." The vandals have destroyed not only Jefferson's grave but those of his wife and two daughters. The memory of the women in the family has been desecrated as well.

The last lines of the preface strike a similar note as Randolph describes three illustrations in the book. First are a portrait of Jefferson by Gilbert Stuart and one of his daughter Martha Jefferson Randolph by Sully. Finally, "the view of Monticello represents the home of Jefferson as it existed during his lifetime, and not as it now is—a ruin." The physical deterioration of the gravesite and the home symbolizes the destruction of Jefferson's reputation by his enemies: "No man's private character has been more foully assailed than Jefferson's." Randolph's task is to impart "to my readers a tithe of that esteem and veneration which I have been taught to feel for him" by her father, Jefferson's grandson and namesake, Thomas Jefferson Randolph, "the person with whom he was most intimate during life."[6]

Judging by the review of her book in the *New York Times*, Randolph succeeded at her task. "We think [*The Domestic Life of Thomas Jefferson*] will forever set at rest all the aspersions upon the private character of the author of the Declaration of Independence, and prove him not only to have been a great statesman, but a good man." The review, however, is not so much an account of Randolph's book as a short biography of Jefferson compiled from Randolph's book and the author's own knowledge. For example, the *Times*

review describes briefly how Jefferson was chosen as one of Virginia's delegates to the Continental Congress and his role in drafting the Declaration of
Independence. Randolph tells us only that "in the year 1775 Jefferson went to
Philadelphia as a member of Congress" and that his mother died on March 31
the next year and "thus . . . did not live to see the great day with whose
glory her son's name is indissolubly connected." Her only explicit mention
of the Declaration of Independence comes in an anecdote at the bottom
of the page, taken from an appendix to Randall's biography: according to
a "gentleman who had been a frequent visitor at Monticello during Mr.
Jefferson's life"—identified by Randall as General J. Spear Smith—because
Congress met near a livery stable, the delegates were pestered by flies that
they continuously had to swat away with handkerchiefs. "So very vexatious
was this annoyance, and to so great an impatience did it arouse the sufferers,
that it hastened, if it did not aid, in inducing them to promptly affix their
signatures to the great document which gave birth to an empire republic."[7]

Both the *Times* reviewer and Randall set out the standard political narrative. Randolph undercuts it. As J. Jefferson Looney's essay in this volume
makes clear, Randolph's biography is not the one that Jefferson would have
written himself or had written for him. Both the short and long lists of
accomplishments and milestones that Jefferson recorded for biographers as
well as the more extensive notes that he compiled concerned politics and
public affairs almost exclusively. He declined to provide one biographer
all the information he requested, saying that "many of the objects of your
enquiry are too minute for public notice. The number, names, and ages of
my children, grandchildren, great grandchildren E'c would produce fatigue
and disgust to your readers."[8]

These are the objects out of which Randolph constructs her biography.
She intends her book to complement Randall's political biography, but her
work cannot help being a commentary on the political narrative as well.
She recognizes that her great-grandfather is remembered for the Declaration of Independence, but she can do no more than allude to the "glory" of
the "great day" and imagine the pride it would have inspired in Jefferson's
mother. She cannot even utter the words "Declaration of Independence" in
this portion of the text, relegating them to a footnote. Moreover, the anecdote recounted there suggests that more than anything, Jefferson and his
colleagues were eager to conclude their business in Philadelphia so that they
could escape the fly-infested meeting room.

In Randolph's recounting of her great-grandfather's life, the political arena is always one from which to flee. Modern readers, of course, are familiar with Jefferson's frequent descriptions to his daughters of the tortures of public life. While holding office he characterized the nation's capital as a "circle of cabal, intrigue and hatred" and "a dreary scene where envy, hatred, malice, revenge, and all the worse passions of men are marshalled to make one another as miserable as possible." He was "disgusted with the jealousies, the hatred, and the rancorous and malignant passions of this scene." Political honors were but "splendid torments."[9] In 1871, when Randolph published her book, however, it was not common knowledge that Jefferson had disparaged public life in this way.

Although Jefferson's family had given Henry Randall access to the family letters, and he used them liberally, he did not quote all the passages that deprecated politics. When he did, he relegated them, for the most part, to the chapter ends. The exception is the letter Jefferson wrote to his daughter Polly on February 17, 1801, as the House continued balloting to select a president.[10] Jefferson told her that a resolution was expected the following day, but that "the scene passing here makes me pant to be away from it—to fly from the circle of cabal, intrigue, and hatred, to one where all is love and peace." Randolph does not know what to make of such a letter, "in which we find strangely blended politics and fatherly love—a longing for retirement and a lurking desire to leave to his children the honor of his having filled the highest office in his country's gift." Randall, however, reprints the letter in context, the balloting in the House, and thereby shows that Jefferson's complaint about "cabal" and "intrigue" was not mere literary fancy at the moment when rumors circulated of Burr's agents busily at work in Albany, others prepared to sell themselves to the highest bidder, and Jefferson's followers talked about the possibility of taking up arms to thwart a Federalist usurpation. Randolph, however, glides over the balloting with phrasing that foretells the happy outcome—a "storm, which for a week convulsed the country with excitement, and shook the young Government to its centre."[11]

With her focus almost wholly on Jefferson's domestic life and no interest in politics, not even as context for that life, Randolph leaves the reader with the impression that Jefferson entered politics only out of "a lurking desire to leave to his children the honor." When Jefferson retired from office after his second term as president, "his whole demeanor betokened the feelings of one who had been relieved of a heavy and wearisome burden." Government service was merely burdensome. It kept Jefferson from those he loved best. Randolph includes the encomiums to family love that have become so familiar over the years. In 1798, for example, Jefferson tells his younger daughter of his impatience to leave Philadelphia "and every thing which can be disgusting, for Monticello and my dear family, comprising every thing which is pleasurable to me in this world." A year earlier, upon learning that Polly was engaged to her cousin John Wayles Eppes, he wrote her rapturously, imagining the future. He wrote his older daughter, Martha, "I now see our fireside formed into a group, no one member of which has a fibre in their composition which can ever produce any jarring or jealousies among us. No irregular passions, no dangerous bias, which may render problematical the future fortunes and happiness of our descendants." Family was the antidote to the poison of political life.[12]

And politics became the explanation for the family's lack of fortune. Repeatedly Randolph tells us that Jefferson's public service cost his family dearly. Upon returning to Monticello at the end of his presidency, "it required but a brief sojourn at home, and a thorough investigation of his affairs, for Jefferson to see that his long-continued absence had told fearfully on the value of his farms; that his long enlistment in the service of his country had been his pecuniary ruin." Although Randolph generally lets Jefferson's correspondence speak for itself (even when clarification of transitions might be helpful), when it comes to what she calls her great-grandfather's "pecuniary embarrassments," she thinks it necessary not only to fill in missing information but to tie it in to an explanation. Jefferson, she notes, was "in public life almost continuously from 1774 to 1809"; no matter how "beneficial to the public his services to his country had been, on himself they were allowed to entail bankruptcy and ruin." She takes the reader through Jefferson's career and a succession of financial reverses. Although Jefferson had added to a handsome inheritance and owned 5,000 acres by 1774, he had also acquired the debt that came along with his wife's dower. Randolph implies, incorrectly, that Jefferson had discharged the dower debt relatively early in his career, but, as Herbert Sloan has explained in his authoritative study, the effort to settle these debts "would drag on for decades."[13]

It is necessary for Randolph, however, that public service, rather than anything to do with the family itself, be the cause of the family's ruin. "When Jefferson resigned as Secretary of State in 1794," she explains, "he hoped he had turned his back forever on public life, and proposed to devote the residue of his days to the restoration of his shattered fortunes." Her great-grandfather returned to public service, however, but only because he was "besieged by deputations of the most distinguished men of the day—old associates of the Revolution, who pressed his country's claim on him with an earnestness and pertinacity not to be resisted, and which finally recalled him to public life." Jefferson's "shattered fortunes" were everyone else's fault rather than his own. When he returned to Monticello in 1809, it was "with hands, as he himself said, as clean as they were empty"—penniless, yet of impeccable character.[14]

Jefferson held the members of his family to the same high but impoverishing standard. Twice, his great-granddaughter tells us in introducing separate letters, he refused to secure government positions for family members. Both times she contrasts Jefferson's practices favorably with those of her own day. The first letter is one from March 1801 in which Jefferson turned down a request from his cousin (and business agent) for a position for his brother, explaining, "The public will never be made to believe than an appointment of a relative is made on the ground of merit alone, uninfluenced by family views; nor can they ever see with approbation offices, the disposal of which they intrust to their Presidents for public purposes, divided out as family property."[15] Here, Jefferson intended to follow Washington's example, not that of Adams, who had "degraded himself infinitely by his conduct on this subject." Jefferson knew that his course "places the relations of the President in a worse situation than if he were a stranger, but the public good, which cannot be effected if its confidence be lost, requires this sacrifice." The only consolation to the leader's family was "sharing in the public esteem," which, Sarah Randolph added, "in an age when nepotism is so rife, may, from its principles, seem now rather out of date." Randolph repeats the point later in her book—which is significant since her own editorial interventions are so infrequent. In introducing a passage from Jefferson's 1825 letter to Joseph Cabell in which he discussed faculty appointments to the University of Virginia, Randolph says it "sounds strangely now in an age in which nepotism is so rife." In that letter Jefferson boasted, "I can say with truth, and with unspeakable comfort, that I never did appoint a relation to office." But here, the explanation was not only principle but also "because I never saw the case in which some one did not offer, or occur, better qualified."[16]

If she read her great-grandfather's letters closely, Randolph might have found them cutting. True, they show Jefferson to be highly principled— precisely the point Randolph wanted to make—and a model contemporary politicians might well emulate. But Jefferson also told his correspondents that his own kin were undeserving, and that anyway, the family that he impoverished would have to subsist off his "public esteem," which is exactly what his descendants tried to do. Jefferson bequeathed his papers to his eldest grandson and namesake, Thomas Jefferson Randolph (Sarah Randolph's father), "as of his own property." In order to "relieve the massive debts that were," as Francis D. Cogliano puts it, "another of Jefferson's legacies," Thomas Jefferson Randolph tried to turn the papers into cash. He published four volumes of the papers as the *Memoir, Correspondence, and Miscellanies from the Papers of Thomas Jefferson.* Preparing the papers for publication was a kind of cottage industry for Jefferson's grandson, his mother, and his sisters. The women spent five to eight hours each day transcribing the documents, which in some cases were already so deteriorated that they had to place a magnifying glass behind the pages in the full light of the noonday sun in order to detect the impression of the pen and ink. "A few lines will sometimes cost as many days," Martha Jefferson Randolph explained.[17]

The family treated the papers as a legacy with a monetary value. In 1848, Thomas Jefferson Randolph sold his grandfather's papers to the United States for $20,000. The family had wanted to withhold three boxes of "private family letters," but Secretary of State James Buchanan insisted that they be deposited with the government. These papers were not returned to the family until late 1870 or early 1871. Whether by accident or design, however, the family kept some of the private correspondence. As Andrew Burstein tells us, in 1851 the family just happened to find "in a dark and entirely forgotten receptacle" a cache of papers including more than 300 letters between Jefferson and his daughters, which they turned over to the biographer Henry Randall. Randall claimed to have the entirety of Jefferson's "family correspondence," including every letter that Jefferson had ever sent his daughter Polly, "not one" of which "has ever been published," along with the account Jefferson's doctor, Robley Dunglison, wrote about Jefferson's final illness and death.[18] When Sarah Randolph published her *Domestic Life* in 1871, she said that her work had been made possible by the government's return of the "family letters and private papers" so that she was "enabled to give in these pages many interesting letters never before published." She claimed that the reader could now see truly private papers, "not . . . ever before published"— and "never before published" enhanced the value of the book.[19]

Randolph's *Domestic Life* is manifestly about love—Jefferson's love for his family and the love they returned to him. Chief among the "outstanding traits of the 'beautiful domestic character' created" in her book, according to Merrill D. Peterson, was Jefferson's "enormous capacity for love." Yet the letters themselves and Randolph's own insertions suggest that this love was not wholly unconflicted. It might be observed that family love never is. As we have already seen, Randolph described politics as an unwelcome intrusion into Jefferson's life. A late-life letter demonstrated "what little interest he took in politics," and there is almost no indication in the letters Randolph includes that even at the peak of his career Jefferson considered public service anything more than an unpleasant and heavy burden.[20]

But the letters also suggest that Jefferson could be both indulgent and withholding. He refused on principle to appoint relatives to public office. His hectoring letters to his young daughters suggested that his love, though abundant, was also contingent. In the first extant letter Jefferson wrote his daughter Martha, he lectured her that "the conviction that you would be more improved in the situation I have placed you than if still with me, has solaced me on my parting with you, which my love for you has rendered a difficult thing. The acquirements which I hope you will make under the tutors I have provided for you will render you more worthy of my love; and if they can not increase it, they will prevent its diminution." And finally, at the end of the letter, in case the message had not been fully clear, Jefferson added a "P.S.—Keep my letters and read them at times, that you may always have present in your mind those things which will endear you to me." Jefferson had left his eleven-year-old daughter in Philadelphia to be educated while he attended Congress in Annapolis. Her mother had died the year before. Her younger sisters remained with their aunt in Virginia.[21] Here was Jefferson's parental style distilled into two sentences: the sacrifices were all his. He was the only one who needed solace; he was the one, implicitly, who was undertaking an expense, all for his daughter's good. She owed him compensation, and if she did not improve—in her studies, in her acquirements, in her love—he would love her less. Her father's love always had to be earned.

We do not know how this motherless girl reacted to her father's letter at the time, but a quarter century later Martha invited a good friend into her bedroom at Monticello, where she showed the friend her father's letters. The friend copied down some of those passages in which Jefferson spoke most strongly about the importance of family love as the antidote to the poison of politics. We know the reaction of Martha's younger sister Polly, the one who was left in the care of her aunt and uncle while her father served his nation, first in the capital and then in Paris. In her first letter to her father, then in Paris, Polly, then five or six, told him, "I want to know what day you are going to come and see me." A few months later, her baby sister died and, Randolph notes, "the death of this child was felt keenly by Jefferson." Once settled in Paris, "he became impatient to have" Polly sent to him. She remained in Virginia, however, until 1787, in part because, as Randolph puts it, "the child herself could not bear the thought of being torn from the kind uncle and aunt, whom she had learned to love so devotedly, to go to a strange land."[22]

Randolph introduces the first of Jefferson's letters to his younger daughter by observing that "it is touching to see how gently her father tries to reconcile her . . . to her separation from her good uncle and aunt, and how he attempts to lure her to France with the promise that she shall have in Paris 'as many dolls and playthings' as she wants." Polly resisted, however. Her aunt had to use, as she told Jefferson, "every stratagem to prevail on her to consent to visit you." Randolph tells us about the ploy that finally got Polly aboard ship, bound across the Atlantic: her cousins boarded with her and played with her "until she had become somewhat at home and acquainted with those around her. Then, while the child was one day asleep, they were all taken away, and before she awoke the vessel had cut loose from her moorings, and was fairly launched on the tedious voyage before her." Randolph does not mention that Polly was not entirely alone; she was accompanied by another girl also torn from her family, her father's fourteen-year-old slave, Sally Hemings.[23]

Whether we view Jefferson's efforts to draw his daughter to Paris as "touching" or not will, no doubt, depend on how each of us understands relationships within families and how we read the transcripts of family love. Abigail Adams, into whose care Polly and Sally Hemings were deposited when their ship arrived in London, observed Polly's distress and described it to her father. Just as she had been tricked into boarding the ship, Polly had to be "decoyed" off it. Once in London, she became so attached to Adams that she would not leave her side. As Adams explained, "she has been so often deceived that she will not quit me a moment least she should be carried away." Moreover, Polly was puzzled that Jefferson had not come to London himself to pick her up but instead sent a French-speaking servant. She told Adams "that as she had left all her Friends in virginia to come over the ocean to see you, she did think you would have taken the pains to have come here for her" and not sent a man "whom she cannot understand."[24]

Randolph does not include the letters Adams wrote Jefferson about his daughter, but she does reproduce a letter that Adams wrote her own sister just after Polly's departure. The little girl spent two weeks with Adams, during which "she would sit, sometimes, and describe to me the parting with her aunt, who brought her up, the obligation she was under to her, and the love she had for her little cousins, till the tears would stream down her cheeks. . . . Her papa would break her heart by making her go again."[25] Many years later, Polly would marry one of those cousins, the son of the aunt who had brought her up.

In his first letter to Polly, when he was trying to attract her to Paris, Jefferson had held out various enticements, not only "as many dolls and playthings" as she wanted but also instruction in how "to play on the harpsichord, to draw, to dance, to read and talk French, and such other things as will make you more worthy of the love of your friends." Just as in Jefferson's first letter to Polly's older sister, a father's love was contingent. "If you always practice these lessons we shall continue to love you as we do now, and it is impossible to love you any more." There is the hint, too, that a daughter's love could be bought—with toys and dolls and expensive lessons. In her first letter to her father, Polly had thanked him for the sashes he had sent her. Such items were the stuff of love. When the women in Jefferson's family reflected upon his perfect love, they often associated it with specific items. Sometimes these were the letters themselves, which, as we have seen, Martha Jefferson Randolph shared with her friend. After her father's death, she kept and used not only his bed but his "down cover-lit" as well. When, late in life, she told a friend who had come to visit her in her sickbed where these objects had come from, "she stopped, choked by emotion and could not restrain her tears, tho' she concealed them by drawing the bedclothes over her face."[26]

Like his daughters, Jefferson's granddaughters associated him with objects, gifts of particular value. As Ellen Randolph Coolidge reminisced to Randall, in a letter that Randolph includes in *The Domestic Life,* "When about fifteen years old, I began to think of a watch, but knew the state of my father's finances promised no such indulgence." This would have been around 1811, after Jefferson had retired to Monticello where his daughter Martha and her children took up residence with him while Martha's husband, Thomas Mann

Randolph, struggled to turn a profit at his own plantation. "One afternoon the letter-bag was brought in," Coolidge continued. "Among the letters was a small packet addressed to my grandfather. It had the Philadelphia mark upon it. I looked at it with indifferent, incurious eye. Three hours after, an elegant lady's watch, with chain and seals, was in my hand, which trembled for very joy. My Bible came from him, my Shakspeare [sic], my first writing-table, my first handsome writing-desk, my first Leghorn hat, my first silk dress. What, in short, of all my small treasures did not come from him?" What, indeed, did not come from Thomas Jefferson? Nor was Coolidge the only grand-daughter who was favored. "My sisters, according to their wants and tastes, were equally thought of, equally provided for. Our grandfather seemed to read our hearts, to see our invisible wishes, to be our good genius, to wave the fairy wand, to brighten our young lives by his goodness and his gifts."[27]

Ellen Coolidge's sister Virginia Trist had similar memories. "Often," she reminisced to her husband, Nicholas, their grandfather "discovered, we knew not how, some cherished object of our desires, and the first intimation we had of his knowing the wish was its unexpected gratification." Among his granddaughters, Jefferson functioned as a cross between an all-seeing god and a wish-granting genie: "Sister Anne gave a silk dress to sister Ellen. Cornelia (then eight or ten years old), going up stairs, involuntarily expressed aloud some feelings which possessed her bosom on the occasion, by saying, 'I never had a silk dress in my life.' The next day a silk dress came from Charlottesville to Cornelia, and (to make the rest of us equally happy) also a pair of pretty dresses for Mary and myself." Another time, after Virginia tore her own dress, Jefferson "himself selected"—and paid for—"another beautiful dress." Every wish became her grandfather's command. She had long coveted a guitar. A neighborhood woman offered to sell her one, but for "so high a price that I never in my dreams aspired to its possession." Yet one morning, when Virginia came down to breakfast, there the guitar was, a gift from her grandfather if only "I would promise to learn to play on it." The memory and the emotions they evoked were vivid more than twenty years later. "I never shall forget my ecstasies. I was but fourteen years old, and the first wish of my heart was unexpectedly gratified."[28]

These gifts came at a price. The extent to which a silk dress here or a guitar there contributed significantly to Jefferson's mountain of debt is hard to gauge. We know that he was not one to deny either himself or his loved ones indulgences such as these. Many years later, his daughter and her children would have to abandon Monticello and the enslaved people who lived at it because they could no longer afford to keep them. Sarah Randolph believed that somehow her grandfather's generosity to others was responsible for the calamity of the loss of Monticello. He had given selflessly of his time to his nation, and after his retirement, he offered hospitality without regard to the expense to "the crowds of visitors which his reputation drew to his house." Randolph insists that Jefferson "was in no wise responsible for having incurred" his debts, and the "pecuniary embarrassments" were the product of "circumstances beyond his control."[29]

In surveying Randolph's *Domestic Life,* Merrill D. Peterson has observed that the Jefferson she describes "knew no happiness outside the bosom of his family." That is certainly the impression her book conveys. As I have suggested elsewhere, that also is what Jefferson wanted his family to believe. His happiness required many sacrifices on their part; at least they could be assured—for he so assured them—that they were the source of his only true happiness. It should be noted that most of these assurances were delivered to the women in Jefferson's family. Indeed, his closest family relationships were almost all with women. Although Randolph is at pains to depict Jefferson as "manly," Peterson believes that "her narrative suggested, nevertheless, that there was something to be said for the other view." He catalogs the qualities that Randolph describes—Jefferson's "unfailing joy in household cares, the raising of children, the arrangements of the house, the cuisine and the garden . . . [and] most of all, the sweetness of his temper, seldom ruffled and almost never broken by anger—these traits would commonly be counted more effeminate than masculine." Peterson is not the only historian before or since to consider Jefferson "effeminate," but as the historian Joseph J. Ellis discovered, such inferences from the documentary record about a historical figure's gender identity can be dangerous. Extrapolating from Henry Adams's observation that "Jefferson's temperament was 'almost feminine,'" Ellis concluded that "for most of his adult life" Jefferson "lacked the capacity for the direct and physical expression of his sexual energies" and hence could not have fathered Sally Hemings's children. Yet we now know—as Ellis has acknowledged—that Jefferson was indeed their father and that Jefferson was fully capable both of picking out dresses for his granddaughters and expressing directly his sexual energies.[30]

What may mislead historians is that, perhaps more than any of the other political leaders of his generation—or many generations—Jefferson had many close attachments to women, from which hundreds of letters survive. By accident of nature, his two surviving white children were both women, and the older of these had six surviving daughters. Perhaps by no accident, Jefferson's bonds to their husbands were not especially strong. In the family circle, there were no men to rival Jefferson for dominance. This family configuration was unusual for the time. Moreover, the bonds between Jefferson and his female relatives were especially close. Yet if these bonds—and his discussions about women's clothing and household arrangements—may make him seem "effeminate," at the same time Jefferson fostered a kind of intellectual development for the women in his family that was less gendered than one might well have expected—particularly of a man like Jefferson, who could betray streaks of misogyny.[31]

Jefferson, to be sure, was not only aware of sexual difference, but in fact constructed it. His early letter to Martha, then eleven, in which he lectured her on proper female grooming, is well known. Randolph includes the key passage in the *Domestic Life:* "be you, from the moment you rise till you go to bed, as cleanly and properly dressed as at the hours of dinner or tea. A lady who has been seen as a sloven or a slut in the morning, will never efface the impression she has made, with all the dress and pageantry she can afterwards involve herself in. Nothing is so disgusting to our sex as a want of cleanliness and delicacy in yours." This from a man who was known "to greet guests in slovenly clothes," "linnen that was much soiled," and worn-out slippers.[32] Different standards applied to women and to men, and women were supposed to work to make themselves attractive to men.

At the same time, Jefferson could instruct his daughters just as he might have a son. When his daughter Martha, then about fifteen, complained about studying Livy, her father encouraged her to redouble her efforts: "We are always equal to what we undertake with resolution." She must remember that she was an American, and that "it is a part of the American character to consider nothing as desperate; to surmount every difficulty by resolution and contrivance." In Europe, one could walk into a shop and purchase everything that was ever needed, but in America, we have to "find the means within ourselves, and not to lean on others. Consider, therefore, the conquering your Livy as an exercise in the habit of surmounting difficulties; a habit which will be necessary to you in the country where you are to live, and without which you will be thought a very helpless animal, and less esteemed." Here was Jefferson, enjoining upon his daughter that most American of traits, self-reliance, to be acquired by the assiduous study of Livy. Two decades later, he praised Martha's young daughter Cornelia on learning to write, because, he explained, it is to writing that "we are indebted for all our reading . . . for the Iliad, the Aeneid," and other works.[33]

Jefferson could cross the gender line in both directions. It was not so much that he was "effeminate" as that he could identify with both women and men. When he worried that his daughter Polly, now married, was too inclined to "withdraw from society"—her husband had told Jefferson that they would not be spending the summer at Monticello—he lectured her from his own experience: "I am convinced our own happiness requires that we should continue to mix with the world . . . and that every person who retires from free communication with it is severely punished afterwards by the state of mind into which he gets." Jefferson was not using "he" generically: he had himself in mind. "From 1793 to 1797," he confessed to his daughter, "I remained closely at home, saw none but those who came there, and at length became very sensible of the ill effect it had on my own mind, and of its direct and irresistible tendency to render me unfit for society." Jefferson was referring to the period when he returned home after his resignation as secretary of state—as Sarah Randolph had put it, turning "his back forever on public life"—in order to "devote the residue of his days to the restoration of his shattered fortunes." This was the only extended period of time that Jefferson spent at Monticello between 1774 and 1809.[34]

Because Jefferson could identify with the women in his family, it is no surprise that they could identify with him and devote their lives to protecting his reputation. That reputation, as we have seen, became their living. Not only did Sarah Randolph publish *The Domestic Life,* but after her father died and he left the family papers to her, she proposed a new edition of Jefferson's writings to the Library of Congress. A new edition was necessary, she testified to Congress, both to correct numerous errors in the nine-volume Henry Augustine Washington edition and, by including the family letters in her possession, "to throw much light upon the private and public life of the great statesman, and present him in many phases of life, heretofore unknown." In 1888, a congressional committee recommended paying Randolph $2,500 a year to prepare a new edition of the Jefferson papers, but then, the subsequent year, it considered buying the family papers outright. While Congress debated, Randolph died and the papers passed to her sister Carolina.[35]

Sarah Randolph believed that the family correspondence provided the key to Jefferson's character. Jefferson himself had taught his family that he had two selves, an "imaginary" one constructed by the public and his real one, known only to them. Twice in the *Domestic Life* we see Jefferson using this defense mechanism to deflect the criticism that stung him so badly. In both cases, the reports come from family members, and, in fact, an Internet search of the Jefferson papers at the Library of Congress does not provide any instance of Jefferson using this wording in his correspondence.[36] There is no reason, however, to doubt his family's memory of this distinctive phrase. One comes from the pen of Thomas Jefferson Randolph, who remembered his grandfather's final days for Henry Randall. As Jefferson lay on his deathbed, he called in the members of his family for a "parting interview." He spoke fondly of his long friendship with James Madison, but also talked about his enemies. "In speaking of the calumnies which his enemies had uttered against his public and private character with such unmitigated and untiring bitterness, he said that he had not considered them as abusing him; they had never known *him*. They had created an imaginary being clothed with odious attributes, to whom they had given his name; and it was against that creature of their imaginations they had levelled their anathemas."[37]

The other instance comes from an anecdote, "told from the most authentic source," that Sarah Randolph recounted about her great-grandfather. Randolph situates the story during Jefferson's first term as president. As he was out riding one day, she tells us, he came upon a pedestrian and struck up a conversation with the man who, not recognizing him, immediately started discussing politics "as was the habit of the day—and began to abuse the President, alluding even to some of the infamous calumnies against his private life." Jefferson asked the stranger, a Kentuckian, if he actually knew the president. No, he did not, but he would "never shrink from meeting Mr. Jefferson should he ever come in my way." Jefferson promised him an introduction if he would meet him at the Executive Mansion the next day. The abashed Kentuckian appeared before Jefferson at the appointed time, saying, "I have called, Mr. Jefferson, to apologize for having said to a stranger—." Before the man could finish, Jefferson disarmed him by making clear that he took no offense at "hard things [said] of an imaginary being who is no relation of mine." He then invited the Kentuckian to stay for dinner.[38]

Two themes from this anecdote recur in *The Domestic Life*. So often, it seems, did Jefferson go unrecognized in public that one might be forgiven for wondering if some of the stories might be apocryphal. At the very least, tales of the unknown Jefferson struck a chord with Sarah Randolph. One of the stories sounds almost like a folk tale. Jefferson stopped one evening at a country inn, where he entered into conversation with a stranger who did not recognize "this plainly-dressed and unassuming traveller." They talked about every topic imaginable—law, medicine, theology—on all of which Jefferson seemed "perfectly acquainted." When the stranger later asked the innkeeper who this astonishing man was, there came the reply, "Oh . . . why I thought you knew the Squire." All the stories about the unrecognized Jefferson speak to his modesty and good nature. In a story told by Thomas Jefferson Randolph, Jefferson once again encountered a stranger when out riding. This time, the president and several companions were returning home to Virginia on horseback, and the stranger asked Jefferson's assistance alone in fording a stream, judging him a good man from his appearance.[39]

Two other anecdotes suggest that in some circumstances Jefferson wanted to be recognized and his authority acknowledged. Sarah Randolph tells us that she knows of only two occasions when Jefferson lost his temper. In one instance, Jefferson and his daughter Martha were crossing a stream by ferry. The two ferrymen began an argument on shore and continued it on the ferry, coming almost to blows. Jefferson "remonstrated with them," but still they raged. Finally, "with his eyes flashing" Jefferson "snatched up an oar" and shouted to the ferrymen to "Row for your lives" or be knocked overboard. The other instance involved Jefferson's "favorite coachman," Jupiter. Jefferson had ordered another slave, a boy, to take one of the horses and go on an errand for his master, but Jupiter considered these horses as his and would not let the boy use one. When the boy told Jefferson about Jupiter's countermand, Jefferson thought the coachman was playing a joke on the boy, so he sent the boy back again, with the same order. Jupiter once again refused. Then, in "an excited tone," Jefferson directed that Jupiter himself appear, whereupon he "received the order and a rebuke from his master in tones and with a look which neither he nor the terrified bystanders ever forgot." This may be the only account we have of Jefferson terrifying anyone; it cannot be an accident that the object of Jefferson's anger was enslaved, nor that the objects of his oar-wielding threat of physical violence were two lower-class men. Jefferson rarely expressed anger, but when he did, it was at those far beneath him in status who had failed to oblige him.[40]

Slaves haunt the pages of the *Domestic Life* like ghosts. They are presences who do not speak, yet appear from time to time, at the edge of the stage.

Randolph nowhere discusses the institution of slavery. The closest she comes is when she reproduces a portion of Duc de la Rochefoucauld-Liancourt's description of his visit to Monticello in 1796. Jefferson's "negroes," we are told, "are nourished, clothed, and treated as well as white servants could be. . . . He animates them by rewards and distinctions; in fine, his superior mind directs the management of his domestic concerns with the same abilities, activity, and regularity which he evinced in the conduct of public affairs." Slavery at Monticello, like its master, is orderly and wholly benign. Randolph mentions also that Jefferson owned 154 slaves, "a very small number in proportion to his landed estate."[41]

Of course there is the now-familiar story about the slaves welcoming Jefferson and his daughters home from Paris, with the slave men unhitching the horses from the carriage and drawing it up the mountain with their "strong black arms up to the foot of the lawn in front of the door at Monticello." Randolph recounts another family story, this one about Polly, who had come to visit her father so sick and weak that she was "carried to Monticello in a litter borne by men." Surely these nameless men were enslaved. Although sometimes Jefferson mentioned particular slaves by name—not just Jupiter, but Critta, Remus, Phill, Davy, Melinda, John, and James—more often the slaves are ghosts. "The house, its contents, and appendages and servants, are as freely subjected to you as to myself," Jefferson offered Polly in an attempt to lure the gravely ill woman back to Monticello. Three years earlier, a similar offer: "I insist that you command and use every thing as if I were with you, and shall be very uneasy if you do not." A few months earlier: "The servants will be here under your commands."[42]

The most haunting ghost, of course, is Sally Hemings, nowhere mentioned but always a presence, the rationale, even, for the book. "No man's private character has been more foully assailed than Jefferson's," Randolph had written on the first pages of her book. Of the "calumnies" that Jefferson's "enemies had uttered against his public and private character," surely none had been more troubling to Jefferson's family than the allegations that he had fathered Sally Hemings's children. When the Kentuckian Jefferson had met while out riding one day had launched into his diatribe against the president, he had alluded "even to some of the infamous calumnies against his private life." Randolph nowhere mentions what these calumnies were, nor does she attempt to refute them with any specificity. Instead, she offers as a rebuttal the entire book, a portrait of "a beautiful domestic character," as if this were the only defense her great-grandfather could ever need.[43]

Here, then, is the importance of the stories about the multiple strangers who, when meeting Jefferson, "did not know who he was," and the invocation of the "imaginary being" created by those who did not know *him*. If Randolph's book is to be accepted as a true portrait of Jefferson, then it must rest on the claim that she and her father and grandmother and her aunts and uncles and the rest of her white kin knew the real man. That is the book's burden.[44]

But did they?

Sarah Randolph reproduces her father's description of his father's death. The scene is deeply moving as we see the old man slipping away. At four in the morning of July 4, as his end approached, Jefferson "called his servants in attendance with a strong and clear voice, perfectly conscious of his wants. He did not speak again." Jefferson's last words, then, were to his slaves, a summoning of them to meet his final needs. Here they are again, the ghosts. At ten in the morning, according to Thomas Jefferson Randolph, his grandfather "fixed his eyes intently upon me, indicating some want, which, most painfully, I could not understand, until his attached servant, Burwell, observed that his head was not so much elevated as he usually desired it." "Upon restoring it to its usual position," Thomas Jefferson Randolph continued, "he seemed satisfied." There, with the end only a few hours away, and with his grandfather staring intently at him, Thomas Jefferson Randolph could not read his grandfather, and it caused him pain. Only Burwell could tell what the dying man needed to make himself comfortable.[45]

Notes

1. Bernard Mayo, ed., *Jefferson Himself: The Personal Narrative of a Many-Sided American* (Boston, 1942). J. Jefferson Looney makes the same point about Mayo's work in his essay in this volume, "'Merely Personal or Private, with Which We Have Nothing to Do': Thomas Jefferson's Autobiographical Writings."

2. Sarah N. Randolph, *The Domestic Life of Thomas Jefferson: Compiled from Family Letters and Reminiscences by his Great-Granddaughter* (New York, 1871), 283, 277.

3. Ibid., vii. Sarah Randolph acknowledges the existence of the Hemings family in only the most oblique ways—for example, by stating in her preface that "no man's private character has been more foully assailed than Jefferson's" (ibid.). It is important to

note that at Monticello, Jefferson had two families, one white and one black, a subject I have explored in "The White Jeffersons," in *Sally Hemings and Thomas Jefferson: History, Memory, and Civic Culture,* ed. Jan Ellen Lewis and Peter S. Onuf (Charlottesville, Va., 1999), 127–60.

4. Randolph, *Domestic Life of Thomas Jefferson,* 275–77.

5. Henry S. Randall, *The Life of Thomas Jefferson,* 3 vols. (New York, 1858), 1:viii, 622; Randolph, *Domestic Life of Thomas Jefferson,* vii. For Randall, see Andrew Burstein, "'Dexterity and Delicacy of Manipulation': Biographers Henry S. Randall and James Parton," in this volume.

6. Randolph, *Domestic Life of Thomas Jefferson,* 431, 432, viii.

7. "Thomas Jefferson," *New York Times,* 3 August 1871; Randolph, *Domestic Life of Thomas Jefferson,* 49–50; Randall, *Life of Thomas Jefferson,* 3:680–81.

8. Quoted in Looney, "'Merely Personal or Private,'" 27.

9. Quoted in Jan Lewis, "'The Blessings of Domestic Society': Thomas Jefferson's Family and the Transformation of American Politics," in *Jeffersonian Legacies,* ed. Peter S. Onuf (Charlottesville, Va., 1993), 114–15. These letters (TJ to Mary Jefferson Eppes, 15 February 1801; TJ to Martha Jefferson Randolph, 8 February 1798; TJ to Martha Jefferson Randolph, 8 June 1797) were published in *The Family Letters of Thomas Jefferson,* ed. Edwin Morris Betts and James Adam Bear Jr. (Columbia, Mo., 1966), 196, 155, 146, and have been cited by many authors.

10. Although he named her Mary at birth, Jefferson later addressed his younger surviving (white) daughter by her nickname Polly, and that is how I identify her as well.

11. Randolph, *Domestic Life of Thomas Jefferson,* 274, 271; Randall, *Life of Thomas Jefferson,* 2:594–602. For the historical context, including predictions of constitutional and paramilitary turmoil, see the essays in James Horn, Jan Ellen Lewis, and Peter S. Onuf, eds., *The Revolution of 1800: Democracy, Race, and the New Republic* (Charlottesville, Va., 2002).

12. Randolph, *Domestic Life of Thomas Jefferson,* 274, 329, 250, 245.

13. Ibid., 329, 397, 399, 408; Herbert E. Sloan, *Principle and Interest: Thomas Jefferson and the Problem of Debt* (New York, 1995), 22.

14. Randolph, *Domestic Life of Thomas Jefferson,* 400.

15. Ibid., 277. This passage illustrates Randolph's method. In introducing the letter she mentions only that George Jefferson was a "kinsman" and that her own ancestor rejected nepotism. George Jefferson had written Thomas Jefferson several weeks earlier to forward, abashedly, a letter from his brother pleading for a government position. George Jefferson came close to begging Jefferson *not* to find an office for his brother, knowing both that Jefferson's Federalist enemies would "censure" him for it and that his brother's qualifications for any office would probably not, as he delicately put it, "stand the test of investigation." George Jefferson's request was a very easy one for Thomas Jefferson to turn down. See George Jefferson to TJ, 4 March 1801, *TJP,* 33: 158–60.

16. Randolph, *Domestic Life of Thomas Jefferson,* 277, 388–89.

17. Paul G. Sifton, "The Provenance of the Thomas Jefferson Papers," *American*

Archivist 40 (1977): 18; Francis D. Cogliano, *Thomas Jefferson: Reputation and Legacy* (Charlottesville, Va., 2006), 81, 82. Cogliano notes that, not surprisingly, the family made a number of errors, which were repeated in subsequent editions of Jefferson's writings.

18. Sifton, "Provenance of the Thomas Jefferson Papers," 20–24; Burstein, "Dexterity and Delicacy of Manipulation," 64. Burstein is quoting from an article published in the *New York Commercial Advertiser* that profiled Randall just before the publication of his biography. A copy of this article can also be found as "Literary Intelligence," *American Publishers' Circular and Literary Gazette* 3 (25 July 1857): 469–70. The family told Randall that the papers had been found "amongst the old, cast-aside account books and other trumpery of a closet connected with Mr. Jefferson's bedroom"—the one "above the alcove, with its two eye-like holes opening into the bedroom" —and then moved to Edgehill, where they remained forgotten for several decades.

19. Randolph, *Domestic Life of Thomas Jefferson,* viii. It is not clear what happened to the cache of papers that the family turned over to Randall and exactly which letters had been held by the government between 1848 and 1870–71. Merrill D. Peterson concluded that "much" that Sarah Randolph "published was taken from Randall's *Life,* for the New Yorker had drawn from the same bundles of family papers and the same wells of family remembrance." See *Jefferson Image,* 232. I thank Jeff Looney for sharing his insights with me.

20. Randolph, *Domestic Life of Thomas Jefferson,* 388; *Jefferson Image,* 232.

21. Randolph, *Domestic Life of Thomas Jefferson,* 69–70; Cynthia A. Kierner, *Martha Jefferson Randolph, Daughter of Monticello: Her Life and Times* (Chapel Hill, N.C., 2012), 42–43.

22. Margaret Bayard Smith, *The First Forty Years of Washington Society,* ed. Gaillard Hunt (New York, 1906), 74–77; Randolph, *Domestic Life of Thomas Jefferson,* 102. I have discussed Smith's transcription of these letters in Jan Lewis, "White Jeffersons," in Lewis and Onuf, *Sally Hemings and Thomas Jefferson,* 130, 158n3. Both Henry Randall and Sarah Randolph include one of these letters, that of 8 June 1797, in their books (Randall, *Life of Thomas Jefferson,* 358; Randolph, *Domestic Life of Thomas Jefferson,* 206). Neither, however, includes Jefferson's letter of 5 February 1801, and it is not clear whether Randall or Randolph had it available. This letter is reproduced in full in Betts and Bear, *Family Letters of Thomas Jefferson,* 194–96, and in *TJP,* 32:556–57.

23. Randolph, *Domestic Life of Thomas Jefferson,* 103, 124, 125; Annette Gordon-Reed, *The Hemingses of Monticello: An American Family* (New York, 2008), 193–95. See also Fawn M. Brodie, *Thomas Jefferson: An Intimate History* (New York, 1974), 216–19.

24. Abigail Adams to TJ, 6 July 1787, *TJP,* 11:551.

25. Randolph, *Domestic Life of Thomas Jefferson,* 126. Randall also includes this letter. See Randall, *Life of Thomas Jefferson,* 1:480.

26. Randolph, *Domestic Life of Thomas Jefferson,* 103–4, 102; Smith, *First Forty Years of Washington Society,* 309.

27. Randolph, *Domestic Life of Thomas Jefferson,* 345; Kierner, *Martha Jefferson Randolph,* 142–56.

28. Randolph, *Domestic Life of Thomas Jefferson,* 347–48. Randall published both of these letters. See *Life of Thomas Jefferson,* 3:347–51.

29. Randolph, *Domestic Life of Thomas Jefferson,* 397, 406. Paul Finkelman, "Jefferson and Slavery: 'Treason Against the Hopes of the World,'" in Onuf, *Jeffersonian Legacies,* 181–221, makes the case for Jefferson's profligacy. Sloan, *Principle and Interest,* describes Jefferson's finances more generally.

30. *Jefferson Image,* 232–33; Jan Lewis, "'The Blessings of Domestic Society': Thomas Jefferson's Family and the Transformation of American Politics," in Onuf, *Jeffersonian Legacies,* 109–46; Joseph J. Ellis, *American Sphinx: The Character of Thomas Jefferson* (New York, 1997), 305; Joseph J. Ellis, "Jefferson: Post-DNA," *WMQ* 57 (2000): 125–38.

31. I have explored this topic in Jan Lewis, "Jefferson, the Family, and Civic Education," in *Thomas Jefferson and the Education of a Citizen,* ed. James Gilreath (Washington, D.C., 1999), 63–75, 324–26, and "Jefferson and Women," in *Seeing Jefferson Anew: In His Time and Ours,* ed. John B. Boles and Randal L. Hall (Charlottesville, Va., 2010), 152–71. See also Brian Steele, "Thomas Jefferson's Gender Frontier," *JAH* 95 (2008): 17–42, and Brian Steele, *Thomas Jefferson and American Nationhood* (New York, 2012), 53–90. For ideas about women's intellectual capacity in this period more generally, see Lucia McMahon, *Mere Equals: The Paradox of Educated Women in the Early American Republic* (Ithaca, N.Y., 2012).

32. Randolph, *Domestic Life of Thomas Jefferson,* 71; Louis-André Pichon, quoted in Jon Meacham, *Thomas Jefferson: The Art of Power* (New York, 2012), 353; William Plumer, quoted in Dumas Malone, *Jefferson the President: First Term, 1801–1805* (Boston, 1970), 371; and R. B. Bernstein, *Thomas Jefferson* (New York, 2003), 140.

33. Randolph, *Domestic Life of Thomas Jefferson,* 115–16, 320.

34. Ibid., 284, 400.

35. Sifton, "Provenance of the Thomas Jefferson Papers," 25. Carolina sold some of the papers to a male cousin and left the rest to female relatives. Some of the family papers were lost in a fire, but the rest were eventually deposited by family members in a series of repositories. See ibid., 27–29.

36. See http://memory.loc.gov/ammem/collections/jefferson_papers/index.html.

37. Randolph, *Domestic Life of Thomas Jefferson,* 425, 427–28. The letter is also reproduced in Randall, *Life of Thomas Jefferson,* 3:544.

38. Randolph, *Domestic Life of Thomas Jefferson,* 289–90.

39. Ibid., 38, 337.

40. Ibid., 321–22. Annette Gordon-Reed informs us that Jupiter's last name was Evans and that he had been Jefferson's boyhood companion and served as his attendant until, at the age of thirty-one, he was replaced in that position by Robert Hemings and moved to the position of custodian of the stables and sometime coachman. See Gordon-Reed, *Hemingses of Monticello,* 95, 124–25.

41. Randolph, *Domestic Life of Thomas Jefferson,* 238, 229. Immediately after enumerating the slaves on Jefferson's plantations, Randolph moved on to list the number of horses, mules, cattle, hogs, and sheep.

42. Ibid., 153, 300, 286, 279, 320, 308–9, 278–79, 244, 298.

43. Ibid., viii, 428, 289, vii.

44. Ibid., 38, 289–90.

45. Ibid., 428. Gordon-Reed notes the presence of the slaves at Jefferson's deathbed. She surmises that among them were not only his personal servant Burwell Colbert but also Sally Hemings. See Gordon-Reed, *Hemingses of Monticello,* 650–51.

5   Painting with a Fine Pencil

Henry Adams's Jefferson

In a famous passage of the *History of the United States during the Administrations of Thomas Jefferson and James Madison,* Henry Adams wrote, "A few broad strokes of the brush would paint the portrait of all the early Presidents with this exception. . . . Jefferson could be painted only touch by touch, with a fine pencil, and the perfection of the likeness depended upon the shifting and uncertain flicker of its semi-transparent shadows."[1] Read closely, it is the key to Adams's portrait of Jefferson, and perhaps to the entire work of history.

Among students of the early republic, Henry Adams is remembered as a critic of Thomas Jefferson.[2] Yet Adams was no Jefferson hater. No Adams could participate in the "Hamilton revival" of the late nineteenth century.[3] Hamilton was a family enemy; Jefferson was a friend, and also a rival. John Quincy Adams sat in the 1808 Republican caucus that nominated James Madison for president, an act that cost Adams his Senate seat, and John Adams and Jefferson renewed their friendship a few years later. In 1877, Henry Adams sent a friend a copy of Henry Cabot Lodge's *Life of George Cabot,* "but I beg you to believe that I sympathize as little with his attacks on Jefferson as with his attacks on the Adamses."[4] In fact, Adams praised Jefferson, writing: "Washington and Jefferson doubtless stand pre-eminent as the representatives of what is best in our national character or its aspirations." And in the *History* Adams recognized that "according to the admitted standards of greatness, Jefferson was a great man." That was no mere ironic concession. Adams continued, "After all deductions on which his enemies might choose to insist, his character could not be denied elevation, versatility, breadth, insight, and delicacy."[5]

What explains the rough treatment Jefferson received in the history? Why has it been so easy to view the *History* as nothing more than a critique of Jefferson? Adams thought that Jefferson, perhaps even more than Washington, was America's "Legislator" in the classical mode, the great man who imposed his stamp on the nation. And that explains the mixed review.

Adams was writing in the 1880s, just as pointillists were stepping beyond impressionism. The pointillists, like Jefferson, were close readers of modern science. They studied the play of light and color. The pointillists hoped that science could help perfect art.[6] At the same time, their art, like modern empirical science, stayed at the surface. When examined up close, a Seurat painting breaks down into a chaos of dots. All that suggested something about the nature of Jefferson's thought, and its limits.

As science marched through the nineteenth century, the confident empiricism of the Enlightenment was losing its sway. An enlightened admirer and practitioner of science, Jefferson had faith that the modern scientific method would provide a sufficient guide to progress. In one letter to Henry Adams's great-grandfather, Jefferson wrote that "a single sense may indeed be sometimes deceived, but rarely, and never all our senses together, with their faculty of reasoning."[7] By the late nineteenth century, Jefferson sounded hopelessly naive, at least to Adams.[8] Adams's description of Jefferson also suggested that Jefferson was hard to describe. One therefore has to read Adams closely to understand his impression of Jefferson. Near the end of the introductory chapters of the *History,* Adams wrote that "Jefferson . . . dreaded so greatly his own reputation as a visionary that he seldom or never uttered his whole thought." A couple of pages later he added, "Jefferson's writings may be searched from beginning to end without revealing the whole measure of the man." To explain Jefferson, therefore, Adams looked for a logic, deeply embedded in his writings, statements, and statecraft. According to Adams, Jefferson set out to create a better nation than history had ever known: "That the United States should become a nation like France, England, or Russia, should conquer the world like Rome, or develop a typical race like the Chinese, was no part of his scheme. He wished to begin a new era." The paramount goal of his statecraft was progress. All Jefferson's tergiversations could be explained in light of that lofty end.[9]

At the same time Adams told the story of Jefferson and America, and of Jefferson's America, Adams wrote another story, which can be only be inferred from the text. That story vindicated Adams's own flesh and blood, at least in certain respects. In other ways, however, Jefferson came out on top. Jefferson had more power; John Adams had more truth. Henry Adams wished to give full credit to Jefferson for his talents and achievements, but he also used his own progenitor implicitly to show Jefferson's limitations and those of the nation, too.

The historian went to great lengths not to mention John Adams in the *History.* He felt uncomfortable writing about his great-grandfather. When Justin Winsor asked him to write about the American Revolution for the "Memorial History of Boston," Adams turned him down, saying it would not be fitting for him to write in praise of his own flesh and blood.[10] It might even be that Adams wrote about the years from 1801 to 1817 because they were the sixteen years between 1765 and his own lifetime when his ancestors would factor least in the story. The second president came up in the *History* every now and then, but somehow the name "John Adams" does not appear in the text for quite some time. As Donald Hall noted several years ago, it is "a neat trick [which would be impossible] were it not for the magic of euphemism." If Adams's goal was to minimize the connection between author and subject, he fails miserably, for "not mentioning the name of your great-grandfather—who was President . . . is roughly like hiring a blimp to fly overhead with *John Adams Was My Great-Grandfather* stenciled on its side in letters thirty feet high."[11]

In his private writings, Adams was sometimes more candid about his admiration for his great-grandfather. On March 3, 1901, the centennial of John Adams's last day as president, he wrote, "I look over to the White House wondering what my old friend Thomas Jefferson would say. It is just a hundred years since he turned my harmless ancestor into the street at midnight, and I think he must wish he hadn't, for there is mighty little left of him; whereas my venerable ancestor has at least me." On the same date fifteen years later the historian made a similar comment.[12] In other words, Henry Adams tended to think of the second and third presidents in tandem.

Elsewhere, he compared John Adams favorably with John Quincy Adams. He did not consider the sixth president "a subject of compassion. His father was worth two of him, and really suffered and enjoyed greatly."[13] He criticized the admiring biography of John Quincy Adams that his brother, Brooks, wrote for overlooking their grandfather's faults: "I will not be as big as brute as J.Q.A. was, but I am ready to go all lengths for his father."[14] In a more comic mood, Henry criticized Brooks's emphasis on the family's

Quincy bloodline, pointing to the family's Boylston blood: "my own theory for Boylston influence is that you and I have the Boylston strain three times repeated. John Adams had it but once. Which accounts for you and us others being three times as damned a fool as John Adams—which seems hard."[15]

There can be little doubt that the Adams-Jefferson contrast was on Henry Adams's mind as he wrote the *History*. In 1882, while hard at work on the project, he contrasted Jefferson with John Adams. Adams's great-grandfather "is a droll figure, and good for Sheridan's school, but T.J. is a case for Beaumarchais; he needs the lightest of touches."[16] Note that this comment gives a comic twist to the remark that gives us our title, and that Adams selected two late eighteenth-century comic playwrights—the English author of *School for Scandal*, and the French author of the *Marriage of Figaro*. Might Adams have penned the latter phrase with the former one fresh in his mind, or vice versa?

Early in the *History*, Adams introduced Jefferson with long passages in the section on the character of the South and near the end of the chapter on "American Ideals."[17] Adams concluded that Jefferson had a philosophy that he adhered to as well as he could in the circumstances he faced. That was a mixed blessing.

Jefferson wished to create the world anew. Human life could be fundamentally rearranged; there was no strong human nature deep beneath the surface radically limiting his project. Forging the American republic was a means to that end. In this new world, interests would rule and, as the sphere of interest extended, bring about a more peaceful, and therefore more free, world. Jefferson had a towering ambition. He "aspired beyond the ambition of nationality, and embraced in his view the whole future of man." The third president hoped "for a time when the world's ruling interests should cease to be local and should become universal; when questions of boundary and nationality should become insignificant; when armies and navies should be reduced to the work of police, and politics should consist only in nonintervention,—he set himself to the task of governing, with this golden age in view." In short, the goal of Jefferson's statecraft was peace: "'Peace is our passion!' This phrase of President Jefferson . . . expressed his true policy." In this vision, the military would become global policeman, in a world where national boundaries would not matter. That explained Jefferson's comment: "Whether we remain one confederacy . . . [was] not very important." The particular characters of nations would wash away into a world of interlocking and harmonious interests. With war safely in the dustbin of history, men would finally be free to pursue happiness.[18]

Were Jefferson's goals reasonable? Adams had his doubts. Those doubts grew, in part from Jefferson's philosophy. Jefferson might believe, for example, that peace was a good, but he had trouble defending that proposition. Explaining what he took to be Jefferson's position, Adams created an imaginary speech from the third president:

> He might be imagined to define democratic progress, in the somewhat affected precision of French philosophy: "Progress is either physical or intellectual. If we can bring it about that men are on the average an inch larger . . . if their brain is an ounce or two heavier, and their life a year or two longer,—that is progress. If fifty years hence the average man shall invariably argue from two ascertained premises where he now jumps to a conclusion from a single supposed revelation,—that is progress! I expect it to be made here, under our democratic stimulants, on a greater scale, until every man is potentially an athlete in body and an Aristotle in mind."[19]

Note the materialism of these ideas. Each marker of progress is something that can be measured, quantified, and analyzed. That is no accident. As Adams's allusion to pointillism implied, Jefferson was a devotee of modern science, following "the somewhat affected precision of French philosophy."[20] This philosophy provided the foundation for the "ideology" Jefferson admired. It presumed a world in which everything worth knowing could be learned via the modern scientific method, and that the world really is, generally speaking, as it appears. In the letter in which Jefferson told John Adams that our senses, "with their faculty of reason," are never deceived, he also reasoned that "on the basis of sensation, of matter and motion, we may erect the fabric of all the certainties we can have or need."[21]

According to Jefferson, the modern scientific method was indeed a sufficient foundation for all human reasoning. All other methods, and all other ideas about the nature of truth—anything that could not be grasped by his materialist philosophy—Jefferson dismissed as false and as a relic of barbarous ages past. By Henry Adams's day, at least in some philosophical circles, Enlightenment empiricism was tending toward nihilism—implying both that the surface is all that is knowable and that it is *not* truth.

Adams silently used his great-grandfather's words to raise questions about Jefferson's philosophy.[22] Immediately after describing Jefferson's ideas, his *History* continued:

> To this doctrine the New Englander replied, "What will you do
> for moral progress?" Every possible answer to this question opened
> a chasm. No doubt Jefferson held the faith that men would improve
> morally with their physical and intellectual growth; but he had
> no idea of any moral improvement other than that which came
> by nature. He could not tolerate a priesthood, a state church, or
> revealed religion. Conservatives, who could tolerate no society
> without such pillars of order, were, from their point of view, right in
> answering, "Give us rather the worst despotism of Europe,—there
> our souls may at least have a chance at salvation!" To their minds,
> vice and virtue were not relative, but fixed terms.[23]

This comment sets up much of what follows in the *History*. Jefferson had "faith that men would improve morally." It was not and—according to the scientific method—could not be a scientific conclusion. It was a faith, not a rationally defensible proposition. The scientific method is merely a method. As such it is amoral. If all reason must follow the modern scientific method, then there can be no rational basis by which to distinguish right from wrong.

In this passage, Henry Adams was paraphrasing his great-grandfather. In "Discourses on Davila," John Adams asked, "Is there a possibility that the government of nations may fall into the hands of men who teach the most disconsolate of all creeds, that men are but fireflies, and that this *all* is without a father? Is this the way to make man, as man, an object of respect? Or is it to make murder as indifferent as shooting a plover?" Were that to happen, Adams asked, "would not one of these, the most credulous of all believers, have reason to pray to his eternal nature or his almighty chance . . . *give us again our popes and hierarchies, Benedictines and Jesuits, with all their superstition and fanaticism, impostures and tyranny*"?[24]

Modern scientific materialism was a danger to all that John Adams held most dear, for it threatened to produce the very nihilism that was gaining philosophic and moral currency in the late nineteenth century. One did not have to read Nietzsche to see that. Jefferson claimed to be a materialist in philosophy and a Unitarian in religion. The Adams family doubted that circle could be squared. What about spirit? Jefferson wrote Henry's great-grandfather, "Jesus taught nothing of it. He told us indeed that 'God is a spirit,' but he has not defined what a spirit is, nor said that it is not *matter*."[25] By contrast, John Adams insisted to Jefferson that "the Saint has as good a right to groan at the Philosopher for asserting that there is nothing but matter in the Universe, As the Philosopher has to laugh at the Saint for saying that there are both Matter and Spirit."[26] John Adams's skepticism pointed to the hole in Jefferson's ideology. It mistook impression for truth. As a practical matter, that often worked, but in time it could cause serious problems.

Henry Adams was doing more than setting up a simple contrast between John Adams and Thomas Jefferson. His great-grandfather did not say exactly the words his great-grandson put into the *History*. The subtle changes Adams introduced to his great-grandfather's words were also part of the story. In the *History*, "Federalism" and "New England" are terms associated with High Federalists like Fisher Ames.[27] John Adams was only in partial agreement with them. He opposed a religious establishment, even if he thought it would be better than the official atheism of the French Revolution. The John Adams passage quoted here does not speak of saving souls, although it does in his great-grandson's version. "Discourses on Davila" was a series of essays on politics, not religion. It was about man's political nature. The *History* vindicated John Adams's understanding of politics more than Jefferson's. Politics could not be ordered by modern science.

Between the lines, the *History* suggested that John Adams was also on to something deeper. Jefferson was a materialist, and he also believed in natural rights. Could those two ideas, which made very different premises about human nature, be reconciled? Or was Jefferson's philosophy built on an act of will more than of reason? In the *History* the American mind resembled Jefferson's mind. That reconciliation, being willful, was possible only on the surface. It was ideology rather than philosophy. That was the gravamen of the line, "Every possible answer to this question opened a chasm."[28] Jefferson, following the modern scientific method, put morality and reason in separate boxes.

According to the *History*, Jefferson's statecraft was successful in some ways but not in others. The Union held together, and it became a nation unlike any other the world had known. At the same time, however, Jefferson's ideology failed. Peaceful coercion could not replace war as a tool of state, and strict construction was impossible in practice. Even so, Jefferson's ideas shaped the American mind.

Readers of the *History* see the failure of Jefferson's political theories, amid the success of American democracy, in Adams's discussion of the Embargo and the Louisiana Purchase. Peace was the end of Jefferson's statecraft, and embargo was the means to that end. In his discussion of Jefferson in the introduction to the *History*, Adams wrote, "Few men have dared to legislate as though eternal peace were at hand, in a world torn by wars and convulsions and drowned in blood; but this was what Jefferson aspired to do." The third president "believed that Americans might safely set an example which the Christian world should be led by interest to respect and at length to imitate. As he conceived a true American policy, war was a blunder, an unnecessary risk; and even in case of robbery and aggression the United States, he believed, had only to stand on the defensive in order to obtain justice in the end. He would not consent to build up a new nationality merely to create more navies and armies, to perpetuate the crimes and follies of Europe." Above all, "the central government at Washington should not be permitted to indulge the miserable ambitions that had made the Old World a hell, and frustrated the hopes of humanity."[29]

Interests could replace war, and commerce could make war obsolete. "Peaceful coercion" was Jefferson's way of war. Regarding the Embargo, Adams let John Randolph explain: "The system of embargo is one system. . . . The system of raising troops and fleets of whatever sort is another and opposite." Jefferson, Adams wrote, was "prepared to risk the fate of mankind on the chance of reasoning far from certain in its details."

Adams credited Jefferson's philanthropy: "The embargo was an experiment in politics well worth making. In the scheme of President Jefferson's statesmanship, non-intercourse was the substitute for war,—the weapon of defense and coercion which saved the cost and danger of supporting army or navy, and spared America from the brutalities of the Old World." No wonder the stakes seemed so high. "Failure of the embargo meant in his mind not only a recurrence to the practice of war," Adams wrote, "but to every social and political evil that war had always brought in its train. In such a case the crimes and corruptions of Europe, which had been the object of his political fears, must, as he believed, sooner or later teem in the fat soil of America. To avert a disaster so vast, was a proper motive for statesmanship."[30]

Jefferson thought that the failure of peaceful coercion meant not only war but also that the United States would have to have the kind of arbitrary government that he hated. With war came reasons of state, and with reasons of state came arbitrary government. War, therefore, brought "not only a recurrence to the practice of war, but to every social and political evil" that came with it. That effort, Adams suggested, was very American. "Except for a few Federalists, every American, from Jefferson and Gallatin down to the poorest squatter, seemed to nourish an idea that he was doing what he could to overthrow the tyranny which the past had fastened on the human mind."[31]

But war could not be eliminated from man's terrestrial history. Jefferson's theory of statecraft died with the failure of the Embargo. Its cost, Adams noted, "exceeded all calculation. Financially, it emptied the treasury, bankrupted the mercantile and agricultural class, and ground the poor beyond endurance. Constitutionally, it overrode every specified limit on arbitrary power and made Congress despotic. . . . Morally, it sapped the nation's vital force, lowering its courage, paralyzing its energy, corrupting its principles. . . . Politically, it cost Jefferson the fruits of eight years painful labor for popularity. . . . Frightful as the cost of this engine was, as a means of coercion the embargo evidently failed."[32]

The federal government would need much more power than Jefferson had hoped it would need. It would need to create permanent armies and navies—with all that they entailed for the size of government and, Jefferson feared, the character of the nation. This was the lesson John Adams had tried to teach Jefferson and his circle, in France and America, from the start of the French Revolution, if not before. It was a lesson recorded on every page of history.[33] Some human truths were, in fact, available to all students of history. In pointing to that conclusion, the *History* vindicated Adams. Broadly speaking, the *History* suggested that the nature of politics did not and could not change. "America began slowly to struggle," Henry Adams wrote, "under the consciousness of pain, toward a conviction that she must bear the common burdens of humanity, and fight with the weapons of other races in the same bloody arena; that she could not much longer delude herself with the hopes of evading the laws of Nature and the instincts of life; and that her new statesmanship which made peace a passion could lead to no better result than had been reached by the barbarous system which made war a duty."[34]

Strict construction was the domestic compliment to the Embargo. It, too, failed—even though it was central to Jefferson's understanding of the federal republic. Adams quoted Jefferson's comment that "the federal government is in truth our foreign government." He then deadpanned, "That these views were new as a system in government could not be denied." As Adams explained, "the national government, as he conceived it, was a foreign department as independent from the domestic department, which belonged to the States, as though they were governments of different nations." The success of such a federation depended upon the belief that the line between foreign and domestic policy, and between federal and state power, was clear and enforceable.[35]

Jefferson preached strict construction but practiced something different. Such a practice was not within him. Adams quoted from Jefferson's draft of the Kentucky Resolutions: "every State has a natural right, in cases not within the compact, to nullify of their own authority all assumptions of power by others within their limits." Elsewhere, Adams added that "the essence of Virginia republicanism lay in a single maxim: THE GOVERNMENT SHALL NOT BE THE FINAL JUDGE OF ITS OWN POWERS." But, Adams noted, Jefferson's "mind shared little in common with the provincialism on which the Virginia and Kentucky Resolutions were founded. His instincts led him to widen rather than to narrow the bounds of every intellectual exercise; and if vested with political authority, he could no more resist the temptation to stretch his powers than he could abstain from using his mind on any subject merely because he might be drawn upon ground supposed to be dangerous."[36] His statecraft spanned over the republican canvas; it was not anchored by anything beneath the surface.

The Jefferson administration supported internal improvements in its early years—"a violation of States-rights theories." Jefferson also used patronage to upend Aaron Burr's faction in New York. Judged by party principles of the 1790s, those were hardly Republican actions. Those were relatively small matters, perhaps to be allowed on the theory that, as Jefferson noted, "we see the wisdom of Solon's remark,—that no more good must be attempted than the nation can bear."[37]

The Louisiana Purchase provided the coup de gras to Jefferson's constitutional theories. Nothing in the Constitution suggested that the U.S. government had the right to acquire territory. Jefferson himself said that the purchase was "an act beyond the Constitution" that could only be authorized by amendment. The government, he said, "must appeal to *the nation* for an additional article to the Constitution approving and confirming an act which the nation has not previously authorized." Absent such a constitutional remedy, Jefferson wrote, the purchase would make the Constitution "a blank paper by construction." But necessity forced Jefferson's hand. No amendment was made. Adams rendered judgment: "The essential point was that for the first time in the national history all parties agreed in admitting that the government could govern." The comment was meant to sting.[38]

According to Jefferson, one could no more presume that the power to make treaties allowed the acquisition of an empire than one could admit that the power to manage the debts of the United States or to regulate commerce among the states implied the right to create a corporation to do so. In the realm of executive power, that line of reasoning was inseparable from the theories that Hamilton embraced in his *Pacificus* essays, which had so angered Jefferson in contretemps over Washington's Neutrality Proclamation. To argue that the power to make treaties, by nature, included the power to acquire land was exactly analogous to Hamilton's argument that the "executive power" described in Article II of the Constitution had a nature, which implied certain prerogatives belonged to it. (It is no coincidence that such reasoning had more in common with classic political science, rather than a political science built upon the modern scientific method, which rejects such teleology.) In the name of progress, Jefferson rejected the idea that government had a nature—so long as there are governments, they must exercise certain powers in order to function, just as a ship must float in order to sail. That was particularly true for the presidency. "The Pope could as safely trifle with the doctrine of apostolic succession," Adams wrote, "as Jefferson with the limits of Executive power."[39]

Adams thus rendered an ironic judgment on Jefferson. The third president was reasonable enough to kill his own theory rather than lose Louisiana. In practice, although never in theory, Jefferson allowed that John Adams had been correct. Governments have a nature. Absent certain powers they simply cannot function, as all of history, including the history of Jefferson's own administration, proved.[40] Moreover, Adams was, albeit ironically, combatting contemporary criticisms of Jefferson, by separating Jefferson from John C. Calhoun, and from secession, rebellion, and slavery.

The lesson of the *History*, however, is *not* that John Adams defeated Thomas Jefferson in the court of history. To be sure, the *History* does imply that American *government* had to retain certain powers that the second president said it needed. Jefferson's ideology was not functional as a governing ideology. But the *History* was not the story of the rise of a government. It was the story of the creation of a democratic "nation," to use Jefferson's term. Note Adams's language: "Failure of the embargo meant *in his mind* not only a recurrence to the practice of war." If it failed, "the crimes and corruptions of Europe . . . *must, as he believed,* sooner or later teem in the fat soil of America." Jefferson was wrong, for the action in America was outside of government. It was, as Madeleine Lee, the heroine of his novel *Democracy,* learns, in "the true democracy of life, her paupers and her prisons, her schools and her hospitals."[41] Keep in mind that Adams was a close student of Alexis de Tocqueville.[42] The story of America was democracy, and the story of democracy was social rather than political. That is what made the United States a new kind of nation.

The real action in American history was outside of government. Immediately before his chapters on the Embargo, Adams interjected two long paragraphs about the steamboat. "A few whose names could be mentioned in one or two lines," he wrote—"Men like Chancellor Livingston, Dr. Mitchell, Joel Barlow,—hailed the 17th of August, 1807, as the beginning of a new era in America, . . . for on that day, at one o'clock in the afternoon, the steamboat 'Clermont,' with Robert Fulton in command, started on her voyage" and "for the first time America could consider herself mistress of her vast resources. Compared with such a step in her progress, the medieval barbarisms of Napoleon and Spencer Perceval signified little more to her than the doings of Achilles and Agamemnon."[43]

The steam engine conquered the problem of distance—the issue of first concern in American history.[44] With steam navigation (and by implication the railroad too) the nation could spread over a theretofore impossible expanse of territory. Many Federalists had reservations about the Louisiana Purchase partly because they feared that no nation could digest so much land and remain free. Jefferson was confident that the United States could subsume the territory with relative ease. His concept of a federal union solved that problem. Such a union, he thought, could remain republican if the national government remained focused solely on foreign affairs. Jefferson was wrong about that, too. Private citizens, using science, and largely outside the workings of politics, made the nation.

Strict construction and peaceful coercion failed; the democratic republic lived. Steam travel, Adams asserted, "separated the colonial from the independent stage of growth." Moreover, modern practical science was the key.

Jefferson was, in a sense, correct. Science made the new republic possible. It also rendered Federalist political wisdom obsolete. It did that, however, by rendering politics a sideshow.[45]

But America also bore Jefferson's stamp. In his discussion of Fulton, Adams noted that democracy was rewriting the rules of history, and doing so in a Jeffersonian manner. "The unfailing mark of a primitive society," he wrote, "was to regard war as the most natural pursuit of man; and history with reason began as a record of war, because, in fact, all other human occupations were secondary to this. The chief sign that Americans had other qualities than the races from which they sprang, was shown by their dislike for war as a profession, and their obstinate attempts to invent other methods for obtaining their ends; but in the actual state of mankind, safety could still be secured only through the power of self-defence."[46]

Europeans dismissed Americans as crass materialists, only out for the next dollar. The *History* refuted that charge. But the nation only succeeded by casting "political philanthropists" like Jefferson aside. Jefferson missed the boat. When the *Clermont* steamed on its way, "government took no notice," even though steam settled "the political and economic problems of America at once." Why should government have paid attention to Fulton? At the time, "the reign of politics showed no sign of ending." In fact, Adams suggested, politics was no longer the story in America. It would soon cease to reign. Adams's great-grandfather's field of expertise was no longer the central concern of history.[47] Jefferson's wish to build a country whose essence was, in a sense, outside of politics was vindicated.

The deeper story of the *History* was the movement from a world ruled by statesmen like Jefferson and his friends to one ruled by middle-class democracy. In the *History*, events often controlled Jefferson's actions. At the same time, however, the *History* showed that America was created, in part, in Jefferson's image. There is a clear family resemblance between the traits Adams ascribed to Jefferson and those he ascribed to the American mind. That was by design. "Whether the figures of history were treated as heroes or as types," as Adams wrote in his final chapter, "they must be taken to represent the people."[48]

But what, exactly, was this new, democratic nation? The *History* presented the United States during the administrations of Jefferson and Madison as a dialectic, anticipating Gordon Wood's *Radicalism of the American*

Revolution by a century. Instead of Wood's "Monarchy," "Republicanism," and "Democracy," however, Adams gave us "Federalism," "Republicanism," and "Democracy."[49] According to Adams, the Federalists were too European to succeed in America. In 1801, "Federalism was already an old-fashioned thing . . . a half-way house between the European past and the American future."[50] Upholding the classic aristocratic view that popular governments could not last, Federalists embraced "the conviction that democracy must soon produce a crisis, as in Greece and Rome, in England and France, when political power must revert to the wise and the good or to the despotism of a military chief." Jefferson and his supporters were the antithesis. They were "political philanthropists" employing enlightened science to save mankind from war and tyranny. They refused "to build up a new nationality merely to create more navies and armies, to perpetuate the crimes and follies of Europe." Democracy would be the synthesis. It was something new under the sun. At the same time, its triumph vindicated key elements of Federalist statecraft. America was new and different, but American politics was not.[51] But politics was, in this new world, no longer so central as it had been.

Middle-class democracy overwhelmed Jeffersonian aristocracy no less than it overwhelmed Federalist aristocracy. In his *Life of Albert Gallatin,* a precursor to the *History,* Adams described how democracy had won its victory: "There are moments in politics, when great results can only be reached by small men,—a maxim which, however paradoxical, may easily be verified. Especially in a democracy the people are apt to become impatient of rule, and will at times obstinately refuse to move at the call of a leader, when, if left to themselves, they will blunder through all obstacles, blindly enough, it is true, but effectually."[52]

By the end of the *History,* democracy had achieved the goals that had eluded statesmen of both parties. By 1817, Adams found, "Not only was the unity of their nation established, but its probable divergence from older societies was also well defined. Already in 1817 the difference between Europe and America was decided." The amorphous force of democracy made the United States a nation and secured its divergence from the pattern of past history—the goals of Jeffersonian Republicanism. At the same time, it made a hash out of Jefferson's theory, and of his hopes for peace. By the end of the War of 1812, Adams wrote, "The traits of American character were fixed." When Adams's grandfather joined the administration of James Monroe, "Old Republicans were at a loss to know whether James Monroe or J. Q. Adams had departed farthest from their original starting points." "In truth," wrote Adams, "parties had outgrown their principles."[53]

The result was a nation with strong passions, but no great ideas. "Except for those theories of government which are popularly represented by the names of Hamilton and Jefferson," Adams wrote in 1878, "no solution of the great problems of American politics has ever been offered to the American people."[54] American political life defied principled explanation. One could describe its surface, but giving it a deeper, coherent meaning was next to impossible.

That very lesson, however, grew naturally in Jeffersonian soil. Jefferson rejected the kind of reasoning that made any nonmaterialist philosophy possible. Moreover, the third president reasoned, if human nature were fixed, in any robust way, then it was impossible to change the world. The trouble, Adams realized, was that Jefferson also upheld the rights of man. Adams could well wonder how one could both reject human nature as the basic material of politics and, at the same time, subscribe to a philosophy that held that certain things are right for man qua man. Jefferson denied that he had to choose. That had important implications for America's future.

As Tocqueville explained, the democratic mind was uncomfortable with fixed standards, for all such standards implied a hierarchy, and the democratic mind had an aversion to hierarchies. Tocqueville, Adams knew, was not claiming anything his great-grandfather had not observed in *Defence of the Constitutions*—which he had helped his father, Charles Francis Adams, edit in the 1850s. In the original edition, the first volume of *Defence* gets to John Adams's account of Book 8 of Plato's *Republic* a bit past the halfway mark. For the most part, the remainder of that volume of *Defence* was (literally) ancient history, which Adams used to demonstrate Plato's argument in practice.[55] He also, of course, argued that checks and balances were necessary to prevent instability and arbitrary government. Along the way, however, he highlighted the same point Plato highlighted in his discussion of democracy—that in democratic regimes men and women are in love with the idea of equality. That meant that all moral ideas, except as they were understood to vindicate equality, were suspect. It also meant that civilization would always be in danger, for it would be difficult to maintain standards of excellence, or even of decency, in such a regime. What could be vulgar to a true democrat? One man's vulgarity is another man's passion.

In short, democracy, classically understood, raised the same moral questions as modern science and modern art. In Henry Adams's youth, the nation had chosen the equal rights of men over the right of men to choose slavery. Would America continue to make the right choice? The nation was young.

Was the United States good? That was the ultimate Adamsian question, and an enduring challenge to any nation built on Jeffersonian ideology. Adams suggested that it was too soon to tell. The *History* ended with a series of questions about the Americans:

> They were intelligent, but what paths would their intelligence
> select? They were quick, but what solution of insoluble problems
> would quickness hurry? They were scientific, and what control
> would their science exercise over their destiny? They were mild, but
> what corruptions would their relaxations bring? They were peaceful,
> but by what machinery were their corruptions to be purged? What
> interests were to vivify a society so vast and uniform? What ideals
> were to ennoble it? What object, besides physical content, must
> a democratic continent aspire to maintain? For the treatment of
> such questions, history required another century of experience.[56]

Jefferson's America left all that open for discussion. Only an Adams, perhaps, would state the matter that starkly. Some day, after the age of democracy had passed, history would render judgment.

Notes

1. Henry Adams, *History of the United States during the Administrations of Thomas Jefferson and James Madison*, 2 vols. (New York, 1986), 1:188.

2. Peter Shaw takes this view in "Blood Is Thicker Than Irony: Henry Adams' History," *New England Quarterly* 40 (1967): 163–87.

3. *Jefferson Image*, 224.

4. H. Adams to Hugh Blair Grigsby, 7 September 1877, in *The Letters of Henry Adams*, ed. J. C. Levenson et al., 6 vols. (Cambridge, Mass., 1982), 2:319. Joyce Appleby notes that Adams told his brother Charles to "leave Jefferson alone!" in his biography of their grandfather. Appleby then adds, "one wishes Henry had followed his own advice." See Joyce Appleby, "Jefferson and His Complex Legacy," in *Jeffersonian Legacies*, ed. Peter S. Onuf (Charlottesville, Va., 1993), 2.

5. H. Adams (quotation), in Ernest Samuels, *Henry Adams* (Cambridge, Mass., 1989), 140; Adams, *History of the United States*, 1:99.

6. According to Robert Rosenblum and H. W. Janson, *19th-Century Art* (New York, 1984), pointillists like Seurat had faith that science could help perfect art through "the full-scale demonstration of new, quasi-scientific theories of painting, which explored what Seurat called Divisionism, by which colors would be divided, or broken down, into their separate component parts, as well as the technique of Pointillism, that is, the application of pigment in atomic dots, or points, of paint, an almost microscopic unit from which the vast whole would be constructed." In his paintings, "this new universe ticks like a Swiss watch, an immaculate image of modular precision consonant with the decade's faith in technological progress" (ibid., 399).

7. TJ to John Adams, 15 August 1820, in *The Adams-Jefferson Letters: The Complete Correspondence between Thomas Jefferson and Abigail and John Adams,* ed. Lester J. Cappon (Chapel Hill, N.C., 1959), 569.

8. Rosenblum and Janson write of Seurat's "quasi-scientific faith that art can be created through rational systems of color, geometry, even emotion" (*19th-Century Art,* 397). In his own day, Henry Adams's contemporary, Herbert Baxter Adams, thought that history could be improved by becoming a science; Henry Adams had his doubts. For more on this, see Richard Samuelson, "The Politics of Scientific History," in *A Political Companion to Henry Adams,* ed. Natalie Taylor (Lexington, Ky., 2010), 153–70.

9. Adams, *History of the United States,* 1:120, 122, 101.

10. H. Adams to Justin Winsor, 25 November 1880, in Levenson et al., *Letters of Henry Adams,* 2:412.

11. Donald Hall, "Henry Adams' History," *Sewanee Review* 95 (1987): 523.

12. H. Adams to Elizabeth Cameron, 3 March 1901, in Levenson et al., *Letters of Henry Adams,* 5:212; H. Adams to Cameron, 1–3 March 1916, ibid., 6:724.

13. H. Adams to Mabel Hooper, 28 January 1896, ibid., 4:364.

14. H. Adams to Brooks Adams, 18 February 1909. This passage is from Henry Adams's critique of Brooks Adams's manuscript biography of John Quincy Adams (p. 67), Adams Family Papers, Massachusetts Historical Society, Boston. For more on Henry Adams's thoughts about his great-grandfather, see my "Henry Adams' Need to Know John Adams," in *Henry Adams and the Need to Know,* ed. William Decker (Boston, 2005), 18–44.

15. H. Adams to Charles Francis Adams Jr., 21 December 1912, in Levenson et al., *Letters of Henry Adams,* 6:574.

16. H. Adams to John Hay, 3 September 1882, ibid., 2:468. The context here is interesting. Adams has finished his *John Randolph.* He did not like "the enforced obligation to take that lunatic monkey *au serieux.* . . . I was obliged to treat him as though he were respectable. For that matter, I am under much the same difficulty with regard to T. Jefferson, who, between ourselves, is a character of comedy. John Adams is a droll figure."

17. As Adams noted in the section on Virginia, immediately after allowing for Jefferson's greatness, "As a leader of democracy he appeared singularly out of place. . . . With manners apparently popular and informal, he led a life of his own, and allowed few persons to share it. His tastes were for that day excessively refined. His instincts were those of a liberal European nobleman, like the Duc de Liancourt, and he built

for himself at Monticello a chateau above contact with man. The rawness of political life was an incessant torture to him, and personal attacks made him keenly unhappy. His true delight was in an intellectual life of science and art." See Adams, *History of the United States,* 1:99.

18. Ibid., 101, 52.

19. Ibid., 122.

20. Once again, this tracks the "quasi-scientific theories of painting," and a "new universe [that] ticks like a Swiss watch." See note 6.

21. TJ to J. Adams, 15 August 1820, in Cappon, *Adams-Jefferson Letters,* 567–69.

22. For some reflection on the philosophical dimensions of the John Adams–Thomas Jefferson contrast, see "Jefferson and Adams," in *A Companion to Thomas Jefferson,* ed. Francis D. Cogliano (Malden, Mass., 2011), and my "Jefferson, Adams and the American Future," *Claremont Review of Books* 11, nos. 1–2 (Winter–Spring, 2010/2011): 65–69.

23. Adams, *History of the United States,* 1:122.

24. J. Adams, "Discourses on Davila," in *Works of John Adams,* ed. Charles Francis Adams, 10 vols. (Boston, 1850–56), 6:281.

25. TJ to J. Adams, 15 August 1820, in Cappon, *Adams-Jefferson Letters,* 567–69.

26. J. Adams to TJ, 12 May 1820, ibid., 564.

27. One could argue that the *History* vindicates John Adams against the High Federalists, too. Exploring that question in detail would be another essay. There is, however, an interesting parallel here. John Adams, in the *History,* is a moderate Federalist, more worthy of respect than the High Federalists. Jefferson, similarly, is a moderate Virginia Republican, more worthy of respect than the Old Republicans.

28. Adams, *History of the United States,* 1:122.

29. Ibid., 101.

30. Ibid., 1075, 100, 1115.

31. Ibid., 119–20. Note that "except for a few Federalists" does not mean "except for all Federalists." In the *History,* the American consensus won in the end. What failed were the ideas that set Jefferson apart from the other great statesmen of the founding era.

32. Ibid., 1125.

33. See, for example, J. Adams to Benjamin Rush, 3 July 1812, in *The Spur of Fame: Dialogues of John Adams and Benjamin Rush, 1805–1813,* ed. John A. Schutz and Douglass Adair (San Marino, Calif., 1966), 249.

34. Adams, *History of the United States,* 1:1126.

35. Ibid., 146, 147.

36. Ibid., 97, 174, 100. For TJ's draft of the Kentucky Resolutions, see "Jefferson's Draft," [before 4 October 1798,] *PTJ,* 30:536–43.

37. Adams, *History of the United States,* 1:205, 159, 161. Of New York patronage politics, and Jefferson's meddling in it, Adams wrote, "on both sides the game was selfish, and belonged rather to the intrigues of Guelfs and Ghibellines in some Italian city of the thirteenth century than to the pure atmosphere of Jefferson's republicanism." See

ibid., 159. The entire second book of John Adams's *Defence of the Constitutions* relates the history of medieval Italian republics.

38. Adams, *History of the United States*, 1:359, 363, 379.

39. Ibid., 362.

40. Henry Adams immediately pointed to the implications of the idea: "If he and his friends were to interpret the treaty-making power as they liked, the time was sure to come when their successors would put so broad an interpretation on other powers of the government as to lead from step to step, until at last Virginia might cower in blood and flames before the shadowy terror called the war-power. With what face could Jefferson then appear before the tribunal of history, and what position could be expect to receive." See ibid., 362. Adams knew that story well. His grandfather had made that very case. See Charles Francis Adams Jr., "John Quincy Adams and Martial Law," *Massachusetts Historical Society Proceedings*, 2d. Ser., 15 (1902): 439.

41. Henry Adams, *Democracy: An American Novel*, in *Democracy and Esther: Two Novels by Henry Adams* (Gloucester, Mass., 1965), 188.

42. He once called Tocqueville "the gospel of my private religion." H. Adams to C. F. Adams Jr., 1 May 1863, in Levenson et al., *Letters of Henry Adams*, 1:350.

43. Adams, *History of the United States*, 1:1019.

44. In the first paragraph of the *History*, Adams writes, "the true political population [of the United States in 1800] consisted of four and a half million free whites, or less than one million able-bodied males, on whose shoulders fell the burden of a continent." See ibid., 5.

45. Ibid., 1019.

46. Ibid., 1020. In his conclusion, Adams notes that "in the American character antipathy to war ranked first among political traits." He continued a few sentences later, "The party of Jefferson and Gallatin was founded on dislike of every function of government necessary in a military system." See ibid., 2:1335.

47. Ibid., 1:112, 1020.

48. Ibid., 2:1335.

49. Those are Wood's three section heads in *The Radicalism of the American Revolution* (New York, 1991). For a more sustained discussion of this reading of the *History*, see my dissertation, "The Adams Family and the American Experiment" (Ph.D. diss., University of Virginia, 2000).

50. Adams, *History of the United States*, 1:353. In his introductory section, Adams wrote of "the common feeling of Europeans, which was echoed by the Federalist society of the United States." See ibid., 114.

51. Ibid., 61, 131, 101.

52. Henry Adams, *The Life of Albert Gallatin* (1879; repr., New York, 1943), 432.

53. Adams, *History of the United States*, 2:1331, 1345, 1277, 1272.

54. Adams, *Life of Albert Gallatin*, 492.

55. John Adams, *Defence of the Constitutions of Government of the United States of America*, 3 vols. (New York, 1971), 1:210. That is the start of Letter 35.

56. Adams, *History of the United States*, 2:1345.

II Rivalry

6   "I Come to Bury Caesar"

Burr Biographers on Jefferson

Nancy Isenberg

The Revolutionary generation loved allusions to the ancients, leading some historians and biographers to bestow classical nicknames on the founders. Parson Mason Weems simultaneously cast George Washington in the image of a saint and as the Roman Cincinnatus. In the first biography of Patrick Henry, William Wirt elevated his subject into the "American Demosthenes." In the 1990s, Joseph Ellis contended that the Sphinx, a wonder of the ancient world, its mysteries symbolized in a simple but hidden riddle, captured the conflicted personae of Thomas Jefferson. According to Ellis, Jefferson's identity was fractured by deep-seated contradictions; the "American Sphinx," like Sybil of the 1976 television film, suffered from a kind of dissociative identity disorder, with competing inner voices that refused to talk to each other. Stanley Elkins and Eric McKitrick, in their oft-cited and deeply biased *The Age of Federalism,* likewise labeled Aaron Burr the eternal "enigma." In their minds, as an anomalous and scandalous figure among the high-minded founders, Burr embodied a corrupting and seductive force.[1]

Such archetypes have persisted because they supply the founders with an air of timeless fascination and hidden mystery. Although Jefferson and Burr represented the top tier of the Republican party in the election of 1800, they have been recast as clashing titans, part of a lost breed of flawed, if captivating, giants never to walk the earth again.[2] Ellis, perhaps unknowingly, was redrawing Jefferson in the image of the enigmatic Burr, reviving the Federalists' language of pathology and subversion that fueled the partisan battles of the 1790s and early 1800s. For the Federalists and their modern-day defenders, Jefferson was and still remains a confounding hypocrite and devious pretender; Burr, always elusive, descends to us as a shape-shifting creature. Seemingly inscrutable, the towering (and teetering) founders defy definition. As the exotic labels "Sphinx" and "enigma" suggest, they can never be pinned down with certainty.

So if Burr has enjoyed—or rather endured—a posthumous reputation nearly as topsy-turvy as that of Jefferson's, he did not have a "fan club" on the order of Jefferson's. Yet several authors who conceived their books with the inescapable knowledge that Aaron Burr was widely thought unheroic and unlovable believed that he was still worth understanding as a sturdy political actor. To Matthew Livingston Davis, Samuel Knapp, and all who succeeded them in characterizing Burr, the names Burr and Jefferson would have to be intertwined, allies and antagonists, standing in historic counterpoint.

In earlier times, most biographers of Burr who undertook the Jefferson-Burr comparison were less troubled by hidden mysteries or opaque person-alities than modern popularizers have tended to be. Matthew Davis, Burr's long-trusted political associate, is arguably the most influential of those who have fashioned Burr's legacy. In 1836, the year Burr died, he published *Memoirs of Aaron Burr* after having been granted by his subject complete authority over his personal papers. He had known Burr for forty years, and had worked closely with him in New York during the formative years of the Republican party. As these things go, however, Davis was an unusual choice to act as executor of Burr's historical legacy. He was not a family member, nor was he Burr's first choice. When Burr was preparing for his 1804 duel with Alexander Hamilton, he designated in his will that his daughter, Theodosia, should gain custody of his personal papers. He then asked his son-in-law, South Carolina planter Joseph Alston, to pen a memoir of him if he did not survive. By 1836, however, both daughter and son-in-law were long dead, and he had no trustworthy heirs to take on the task.[3]

Other qualities predisposed Burr to anoint Davis his biographer. The younger man had acquired a reputation as a raconteur in Washington circles, telling stories about the early days of partisan politics. He acted, at the same time, as a gossip columnist, writing for New York and London papers under the pen name of "The Spy in Washington."[4] Burr solicited the publicly active Davis to publish his papers in order to correct the historical record.

In 1830, at seventy-four, Burr urged Davis to read Thomas Jefferson Ran-dolph's just-published edited collection of his grandfather's papers. He even marked the particular passages that he wanted Davis to pay attention to. Remarkably, Davis wrote thirty-six pages of notes, expressing his shock in heated outbursts.[5] The Jefferson he discovered in these papers was a man he loathed, a politician who repeatedly twisted the truth. His uncensored commentary reveals Davis shaping Burr's *Memoirs* as a challenge to Jefferson's record of the past; he was prosecuting a "paper war" against Jefferson's published papers.[6] Jefferson loomed over Davis's biographical portrait of Burr, and not simply as one of the cast of characters in Burr's life. He was a formidable, antagonistic presence informing the overall narrative. His hypocrisy had to be exposed and refuted for Burr's public life to be authoritatively rendered.

Davis's version of the *Memoirs* is a strangely divided work. It was published in two volumes: the first addressed his subject's early years, war experiences, and family life; the second focused more on Burr's legal and political career. Jefferson's name does not even appear until the last couple of pages of the first volume, as Davis foregrounds what he will cover in greater detail in the second volume. The two volumes thus divide Burr's life into pre- and post-Jefferson stages. Davis implies that Burr's fateful alliance with Jefferson in the presidential race placed the two on very different paths: "the election of Mr. Jefferson and the ruin of Colonel Burr."[7]

The election of 1800 is the centerpiece of Davis's narrative. Even the illustrations point to its centrality. The frontispiece of volume 1 features John Vanderlyn's portrait of Burr in 1802; volume 2 opens with the same artist's boyish profile of Theodosia Burr Alston (she is a carbon copy of the paterfamilias), painted at the same time. In that crucial year, the vice president's enemies had just begun a concerted campaign to discredit him. The previous fall, Davis had made an ill-timed visit to Monticello to plead with the new president for the patronage post of naval officer in the New York custom house. Failing in his mission, he left the mountaintop humiliated, knowing his dismissal was a clear sign that Burr had lost Jefferson's favor, too.[8]

In his preface to the first volume and subsequently in the text, Davis makes a point of telling readers that, after Burr's death, he threw a large number of Burr's personal letters in the fireplace. In particular, he had chosen to destroy virtually all of Burr's correspondence with women. Davis proudly confessed that he had done so to protect the reputation of several ladies. By way of explanation, he compared Burr to Lord Byron, whose literary executor had done similarly after the poet's death in 1824. According to Davis, Burr had kept the letters as "trophies of his victories." Moralizing, Davis added that he was disturbed that Burr had mingled missives of his female correspondents without regard to their reputations, promiscuously combining "productions of highly cultivated minds" with the lowbrow scribbling of women (some, perhaps, in the sex trade) who were within Burr's orbit. Purging letters enabled Davis to claim the high ground, voicing his disgust and then erasing all traces of that which repelled his refined sensibility. From this point forward, as he told his readers, Burr's "revolting trait . . . will not be referred to again."[9]

Davis's prudery was that of a man who protested too much. This chivalrous defender of unsullied womanhood was himself an investor in several New York City brothels. The historian Jeffrey Pasley has conjectured that Davis's mother, who ran a boardinghouse, may have offered men more than food and lodging. A thriving culture of prostitution had long existed in the vibrant port, and at no time during his earlier acquaintance with Burr did Davis lash out against his patron's "licentiousness." He may have been responding to Burr's rather public divorce trial, which took place just before his death. His soon-to-be ex-wife, Eliza Jumel, charged him with adultery, and New Yorkers were entertained by the racy testimony of Jumel's spying maid, who offered up graphic details of one of the old man's supposed sexual liaisons. In Davis's biography, Burr's imprudent marriage to Jumel is not mentioned once.[10]

Davis's decision to compare Burr to Lord Byron may offer the best clue to his interpretative pose. Willing to concede that his Byronesque Burr was a flawed, passionate man, Davis meant to subordinate the libertine narrative to the record of one "so eminent as a soldier, as a statesman, and as a professional man." Making it clear that his Burr was a bona fide hero, Davis could now proceed to highlight the New Yorker's genuine triumphs in law and politics in a world of men like himself, whose dalliances with women were of no lasting significance.[11]

Davis was passionate about politics, and especially the birth of the Republican party. His goal was to rescue Burr and the Burrites from Jefferson's Virginia-centered version of the past. In his extended commentary on Jefferson's newly published papers, Davis explicitly listed several reasons for the "ruin of the vice president." The first was the election tie. Jefferson and Burr had each received seventy-three electoral votes, putting both men ahead of the incumbent John Adams. The experience, according to Davis, so embittered Jefferson that he quickly became jealous and distrustful of Burr, "because the federal party had menaced him [Jefferson] with the loss of the election, and had actually driven him into terms of compromise with them, notwithstanding all his asseverations to the contrary." Consumed with a desire for revenge, Jefferson blamed Burr for what were in fact the devious actions of Federalists; he had been forced to make a deal with his enemies, and then turned on his vice president, ironically blaming Burr for causing him to lie about the whole embarrassing episode!

The second reason for pushing Burr aside, in Davis's mind, was Jefferson's determination to put James Madison, his fellow Virginian and trusted lieutenant, in the president's chair after he retired from office. To accomplish this, the president played off the competing Republican factions in New York state politics, all to Burr's detriment. The Clintonians and Livingstons felt no measurable loyalty to Burr and were easily spurred on to destroy him. Their minds were "poisoned," wrote Davis, their "jealousy and distrust being awakened, by insinuations and innuendoes." Governor George Clinton and Chancellor Robert Livingston, holding the two most powerful offices in New York, had earlier united with Burr out of interest alone. Predictably, Hamilton joined in the effort to diminish their common rival, "entertaining a hope that they would regain lost power and considering Mr. Burr, very justly, a formidable obstacle in their way."[12]

Six years after T. J. Randolph's edition of the Jefferson papers, Davis defined his calling as the honest bearer of an uncomfortable truth, righting historical wrongs. In Burr's *Memoirs,* he intended to draw aside the curtain that obscured the "mystery" of the election of 1800, revealing what really happened during the secret negotiations that broke the tie in the House of Representatives and secured the presidency for Jefferson. Challenging the conventional wisdom that Burr had intrigued with Federalists to subvert the Republicans' clear intent, Davis pointed an accusatory finger at Jefferson for having brokered a deal with James Bayard of Delaware, lone representative of his state and ringleader of the Federalists in Congress.

To prove his charges, Davis reprinted a series of legal depositions taken from Bayard and from Samuel Smith of Maryland, the two men who had negotiated the deal. Bayard confessed that Jefferson soiled his hands to secure the election, and that Burr was completely innocent. For Davis, Jefferson's larger crime lay in having advanced his ambition at Burr's expense. Without Burr's active engagement, Jefferson would have never won New York's electoral votes and defeated Adams. Jefferson had shown his gratitude by exiling Burr from the party and willfully destroying his political career.[13]

After reading Jefferson's papers, Davis concluded that the president was a man devoid of honor.[14] Compiling evidence of Jefferson's moral deficiency, he fixed on the official statement of Dr. Erich Bollmann presented during Burr's treason trial in 1807. The German-born Bollmann was part of Burr's abortive Mexican filibuster project. During a private meeting with the president at the time of the treason trial, Bollmann agreed to prepare a written statement about his dealings with Burr, but only if Jefferson gave his word that he would not use this information to compel Bollmann's testimony before the grand jury. The German did not want to be coerced into accepting a pardon. Jefferson then proceeded to violate their agreement. Appalled by the president's lack of honor, Bollmann did more than refuse the pardon. He prepared a new statement, read by one of Burr's attorneys, that unmasked the Virginian's underhanded methods. He posed a rhetorical question: "Is *life,* in Mr. Jefferson's opinion, *all;* and *character* and *reputation,* which alone can make it desirable, nothing?" Blending irony with disgust, Davis cataloged this episode as one among "numerous instances of Mr. Jefferson's idea of *honour* and *morality.*"[15]

The portrait he painted of Jefferson is dark and brooding. In linking the election controversy to Jefferson's later charge of treason against Burr, Davis highlighted the president's pathological hatred: "Mr. Jefferson's malignity towards Colonel Burr never ceased but with his last breath. His writings abound with proof of that malignity, smothered, but rankling in his heart." The treason trial restaged the dynamic of the election of 1800 in that Burr (as odd as it sounds) rescued Jefferson. As much as Burr's remarkable talents as a lawyer saved him from conviction in 1807, to Davis he saved Jefferson from his own worst impulses. Had the president succeeded in convicting Burr, he would have left an even darker "stain" on the nation's reputation by corrupting the judicial process.[16]

Burr was a man worthy of admiration, and Jefferson simply was not. The qualities that drew Davis to Burr were his skills in "execution," his "sagacity," and his remarkable "fortitude" in accomplishing what might have seemed impossible to lesser men. Burr was a man of action. He was also known for his unflinching loyalty to political allies and personal friends alike. For Davis, Burr represented a better disciple of democracy than Jefferson, because he mixed easily and saw beyond class differences.[17]

Although Davis was born to a lower-class family, had no formal education, and had risen through the printing trade, Burr had never made him feel inferior. The same could not be said about Jefferson, as Davis learned when he journeyed to Monticello in 1801. In later years, he told a story that encapsulated his feelings. During the visit, Jefferson caught a large fly in his hand. Holding up the captive insect, he remarked on its unequal parts, its large head and small body. But this was not a science lesson. The president was comparing the supplicant from New York to that fly, viewing him as someone whose aspirations were larger than his natural station. To Jefferson, Davis was nothing more than an annoying pest. Or so Davis believed, as he watched the fly dangle before him.[18]

If he found some of Jefferson's actions befuddling, the biographer had little trouble explaining them. In his 1830 commentary on Jefferson's papers, Davis pointed out Jefferson's talent for deception. He cited Federalist Oliver Wolcott's remark that he was "the greatest liar, he had ever known in the course of his life." Davis also felt that Jefferson was "very *pliant* and *supple,* if not sycophantic, when he had an end to accomplish." Jefferson could woo; he could seduce. In contrast, Burr's victories came through his unflagging energy, coolness under pressure, and meticulous execution. While others painted Burr as a devious Chesterfieldian, Jefferson was the true Chesterfieldian, the courtier who would say anything to convince an unsuspecting mark to do his bidding.[19]

Of all the adjectives that Davis used to describe Jefferson, the most telling was "Jesuitical." Not an outright liar, Jefferson was a gifted dissembler, a man for whom equivocation and rationalization came easily. He could spin his words in such a way to conceal his true intentions. Reading Jefferson's papers, Davis made special note of two such instances. One was Jefferson's habit of voicing his desire to retire from political life, his rhetorical pose of "always disclaiming any wish to fill public stations yet always ready to accept them." Davis observed that he could only find one post that Jefferson had ever rejected—his longing for the simple life of family and farm seemed insincere. Indeed, he was completely comfortable exercising power, displaying what Davis described as "great *tact* in managing men and parties." Jefferson was no Cincinnatus: a humble farmer on certain days, perhaps, but in no way selfless.[20]

Jefferson was equally disingenuous in claiming never to have written for the newspapers. He acted as though this sordid trade was beneath him. After reading his papers, Davis found that Jefferson had regularly recruited allies to write for him. Madison and others served as his amanuenses, parroting his views and tarring his enemies. "There was no man living," Davis reckoned, "who placed more confidence" in the newspapers than Jefferson. He was as much a politician as Hamilton or Burr, only lacking their candor. Indeed, Jefferson was less a man of mystery than of man of intellectual casuistry, and less a riddle than a carefully practiced master of sophistry. Unlike Professor Ellis, Davis was certain that Jefferson knew precisely what he was doing, ensuring his leadership by carefully crafting his public image and adeptly "managing men and parties."[21]

In the *Memoirs*, Davis took one of Jefferson's most famous passages on Burr's character as the best example of Jeffersonian deceit. Writing in his "Anas," Jefferson claimed that, from the time he first met Burr, "*His conduct very soon inspired me with distrust. I habitually cautioned Mr. Madison against trusting him too much.*" He wrote this in 1804. His point was that he had been wary of Burr from the early 1790s, when Burr was first elected a U.S. senator from New York. Davis disputed this belated rendering with Jefferson's own words. He cites a letter Jefferson wrote to Burr in 1797, in which he acknowledged his "esteem" for Burr. Which observation was more honest? The earlier letter either proved that Jefferson held Burr in "high regard" and "placed confidence in him" or that in 1797 he "unnecessarily and uninvited, made professions that were false and deceptive." Either he played the supplicant when he needed Burr or he told a whopper in 1804. Jefferson could not have it both ways. Was he all things to all men, or was the real Jefferson never there at all? Davis cut through the misdirection, concluding that the "*Anas*" was doctored evidence. After the election tie fiasco, Jefferson lost the ability to write without bias about Burr.[22]

The only classical allusion Davis deployed occurs at the end of volume 1. But instead of citing Sallust or Cicero, he quotes from Shakespeare's *Julius Caesar,* closing the book with the epigrammatic "*I come to bury Caesar, not to praise him.*" These are the words of Mark Antony, as imagined by Shakespeare, in giving his funeral eulogy for the dead emperor. The quote makes perfect sense, as the *Memoirs* is nothing so much as a funeral dirge for Aaron Burr.[23]

There is more to Shakespeare's quote than meets the eye. Antony was refusing to directly refute what Brutus had said about Caesar, while indirectly undercutting the negative sentiments expressed by the conspirators by offering to "speak what I do know." Davis, too, spoke from personal knowledge, which he privileged over all else—and especially the rumor-mongering. As Antony's oration memorably puts it: "The good is oft interred with their bones."[24] Davis would recover the good about Burr.[25]

Ironically, Davis's allusion to Caesar may even be better suited to the character that he constructed for Jefferson. It is he who emerges in the narrative as a power-hungry imperial president bent on destroying his honorable rival. It is Jefferson, no less than Burr, who has to be disinterred and who deserves a close forensic examination by an ostensibly objective biographer. Davis could not resurrect Burr without reburying Jefferson in a new, less glorifying, literary coffin.

Burr had two other nineteenth-century biographers, Boston attorney Samuel Knapp and New York journalist James Parton. Knapp's *The Life of Aaron Burr* (1835) appeared one year before Davis's two-volume work, and just before Burr died. Knapp, a prolific writer, emphasized the value of publishing while his subject was still alive, for if "misrepresented by his biographer," then the "error may be corrected, or a false judgment reversed." Knapp seems to have had the approval of Burr, claiming a personal acquaintance. Without a political ax to grind, he saw his task as offering a balanced interpretation, unencumbered by the "baleful effects of party spirit." He intended to examine "all opinions," convinced that in the current climate, some opinions were "*overrated, some underrated,* and *not a few grossly misrepresented* by all parties."[26]

Knapp's nonpartisan pose was probably overstated. As a New Englander and an admirer of John and Abigail Adams, he most likely had some sympathy for the Federalist critique of Jefferson. He was suspicious of manufactured public opinion and the way that rumors and lies could destroy a man's reputation. In that vein, he opened his biography with the fable of Psapho (which Knapp spelled with an "O"), the Libyan king known for training his birds to say "Opsapho is a God." The birds thus became an oracle, and Psapho's people were convinced that their king was divinely favored. But it was all a "trick to gull the Lybians," Knapp reminded his readers; the king's acclaim and authority rested on a false foundation. If Knapp was comparing Jefferson to the Libyan king, the story applied to Burr as well. If the birds had been taught to parrot Psapho is a "demon," he sarcastically observed, then the king would have been massacred by his people and hated by mankind.

Americans blindly worshipped Jefferson, and despised Burr, because they, too, had been misled by "tricks" that succeeded in distorting the portraits of both men.[27]

Excess adoration was a danger to the Republic. Knapp may have been less interested in partisan politics, but he agreed that Jefferson first felt a "deep resentment" toward Burr after the election of 1800. As a lawyer, Knapp was outraged by Jefferson's dictatorial behavior during Burr's treason trial. Beyond his personal need to reap revenge, the president had exposed a deeply flawed understanding of justice.

As any good lawyer would do, Knapp introduced an incriminating piece of evidence. To convict Jefferson, he reprinted an 1807 letter to prosecutor George Hay. In it, Jefferson accused the presiding judge, Chief Justice John Marshall, of allowing Burr to become a "rallying point of the disaffected and worthless." The president could not conceive that any but the most depraved could condone Burr's activities. To Knapp, Jefferson's agenda was both transparent and deadly: he would not stop until he had removed the chief justice and packed the bench with his "parasites." He had tried to suspend habeas corpus, and during the trial itself, he worked to undermine due process. Destroying what he could not control, Knapp's Jefferson had become a deranged demagogue, with a "peculiarly organized mind."[28]

Nonetheless, Knapp saw a silver lining in this story. He believed the time was right for his biography because "softer breezes of public opinion" were just now reassessing the nearly eighty-year-old man's legacy. Burr's future looked brighter, because the "searching minds" of "rising generations" would reverse the "erroneous" verdict of the Revolutionary generation. Times were changing. Or so the biographer believed.[29]

Knapp's prediction was as wrong as it could be. In 1857, when Parton completed his *Life and Times of Aaron Burr*, the work was attacked for its all too sunny portrait of this "gifted, unprincipled, and wretched man," as one reviewer put it. Owing to this criticism, the biographer felt obliged to defend his balanced approach by arguing in the 1867 edition that Burr's life presented a good moral lesson to American readers. That is, in spite of the remarkable gifts of intelligence, courage, and diligence, Burr had one undeniable flaw: the lack of a "CONSCIENCE." For Parton, human beings were more complicated. He opposed overmoralized treatments of historical figures, their reduction to either heroes or villains. Even if later editions of his *Burr* opened with the aforementioned caveat, Parton believed that the biographer's purpose was to sift through all available information and find the truth.

Although Parton never met Burr, America's first professional biographer spent three years talking to Burr's former acquaintances. He privileged their insights over dense, dry documents. Parton was a modern Plutarch, one reviewer lauded, a historical interpreter who reassembled his subjects' lives by drawing on their less celebrated moments and exploiting seemingly innocuous anecdotes. What set his biography apart, Parton felt, was that he had penetrated the real man behind the facade to rescue Burr from being permanently identified as (that word again) a "baffling enigma." To label someone an "enigma" was a weak excuse for failing to dig deep enough. Not surprisingly, larger-than-life classical allusions do not appear in Parton's *Burr.* His biographical subjects were "specimens" to be studied rather than models for imitation.[30]

Yet Parton, for all his claims of originality, repeated almost all of Davis's arguments. Once again, Burr was completely innocent of intriguing for the presidency; Jefferson wished to make Madison his successor. By the time Jefferson recorded his account of Burr in the *"Anas,"* he had a "dislike of Burr that was extreme, perhaps morbid." Little separated Davis's choice of adjectives from Parton's: the former's "malignity" became the latter's "morbid" in describing Jefferson's pathological hatred.

Writing in the 1850s, Parton cleverly redefined American democracy as "the fruit of Jefferson's ideas and Burr's tactics." The period from the Constitution to the annexation of Texas was now the age of Jefferson *and* Burr. In striking fashion, Parton described the two men as equally indispensable in shaping the course of history. Parton praised Jefferson's talents, the "breadth and liberality" of his thinking; at the same time, he exposed his darker impulses. Beneath his friendly and unimposing manner, Jefferson was an ideologue, holding back the convictions that flowed like "white hot lava" through his veins. Jefferson was a man of opinions, not a man of action, a leader to be admired, but an "inexecutive man in an executive station." This characterization would soften by the time Parton got around to writing a biography of Jefferson.[31]

In *The Life and Times of Aaron Burr,* Parton's approach was to diminish Jefferson's grandeur without appearing to do so. Jefferson's political presence is muted until the time of Burr's treason trial, when the president appears in a more desperate light, fearing public "ridicule" if his charges against Burr did not stand. His November 1806 proclamation against Burr had sent shock waves across the nation, frightening citizens by declaring that civil war was brewing in the western states. Parton quoted a letter from Jefferson to James Bowdoin, his minister to Spain, in which he asserted that "Burr's enterprise is the most extraordinary since the days of Don Quixote," and that Burr meant to place himself "on the throne of Montezuma, and extend his empire to the Alleghany." Without missing a beat, the purportedly neutral biographer exclaimed: "How nonsensical is this!" He asked his readers to ponder the president's logic: how could one man induce every American in the western states to "yield in submission to a usurper"?

Parton echoed Knapp's outrage in concluding that Jefferson showed the signs of a mind that was "absurdly excited." Imagining conspiracies everywhere, Jefferson proceeded to accuse Marshall and the Federalists of rallying to Burr's side to topple the Republic and establish a monarchy. Like Knapp, Parton saw Jefferson, not the men he appointed, as the "real prosecutor" of Burr. Summing up Jefferson's behavior during the treason trial, Parton returned to Davis's favorite theme that Jefferson owed his presidency to Burr. The twisted rivalry between these two previously allied politicians could not be simply set forth. In Parton's cumbersome words, it was the prosecutor of Burr who was the "President of the United States, who was made President . . . by Aaron Burr's tact and vigilance, and who was therefore able to wield against Aaron Burr the power and resources of the United States."[32]

The twentieth century brought new Burr biographers, many claiming to have uncovered new sources. One of the "best biographies in print," according to the *New York Times* in 1961, was Nathan Schachner's single-volume study, published in 1937. A graceful writer with keen insights, Schachner understood that both Burr and Jefferson were political animals. He redefined "enigma," granting the word a positive meaning. What made Burr different from his peers was his "too cool-headed, too analytical" approach to politics. Refusing to be caught up in party dogmas, or swayed by "violent hatreds," Schachner's Burr treated politics as his "life-work," a career, and it was this trait that set him apart.[33]

Schachner saw Jefferson similarly. The third president had "scares" after the 1801 election tie, especially the embarrassment of having to constantly disavow that he had made a deal with the Federalists. Jefferson's need to parse the meaning of Samuel Smith's explanation, quibbling over Smith's statement that he had been "directly *authorized*" by him to come to terms with

Bayard, rang false to Schachner. "Jefferson was too good of a politician," he concluded, not to have realized what Smith wanted from him. Schachner's approach provided a breath of fresh air. In discussing the Burr-Jefferson relationship, he dismissed the tiresome framework that required condemnation of one or the other's moral character. At least up to the treason trial.[34]

Here, Schachner revived all the old complaints of previous biographers. Jefferson's decision to issue a proclamation, pointing to Burr's intrigue without naming names, created a conspiracy in print. Schachner characterized this as a "strange episode in the life of a great figure." Jefferson had become the "philosopher displaying his spleen," "the ardent prophet of the Bill of Rights tearing every constitutional guaranty of personal liberty to shreds," and "the disciple of the Enlightenment adopting the Jesuitical doctrine that the end justifies the means!" But, as it turned out, Schachner's assessment was even more damning than the earlier charges: Jefferson never sincerely believed that Burr was guilty, he said, despite the public pretense. For Schachner, Jefferson's political skills and literary finesse ultimately betrayed him, for it was his ability to manufacture a conspiracy where none existed that forced him to pursue Burr's conviction to the bitter end.[35]

Milton Lomask published his biography of Burr in two volumes (1979, 1982). Lomask was a popular writer, not a trained historian, but he had access to many of the documents held by Mary-Jo Kline, editor of the Burr Papers project. Despite such material, his biography effectively retreated to the didacticism of Parson Weems.

Lomask began his career as a journalist before writing biographies and inspirational books about Catholic saints, theologians, and bishops, as well as a series of children's books. Comfortable with Catholic typology, Lomask reconstructed Burr's life as an allegory. He borrowed from Parton in foreshadowing Burr's downfall as "the American incarnation of Lord Chesterfield." This same comparison informs his reconstruction of the Burr-Jefferson relationship.[36]

The Chesterfieldian Burr is a conflation of several stereotypes: the proud aristocrat, indulgent spendthrift, and pleasure-seeker—a cipher without a core set of principles. Lomask has these traits emerge everywhere in Burr's experience. He asserts that when they first met in 1776, George Washington found Burr's "air of superiority" annoying; he imagines that this one trait explained Washington's enduring dislike of Burr. The problem is that it is all factually barren guesswork. If the younger Revolutionary officer was so haughty, why did the other Continental army commanders he served under view Burr differently? Why did General Israel Putnam, Colonel William Malcolm, and General Alexander McDougall—all men whose class backgrounds were beneath that of Washington—find him loyal, not haughty in the least? Why did they appreciate Burr's direct, no-nonsense approach to conducting war?

Lomask never bothered to read Burr's military correspondence before pronouncing him Chesterfieldian. His only evidence for Burr's haughty manner (which he admits) is the later opinion ("two and a half decades" later) expressed by U.S. senator William Plumer, a Federalist gossip, ally of Hamilton, and enemy of Burr. And Plumer didn't even know Burr during the war.[37]

Chesterfield's *Letters to his Son* (1774) was a widely popular guide to Anglo-American manners, and little of Burr's personal style actually fit the mold. Indeed, the image of Burr as a man of pleasure who lived too well could as easily apply to Jefferson, who described himself as an Epicurean, drank French wines, lived in a mansion, and died in debt.[38]

Let us, then, set the record straight. The Chesterfieldian label was deployed by Burr's enemies to caricature him as a man of surfaces, a dandy who cavalierly mixed pleasure with business. It was meant to satirize, to diminish him for political advantage. As overly simplistic were caricatures of Jefferson by his contemporaneous detractors as a wild-eyed philosopher. According to Lomask, Burr's "blithe" Chesterfieldian pose, "more than any single thing," earned him the "profound hatred of Thomas Jefferson, whose view was that politics was a solemn duty and service to mankind."[39]

Lomask's Jefferson is as naively derived as his Burr, a "reluctant" politician who priggishly refuses to show Burr gratitude for delivering New York in 1800. While Lomask concedes that Jefferson had to have had a "personal vendetta" against Burr by the time of the treason trial, this Jefferson is less of an actor than someone overtaken by his suspicions of the cagey Chesterfieldian. Burr never steps outside that straitjacket. His love of flattery fuels his narcissistic western adventure. For this Catholic moralist, Burr was the dandy as enigma, and Jefferson was equally insubstantial. Temperamental, perhaps a little "womanish," as Hamilton claimed, Lomask's Jefferson was more than willing to try Burr as a traitor for something as frivolous as maintaining a blithe demeanor.[40]

As a biographer, Lomask had competition not from the academy but from the literary market. Gore Vidal's *Burr: A Novel*, published in 1973, reached more American readers than any previous portrait of Burr. Vidal's novel relied on historical documents, and as he wrote in his afterword, he chose to write a historical novel, instead of a history, because he could "attribute motive—something the conscientious historian or biographer ought never to do." Blending history and fiction, Vidal allowed readers to assume he was writing a biography, despite his declaration to the contrary. There was an added benefit to fiction: the freedom to indulge irreverence toward the founders. The time was ripe, insofar as Vidal's *Burr* came on the heels of the popular musical *1776*, a farce about the Continental Congress, released as a Hollywood film one year earlier.

Burr was still mesmerizing, but what made Vidal's account different was that he allowed the New Yorker to control the narrative of his life. Much of his novel has an older and omniscient Burr making observations about his past and his peers. He is a three-dimensional figure—wise, a bit cynical, and with the advantage of hindsight—a brilliant adversary of Jefferson.[41]

Vidal's portrait of Jefferson is downright laugh-out-loud nefarious. The author embellishes Davis's Jefferson to make him even more suspicious. Jefferson finally seems fleshy, with his "freckled fox face," a "large limp hand," and a "thin-lipped smile." He is the *salonnière* of the dinner party who keeps people on the edge of their seats, dropping his voice "so low" that all the guests are obliged to lean "forward across our glasses to hear his sudden warning." Vidal's talent lies in diminishing Jefferson with pithy statements; the Virginian becomes a Jedi Jesuitical master, endowed with the questionable gift of "believing implicitly anything he himself said at the moment he said it." He is an American Napoleon (the same man to whom Burr was routinely compared during his filibustering scheme); this Jefferson was, in Vidal's words, "a fascinating actor but far more subtle than the Corsican." As a master of disguises, the Virginian transformed himself from the "French exquisite" during his years in Europe to a man of the people dressed in old slippers and a frayed jacket.[42]

Vidal brought Davis's charges to life. The reader can just imagine Jefferson in a drawing room, engaging in flattery and enrapturing his listeners, until he becomes angry and flashes that "petulant look about the slit of his mouth." Vidal introduces Madison as the meek but reasonable ally who knows his place as "second fiddle," and acts as Jefferson's therapist, explaining his faults. Cast as "everyone's bachelor friend," Madison is defanged and neutered, clearly no rival for the socially aggressive Jefferson.[43]

Yet Vidal dramatically breaks with Burr's past biographers in making all of the historical figures he presents highly sexualized beings. He repeats an old rumor that Martin Van Buren was Burr's bastard son. He has a famous New York madam describe Hamilton as a man who never bothered with foreplay: "he would leap upon a girl and before she knew what was happening he was pulling up his breeches and out the door." Henrietta Colden, an educated New Yorker, served as the mistress of both Hamilton and Jefferson in *Burr*. None of this can be proven, of course, and Vidal might have been shocked to learn that it was actually the not-so-shy little Madison who courted the widow Colden.[44]

Vidal drops numerous hints that Burr's relationship with his daughter Theodosia verged on incest. Jefferson, too, is painted as a plantation "Sultan," and Monticello the seat of his biracial harem. During Burr's visit there in 1795, the New Yorker voices discomfort in seeing so many of Jefferson's slaves with "skins a good deal fairer than my own." Sally Hemings was both Jefferson's "concubine" and "his sister-in law." Vidal has Burr describe Hemings as everything Jefferson wanted in a wife, "submissive, shy, and rather stupid."[45]

There is nothing appealing about Vidal's Jefferson. He is more of a Turkish emperor than Burr's enemies ever imagined him to be. He is not just an "embryo-Caesar," as Hamilton aggressively labeled Burr, but by the time of Burr's treason trial, a "Caesar, born full-grown and regnant." Vidal has Jefferson fabricate evidence, threaten witnesses, and wield the tool of every dictator, martial law.

The novelist is especially harsh in blasting Jefferson's view of the Constitution as a "convenience when it allowed him to do what he wanted to do, and a monarchical document when it stayed his hand." Buying Louisiana, trying to steal Florida, and dreaming of annexing Cuba, Jefferson exceeded the executive power of the "two monarchists," Washington and Adams, whom he had railed against as dangerous to the Republic. In this way, Vidal channels all of Davis's criticisms and allows his readers to visualize Jefferson as the ultimate Hollywood villain—the antithesis of every democratic principle he supposedly stood for. To cap it off, Jefferson is the unfeeling brute who whips his horse mercilessly and, when flushed with anger, causes his pet mockingbird to fly from his shoulder in fear.[46]

Biographers of Burr have all aimed their verbal pistols at Jefferson in one way or another. Just to begin a discussion of Burr as a viable political adversary, the glare of Jefferson's imagined halo needs to be dimmed. Conjuring all the dark, repressed passions of film noir, Vidal went so far as to compare Jefferson's behavior to that of an "estranged lover." The consuming obsession with personality by all of the aforementioned writers has masked the unruly contingencies of the real political environment in which these historical actors lived and operated. The unstable Republican party that brought Jefferson and Burr together in the first place is marginalized in every one of their narratives. Sectional conflict, the influence of state politics, and unpredictable discursive forces constructing their identities in the public sphere all get short shrift. We are left with single-minded creatures of ambition.

In truth, Burr and Jefferson made their decisions based on imperfect information. They were savvy politicians who took risks, built alliances, occasionally (and sometimes dramatically) miscalculated, and never stopped trying to shape their legacies. Their story of the election of 1800 is less an Olympian struggle between flawed giants than the failure of constitutional design. Furthermore, Burr and Jefferson need to be seen as two among a host of players engaged in the larger contest between the two proud states of New York and Virginia. Their philosophies on western expansion were more alike than different. In intellectual terms, both were devoted men of the Enlightenment. It is only in the pungent prose of their enemies that Burr and Jefferson ever became enigmatic.

Notes

1. For the importance of classical pseudonyms, see Eran Shalev, "Ancient Masks, American Founders: Classical Pseudonyms during the American Revolution and the Early American Republic," *JER* 23 (2003): 151–72, esp. 160, 165, 170–72; also see Garry Wills, *Cincinnatus: George Washington and the Enlightenment* (New York, 1984); Maurie D. Mcinnis, "George Washington: Cincinnatus or Marcus Aurelius?," in *Thomas Jefferson, the Classical World, and Early America*, ed. Peter S. Onuf and Nicholas P. Cole (Charlottesville, Va., 2011), 151–52; William Wirt, *Sketches of the Life and Character of Patrick Henry* (Philadelphia, 1817), 54, 125; Joseph J. Ellis, *American Sphinx: The Character of Thomas Jefferson* (New York, 1997), 10, 13, 89–90, 301–2; Stanley Elkins and Eric

McKitrick, *The Age of Federalism: The Early Republic, 1788–1800* (New York, 1993), 743–44. Elkins and McKitrick borrowed the "enigma" metaphor from John Stagg's review essay, and he in turn borrowed the metaphor from the nineteenth-century biographer James Parton, whose work I address later in this essay.

When Elkins and McKitrick insist that "Aaron Burr was *not* a representative man of his time. He was certainly a deviant type," they engage in further distortion. They proceed to say that Burr's story "tantalizes," and that somehow the other "founders" were different from Burr because they lived "in settings devoid of décor or scenery." (Anyone who has visited Monticello, or has read of the pomp and circumstance surrounding Washington's presidency, should recognize this as a ridiculous suggestion.) Elkins and McKitrick reduce Burr's "fascination with women," and his status as "a man of genuine culture" who "read everything," to surface acquirements. They then contend that "everything he said or wrote—even when lying, which he did often and with great finesse—showed a lively and piquant intelligence." These are all irresponsible and ill-informed statements: the idea that Burr lied more than Hamilton or Jefferson contradicts the historical evidence, and yet the authors assume that the "real" founders, as representative men of the age, were men of virtue and talents apart, whose lies somehow do not reflect on their larger character. Elkins and McKitrick issue their accusations absent of evidence or proof, their biases derived from a Hamilton-centric vision of the early republic, requiring Burr to be cast as a villain. At the same time, they echo the scandalmongering prose of the day, evidently unaware of the origins of their biased portraits. They repeat the common trope used by Burr's enemies that tarred him as dandyish, part of an eighteenth-century rhetorical ploy aimed at feminizing a political enemy in order to dismiss him.

Stagg repeats a similar set of charges, without evidence, that Burr was "an ambitious man who concealed himself behind a polished, aristocratic demeanor." Again, without evidence, Stagg would have it believed that understanding Burr is not a "matter of documentation," but a matter of assessing "his remote, self-absorbed, almost narcissistic personality." It is contrary to the very nature of historical scholarship to reduce any historical actor to a series of highly biased caricatures. In claiming that a "known" personality substitutes for evidence, scholars relieve themselves of due diligence and ratify inherited assumptions. A lack of objectivity and dismissal of scholarly rules of evidence are unfortunately common in most assessments of Burr. See J. C. A. Stagg, "The Enigma of Aaron Burr," *Reviews in American History* 12, no. 3 (September 1984): 378–82. I discuss these problems in *Fallen Founder: The Life of Aaron Burr* (New York, 2007), 405–14, and "The 'Little Emperor': Aaron Burr, Dandyism, and the Sexual Politics of Treason," in *Beyond the Founders: New Approaches to the Political History of the Early American Republic*, ed. Jeffrey L. Pasley, Andrew W. Robertson, and David Waldstreicher (Chapel Hill, N.C., 2004), 129–58.

2. The desire of biographers to celebrate the founders as otherworldly began early. In D. B. Warden's 1808 essay "Life of Washington," he not only compares Washington to Cincinnatus but also ends his piece with the following appeal to his irreproducible greatness: "For if we take him but for all in all, We ne'er shall look upon his like again."

This quote was a slight variation of Horatio's words to Hamlet about his father. See D. B. Warden, "Life of General Washington," *The Belfast Monthly Magazine* 1 (1808): 37–40. The Shakespeare quote was used as toast to Washington in New York City in 1811. See *Public Advertiser*, 6 July 1811.

3. Matthew L. Davis, *Memoirs of Aaron Burr. With Miscellaneous Selections from his Correspondence,* 2 vols. (New York, 1836), 1:iii–iv; Isenberg, *Fallen Founder,* 198, 263–64, 467n62.

4. On Davis's activities in the 1830s, see Jeffrey L. Pasley, "Matthew Livingston Davis's Notes from the Political Underground: The Conflict of Political Values in the Early American Republic," http://pasleybrothers.com/jeff/writings/davisv2.htm, 4, 24n11.

5. Davis, *Memoirs of Aaron Burr,* 1:iii. Davis's running commentary on Jefferson's *Memoir, Correspondence, and Miscellanies,* edited by his grandson Thomas Jefferson Randolph, is oddly enough located in vol. 57 of the Rufus King Papers, New-York Historical Society (hereafter cited as Davis, "Commentary on Jefferson's *Memoir*"). I want to thank Jeff Pasley for telling me about this source.

6. For the importance of the paper war in the early republic, see Joanne B. Freeman, *Affairs of Honor: National Politics in the New Republic* (New Haven, Conn., 2001), 105–58.

7. Davis, *Memoirs of Aaron Burr,* 1:435.

8. Isenberg, *Fallen Founder,* 231; Pasley, "Matthew Livingston Davis's Notes" 14, 16–17. The illustrations were "A. Burr, Vice President of the United States," and "Mrs. Theodosia Burr Alston," both based on paintings by the artist and Burr's good friend John Vanderlyn, and reproduced by the engraver J. A. O'Neil in New York, 1802.

9. Davis, *Memoirs of Aaron Burr,* 1:v–vii, 91–92.

10. On Davis's background, see Pasley, "Matthew Livingston Davis's Notes," 5, 25–26n16. At the age of seventy-seven, in 1833, Burr married Eliza Jumel, the mistress, wife, and widow of the wealthy wine merchant Stephen Jumel. Burr and Jumel separated six months later, and a year after that Jumel sued for divorce. Jumel's maid, Mariah Johnson, gave graphic (most likely fabricated) details of Burr's sexual liaisons with Jane McManus. When Burr died, an obituary described him as a "successful ladies' man" without parallel in this country. See Isenberg, *Fallen Founder,* 400–404, 520n5.

11. Davis, *Memoirs of Aaron Burr,* 1:91–92. Thomas Moore published *The Works of Lord Byron: With His Letters and Journals, and His Life* in 1835. Moore was responsible, along with his publisher, John Murray, for allowing Byron's memoirs to be destroyed. It is highly likely that Moore's action gave Davis the idea for burning Burr's letters. Also see Jeffrey Vail, *The Literary Relationship of Lord Byron and Thomas Moore* (Baltimore, 2001), and Ronan Kelly, *Bard of Erin: The Life of Thomas Moore* (New York, 2008).

12. Davis, "Commentary on Jefferson's *Memoir*," 29–34. Davis repeated these arguments in *Memoirs of Aaron Burr,* 2:76, 89.

13. The depositions were taken as part of two suits. One suit was brought by Burr against James Cheetham for libel. Cheetham was editor of the New York newspaper the *American Citizen* and author of several pamphlets that accused Burr of intriguing

with the Federalists to secure the presidency for himself. Bayard also gave a deposition in an 1806 suit involving James Gillespie and Abraham Smith, in which he admitted to making a deal with Jefferson, using Samuel Smith as his intermediary. Smith's deposition confirmed what Bayard had said in his deposition. Davis, *Memoirs of Aaron Burr*, 1:436, 2:100, 105, 127, 131–32, 136; Isenberg, *Fallen Founder*, 219–20.

14. Davis, "Commentary on Jefferson's *Memoir*," 15.

15. Davis, *Memoirs of Aaron Burr*, 2:387–90; Isenberg, *Fallen Founder*, 303, 346–47.

16. Davis, *Memoirs of Aaron Burr*, 2:24, 139.

17. Ibid., 1:406, 2:16–17, 60, 66.

18. Pasley, "Matthew Livingston Davis's Notes," 5–6, 17. The story of his encounter with Jefferson was published in the *New York Herald* in 1850, the same year Davis died.

19. Davis, "Commentary on Jefferson's *Memoir*," 8–9.

20. Ibid., 8, 17, 19, 24.

21. Ibid., 8, 25–26.

22. Davis, *Memoirs of Aaron Burr*, 2:139–40; Davis, "Commentaries on Jefferson's *Memoir*," 23.

23. Davis, *Memoirs of Aaron Burr*, 1:436.

24. The passage is from Shakespeare's *Julius Caesar*, act 3, scene 2, the famous oration by Mark Antony:

Friends, Romans, countrymen, lend me your ears;
I come to bury Caesar, not to praise him;
The evil that men do lives after them,
The good is oft interred with their bones,
I speak not to disprove what Brutus spoke,
But here I am to speak what I do know.

25. In the preface, Davis noted that Burr did not wish to conceal any part of his life, and as a biographer, he wanted to provide an accurate portrait of Burr's character based on documentary testimony. See Davis, *Memoirs of Aaron Burr*, 1:iv–v, 236.

26. Samuel L. Knapp, *The Life of Aaron Burr* (New York, 1835), vii–viii, 202; Ben Harris McClary, "Samuel Lorenzo Knapp and Early American Biography," *Proceedings of the American Antiquarian Society* 95 (1985): 39–67, esp. 50–55, 49, 65.

27. Knapp, *Life of Aaron Burr*, iii–iv, 201. For his relationship with the Adamses, see McClary, "Samuel Lorenzo Knapp," 45, 49–50, 52, 54, 63. In a critical review of Knapp's biography, the reviewer mocked his writing style, observing that "classical allusions are thrown out as freely as the peltings of a Roman Carnival." See *The New England Magazine* 9 (1835): 143. Psapho was a common literary reference. It was first mentioned by the Dutch humanist Desiderius Erasmus in his *Adagia* (1500) and was used by poets into the nineteenth century. For a view on Psapho similar to Knapp's, see "Analects of Literature," *The North American Magazine* 1 (1833): 259; also see Joseph Twadell Shipley, *Dictionary of World Literature: Criticism, Forms, and Technique* (New York, 1964), 462.

28. Knapp, *Life of Aaron Burr,* 89, 182–83, 185–86, 188.

29. Ibid., 202.

30. James Parton, *The Life and Times of Aaron Burr* (Boston and New York, 1857; rev. ed., 1892), viii–ix, xi–xiii; "The Biographical Writings of James Parton," *The North American Review* 104 (1867): 601; Scott Casper, *Constructing American Lives: Biography and Culture in Nineteenth-Century America* (Chapel Hill, N.C., 1999), 231–32.

31. Parton contends that Burr's management and Adams's mismanagement, "more than all others, hastened the republican triumph." See Parton, *Life and Times of Aaron Burr,* 1:196, 207–8, 215–17, 225, 294, 306, 317, 330.

32. Ibid., 2:104–6.

33. Nathan Schachner, *Aaron Burr: A Biography* (New York, 1937), 103; also see the brief mention in the *New York Times,* 5 March 1961.

34. Like Davis, Schachner claimed that Burr had won the election for Jefferson. He also noted that "Jefferson had a positive talent for effective evasion." See Schachner, *Aaron Burr,* 169, 187, 207–8, 217.

35. It is interesting that Schachner came up with the same word ("Jesuitical") that Davis had only used in his unpublished commentary on Thomas Jefferson Randolph's *Memoir, Correspondence, and Miscellanies.* Concerning Burr's western "conspiracy," Jefferson comes across not as a man with a disorganized mind, but as one who attempts to control the national narrative on Burr's activities in the West. Schachner describes him as a "master of the gentle art of leading public opinion." See Schachner, *Aaron Burr,* 352, 355, 387–91, 399, 401, 406.

36. On Lomask's writing career, see Walter Romig, *The Book of Catholic Authors: Informal Portraits of Famous Modern Catholic Writers,* 6th Ser. (Detroit, 1960), 247–51; Milton Lomask, *Aaron Burr: The Years from Princeton to Vice President, 1756–1805* (New York, 1979), 68, 97; Parton, *Life and Times of Aaron Burr,* 1:63.

37. Lomask, *Aaron Burr,* 44–45.

38. Lomask contends that "Burr seems to have taken everything in [Chesterfield's] *Letters* at face value." Yet he does not know that Burr's favorite author, Mary Wollstonecraft, offered a scathing rebuke of Chesterfield's code of conduct. See ibid., 68–69, 97, 107, 111; also see C. Hemphill, *Bowing the Necessities: A History of Manners in America, 1620–1860* (New York, 1999); for Jefferson's Epicurean tastes, see Andrew Burstein, *Jefferson's Secrets: Death and Desire at Monticello* (New York, 2005), 166, 288; also see Isenberg, *Fallen Founder,* 74–75, 81, 123.

39. Milton Lomask, *Aaron Burr: The Conspiracy and Years of Exile, 1805–1836* (New York, 1982), xv–xvi, 107. For the Chesterfieldian slur used against Burr, see "Portrait of Burr," *Port Folio,* 16 May 1807; Federalists attacked Burr as a hedonistic aristocrat as early as 1795, so it is not surprising that this charge found its way into the Federalist *Port Folio.* Lomask unknowingly echoes what New York newspaper editor James Cheetham wrote in his scathing portrait of Burr as an enigma: "so mutable, capricious, versatile, unsteady and unfixed, one to which no determinate name can be given . . . from his *Debut* on political life, he has been everything and nothing." See James Cheetham, *A View of the Political Conduct of Aaron Burr* (New York, 1802), 5, 15–16, 24–25, 35. Also

see Lomask, *Aaron Burr*, 200, 107, 131; Isenberg, *Fallen Founder*, 138–39, 224, 231–32, 245, 248, 254–55, 273, 408, 410–12; Isenberg, "'Little Emperor,'" 129–58.

40. Lomask, *Aaron Burr*, 201, 303; Lomask, *Aaron Burr: The Conspiracy*, 56, 107, 201.

41. Gore Vidal, *Burr: A Novel* (New York, 1973), 11, 563.

42. Ibid., 200–203, 206.

43. Ibid., 208, 234, 242, 244, 268, 334.

44. Ibid., 21–23, 38, 200. For Colden's relationship with Madison, see Andrew Burstein and Nancy Isenberg, *Madison and Jefferson* (New York, 2010), 192–93.

45. On incest, see Vidal, *Burr,* 35, 136, 157, 345–46, 351, 356; on slavery, women, and Sally Hemings, see ibid., 256–57, 264.

46. Ibid., 256, 258–59, 265, 422.

Punching the Ticket

Hamilton Biographers and the Sins of Thomas Jefferson

JOANNE B. FREEMAN

On July 13, 1804, Gouverneur Morris was a frustrated eulogist. Asked to deliver the funeral oration for his friend Alexander Hamilton, he kept running aground. First, there was Hamilton's illegitimate birth; somehow, that had to be passed over. Then there was Hamilton's problematic politics; he admired the British monarchy and had serious doubts about the Constitution, and had said so "long and loudly." His financial system—his life's work—was widely (and to Morris, unjustly) hated. He had confessed to the world an adulterous affair. And then there was his personality; Hamilton was "indiscreet, vain, and opinionated," which had to be acknowledged or "the character will be incomplete."[1]

As Morris knew all too well, Hamilton's reputation is trailed by many tin cans. More often than not, Hamilton provided the string. But one tin can has proven heavier than most: Hamilton's discomfort with democracy. Even today, some people believe that he called the American people a "great beast," a claim based on fourth-hand hearsay reported sixty years after the "fact."[2]

In truth, Hamilton's thoughts about democracy were more complex, particularly given that the new republic was an evolving experiment in representative democracy.[3] Although he acknowledged the importance of popular politics in the new nation, and actively appealed to the public in the press, Hamilton was never entirely comfortable with the politics of the street. He disliked the disorder of popular unrest, distrusted the impact of popular protest, and disdained wooing the masses. Worse, he rarely hesitated to say so. Indeed, he saw his distrust of democracy as the height of responsible governance, a vital anchoring counterweight to the flighty whirlwind of democratic excess. The Federalists' leading spirit, he virtually embodied this mentality—the gradual decline of both his reputation and his party revealing the degree to which he was swimming against the democratic tide.

And so his reputation has passed through the centuries: the aristocratic yin to Thomas Jefferson's democratic yang. More often than not, in the American historical narrative, Hamilton has stood as a strong-state doubter of democracy, unquestionably important to the national superstructure but detached from the ideals at the heart of America's sense of self. Forever paired with Jefferson on a "seesaw of prestige," he often sits in Jefferson's shadow, rising in esteem when his ideals and policies prove useful, then sinking into oblivion when their purpose has been served.[4] For Americans, praise for democracy rarely falls out of fashion; Jefferson's contributions rarely fall out of mind. Hamilton's reputation has traveled a more tangled path.

Perhaps this explains the ardent advocacy of many Hamilton biographers.[5] Beyond exploring his life and politics, they champion his cause: rescuing him from oblivion, redeeming his reputation, and decrying his shaky membership in the Founder Hall of Fame. Pleading the case for their historical underdog, these biographers seem to have their chins up and their fists poised and ready, awaiting an inevitable full-force Jeffersonian blow— a mindset fittingly characteristic of Hamilton.

By far, the biggest obstacle to Hamilton's fight for fame is his democracy problem. Confronted with this hurdle, many Hamilton biographers accentuate the positive. They praise his talents and accomplishments, heralding the high points of his brief and crowded life. They highlight the dramatic details of his rags-to-riches life story. They focus on his legacy, celebrating how his bold policies and unerringly national vision paved the way for modern America. In essence, they brush his problem politics aside.

But it's one thing to play a game of distraction and quite another to look the monster in the eye. Hamilton's biographical smoke screen of talents and merits can't erase his democracy problem. And the foremost symbol of that problem is Jefferson, America's touchstone of democracy. Thus the strategy of many Hamilton biographers: eager to explain and justify Hamilton's democratic discomfort, they highlight Jefferson's democratic excesses, depicting him as the scheming demagogue that Hamilton believed him to be.

And Hamilton *did* consider Jefferson a demagogue, the veritable embodiment of democracy's most serious vulnerability. Consider Hamilton's pitch for Jefferson's presidential run in 1800: "I admit that his politics are tinctured with fanaticism, that he is too much in earnest in his democracy, that he has been a mischevous enemy to the principle measures of our past administration, that he is crafty & persevering in his objects, that he is not scrupulous about the means of success, nor very mindful of truth, and that he is a contemptible hypocrite."[6] So why vote for Jefferson? He was such an inveterate demagogue, Hamilton argued, that he would temper his measures for fear of damaging his popularity. Faced with the exceedingly distasteful task of promoting Jefferson, Hamilton managed it only after coursing down a runway of Jeffersonian sins.

Biographers eager to advocate Hamilton course down that same runway. They create looking-glass Jeffersons as seen through Hamilton's eyes. They depict Jefferson as democracy run amuck, its inherent instabilities brought to life. In Hamilton biographies, Jefferson is a Scheming Politician: a Machiavellian manipulator of men. He's a Slovenly Demagogue: a pandering, posturing "man of the people" whose honeyed words and deliberately shabby clothes captivated the masses. He's a Slaveholding Aristocrat: a rhetoric-spewing lord of the manor desperately clinging to an agrarian slavery-infested world. Or—most extreme of all—in the eyes of Hamilton's sons, Jefferson was a Soulless Villain: a ruthless politico who stopped at nothing to get ahead.

In essence, Jefferson's supposed sins do biographical magic; they justify Hamilton's democratic doubts. They also turn Hamilton's alleged sins into virtues. Compared with Jefferson the schemer, Hamilton seems admirably frank, although that frankness sometimes did him damage. Compared with Jefferson the demagogue, Hamilton seems virtuously oblivious to popular acclaim. Compared with Jefferson the slaveholder, Hamilton is a social revolutionary fostering a dynamic economy brimming with opportunities for all. The flattering glow of Jefferson's sins doesn't make Hamilton seem cuddly, but it does the next best thing: it transforms him into a democrat despite himself, which is magic indeed.

It also does one thing more. In battering Jefferson and flattering Hamilton, each generation of Hamilton biographers has said a lot about itself. Post–Civil War biographers valued Hamilton's aggressive nationalism and scorned Jefferson's politics of indirection. Fueled by their reform-minded agenda, Progressive writers praised Hamilton's constructive sweeping statesmanship and denounced Jefferson's demagoguery. In the shadow of an alleged Communist threat, Cold War writers glorified Hamiltonian capitalism and spurned Jeffersonian agrarianism. And given the current deep distrust of political insiders and alien "outsiders," recent writers have transformed Hamilton into America's founding immigrant battling a privileged insider Jefferson.

To some degree, all of these writers have seen themselves in Hamilton, but none more so than his first generation of biographers. Grappling for the soul of a nascent republic shaped by their friends and fathers, in writing about Hamilton they sang a song of themselves.

The first Hamilton biographer to champion his cause was his third surviving son, John Church Hamilton, who did so with a vengeance.[7] His seven-volume, 4,000-page *History of the Republic of the United States* (1857–64) argued that Alexander Hamilton *was* the Republic; more than any other founder, he gave it life. Given the inherent rightness of Hamilton's cause, his opponents by definition were enemies of the state, motivated by selfish desires alone. And none was more selfish—more mean, rotten, and nasty—than Jefferson, a man of boundless ambition, a defamer of reputations, a master manipulator, a cant-spewing demagogue. This Jefferson has no redeeming virtues—not a one. The first major Hamilton biography, *History of the Republic,* set the Jefferson-bashing bar high.[8]

It was easy to see the inner alchemy at play. As one reviewer wrote, John Church Hamilton was the "faithful depositary" of his father's "political antipathies" distilled down to their vicious, vituperative essence. Alexander Hamilton's entire family heeded the same call; John Church's *History* was part of their ongoing quest to earn Hamilton the recognition that they felt he deserved. The enterprise's heart and soul was Hamilton's widow, Elizabeth. From Hamilton's death in 1804 until her death in 1854 at the age of ninety-seven, she conducted a nonstop campaign preaching the gospel of Hamilton. For decades, she turned from one Federalist to another, seeking a biographer to ensure her husband's fame, only to be disappointed time and again by men who were too busy, too sick, too daunted, or—in the case of Timothy Pickering—too dead to write. (He died before he finished.)[9] Elizabeth's crusade to prove Hamilton's authorship of George Washington's Farewell Address was so widely known and so fervently pursued that leading Federalists hid incriminating documents from her to preserve Washington's pedestal of greatness.[10] Hamilton's sons supported her efforts with fist-clenched belligerence. Egged on by their mother, their pride, and a bottomless pit of indignation, Hamilton's two oldest sons, Alexander and James, routinely leaped to their father's defense, leaving a stream of newspaper screeds, abusive letters, and lawsuits in their wake.[11]

John Church went the extra mile. Over the course of roughly thirty years, he published seventeen volumes about his father: two volumes of an unfinished four-volume biography, the seven-volume *History*, a seven-volume edition of his father's papers, and an edition of *The Federalist* so dedicated to glorifying his father that it even inflates the size of his name on the title page.[12] He also collected his father's papers, cataloged his portraits, erected monuments, and dedicated memorials. Though trained as a lawyer, John Church claimed dad-defending as a calling.[13]

Spurring his efforts was a slow but steady outpouring of books about Hamilton's foremost foes, Jefferson and James Madison. Thomas Jefferson Randolph's *Memoir, Correspondence, and Miscellanies from the Papers of Thomas Jefferson* (1829) was the first in a series of slaps at Hamilton's reputation that included George Tucker's *Life of Thomas Jefferson* (1837), Henry D. Gilpin's *Papers of James Madison* (1840), Henry Stephens Randall's *Life of Thomas Jefferson* (1858), and William Cabell Rives's unfinished *History of the Life and Times of James Madison* (1859–68).

John Church Hamilton returned the favor in his *History*. For its unadulterated Hamiltonian spite, it stands alone. His goal was threefold: to celebrate his father's accomplishments, to vindicate his father's name, and to reduce the reputations of his father's enemies to smoldering rubble. To say that he went too far is a colossal understatement. He credited his father with virtually every major accomplishment of the founding era. (One reviewer deemed it lucky that Hamilton couldn't have been in Philadelphia in 1776, or he would have gotten credit for the Declaration of Independence as well.)[14] He refuted accusations in excruciating detail; even his footnotes had footnotes. And he attacked Madison, Jefferson, and their biographers tooth and nail: countering every charge, checking every claim, even getting permission from the State Department to read Jefferson's and Madison's manuscript letters, then highlighting how strategic edits had masked their true "spirit, tone, and objects" when published.[15]

But John Church didn't rely on evidence alone. He also engaged in no-holds-barred character attacks. He maligned the motives of Madison, a good man who had been "bound as with a spell" by Jefferson's wily charms to betray Madison's former friend Hamilton. With words dripping with wounded indignation, John Church mapped Madison's moments of treachery, highlighting one above all: he accused Madison of doctoring his Federal Convention notes to prove Hamilton a monarchist, a charge that haunts Hamilton even today. Madison was guilty of "presenting his own views prominently" and "distorting or suppressing the views of others," John Church charged, parsing Madison's every word with mind-numbing detail in footnotes extending for pages. Madison, a man whose "powers of good were great," had defamed himself and discredited his writings. The future "student of American History" should take care.[16]

This dire pronouncement was nothing compared with the shower of insults that John Church rained down on Jefferson; if Hamilton walked with the angels, then Jefferson was the devil incarnate. As a politician, he was despicable: a hypocrite who masked his ambitions behind a false love of retirement; a Machiavellian genius who used men as tools; a demagogue who wooed the gullible masses. Jefferson was no less contemptible a person: a coward who fled the British when he was governor of Virginia; a hedonist "keenly alive . . . to every form of gratification"; a poser ("Franklin was a Savant—Jefferson would be thought one"); a pathological liar; an aristocrat who supported the spread of slavery; and no Christian. And he was ugly: his "easy, flexile manners" made up for "an appearance not well favored." All told, the "careful student of American history" should know that to Jefferson "may be traced every heresy which has infected the counsels of this country."[17]

Clearly, John Church Hamilton was addressing the ages. He wanted the historical "truth" to be known, but to accomplish this higher purpose, he couldn't just defame Hamilton's enemies; he also had to discredit their biographers. Sometimes he quoted them against themselves. (As one reviewer put it, the biographies provided the facts, and John Church furnished "the sneer and the inuendo.")[18] More often, he staged frontal assaults, not only in the text and footnotes but also in appendixes containing tangential but (he hoped) damning evidence, like a letter from Henry Randall promising fair treatment of Hamilton "in the spirit of history"—to John Church, a promise broken.[19]

In essence, in his running commentary, John Church attacked Jefferson and Madison through their biographers, who returned the favor by fighting Hamilton through his son. Given that these biographers were publishing volumes concurrently, this battle unfolded one invective-filled tome at a time. In one volume, an outraged William Cabell Rives chastised John

Church for posthumously attacking Madison with charges "of the grossest and most offensive nature" that no one with "the slightest faith in the principles of truth and honor" could believe. Hamilton's response in his next volume revealed his personal investment in this fight. This was no posthumous attack, he insisted; it was a "vindication of a father by a son from some of the *posthumous* libels of James Madison upon Hamilton."[20]

In the end, Hamilton's *History* was so extreme that it defeated itself. Reviewers savaged it; one called it a sterling example of a rare literary genre: the "comic biography."[21] But it did future Hamilton biographers a service. Few deemed it balanced (although some did, hinting at the depths of future Jefferson-bashing vitriol). But they *did* consider it a handy mine of anti-Jefferson fodder, with ammunition enough for generations to come.

The last volume of Hamilton's *History* (1864) foreshadowed the next batch of Hamilton biographies. "Had Hamilton's views prevailed," John Church charged, the Civil War "could not have taken place."[22] With that bloody trial's end, Hamilton became a nationalistic seer warning against disunion.[23] Thus the surge of Hamilton biographies in the 1880s. After decades of little but the raging Hamilton boys, at least six biographies appeared between 1879 and 1898, plus an edition of Hamilton's writings.[24] Although they sometimes judged Hamilton's politics self-defeating, even the unfriendliest of these biographers deemed his policies invariably right. Hamilton's—not Jefferson's—national vision had prevailed. As Henry Cabot Lodge wrote in *Alexander Hamilton* (1882), in the end, "the great Federalist has the advantage."[25]

Lodge spent much of the 1880s trying to make just that point.[26] The scion of two of Boston's first families, a party-line Republican senator for almost twenty years, he was an unapologetic latter-day Federalist who saw untamed democracy as an open threat to the Republic's strength and dignity. Hamilton, ever a proponent of "strength and order," had rightly tried to counter America's postrevolutionary democratic drift.[27]

Lodge admired Hamilton for many reasons: his nationalism, his conservatism, and his persistence in the face of "relentless opposition." But he was particularly impressed by Hamilton's style of leadership. Hamilton was practical, bold, straightforward, a "fighting man" sometimes to a fault; he stumbled because of "his desire to force things through, and . . . his impatience of delay or of concession, when dealing with other men." To Lodge, all of Hamilton's strengths were on display during the debate over the Constitution. Hamilton had preferred an "aristocratic" republic in the British mold. But when he couldn't get his way, he had taken what he could get. Had Hamilton

> been an agitator, or a sentimentalist of muddy morals and high purposes, a visionary and an idealist, he would have stood up and howled against this Constitution, which was not what he wanted. . . . As he was none of these things, but a patriotic man of clear and practical mind, he knew that the first rule of successful and beneficial statesmanship was not to sulk because one cannot have just what one wants, but to take the best thing obtainable, and sustain it to the uttermost.[28]

Lodge the politician was appraising Hamilton as a fellow toiler in the field.

Given Lodge's dislike of sentimentalists, visionaries, and idealists, it's not hard to guess what he thought of Jefferson. But he saw one sin more: Jefferson was a conniving politician, "silent, subtle, retiring, making no speeches, and printing no essays, but doing a good deal of quiet talking and shrewd letter-writing, toiling in the dark and managing men." As a statesman, Jefferson was "inconsistent, supple, feminine, and illogical," the polar opposite of the "consistent, strong, masculine, and logical" Hamilton.[29] For Lodge, as for most Gilded Age Hamilton biographers, Jefferson was a Scheming Politician.

In this cluster of post–Civil War biographies, political methods mattered. The Civil War had proven the power of a strong national government joined with bold, positive statecraft. These mostly northern biographers wanted to drive this lesson home. (By contrast, they barely mentioned Jefferson's states' rights principles.) They praised Hamilton's political style to the skies and condemned Jefferson's as cowardly and Machiavellian, a strategy that had the added benefit of pinning one of Hamilton's alleged sins on Jefferson. In this telling, Hamilton—so often condemned as an unscrupulous wheeler-dealer—was admirably frank in his methods. Jefferson, not Hamilton, was the master manipulator.

Consider, for example, the Hamilton biography by John Torrey Morse Jr., editor of the "American Statesmen" series that included Lodge's *Hamilton*. Morse's portrait of Hamilton was so adoring that even Lodge thought it had "gone too far."[30] John Church Hamilton had got it right, Morse claimed, but he had buried the truth in seven dense volumes. Morse wanted to distill Hamilton for the masses in an equally "impartial" history.[31]

Like Lodge, Morse thought that Jefferson was "a theorist, not a practical man." He had "an uncontrollable passion for thinking," forever inventing starry-eyed ideas that were "quite fascinating on paper" but wouldn't work in "the world of real men." In one vital way, however, Jefferson wasn't a theorist. He knew how to manipulate people, and therein lay the key to his success. To Morse, as to many of Hamilton's Gilded Age biographers, given the inherent rightness of Hamilton's policies, Jefferson's successes stemmed from dirty politics. "Such a master of party politics as Jefferson has never lived in this country," Morse declared. Jefferson knew how to use men, "acknowledging or denying his connection with them as he saw fit." But his real gift was in writing letters so cunningly "poisonous" that he would have "called forth the sincere admiration of Machiavelli."[32]

For these biographers, the epitome of Jefferson's method was his "Anas," as contained in the fourth volume of Randolph's edition of Jefferson's papers. In retirement, Jefferson had spent years arranging some of his letters into a "true" history of Washington's administration, to be planted amid his papers and discovered after his death.[33] To cast light on his letters, he interwove informal memoranda recording bits of gossip and dinner conversations. Unfortunately for Jefferson, Randolph dismantled his history and published the memoranda at the end of his fourth volume in a separate section titled "Anas" (Latin for a collection of table talk, anecdotes, and gossip), lobbing a historical bombshell that wounded Jefferson's reputation forever after. Hamilton biographers couldn't get enough of it. As Morse put it, the "Anas" was "a blunderbuss which the aged man loaded to the very muzzle with garbled gossip, but carefully forbade to be discharged until he himself should have secured the safe refuge of the grave."[34] It revealed "the true Jefferson in strong lines and gorgeous colours," wrote a later biographer: "Jefferson the skillful politician, the ingenious sophist, the intriguer against his enemies, the distorter of evidence and of facts; above all, perhaps, Jefferson the unforgiving." The "Anas" provided a description of Jefferson's character "to which his bitterest enemy would not wish to add a line."[35]

By far, the most noted part of the "Anas" was Jefferson's claim to have been duped by Hamilton into supporting the assumption of state debts, a charge that has raised the hackles of Hamilton biographers for generations.[36]

To Hamilton's Gilded Age chroniclers, the idea that Jefferson, the master manipulator of men, was fooled by the straightforward-to-the-point-of-indiscretion Hamilton was laughable. "It is impossible to resist pausing over this statement," Lodge snickered, "for it is one of the most amusing ever made even by Jefferson, and shows a confidence in the credulity of posterity which is not flattering."[37] Here Lodge drove the Scheming Politician argument home. Not only had Jefferson manipulated his contemporaries, but he had tried to manipulate posterity as well. By Lodge's account, Jefferson's biographers, his politics, and even his very words could not be trusted.

Certainly, Frederick Scott Oliver—a leading Hamilton biographer in the next batch of biographies—didn't trust Jefferson's words. A British businessman who admitted that he had "little real knowledge of history," he had stumbled across Gertrude Atherton's romantic biographical novel, *The Conqueror: Being the True and Romantic Story of Alexander Hamilton* (1902), became enamored of Hamilton, and never recovered, ultimately writing the most influential Hamilton biography of the early twentieth century: *Alexander Hamilton: An Essay on American Union* (1906).[38] To Oliver, Hamilton held the answer to Britain's turn-of-the-century crisis of empire: Hamilton's "aim was to make a nation: our aim is to make an empire."[39] Hamilton's "aggressive, constructive" statecraft, so lauded by earlier biographers, had been vital to his success, but so had his federal outlook and ardent nationalism—to Oliver, the twin keys to turning Britain's "voluntary league of states" into "a firm Union." Oliver intended his biography to be a kind of political manual, and he partly succeeded. In Ireland and South Africa, both grappling with creating a unitary state, his book was widely discussed. "I shall never forget the effect which *Alexander Hamilton* had on me when I read it," acknowledged one South African official.[40]

Oliver's work was no less admired in America. Republicans generally and Progressives specifically shared some of Oliver's (and Hamilton's) views. Republicans admired Hamilton's nationalism and commercial policies; Progressives, whatever their party, liked his sweeping, constructive style of national statesmanship. Oliver placed Hamilton on a scale of world values, giving Hamilton's views universal significance.[41] Imperialists took heart. Prominent Oliver fans included Theodore Roosevelt, Warren G. Harding, Woodrow Wilson, and Walter Lippmann, among others.[42] A host of Hamilton biographies followed in Oliver's wake.[43]

As suggested by Oliver's love of *The Conqueror,* among influential Hamilton studies at the turn of the century, Atherton's novel ran a close second. Oliver's response was typical of many (and Atherton returned the favor, declaring that his book deserved "immediate rank as a classic").[44] The first biographer to depict Hamilton "the man," Atherton singlehandedly made him a romantic hero.[45] In Theodore Roosevelt's words, Hamilton had "the touch of the heroic, the touch of the purple, the touch of the gallant, the dashing, the picturesque."[46]

Grounding her work in extensive research, including interviews with Hamilton descendants (who were still howling about the Farewell Address) and a trip to the Caribbean (making her the first person to document Hamilton's childhood), Atherton situated her book in a netherworld between fiction and history, describing it as a biography written "in a more flexible manner"—a history intended to read like a novel.[47] Some critics savaged her method. As one charged, "in the jumble of historical personages, authentic documents, love-making that did occur, and love-making that never took place; scandals that are a part of our history and scandals that arose in Mrs. Atherton's prolific brain, you can't for the life of you tell where fact and fiction part company or meet."[48] But many people loved the book for just that reason. *The Conqueror* was a romantic, character-driven history-novel that was fun to read. And Hamilton's life adapted admirably to fiction. Born in obscurity in the Caribbean, raising himself to power by his talents and merits, battling seemingly unbeatable odds, a one-man army of game-changing policies with a risqué love life who fell meteorically from power and died in a duel: it's hard to imagine a historical character better suited to romantic fiction.

Atherton's idealized Hamilton was a democrat. Compared with Jefferson, he was "by far the truer Democrat of the two, because he had the good of the entire Republic at heart."[49] Other Progressive Era biographers agreed: Hamilton's constructive means promoted democratic ends.[50] He himself may have distrusted democracy, but his energetic statecraft served the national good; he was a Progressive at heart.

Yet even these admirers had to wrestle with Hamilton's blind spot: his distrust of democracy. Hamilton's aristocratic streak has long clouded the sunny skies of Hamilton biographies, but in this period—so focused on promoting the public welfare—it stood out. Some biographers confronted the problem head-on, transforming his vice into a virtue. Oliver summed up this argument nicely: "It was Hamilton's most fatal weakness as a politician, and one of his chief virtues as a statesman, that he was indifferent to popularity."[51]

Which brings us back to Jefferson. If Hamilton was an expansive democratic nationalist who grounded his politics on principles rather than demagoguery, Jefferson, by comparison, was the king of demagoguery, exploiting democracy's inherent weaknesses to his own advantage. Using honeyed words expressing abstract American ideals, Jefferson seduced the unthinking masses. One biographer's description of Jefferson as "anarchistic" revealed the fear at the heart of this portrait.[52] Jefferson was the same sort of dangerous ideologue who was currently wreaking havoc on the world stage. The early twentieth century saw the rise of Thomas Jefferson, the Slovenly Demagogue.

Oliver proved a master of this brand of Jefferson-bashing. An Englishman with no particular affection for American democracy, he had an easy time damning Jefferson and his ideals at one stroke.[53] Even so, he couldn't deny democracy's logic and appeal, which he tried to pin down in his analysis of Jefferson. To Oliver, this "Touchstone of Democracy" was a kind of "Don Quixote; with this difference, that half the world shared his illusions."[54] Jefferson doubtless believed the gospel that he preached, but it was all words and fancies. He was

> a reader of books, weaver of fanciful philosophies, an accepter of general principles, a worshipper of words, a hater of the confusion of things. He loved everything that was "free," or that called itself "free," with the passionate unreasonableness of a collector of Stuart relics. His fundamental belief (if we may use these words to describe opinions which never at any point touched a firm bottom, but merely swam like a kind of "sud" upon the stream of expediency) was a set of formulas which he had learned by rote during his official career in France.[55]

Continuing in this vein for a full thirty pages, Oliver grappled with the rhetoric and realities of democracy, American-style.

Yet political success in a democracy required more than pretty words; it relied on the heartfelt faith of the masses. By Oliver's account, here Jefferson the "great actor" excelled. He played the role of the "common man" with a remarkable flair, even dressing the part. His allegedly "slovenly" dress may have fooled his contemporaries into thinking him "a great nature contemptuous of trifles," but Oliver knew it for the costume that it was.[56] Jefferson's "studiously unkempt" appearance—the "little outward forms of democracy in which Jefferson took an uncouth delight"—showed "the ingenuity of a great actor who had carefully weighed the value of the meanest accessories."[57] His "not over-clean" clothes, mentioned by more than one Hamilton biographer, were propaganda.[58]

To Oliver, Jefferson's politics were equally strategic. Like all "great showmen," he had a "*flair* for what was or might be made popular. . . . He knew what the people wanted, and he knew also what it was easy and possible to educate it to want."[59] As Hamilton idolater Arthur Vandenberg sneered in his aptly named *The Greatest American, Alexander Hamilton* (1921), Jefferson was the nation's "first great 'Commoner' in every literal application of that word." Vandenberg, a journalist (soon to be a Republican senator from Michigan), had asked a host of politicians, journalists, scholars, and other noteworthies to name "the greatest American," and was horrified that only one person chose Hamilton. To Vandenberg, Jefferson's "greatest impress upon history" was "in the role of exaggerated democracy." Hamilton, on the other hand, "believed in safe-guarding democracy against its own passions" as promoted by men like Jefferson. Not surprisingly, Vandenberg loved Oliver's *Hamilton*.[60]

Although they acknowledged Jefferson's democratic credentials, these biographers thought that he had planned himself into power, becoming America's darling by posturing and playacting.[61] By contrast, Hamilton—so admirably indifferent to popularity—had given the nation a dose of what it needed, thereby laying the foundations of good government. Jefferson was all words, living and dying "in the odour of phrases"; Hamilton stood for "business against nonsense."[62] He was a man of action who "carried his projects to completion in the face of a relentless opposition, and against the mistaken wishes of a large part of the people."[63]

Here was the power of the Slovenly Demagogue approach. It made Hamilton's distrust of democracy a virtue, not a vice. By defending his principles, expounding his policies, and disdaining demagogic trickery, he had contributed to his own obscurity while serving the public good. To the American public, Hamilton was a "master," but Jefferson was a "friend," and it was "useless to point to the ledger account of benefits conferred."[64] To these biographers, this difference was to blame for Hamilton's foundering reputation.

Depicting Jefferson as a Slovenly Demagogue enabled Hamilton's biographers to highlight this injustice and Hamilton's selflessness as well. It also justified their biographical efforts. They were righting a wrong, revealing to the American people the "master spirit" of America's founding, a true statemaker, perhaps *the* greatest American.[65] As removed as these works were from John Church Hamilton's seven-volume tirade, they were spreading his message.

Toward the end of *Hamilton,* Oliver glanced at an idea that gained popularity in the next set of Hamilton biographies. Speaking of Jefferson, he wrote: "Freedom and fraternity were ever on his lips, so that not only his followers in the North, but possibly even he himself, came to forget that he was a Virginian slave-owner to the last."[66] The paradox of Jefferson the democratic slaveholder flavored the next group of Hamilton studies, but not before decades of relative oblivion for Hamilton, whose reputation tumbled with the stock market crash of 1929 and didn't recover until the Cold War. In the shadow of an alleged Communist threat, with American postwar prosperity booming, Hamilton became a prophet of the glories of capitalism, and Jefferson, a dedicated opponent to Hamilton's financial system, became a backward-looking agrarian clinging to an outmoded slave regime. The Cold War saw the emergence of Thomas Jefferson, Slaveholding Aristocrat.[67]

In a sense, these dips of the seesaw were only natural. Given the level of adulation for Hamilton before the Depression, his link with moneyed men, his seeming indifference to the everyday struggles of the common man, the degree to which Republicans claimed him as their own, and perhaps most damning of all, the ardent public appreciation voiced by Presidents Warren G. Harding and Calvin Coolidge, the economy's collapse couldn't help but bring Hamilton down. "When the great crash came," notes Stephen Knott in his study of Hamilton's reputation, "Alexander Hamilton might as well have been the chairman of the Republican National Committee."[68]

Meanwhile, Jefferson's reputation was on the rise for many reasons: the sesquicentennial of the Declaration of Independence; the centennial of his death; the Democratic Party's desire for a "founder" mascot; and the publication of Claude Bowers's wildly popular *Jefferson and Hamilton* (1925).[69] A dramatic novelistic retelling of the two men's clash, it ingeniously glorified the very things that had tarred Jefferson's reputation for decades. Glorying in Jefferson's sneaky backroom politicking, Bowers praised him as a master politician. Franklin Delano Roosevelt's enthusiastic claiming of the Jeffersonian mantle sealed the deal.

Jefferson was up and Hamilton was down for a good thirty years. And then came the Cold War and the bicentennial of Hamilton's birth in 1955 (or 1957; Hamilton's precise birthdate is unknown).[70] Hamilton the capitalist leaped to the fore, championing the American way against Communism, which—by some accounts—was inherently Jeffersonian. Although Jefferson's commitment to individual rights was praiseworthy, noted Louis Hacker in *Alexander Hamilton in the American Tradition* (1957), his "utopianism" and egalitarianism had taken a dangerous turn in modern times, making Communism palatable to the masses. The modern Jeffersonian, "in order to achieve his conception of 'equality,' was willing to run the risks of oppression."[71]

Hacker's logic hints at the main trend in Cold War Hamilton biographies. Hamilton the capitalist had generated a fluid society with opportunities for all; he was a social revolutionary. Jefferson, by contrast, was a nostalgic devotee of a static agrarian past that benefited southern oligarchs alone. In essence, Jefferson was an aristocrat.[72] Once again, as in Progressive Era biographies, Hamilton was the truer democrat of the two. Broadus Mitchell, one of the period's foremost Hamilton biographers, said so outright. Citing a letter in which Hamilton acknowledged that the Federalists had never learned to pander to the public, Mitchell asked: "If Hamilton's estimate was just (as certainly it was sincere), who was the democrat? Was it better service to the people to engage their wits, or to trick their confidence?"[73] Here was yet another spin on the perennial problem of Hamilton's relations with the masses. By not being a demagogue, Hamilton was a democrat.

Once again, Jefferson was assuming the weight of a charge usually made against Hamilton. Jefferson, not Hamilton, sided with the elite and moneyed classes, in act and implication if not in word. Hamilton, by contrast, was a democratic striver. Along similar lines, Jefferson, not Hamilton, was the real conservative. Even Jacob Cooke, whose *Alexander Hamilton* (1982)— along with John C. Miller's *Alexander Hamilton: Portrait of Paradox* (1959)— was one of the more balanced studies of the period, argued this point with passion. "For the sake of easy labeling," historians had depicted Jefferson as "the new nation's paradigmatic reformer, its most prominent (but somehow 'gentle') radical, and the father of American democracy." But focus on different aspects of Jefferson's thoughts and practices and "the contours of the familiar portrait change," revealing Jefferson as "the prototypical American conservative." Although Jefferson insisted that "a revolution every twenty years would be a good thing," he was "a steadfast supporter of the status quo" who aimed to preserve his agrarian way of life.[74] Jefferson wanted "a mechanical, mathematically definable, and predictable social order," agreed the ardently Hamiltonian historian Forrest McDonald in *Alexander Hamilton: A Biography* (1979): "the only privilege that he ever seriously opposed was privilege that threatened the security of his own little world."[75]

The most remarkable aspect of this conservative consensus is that scholars from across the political spectrum concurred in it. The conservative McDonald admired Hamilton for being a "true revolutionary" who created the conditions for a capitalistic free-market economy that ensured American greatness. Had Jefferson's principles prevailed, the nation would have collapsed into "a collection of banana republics."[76] At the other end of the spectrum, the economic historian Broadus Mitchell, the 1934 Socialist candidate for governor of Maryland, in 1957 and 1962 published a two-volume biography praising Hamilton for using the power of the state to encourage social organization and enforce the "community's will." Unlike Jefferson, who focused on "the immunities of the individual"—a "naked, excessively vulnerable" form of freedom—Hamilton understood that "the safety of the individual is in the security of the mass."[77] Indeed, Mitchell went further, extolling Hamilton as one of several "American Radicals Nobody Knows" who planted the seeds of modern socialism.[78]

The distance between McDonald's and Mitchell's politics couldn't be greater, yet in their praise of Hamilton and their distaste for Jefferson they were soul mates.[79] They were also southerners with deeply conflicted feelings about the South, perhaps a partial explanation for their meeting of the minds. McDonald—a Texas-born historian who taught at the University of Alabama for twenty-six years—said as much in an odd, passionate epilogue to his odd, passionate biography. Musing on the checkered fate of Hamilton's reputation, he pinpointed the North as a Hamiltonian success story, then shifted his gaze southward. Unlike the North, the South had adopted "Jeffersonian rules" grounded on slavery and the "mystique of the land." As a result, the Civil War left the South "a wretched and accursed backwater" while the North advanced to Hamiltonian greatness.[80] In his glowing review of McDonald's book, Mitchell—Kentucky born and raised—praised this "feeling" passage, and for good reason; Mitchell had been wrestling with the history and meaning of the South for decades.[81] Both men were struck by the contrast between the South's bitter realities and its mythic sense of self. There's a poignant irony at play here: two southern Hamilton admirers were decrying the false front of Jeffersonian rhetoric and myth-making. They were southerners who felt betrayed by Jefferson.

The Cold War, civil rights era Jefferson would have a tough time getting past the bitter fact of slavery (although interestingly, Sally Hemings doesn't appear in Hamilton biographies until the turn of the twenty-first century).[82] McDonald and Mitchell raked Jefferson over the coals on this count. Mitchell highlighted the "cruel contradiction of a philosopher writing 'free and equal' and calling to a chattel slave to bring the blotting sand."[83] McDonald called Jefferson "an intellectual dilettante and frequenter of salons—which the labor of his slaves permitted him to be."[84] Both men were probing the open wound of one of Jefferson's central paradoxes: the clash between rhetoric and reality, and the ways that generations of Americans had bought the former and overlooked the latter.

More recently, Ron Chernow pushed this paradox further in his blockbuster *Alexander Hamilton* (2004). Claiming that Jefferson wanted the national capital in the South because it would distance it from "abolitionist forces," he introduces a reality that never was.[85] But his claim hints at how Hamilton's reputation has benefited from Jefferson's vulnerability on this score. In stark contrast to Jefferson's backwardness concerning slavery, Hamilton has become an abolitionist. Celebrating Hamilton as the prophetic founder of modern America, some recent biographers focus on his opposition to slavery, claiming his modernity on that count as well.[86] Depicting Hamilton as an antislavery crusader makes him seem far less disdainfully detached from the masses. In a sublime stroke of historiographic irony, Jefferson may have loosed the tie of Hamilton's heaviest tin can.

Of course, Jefferson was attacked as a rhetoric-spewing slaveholder long before the twentieth century. John Church Hamilton well knew the charge's power. An antislavery Democrat, he placed the blame for the persistence of American slavery squarely on Jefferson's shoulders. As he put it in a newspaper article in 1869, Jefferson's presidential win in 1801 had "established the dominion of the slave power and the continuance of slavery in this republic for sixty years."[87]

John Church pressed his point in an 1864 speech entitled "The Slave

Power: Its Heresies and Injuries to the American People." Singling out Jefferson as the "especial personification" of Virginia, he turned to the ever-handy fourth volume of Randolph's *Memoir* and read aloud two letters in which Jefferson worried that southern boys schooled in northern colleges would lose their states' rights principles and support federal intervention against slavery in Missouri.[88] These letters, he thought, revealed an ugly truth: "While the liberation of the slave was a mere distant, speculative philanthropy—an utopian vision—it all was well enough to preach a possible emancipation," but when the "extension of the slave power" was at hand, Jefferson wrote "iron words, significant of the hand-cuff and the dungeon-gratings."[89] To Hamilton, Jefferson represented "an oligarchic—aristocratic SLAVE POWER."

It's all there: Jefferson the Deceiver, Jefferson the Demagogue, Jefferson the Slaveholding Aristocrat. Although these charges have ebbed and flowed over time, they've had remarkable staying power. The most recent major Hamilton biography, Chernow's *Hamilton*, strikes these chords and more. The end result is a not-quite-believable, larger-than-life Hamilton.

In part, this is a biographer's risk and right; it's natural to get caught up in the life and reputation of one's historical subject, and—depending on the circumstances—logical to champion that subject's cause. But extol too much and credibility suffers, as John Church Hamilton showed all too well. Balance is everything when unraveling the meaning of a life.

Yet balance seems elusory concerning Hamilton and Jefferson. Both men were so enmeshed in the American experiment, so personally invested in its outcome, so passionately devoted to their worldviews, so skilled at dropping hostile bon mots, and so fundamentally opposed to each other in so many ways, that explaining the logic behind one man's life and career makes it difficult not to denigrate the other. Their seesawing reputations only press that point.

Jefferson has had an easier time of this than Hamilton. Uncomfortable with open displays of power, a spokesman for the rights of the democratic many, he sits more naturally in the American tradition. Hamilton's undisguised admiration of power, his pragmatic eagerness to harness elite interests to those of the state, his unwillingness to woo the masses: on these counts and more, it can be difficult for Americans to embrace him. Current biographical trends—and a Broadway musical—have made it easier, depicting him as a prototypical American immigrant who grew up poor and disadvantaged on the "mean streets" of St. Croix and pulled himself up by his bootstraps to earn acclaim and power. His rise and fall seem inherently American, his life course attuned to modern sensibilities. It's hard to resist the power of this dramatic arc, particularly given our polarized politics and the Trump administration's focus on determining precisely who is—and isn't—American. In some ways, this Alger-esque Hamilton feels like a redemptive anodyne in ugly times. But depicting Hamilton's life as a Horatio Alger success story makes him a man out of time, stripping him of challenges in the context of his time, simplifying and modernizing his ambitions, warping the ambitions and sensibilities of his foes, and—perhaps most noteworthy of all—neglecting the complex ethos and implications of his politics.

This isn't to say that Jefferson's politics aren't problematic. In many ways, the foremost Hamiltonian charges are true. Jefferson *was* a sneaky politician; he understood that government in the American republic was government by "sleight of hand."[90] He *did* court popular approval, keeping a close eye on the American public's mood and desires and acting accordingly. And he *was* an aristocratic slaveholder who managed to cast American democratic ideals in visionary language that people the world over could appreciate for its message. There are many cracks in the armor of Jefferson's reputation, but it's hard to attack him for playing America's democratic game so well.

Hamilton couldn't—wouldn't—play that game, and his reputation has suffered for it. Regardless of his good intentions, his discomfort with democracy generally keeps him at arm's length. Try as one might to claim this failing as a virtue, it's a tough case to make in a democratic republic. Add his penchant for talking too much, pushing too hard, and angering too many, and it's no wonder that his reputation has often been problematic. While Americans of all political stripes honor Jefferson, more often than not, Hamilton has been the sometime friend of a select few.

At present, however, his reputation is riding high, and for good reason. Amid the nation's highly polarized politics, our Hamilton isn't much of a politician at all. He's a blend of modernistic seer and immigrant success story—a spin that appeals to capitalist conservatives and immigrant-friendly liberals alike. He's an uber American who reflects our hopes and fears about American identity. Our Jefferson, on the other hand, bears the weight of our race problems. He is a slaveholder above all else.

And so Hamilton's reputation continues to rise and fall. In 1802, when a dejected Hamilton told Gouverneur Morris that "this American World is not made for me," he knew whereof he spoke. Morris hit the nail on the head in his reply: "I can only say that your Talents, if not your Birth, entitle you to the Rank of an American Citizen."[91] And indeed, even today, Hamilton's talents—not his politics—earn the most applause.

Notes

This essay's title is inspired by Peter Onuf's habit of jokingly referring to Jefferson as "meal ticket."

1. Gouverneur Morris, diary entry, 12–14 July 1804, in *The Diary and Letters of Gouverneur Morris,* ed. Anne Cary Morris, 2 vols. (New York, 1888), 2:456–57, 525–26.

2. Stephen F. Knott, *Alexander Hamilton and the Persistence of Myth* (Lawrence, Kan., 2002), 74, 155, 173, 207. Knott's book is the preeminent study of Hamilton's reputation over time. Hamilton allegedly said this at a dinner party; an alleged dinner guest told someone, who told Massachusetts Federalist Theophilus Parsons, who told his namesake son, who included it in *Memoir of Theophilus Parsons* (Boston, 1859), where Henry Adams read it and included it in *History of the United States of America during the First Administration of Thomas Jefferson,* 2 vols. (New York, 1889), 1:85.

3. Gerald Stourzh, *Alexander Hamilton and the Idea of Republican Government* (Stanford, Calif., 1970), esp. 38–56. See also Michael P. Federici, *The Political Philosophy of Alexander Hamilton* (Baltimore, 2012), esp. 214–37.

4. Douglass Adair, "The Authorship of the Disputed Federalist Papers," *WMQ* 1 (1944): 106, discussing Hamilton's and James Madison's seesawing reputations. See also *Jefferson Image*; Knott, *Alexander Hamilton*; John S. Pancake, *Thomas Jefferson and Alexander Hamilton* (Woodbury, N.Y., 1974), 371–403. On "founder" biography trends, see R. B. Bernstein, *The Founding Fathers Reconsidered* (New York, 2009), 123–43.

5. For an early list, see Paul Leicester Ford, *Bibliotheca Hamiltoniana* (New York, 1886). For the purposes of this essay, monographs that study one aspect of Hamilton's thought aren't counted as biographies.

6. Hamilton to James Bayard, 16 January 1801, in *Alexander Hamilton: Writings,* ed. Joanne B. Freeman (New York, 2001), 977; also Hamilton to Edward Carrington, 26 May 1792, ibid., 751.

7. Hamilton first championed his father in an unfinished four-volume biography. John C. Hamilton, *The Life of Alexander Hamilton,* 2 vols. (New York, 1834, 1840). Two Hamilton biographies predate John C. Hamilton's completed *History of the Republic of the United States of America, as Traced in the Writings of Alexander Hamilton and of his Contemporaries,* 7 vols. (New York, 1857–64): James Renwick's "short sketch" in *Lives of John Jay and Alexander Hamilton* (New York, 1840); and Samuel M. Schmucker, *Life and Times of Alexander Hamilton* (Philadelphia, 1857).

8. On J. C. Hamilton's *History,* see *Jefferson Image,* 224–25.

9. Intended biographers included Reverend John M. Mason, Joseph Hopkinson, Timothy Pickering, Francis Baylies, and Frank Lister Hawks, who ultimately published

an edition of Hamilton's writings. Hawks, a North Carolina Episcopal minister and editor of the *New York Review,* may have attracted Elizabeth Hamilton's notice with his fifty-two-page attack on George Tucker's *Life of Thomas Jefferson* (2 vols. [Philadelphia, 1837]) in the *Review* in 1837. *Jefferson Image,* 127–29; Frank Lister Hawks, *The Official and Other Papers of the Late Major-General Alexander Hamilton* (New York, 1842), iii.

10. On Elizabeth Hamilton's Farewell Address campaign, see Harold C. Syrett, ed., *Papers of Alexander Hamilton,* 27 vols. (New York, 1961–87), 20:169–73; Allan McLane Hamilton, *The Intimate Life of Alexander Hamilton* (New York, 1910), 110–12; Victor Hugo Palsits, *Washington's Farewell Address* (New York, 1935), passim; Rufus King to Charles King, 26 November 1825, and Bushrod Washington to Charles King, 6 October 1825, in *Life and Correspondence of Rufus King,* ed. Charles King, 6 vols. (New York, 1896–97), 6:617–20; James Hamilton, *Reminiscences of James A. Hamilton; or, Men and Events, at Home and Abroad, during Three Quarters of a Century* (New York, 1869), 24–35. For her sworn statement asserting Hamilton's authorship of the address, see Hamilton, *Intimate Life of Alexander Hamilton,* 110–12. In 1825, the Hamiltons sued Rufus King for withholding Hamilton documents concerning the address, but dropped the suit when King surrendered them.

11. James defended his father in *Reminiscences;* Alexander did so in the *New-York Evening Post* in 1829, and sent a threatening letter to William Plumer for suggesting that Hamilton had agreed to attend a meeting in 1804 of New England Federalists contemplating disunion (although Plumer thought that Hamilton planned to *denounce* disunion). John Quincy Adams, diary entry, 27 April 1839, in *Memoirs of John Quincy Adams, Comprising Portions of His Diary From 1795 to 1848,* ed. Charles Francis Adams, 12 vols. (Philadelphia, 1874–77), 8:145; Plumer to Alexander Hamilton Jr., 27 March 1829, and Plumer to John Quincy Adams, 27 March 1829, William Plumer Papers, Lib. Cong.

12. Hamilton, *Life of Alexander Hamilton;* John C. Hamilton, ed., *The Works of Alexander Hamilton,* 7 vols. (New York, 1850–51); Hamilton, *History;* John C. Hamilton, ed., *The Federalist: A Commentary on the Constitution of the United States* (Philadelphia, 1864). On the typeface, see Paul Leicester Ford, ed., *Pamphlets on the Constitution of the United States, Published during its Discussion by the People, 1787–1788* (New York, 1888), 405.

13. On portrait collecting, see *Harper's Bazaar,* 10 August 1878, 507.

14. *Atlantic Monthly* 1 (February 1858): 507–9. *New York Courier and Enquirer* editor James Watson Webb attacked J. C. Hamilton, who credited his father with Washington's wartime achievements. See Webb to Hamilton, 12 January 1857, James Watson Webb Papers, Sterling Memorial Library, Yale University.

15. Hamilton, *History,* 4:iii.

16. Ibid., 3:284–86, 338–39, passim, 4:422, passim. Madison was stunned by what J. C. Hamilton planned to write. Nicholas P. Trist to Martin Van Buren, 31 May 1857, Special Collections Library, University of Virginia. For a recent study of the ways in which Madison *did* revise his notes, see Mary Sarah Bilder, *Madison's Hand: Revising the Constitutional Convention* (Cambridge, Mass., 2015).

17. Hamilton, *History,* 4:110, 217, 463, 3:63, 4:116, 118, 123–24, 497, 417, 3:61, 6:37.

18. "Editors' Table," *Russell's Magazine* 5 (September 1859): 560–62.

19. Randall to Hamilton, 21 December 1853, in Hamilton, *History,* 7:856.

20. Ibid., 6:611; William C. Rives, *History of the Life and Times of James Madison,* 3 vols. (Boston, 1859–70), 1:443. Randall relished his own fight with Hamilton; see Randall to Hugh Blair Grigsby, 8 and 12 March 1858, in "New Letters Between Hugh Blair Grigsby and Henry Stephen Randall, 1858–1861," George Green Shackelford, ed., *VMHB* 64 (1956): 331–35. See also *Jefferson Image,* 149–61; Scott E. Casper, *Constructing American Lives: Biography and Culture in Nineteenth-Century America* (Chapel Hill, N.C., 1999), 186–92.

21. *Atlantic Monthly* 1 (February 1858): 507–9; Greeley to Randall, 18 March 1858, "New Letters," 335–36n.

22. Hamilton, *History,* 7:694.

23. John Torrey Morse Jr., *Life of Alexander Hamilton,* 2 vols. (Boston, 1882 [orig. ed., 1876]), 1:174; Arthur Vandenberg, *The Greatest American: Alexander Hamilton* (New York, 1921), 286; Frederick Scott Oliver, *Alexander Hamilton: An Essay on American Union* (London, 1907), 144–45. On the war's intellectual impact, see Henry Cabot Lodge, *Early Memories* (New York, 1913), 123; *Jefferson Image,* 222–26.

24. Gilded Age biographies also include George Shea, *Life and Epoch of Alexander Hamilton: A Historical Study* (Boston, 1879); Edward S. Ellis, *Alexander Hamilton: A Character Sketch* (Chicago, 1898); William Graham Sumner, *Alexander Hamilton* (New York, 1890); Lewis Boutell, *Alexander Hamilton: The Constructive Statesman* (Chicago, 1890); James Schouler, *Alexander Hamilton* (Boston, 1901); Charles A. Conant, *Alexander Hamilton* (Boston, 1901). See also Knott, *Alexander Hamilton,* 47–84.

25. Henry Cabot Lodge, *Alexander Hamilton* (Boston, 1898), 280.

26. Lodge also edited *The Works of Alexander Hamilton,* 9 vols. (New York, 1885–86).

27. Lodge, *Alexander Hamilton,* 89, 44–45. See also William Widenor, *Henry Cabot Lodge and the Search for an American Foreign Policy* (Berkeley, Calif., 1980); Richard Immerman, *Empire for Liberty: A History of American Imperialism from Benjamin Franklin to Paul Wolfowitz* (Princeton, N. J., 2010), 129–33; *Jefferson Image,* 225–26; Knott, *Alexander Hamilton,* 71–72.

28. Lodge, *Alexander Hamilton,* 280, 147, 81, 63.

29. Henry Cabot Lodge, review of Morse, *Life of Alexander Hamilton, North American Review* 123 (July 1876): 125.

30. Ibid., 115. See also Knott, *Alexander Hamilton,* 70–71. Morse later wrote an unfriendly life of Jefferson for his "American Statesmen" series.

31. Morse, *Life of Alexander Hamilton,* 1:viii.

32. Ibid., 407, 409–10, 414–16, 2:2.

33. On the "Anas," see Joanne B. Freeman, *Affairs of Honor: National Politics in the New Republic* (New Haven, Conn., 2001), 62–104, 269–70, 276–77; *Jefferson Image,* 32–35.

34. Morse, *Life of Alexander Hamilton,* 1:414–16.

35. Oliver, *Alexander Hamilton,* 269.

36. Thomas Jefferson Randolph, ed., *Memoir, Correspondence, and Miscellanies from the Papers of Thomas Jefferson*, 4 vols. (Charlottesville, Va., 1829), 4:447. Also Morse, *Life of Alexander Hamilton*, 1:414–16; Henry Jones Ford, *Alexander Hamilton* (New York, 1920), 264–65; Vandenberg, *Greatest American*, 187; John C. Miller, *Alexander Hamilton: Portrait in Paradox* (New York, 1959), 250; Broadus Mitchell, *Alexander Hamilton: The National Adventure, 1788–1804* (New York, 1962), 82–83; Ron Chernow, *Alexander Hamilton* (New York, 2004), 330. See also Broadus Mitchell, *Alexander Hamilton: Youth to Maturity, 1755–1788* (New York, 1957).

37. Lodge, *Alexander Hamilton*, 125–26.

38. F. S. Oliver to Gertrude Atherton, [undated,] in Gertrude Atherton, *Adventures of a Novelist* (New York, 1932), 461; Gertrude Atherton, *The Conqueror* (New York, 1902). Oliver deeply identified with Hamilton, writing a series of newspaper articles on South African union under the name "Pacificus." John D. Fair, "F. S. Oliver, *Alexander Hamilton*, and the 'American Plan' for Resolving Britain's Constitutional Crisis, 1903–1921," *Twentieth Century British History* 10 (1999): 12. On Hamilton and Oliver's broader goals, see ibid.; Oliver to Gertrude Atherton, [undated,] in Atherton, *Adventures of a Novelist*, 448.

39. Oliver, *Alexander Hamilton*, 461.

40. Fair, "F. S. Oliver," 8, 22. On Oliver's influence in South Africa, see "The Irish Free States and British 'Empire' Defence," *Fortnightly Review* (September 1922): 406 ("Louis Botha was the George Washington, and J. C. Smuts was the Alexander Hamilton"). See also Alvin Jackson, *Home Rule: An Irish History, 1800–2000* (New York, 2003), 187; John Kendle, *Federal Britain: A History* (London, 1997), 81; Richard Jebb, "Twelve Months of Imperial Evolution," *Proceedings of the Royal Colonial Institute* 39 (1907–8): 5–6.

41. Oliver, *Alexander Hamilton*, 5–6; Ford, *Alexander Hamilton*, 355–56; "The Book of the Week," *Outlook*, 2 June 1906, 751. See also "An English View of an American Statesman," ibid., 3 November 1906, 578–79.

42. *Jefferson Image*, 336–39; Knott, *Alexander Hamilton*, 85–99; John M. Cooper Jr., *The Warrior and the Priest: Woodrow Wilson and Theodore Roosevelt* (Cambridge, Mass., 1983), 135; Barry Riccio, *Walter Lippmann: Odyssey of a Liberal* (New Brunswick, N.J., 1994), 62; Walter Lippmann, *Public Opinion* (New York, 1922), 218; Randolph Downes, *The Rise of Warren Gamaliel Harding, 1865–1920* (Columbus, Ohio, 1970), 10; Theodore Roosevelt to Oliver, 9 August 1906, in *Theodore Roosevelt and His Time Shown in His Own Letters,* ed. Joseph Bucklin Bishop, 2 vols. (New York, 1920), 2:22–24.

43. Hamilton biographies published between 1902 and 1939 also include Hamilton, *Intimate Life of Alexander Hamilton;* William S. Culbertson, *Alexander Hamilton: An Essay* (New Haven, Conn., 1911); Ford, *Alexander Hamilton*; Robert Irving Warshow, *Alexander Hamilton: First American Business Man* (New York, 1931); Clifford Smyth, *Alexander Hamilton, the Little Lion of the Treasury* (New York, 1931); Johan J. Smertenko, *Alexander Hamilton* (New York, 1932); Ralph Edward Bailey, *An American Colossus: The Singular Career of Alexander Hamilton* (Boston, 1933); David Loth, *Alexander Hamilton: Portrait of a Prodigy* (New York, 1939).

44. Atherton, review of Oliver, *Alexander Hamilton, North American Review* 183 (7 September 1906): 404.

45. Gertrude Atherton, "The Hunt for Hamilton's Mother," *North American Review* 175 (August 1902): 229–42, quote at 229; Knott, *Alexander Hamilton*, 85–86.

46. Roosevelt to Gouverneur Morris, 28 November 1910, in *The Many Faces of Alexander Hamilton: The Life and Legacy of America's Most Elusive Founding Father*, ed. Douglas Ambrose and Robert W. T. Martin (New York, 2007), 37; Justin Wintle and Richard Kenin, eds., *The Dictionary of Biographical Quotation of British and American Subjects* (London, 1978), 354.

47. Atherton, *Conqueror*, ix; Atherton, *Adventures of a Novelist*, 316. On Atherton and the address, see ibid., 317; Hamilton's grandson showed her documents proving Hamilton's authorship. On Atherton's Caribbean research, see ibid., 316–39.

48. Frederick James Gregg, "Mrs. Gertrude Atherton's 'Flexible Manner,'" *The Book Buyer: A Review and Record of Current Literature* 3 (April 1902): 219–20. For positive reviews (provided by Atherton), see Atherton, *Adventures of a Novelist*, 345–46.

49. Atherton, review of Oliver, *Alexander Hamilton*, 404. See also John C. Rose, "Hamilton the Democrat," *Weekly Review* 2 (30 June 1920): 678–79.

50. Culbertson, *Alexander Hamilton*, 8; *Jefferson Image*, 333–46.

51. Oliver, *Alexander Hamilton*, 121; Lodge, *Alexander Hamilton*, 275–76.

52. Hamilton, *Intimate Life of Alexander Hamilton*, 49, 299.

53. See also Christopher J. Riethmuller, *Alexander Hamilton and His Contemporaries, or, Rise of the American Constitution* (London, 1864), 430–32.

54. Oliver, *Alexander Hamilton*, 254–57.

55. Ibid., 279.

56. Ibid., 251–53; Atherton, *Conqueror*, 345. British minister Anthony Merry accused Jefferson of "utter slovenliness." After visiting Jefferson, Daniel Webster and Mahlon Dickerson noted that his clothes *weren't* slovenly, suggesting that they expected otherwise. (Webster described Jefferson's clothes as "very much neglected.") Josiah Quincy, diary entry, January 1806, in Edmund Quincy, *Life of Josiah Quincy* (Boston, 1869), 92–93; Webster, [Memorandum of Mr. Jefferson's conversations,] December 1824, in *The Writings and Speeches of Daniel Webster*, 18 vols. (Boston, 1903), 17:364; Dickerson to Silas Dickerson, 21 April 1802, in *Letters of the Lewis and Clark Expedition, with Related Documents, 1783–1854*, ed. Donald Dean Jackson, 2 vols. (Urbana, Ill., 1978), 2:677. See also 10 November 1804, *William Plumer's Memorandum of Proceedings in the United States Senate, 1803–1807* (New York, 1923), 193 and passim.

57. Oliver, *Alexander Hamilton*, 251–53.

58. Ibid., 252; Atherton, *Conqueror*, 345. Chernow calls Jefferson's clothes "almost sloppy." Chernow, *Alexander Hamilton*, 311.

59. Oliver, *Alexander Hamilton*, 251–53, 258–59.

60. Vandenberg, *Greatest American*, 55, 118, xvi. Hamilton's sole fan was Myron Herrick, ex-governor of Ohio and ambassador to France.

61. Ibid., 102.

62. Oliver, *Alexander Hamilton,* 121, 256–57.

63. Lodge, *Alexander Hamilton,* 275–76, 280.

64. Oliver, *Alexander Hamilton,* 256–57.

65. Ibid., 5–6; Sumner, *Alexander Hamilton,* iii; Vandenberg, *Greatest American.* See also Schmucker, *Life and Times of Alexander Hamilton*; Ford, *Alexander Hamilton*; Forrest McDonald, *Alexander Hamilton: A Biography* (New York, 1979).

66. Oliver, *Alexander Hamilton,* 256–57.

67. Biographies published between 1946 and 2007 also include Nathan Schachner, *Alexander Hamilton* (New York, 1946); Stuart G. Brown, *Alexander Hamilton* (New York, 1967); Robert A. Hendrickson, *Hamilton* (New York, 1976); James Thomas Flexner, *The Young Hamilton: A Biography* (Boston, 1978); Robert A. Hendrickson, *The Rise and Fall of Alexander Hamilton* (New York, 1981); Jacob Ernest Cooke, *Alexander Hamilton* (New York, 1982); Marie B. Hecht, *Odd Destiny: The Life of Alexander Hamilton* (New York, 1982); Noemie Emery, *Alexander Hamilton: An Intimate Portrait* (New York, 1982); Richard Brookhiser, *Alexander Hamilton: American* (New York, 1999); Willard Sterne Randall, *Alexander Hamilton: A Life* (New York, 2003); Joseph A. Murray, *Alexander Hamilton: America's Forgotten Founder* (New York, 2007). Children's and young adult books include Milton Lomask, *Odd Destiny: A Life of Alexander Hamilton* (New York, 1969); Steven O'Brien, *Alexander Hamilton* (New York, 1989); Nancy Whitelaw, *More Perfect Union: The Story of Alexander Hamilton* (Greensboro, N.C., 1997); Stuart A. Kallen, *Alexander Hamilton* (Edina, Minn., 2001).

68. Knott, *Alexander Hamilton,* 113. On Hamilton's crash, see ibid., 113–40.

69. See also *Jefferson Image,* 347–55.

70. Hamilton commemorators claimed 1757 as the year of Hamilton's birth, but he may have been born in 1755.

71. Louis M. Hacker, *Alexander Hamilton in the American Tradition* (New York, 1957), 6–7, 253. See also Knott, *Alexander Hamilton,* 149–50.

72. Miller, *Alexander Hamilton,* 249; Cooke, *Alexander Hamilton,* 109, 115, 122; Chernow, *Alexander Hamilton,* 312. Brookhiser makes the same point with the word "squire," as does McDonald by referencing the "Virginia oligarchy." Brookhiser, *Alexander Hamilton,* 79; McDonald, *Alexander Hamilton,* 212.

73. Mitchell, *Alexander Hamilton: The National Adventure,* 513.

74. Cooke, *Alexander Hamilton,* 115. See also Knott, *Alexander Hamilton,* 196–98.

75. McDonald, *Alexander Hamilton,* 212; Miller, *Alexander Hamilton,* 314.

76. McDonald, "The Founding Fathers and the Economic Order," speech delivered to Economic Club of Indianapolis, 19 April 2006, http://oll.libertyfund.org/index.php?Itemid=267&id=177&option=com_content&task=view. See also Knott, *Alexander Hamilton,* 185–87.

77. Knott, *Alexander Hamilton,* 150; Mitchell, *Alexander Hamilton: The National Adventure,* 218, 545.

78. Daniel Joseph Singal, "Broadus Mitchell and the Persistence of New South Thought," *Journal of Southern History* 45 (1979): 378–79; Broadus Mitchell, "American

Radicals Nobody Knows," *South Atlantic Quarterly* 34 (1935): 394–401. See also Stephen Kurtz's review of Mitchell, *Alexander Hamilton: The National Adventure, Political Science Quarterly* 78 (1963): 465–67.

79. Mitchell, review of McDonald, *Alexander Hamilton, Presidential Studies Quarterly* 10 (1980): 498–99.

80. McDonald, *Alexander Hamilton,* 362.

81. Mitchell, review of McDonald, *Alexander Hamilton;* Singal, "Broadus Mitchell." Remarkably (but revealingly), Mitchell deemed McDonald's *highly* partial biography impartial.

82. Brookhiser, *Alexander Hamilton,* and Chernow, *Alexander Hamilton,* seem to be the first Hamilton biographies to mention Hemings.

83. Mitchell, *Alexander Hamilton: The National Adventure,* 118.

84. McDonald, *Alexander Hamilton,* 212.

85. Chernow, *Alexander Hamilton,* 326.

86. Ibid., 210–16, 580–82; Miller, *Alexander Hamilton,* 122; McDonald, *Alexander Hamilton,* 34, 177. See also James Oliver Horton, "Alexander Hamilton: Slavery and Race in a Revolutionary Generation," *New-York Journal of American History* 3 (2004): 16–24; Rob Weston, "Alexander Hamilton and the Abolition of Slavery in New York," *Afro-Americans in New York Life and History* 18 (1994): 31–45; David Gellman, "The Problem of Abolition in the Age of Nation Building: New York's Founding Fathers Reconsidered," lecture at New-York Historical Society, 10 December 2004; Shane White, *Somewhat More Independent: The End of Slavery in New York City, 1770–1810* (Athens, Ga., 1991). *Papers of Alexander Hamilton* editor Harold C. Syrett accused McDonald of exaggerating Hamilton's abolitionism. Syrett, review of McDonald, *Alexander Hamilton, JAH* 67 (1981): 911–13; see also Michael Chan, "Alexander Hamilton on Slavery," *Review of Politics* 66 (2004): 507–31.

87. *Washington Chronicle,* 2 February 1869, in H. Rpt. 31, Select Committee on Alleged New York Election Frauds, "Alleged New York Election Frauds," 40th Cong., 3d sess. (Washington, D.C.: Government Printing Office, 1869), 91n.

88. Jefferson to Joseph C. Cabell, 31 January 1821; Jefferson to Breckenridge, 15 February 1821, in Randolph, *Memoir, Correspondence, and Miscellanies,* 4:341–43.

89. John Church Hamilton, *The Slave Power: Its Heresies and Injuries to the American People* (New York, 1864), 2–3.

90. *New York Journal,* 16 November 1791.

91. Hamilton to Morris, 29 February 1802; Morris to Hamilton, 11 March 1802, in Syrett, *Papers of Alexander Hamilton,* 25:545, 560.

III History

8   Consulting the Timeless Oracle

The Thomas Jeffersons of Claude Bowers and Albert Jay Nock

BRIAN STEELE

Jefferson would long regret that the Federalists had beaten the Republicans in the race to produce a history that would shape the public's memory of the 1790s. The Republicans, he said, had been foolishly "depending on truth to make itself known, while history is taking a contrary set which may become too inveterate for correction." For Jefferson, *history* ought always to be aligned with *truth,* but he knew the two were always in potential tension. In particular, he understood that historians could shape narratives about the past in ways that might obscure the truth, particularly if political motives nudged them in one direction or the other. Unfortunately, Jefferson believed, Republicans had been "too careless of our future reputation, while our tories will omit nothing to place us in the wrong." Already John Marshall's *Life of Washington,* which Jefferson called a "five-volumed libel," was casting its dark design over the opinions of the public.[1]

Marshall's work, Jefferson believed, deceived in two distinct ways. First, by mischaracterizing Jefferson's Republicans as primarily animated by hostility to federal authority, national dignity, and union (as well as a near-treasonous attachment to France), it ignored what Jefferson considered the true sources of party conflict: Republican determination to preserve the Republic founded in 1776 against Federalist dreams of converting it into a monarchy on the British model. Second, it miscast Jefferson as a two-faced schemer who so much craved power that, to obtain it, he cultivated a deceptive image of himself as a reluctant statesman who preferred over public life his family, his farm, and his books. Marshall's biography, Jefferson argued, "pretends to have been compiled from authentic and unpublished documents." But history, he knew, could "be made to wear any hue, with which the passions of the compiler, royalist or republican, may chuse to tinge it."[2] "History," Jefferson later noted, "may distort truth, and will distort it for a time, by the superior efforts at justification of those who are conscious of needing it most."[3]

As early as 1802, Jefferson began looking for ways to challenge Federalist distortions, primarily through the encouragement of alternate Republican histories of the 1790s. Such histories would tell the truth by describing the party conflict precisely as Jefferson would: a contest between the forces of republicanism and Americanism on the one side and those of monarchy, aristocracy, priestcraft, and Anglomania on the other; between the popular majority and the self-interested minority. Similarly, they would portray his role as he had taken care to play it. Seeking neither glory nor power, and with great reluctance, he had abandoned his private pursuits of happiness to rescue fellow citizens from a counterrevolutionary "reign of witches."[4]

Despite Jefferson's efforts, during his lifetime a powerful Republican antidote to the histories of Marshall and other Federalist writers never quite materialized. If he had been able to hold on for another century, however, he might very well have been pleased with both Claude Bowers's 1925 *Jefferson and Hamilton: The Struggle for Democracy in America* and Albert Jay Nock's 1926 *Jefferson.* In some respects, these books were as different as the authors who wrote them. On the other hand, each addressed what Jefferson considered a significant failure of Federalist historiography. While Bowers, in the first installment of what would grow to a three-volume study of Jefferson's life, corrected Marshall's mischaracterization of the struggle of the 1790s, Nock dramatically revised Marshall's portrayal of Jefferson as an ambitious man with a thirst for power. Yet, for all their success in attending to Jefferson's late-life anxieties about Federalist historiography (itself a questionable project for a historian), each writer to no inconsiderable degree considered himself to be waging Jefferson's own battles in the twentieth century. In the process, each also projected onto Jefferson, perhaps inadvertently, his own (very different) ideological imperatives in a world that Jefferson could not have imagined.

As a high school senior in 1898, Bowers won the Indiana High School Oratorical Contest with a speech about Alexander Hamilton, preparation for which led him, paradoxically, to a lifelong admiration of Jefferson.[5] After graduation, he became a Democratic Party operative and columnist who spent his life tirelessly weaving a narrative continuity—spiritual and actual—between the party Jefferson formed and the one he himself served to his last days.

For Bowers, Jefferson's legacy would be carried and perpetuated—as it had always been, he thought—by the Democrats. In 1900, when he was twenty, he published two articles that struck the note he would hold throughout his long career: the Jefferson-Hamilton struggle not only shaped the early republic but remained the fundamental struggle of American politics and thought. The syllogism went something like this: Jefferson, he asserted, "was as unlike Hamilton as democracy is unlike aristocracy." The present Republicans, the party of the trusts, were obviously hostile to "the people." Therefore, the Democrats must be the party of Jefferson, and the current Republican worldview could be traced directly back to the source of all hostility to democracy in America: "Hamiltonian plutocracy." Accordingly, only "Jeffersonian democracy," Bowers insisted, "will yet blot from the statutes that class legislation which breeds monopoly."[6]

Bowers never really deviated from this line, and his 1925 book—combined with his speeches from the 1920s—is a continuation of the same story he told in those periodical pieces from the turn of the century. He wrote his history books in a way he considered faithful to the truth, but also to lend scholarly support to Democratic Party claims on American affections.[7] The goal was always to ensure that Democrats in the twentieth century would continue to hold their heads high as the party of Jefferson.[8]

It was in his oratory—for which he became known and widely sought—that he made these connections most explicit. In his 1924 Jackson Day speech, Bowers insisted that "there is scarcely a domestic issue that Jefferson thought for and Jackson fought for and Wilson wrought for that is not a vital living issue at this hour."[9] In an era of political apathy and declining party affiliation in which the Democrats were nominating for the office of chief executive men who could compete with Calvin Coolidge for conservatism, Bowers saw it as his mission to remind Democrats what made them unique.[10] The bottom line was that they had always stood "for democracy and against the oligarchy of a privileged class." This struggle, Bowers asserted, remained the fundamental issue of all American politics.[11] If you supported the people, you were with Jefferson; and if you were with Jefferson, you had to be a Democrat with a capital "D." In *Jefferson and Hamilton*, Bowers told his readers that the basic story of the 1790s revolved around the question of whether the United States would be "not only a republic, but a democratic republic." "That," he insisted, "was the real issue between Jefferson and Hamilton." Their dispute was a "clear-cut fight between democracy and aristocracy."[12]

For Bowers, who wrote history in the heroic vein, the battle ultimately boiled down to the conflict between these two great representatives of opposing historical forces. Hamilton was great, "Homeric," even, as Bowers later put it in his 1936 *Jefferson in Power*, and "no Federalist" after him would be worthy "to wear his mantle or to wield his mighty sword." He had no patience with the Federalist leaders who toyed with "treason" and "secession" during Jefferson's presidency and led the party to its "death struggle."[13] Hamilton's flaw, and what differentiated him from Jefferson, was "his lack of sympathy for, and understanding of, the American spirit." Bowers endorsed Hamilton's own assessment that the "American world" simply "was not made for" him, and Adams's that Hamilton was "ignorant of the character of this nation."[14] Because Hamilton was "temperamentally hostile to democracy," and, like other Federalists, "neither had nor sought contact with the average man," he naturally strove to create "an alliance between government and men of wealth."[15] No conspiracy theory was necessary to explain his financial program of privileging the moneyed minority: there really was "nothing diabolical" about it. His worldview quite naturally dictated his policy.[16]

While Bowers's depiction of Hamilton's hostility to the Constitution, his preference for monarchy, and his complete lack of comprehension of the American people more or less replicated the analysis offered up in Jefferson's "Anas," Bowers's "portrait" of Jefferson offered the precise contrast.[17] Since Jefferson's father was an "ardent Whig with advanced democratic ideas" who "manifested sympathy for the plain people," Jefferson's affinity for "democracy was inherent." He arrived in Williamsburg—"the headquarters of the aristocracy"—immediately identified himself with the "growing democratic movement of small farmers," and spent his college years "burnishing his weapons for the fight."[18]

Jefferson's sympathy for the common man is so prominent in this account that Bowers even found a kind of significance in the fact that he wrote the Declaration of Independence "in the house of a bricklayer." By the time Jefferson finished his reforms in Virginia (through which he became "the first American to invite the hate of a class") he had "made himself," Bowers insisted, "one of the foremost democrats of all times."[19]

Well before he encountered Hamilton, Bowers maintained, Jefferson was animated by an entirely different rationale and set of convictions: devoted to democracy, Jefferson was completely in tune with the very American "spirit" that Hamilton never understood. This was an argument Bowers would later extend with his 1945 *Young Jefferson,* which insisted that Jefferson's democratic vision for America "had been thought out, formulated, and clearly and concisely expressed before the establishment of the Constitution," and certainly well "before the inauguration of Washington."[20] No wonder, then, that when he arrived in New York in March 1790 and learned about Hamilton's plans to ingratiate the rich and powerful, he went right to work mobilizing a party to "harness" the "fervent spirit of democracy running through the land."[21] Mobilization was essential, Bowers argued, for the people, although democratic in sentiment, were not ready to resist Federalists who had wealth and power on their side. The problem Jefferson faced was "how to reach, galvanize, vitalize, organize this great widely scattered mass of unimportant, inarticulate individuals."[22]

Fortunately, Bowers's Jefferson was a "master politician." Bowers was insistent that the very traits the Federalists—and later historians who admired them—condemned as duplicitous in Jefferson were actually assets, and he turned all of what had been read as Jefferson's character flaws into virtues. Bowers's Jefferson was rarely naive about power or shy about using it. His "working under cover," which "enraged his foes" and "enrages them still," Bowers called "cleverness." If political attacks ostensibly orchestrated by his "lieutenants" were "so often traced finally to Jefferson," if "he was as elusive as a shadow," this only meant that he had made himself "difficult to trap." What Federalist historians labeled "sneaking under-hand methods" Bowers called "artfulness."

Jefferson turned out to be "a master in the personal management of men." He knew them "at a glance," Bowers insisted, and consequently "never had to raise his voice to get his junior officers to act." He was, Bowers wrote, "the first 'easy boss' in American politics."[23] Jefferson "was without a peer in the mastery of men. He intuitively knew men, and when bent upon it could usually bend them to his will." His Jefferson "was a psychologist and could easily probe the minds and hearts of those he met." He was also unparalleled in his knowledge of "mass psychology," for "when a measure was passed or a policy adopted in Philadelphia, he knew the reactions in the woods of Georgia without waiting for letters." Jefferson "had a genius for gently and imperceptibly insinuating his own views into the minds of others and leaving them with the impression that they had conceived the ideas and convinced Jefferson."

If to some "he seemed motionless, it was because by a nod or look he had put his forces on the march." But he was no "'Miss Nancy' or . . . 'Sister Sue.'" He was "a stickler for party regularity" and was the "first consummate practical politician of the Republic." You would never catch Jefferson "underestimat[ing] the foe." Because "he was not an idealist in his methods," "his enemies" charged him with dishonesty. But Bowers exalted the role of the pragmatic politician. It was not something to shrink from, and his Jefferson never did, for "he was hard-headed and looked clear-eyed at the realities about him. He was cunning, for without cunning he could not have overcome a foe so powerfully entrenched." The Federalists hated his savvy, but of course they did; no one enjoyed being foiled again and again.[24] By 1800, Bowers informed his readers, Jefferson's "work was done." He could return "to his beloved hilltop" confident that he had so perfectly "created the machinery, trained the mechanics, supplied the munitions of victory," and "found means for financing the enterprise," that he could leave "the work" of the campaign "with his lieutenants."[25] The seemingly spontaneous "Revolution of 1800" had been carefully managed.

Consistent with his goal of "re-creat[ing] . . . an heroic, picturesque, and lusty age," Bowers's narrative is replete with military metaphors and overly dramatized descriptions of the familiar events of the 1790s.[26] His Federalists are fanatical in their passion against democracy. Federalist "Hysterics"—the title of one chapter—led to the Adams administration's "Reign of Terror"— the title of another: "'Heads, more heads!' screamed Marat from his tub. 'Heads, more heads!' echoed Pickering from his office."[27] In a later essay, Bowers described the Alien and Sedition Acts as an effort "to make the individual a mere cog in the machinery of a police State" and said that the last two years of the Adams administration saw "storm troopers, not unlike those of Hitler, roam[ing] the country." "Yes," Bowers intoned, "for two years we were setting the pattern for the Stalin's, the Hitler's, and the Mussolini's."[28] (His 1936 *Jefferson in Power* observed with no little satisfaction that, after Jefferson assumed office, "citizens . . . were . . . no longer . . . dragged from their beds at midnight and carried into the country through the rain to be cast into loathsome cells because of criticism of those in power."[29]) It seems worth noting that most reviewers in professional journals thought Bowers's book was the best scholarly treatment of the 1790s to date and seemed on the whole more impressed than put off by the vivid style that assaults our perhaps more jaded sensibilities as melodramatic. But what is not to be missed is Bowers's central contention: that Jefferson and Hamilton fought in the eighteenth century the opening salvo of a battle that, even in the twentieth century, continued to rage in American political life so that, as he put it in the book's last sentence, the "spirits of Jefferson and Hamilton still stalk the ways of men—still fighting."[30]

No wonder Franklin Roosevelt was "breathless" when he put the book down. For those disposed to hear his message, Bowers had done more than retell the story of the 1790s; he had clearly explained the current political moment—one of triumph for Republicans and lethargy for Democrats. Yes, Roosevelt added in his admiring review of the book, the "same contending forces" seemed again to be "mobilizing" for war. "Hamiltons we have today." That much was clear. "Is there," he wondered, "a Jefferson on the horizon?"[31] What Roosevelt seemed to have learned from Bowers (who got an ambassadorship out of it when Roosevelt became president years later) was how to think about current politics in terms of historical continuities.[32] Bowers taught Roosevelt two broad lessons. The first was that the political struggles of the 1920s were in their essence the same as those of the 1790s. Roosevelt acknowledged his new awareness, telling a friend shortly after his review appeared that "we are approaching a period similar to that from 1790–1800 when Alexander Hamilton ran the federal government for the primary good of the chambers of commerce, the speculators and the inside ring of the national government." The second lesson was logically implied in the first: Jefferson's "principles," as Roosevelt told a radio audience in April 1930, were "as applicable today as they were in the early days of the country." Such a message seemed calculated to offer hope to Democrats beleaguered by the 1920s, an age of declining political engagement that witnessed a sharp drop in party identification, a time of hostility to public oversight of private power that witnessed the exaltation of big business, the increasingly uneven distribution of wealth, and the rise of oligopoly. If, in the face of Hamiltonian plutocracy, Jefferson "brought the government back to the hands of the average voter," as Roosevelt put it, then surely his day's Democrats—if they were still committed to Jefferson's principles—could strip power from the interests and hand it back to the people.[33]

Bowers thanked Roosevelt for his review, telling him that he had understood his exact intentions. His book aimed "to recall the party of Jefferson to the real meaning of Jeffersonian Democracy."[34] In 1925, possibly in response to his reading of Bowers, Roosevelt wrote an open letter to Democratic Party leaders in which he called for the restoration of "the clear line of demarcation which differentiated the political thought of Jefferson on the one side, and of Hamilton on the other." Democrats had to claim Jefferson's mantle, to begin once again to "make it clear that" their party "seeks primarily the good of the average citizen through the free rule of the whole electorate, as opposed to the Republican party which seeks a mere moneyed prosperity of the nation through the control of government by a self-appointed aristocracy of wealth and of social and economic power."[35]

In his keynote address to the 1928 Democratic convention in Houston, Bowers reiterated these themes, telling the assembled delegates that "there is not a major evil of which the American people are complaining now that is not due to the triumph of the Hamiltonian conception of the state." The solution was as clear as the diagnosis: "The people must determine whether they will entrust their interest to those who believe that governments are strong in proportion as they are made profitable to the powerful or to the Jeffersonians, who believe that governments are created for the service of mankind."[36]

Roosevelt's review of Bowers may have been the most famous—and ultimately consequential. But perhaps the most insightful and provocative was by an elusive social critic whose own book on Jefferson would be published just a few months after Bowers's appeared. Albert Jay Nock noted that the book placed Bowers "in the front rank of archivist-journalist historians," which, coming from Nock, was less a compliment than it might have first appeared.[37] The book, he wrote, was "as accurate as any piece of journalism could and should be." But such an approach remained inadequate, for it was "only by a sheer journalistic convention" that "the struggle of 1790–1800" could "be represented as a struggle for democracy." Instead, Nock viewed the contest as "between a debtor and producing class, largely agrarian, and a monopolist-capitalist exploiting class." For good measure, Nock wanted it to be known that, notwithstanding Bowers's claims to the contrary, "there was never a struggle for democracy in all our history." Nock thus artfully undermined the first major premise of Bowers's book. But he was hardly finished. For "the view of Mr. Jefferson as a most astute and adroit machine politician, manipulator, organizer, party manager, is purely conventional, and Mr. Bowers has laid much more stress on it than the facts warrant." Nock insisted that he was offering the reader only "two or three grains of salt" with which to digest Bowers's book. But, in reality, he had dismissed everything that made Bowers's Jefferson distinctive and presaged his own— entirely different—account of Jefferson.[38]

For his part, Bowers, who reviewed Nock's own *Jefferson* the following year, seemed to have trouble placing Nock's approach. And for good reason. Nock's book was clearly an appreciation of sorts, but his Jefferson bore little relation to Bowers's or anyone else's, precisely. He noted that Nock's was an "economic interpretation" of the period, but was not quite sure what to make of that except to say that "the writer is evidently impatient of politics." Bowers was more comfortable noting that Nock's Jefferson "emerges distinctly as the champion of the producers against the exploiters." Yet Nock had failed "to appreciate his subject's consummate genius as a political leader, propagandist, organizer, and drill master," but, he conceded, as a friendly explanation for Nock's apparent ignorance of much of what Bowers considered important, Nock was simply "not concerned with that phase."[39] Bowers was more generous to Nock than Nock had been to him, admitting that a focus on the illustrious political career had often blinded historians to Jefferson's "cultural brilliance" and the "ineffable charm of his personality." But he may have missed Nock's point, which was not simply to describe a different aspect of Jefferson that interested him but to say that Jefferson himself was, in point of fact, not at all "concerned with" the "phase" on which Bowers rested his entire reading. Dumas Malone's summary was much closer to the target. "The real Jefferson" in Nock's portrait, Malone wrote, was the private Jefferson, the "man of science," uncomfortable and "reluctant" to participate in politics, "accidental" as a statesman, and not really a "doctrinaire" democrat at all.[40] Indeed, Nock's goal, as he told a friend around the time of publication of his own *Jefferson,* was nothing less than to "quietly and persistently undermine . . . the strongholds of superstition" in Jefferson scholarship, and the superstitions he was interested in undermining would be precisely those that Bowers held dear.[41]

Unlike Bowers, who maintained a fundamental faith in the American political system and a fairly consistent stance throughout his life, Nock, by the time he came to write his book, was a deeply disillusioned progressive who was on the verge of losing faith with American politics and with the American public itself, trying desperately—in the end, unsuccessfully—to maintain hope without cynicism in the face of open-eyed analysis.[42] A former Episcopal priest who had abandoned the ministry, Nock had spent a couple of decades in reformist journalism writing for the *Atlantic,* the *Nation,* the *American Magazine,* and, eventually, editing his own magazine, the *Freeman.* In his early work, Nock displayed the progressive's sense that something was deeply wrong with the world. His 1915 essay, "Peace, the Aristocrat," described the miserable lives of the American working class in sympathetic terms on its way to a powerful critique of the pacifist movement, with which Nock nevertheless remained in sympathy. Pacifists would never get much support from the masses as long as the working class remained so downgraded. War, he said, was simply a much more interesting alternative to most of them than a peace in which they were simply exploited labor. War offered the prospect of equality and purpose, as well as a cleaning of the slate, a fresh start. So "the first practical step toward permanent peace," Nock argued, "is to bring about a more diffused material well-being." Peace, he said, was no doubt "very interesting" to Andrew Carnegie. But it could never "compete with war for the suffrage of such as can, by the hardest work, earn no more than two dollars a day" in one of Carnegie's factories.[43] In a trenchant 1913 essay on a lynching in Coatesville, Pennsylvania, Nock made clear his sense that the "industrial system" itself was responsible for "producing" what he called "*an upper class materialized, a middle class vulgarized, a lower class brutalized.*" Civilization, he said, depended on "a diffused material well-being." Without it, racial hostility and brutality were simply to be expected. Even the prosecution of the perpetrators of the murder would not resolve the underlying problem that had led to the crime.[44]

Nock's caution about state interference had always kept him from proposing anything in the way of general solutions outside of championing Henry George's single tax on land value, itself designed specifically to reduce economic inequality without an increase in government bureaucracy.[45] Eventually, Nock's hostility to the state became the primary impulse trumping his initial concern for the condition of the working class, his sympathetic analysis of the material deprivation of the poor replaced by a disdain for their lack of taste and judgment. Increasingly convinced that more government resulted in less liberty, popular support for Woodrow Wilson's world war and then Franklin Roosevelt's New Deal drove him to despair. By 1936, the world was, for him, divided into "the masses"—who have "neither the force of intellect to apprehend the principles issuing in what we know as the humane life, nor the force of character to adhere to those principles steadily and strictly as laws of conduct"—and those he called "the Remnant," people "who by force of intellect are able to apprehend these principles, and by force of character are able, at least measurably, to cleave to them."[46] And even this was a kinder, gentler way of describing what essentially descended into a bemused misanthropy not only skeptical about whether most humans were capable of progress and self-government, but comfortable wondering whether most *Homo sapiens* possessed any humanity at all.[47]

So his book on Jefferson was written in the midst of a significant transition in his thought, which had never been particularly systematic or always even consistent. If Bowers crafted a Jefferson that could energize and serve the aims of a political party (*Jefferson in Power,* the second installment of his trilogy, appeared in time for Roosevelt's 1936 reelection), Nock portrayed Jefferson as an anarchist individualist who was more interested in the cultivated life than in public service. He was also faintly elitist: radical but, as Nock once wrote admiringly, possessing "Tory manners." A Jefferson, in other words, in Nock's own image.[48]

If Bowers's Jefferson showed up in Williamsburg looking for a fight with the aristocracy, Nock's found there the company of a small circle of like-minded seekers of the good life who considered themselves "marooned" in the otherwise "rather dull" atmosphere of the capital. Bowers's Jefferson spent his college years preparing for political life; Nock's Jefferson spent fifteen hours per day studying, resisting any pressure to hang out with the ordinary people of the town, sharing Nock's own distaste for law and politics, and sharply distinguishing justice from the practice of law. Nock's Jefferson went to France because he thought the few light duties required of a diplomat might afford him the leisure essential to the pursuit of science and art. "More or less against the government under any and all circumstances," Nock's Jefferson assumed that "the true business of life . . . lay outside the routine of politics and diplomacy." While Bowers's Jefferson was a master in the drawing room or at the dinner table, a gregarious manipulator of men, Nock's Jefferson had little time or interest in "leadership" and was "alone in spirit [even] when he had company about him."[49]

Bowers's Jefferson was a strict disciplinarian and "stickler for party regularity." Nock's wouldn't even "go to heaven" if he had to do so "with a party" since he had, as Jefferson put it in a line Nock appreciated, "never submitted the whole system of my opinions to the creed of any party of men whatever."[50] Where Bowers's Jefferson was quick to size up the political situation upon his arrival in New York, Nock's was "slow to apprehend" the implications of the Constitution much less the cunning of Hamilton. Nock's Jefferson simply did not understand the fundamental issues at stake in the 1790s; he tended to focus on the superficial trappings (Hamilton's alleged preference for monarchy and his Anglomania, for example) and ignore the underlying economic rationale of the Federalist program, which was, Nock echoed Charles Beard, designed to use the government to serve the interests of financiers and speculators. Jefferson represented the class interest of producers but without much consciousness of doing so. His opposition to Hamilton was instinctual and procedural rather than informed by an understanding of competing interests. He was hardly the "master politician" of Bowers's story. Bowers's Jefferson was committed to an ideology of democratic freedom that led in obvious policy directions; Nock's had a class interest that made him remarkably flexible with policy.[51] In any case, his conflict with Hamilton had almost nothing to do with democracy; he was barely more democratic than Hamilton, and his educational policies were animated by an elitist bias that Nock found particularly refreshing. Nock never tired of repeating Jefferson's line describing his educational program as a raking of genius from the "rubbish" of ordinary citizens.[52]

If Bowers's Jefferson was always ready for political combat, Nock's "always" lost in cabinet discussions because "contention of any kind was distasteful to him, as having at best a touch of vulgarity about it."[53] Bowers's Jefferson was a natural leader; Nock's found himself in leadership roles "quite alien to his natural bent" and, like Nock himself, "loathed and shunned" the prospect of holding "power over others."[54] And "the one public office that exactly suited him" was the one Jefferson told Benjamin Rush would "give me philosophical evenings in the winter, and rural days in summer": he was, Nock observed, "a born Vice-President."[55] Bowers's Jefferson fought to restore the government to the service of the people; Nock's found himself in charge of a state that would continue to be the instrument for the exclusive benefit of an economic class.[56] Bowers's Jefferson, the "architect of American ideals," stood for everything that made America worth fighting for. Nock's was a voice in the wilderness of American Babbitry. Jefferson, Nock wrote in 1930, formulated "the doctrine that should have been Americanism, but never was."[57]

Although Merrill Peterson later called Nock's biography the "more enduring" of the two classics, he did not endorse Nock's portrait wholesale or dismiss the significance of Bowers's work.[58] As Peterson noted, Bowers's book on Jefferson—and, in particular, its appropriation by Roosevelt—in many ways made the later appreciation of Nock's portrait possible. Peterson suggested that Bowers, in offering a mythology that would resurrect for Democrats an "awareness of the elemental differences between them and the Republicans," freed Franklin Roosevelt, paradoxically perhaps, to embrace a less partisan Jefferson who could now stand as an exemplar of American values and the embodiment of national aspirations.[59] A less partisan Jefferson would transform the early republic into not only hallowed but also safe ground for all Americans.

Roosevelt signaled this transition at the 1932 Jefferson Day dinner where he noted that, "while economic changes of a century have changed the necessary methods of government action, the principles of that action are still wholly [Jefferson's] own."[60] Roosevelt implied that all those committed to Jeffersonian ends might join in pursuing them by whatever means emerged in the course of deliberation. True to this projection, Roosevelt began working to create a new progressive coalition that to some degree undermined the regular party organization, making Bowers and many other Democrats, with their traditional views of party loyalty, instantly "Old."[61] Only one year into his administration, Roosevelt declined participation in the 1934 Jefferson Day dinner itself precisely because "the recovery and reconstruction program is being accomplished by men and women of all parties." "I have," he noted, "repeatedly appealed to Republicans as much as to Democrats to do their part." Roosevelt now insisted, in a kind of epitaph for Bowers's inclination for turning one's position on the Jefferson-Hamilton conflict into a straightforward and uncomplicated referendum on current politics, that "much as we love Thomas Jefferson we should not celebrate him in a partisan way."[62]

Bowers, party loyalist that he was, continued to endorse the New Deal, and later Cold War liberalism, generally, all while continuing to write in the same old vein about Jefferson while holding a day job as ambassador to Spain and later Chile. (He even threatened to fire any staff member who actively criticized the New Deal in front of foreigners.)[63]

But this transcendent Jefferson—symbolized, as Peterson noted, in the Jefferson Memorial that, interestingly enough, focused its attention on the very aspects of Jefferson's life that Nock appreciated, such as Jefferson's hostility to coercion of human thought, his embrace of the libertarian principles articulated in the Declaration, his humanistic quest for truth—also made possible a pragmatic experimentation with the state that Nock would find utterly incompatible with his (increasingly doctrinaire) Jeffersonianism and threatening to civilization itself. Even as Roosevelt wrapped himself in Jefferson's mantle, Nock and his small circle of friends—including H. L. Mencken—came to the conclusion that, as Mencken put it, "Jefferson would have killed himself if he could have seen ahead to Roosevelt II."[64] After Nock died in 1945, he joined Jefferson as a patron saint of the conservative intellectual movement that arose in response to the New Deal.[65]

What Nock hated about the Roosevelt administration was precisely its carelessness about means toward ends; he assumed that any strengthening of the state would, by the logic of the state's design, undermine individual liberty and economic prosperity. "Any thoughtful observer"—a common expression of Nock's, by which he meant himself and a handful of other people—could see that it was impossible to pursue happiness in the way Jefferson intended as long as the state insisted on venturing "into the sphere of positive regulation." Jefferson's entire life, Nock asserted in 1935, had been devoted to opposing such meddling. When the state moves beyond its role as night-watchman, protecting rights and preventing interference with individuals' freedom to pursue happiness, and instead acts to cultivate capacities and enhance capabilities for the better realization of those pursuits, Nock asserted, it positions itself against the "political theory . . . set forth in the Declaration."[66] Nock's relatively unpolitical Jefferson had suddenly become politically animated in opposition to the New Deal, although, it must be said, with much greater understanding than he ever demonstrated in opposing Hamilton. To be sure, Nock's hostility to politics and the positive state predated the New Deal, but the intensity—and even stridency—of the hostility was ramped up with the election of Roosevelt.[67]

Nock's deep concern that the "underserving poor" might not be sufficiently distinguished from the "deserving" animated his opposition to the welfare state at the height of the Great Depression.[68] His 1935 book, *Our Enemy, the State,* which remains a classic among modern libertarians, suggested that "students of politics" and thoughtful people in general should have no trouble seeing that the state could never be used to achieve what Bowers described as "the equal benefit of all the people" or "the protection of the public against the exploitation of the powerful monopolies"; instead, the state, by definition, could only exploit in the service of particular economic interests.[69] His analysis of the state, pulled directly from his reading of Franz Oppenheimer, assumed that the state's very rationale was conquest and exploitation, "a mere device for taking money out of one man's pocket and putting it into another's."[70] In such a reading, republicanism itself was no solution. When wedded to the state, republicanism was, in fact, particularly insidious because it "permits the individual to persuade himself that the State is his creation, that State action is his action, that when it expresses itself it expresses him, and when it is glorified he is glorified."[71] For Nock, the language of popular sovereignty was little more than a manipulation of public opinion. The state was merely the organization of what he called the "political means" of securing resources by stealing from those who had employed the "economic means" of earning a living by producing wealth. Nock could not imagine, as Jefferson and Bowers could, a government that served the interests of the people. The state, in his reading, could not resist being captured by powerful special interests aiming to extract resources from the "producing classes."

Nock seemed indifferent to the fact that, in 1935, his "exploited" class was the business elite that had accumulated so much economic and political power in the 1920s; the state's redistribution in favor of the working classes and the unemployed was a threat to liberty not to be borne. He could understand such a program only in terms of the state's "conquest" of the economic resources of the successful, an "erection of poverty and mendicancy into a permanent political asset," and a "floundering progress toward collectivism."[72] If his 1920s Jefferson understood that *either* government or landlord could take from workers "an unjust proportion of their labor," by the 1930s Nock had come to believe that, as Russell Kirk later characterized his position in the 1930s, "centralized political power, rather than selfish economic interest, had become the principal menace to American freedom."[73] By this point, Nock was insisting that, as he put it, "the superficial distinctions of Fascism, Bolshevism, [and] Hitlerism" could interest only simple-minded "journalists and publicists." Only "the serious student" recognized in all those systems "the one root-idea of a complete conversion of social power into State power."[74] In the 1920s, Nock had believed that Jefferson's objections to Federalist uses of power were never "to strength, but to irresponsibility; not to centralization in itself, but" to use of the state "as an engine of exploitation," an exploitation that a republicanized state might check.[75] By 1943, Nock seemed to recall only that "Mr. Jefferson" embraced "the elementary truth . . . that in proportion as you give the State power to do things for you, you give it power to do things to you."[76]

What Stuart Sherman, literary critic for the *New York Herald Tribune,* in the 1920s identified as Nock's "philosophical disdain" and "amused superiority" became ever more prominent in his writing. His memoir described the process by which he eventually "parted company" with those who imagined that most people were susceptible of further cultivation, education, moral improvement, and self-government.[77] In the 1920s, Nock had blamed Jefferson for misleading the American public into an "overconfidence in literacy."[78] In his later work, Nock seemed delighted to discover that Jefferson was actually a kind of elitist like himself whose "scheme of public education" was "more mercilessly selective than any that has ever been proposed for any public system in this country." Jefferson, he thought, might have "risked a wry smile at the spectacle of our colleges annually turning out whole battalions of bachelors in the liberal arts who could no more read their diplomas than they could decipher the Minoan linear script."[79]

Nock concluded that Americans, devoted wholesale, as they seemed to be, to the pursuit of money, had become resistant to—if not utterly incapable of—cultivated taste or the desire to live the kind of good life to which Jefferson aspired.[80] Nock, who more or less gave up on America, eventually claimed no country.[81] His book on Jefferson—with its Thoreauian emphasis on the sovereignty of the individual—largely ignored the Declaration of Independence, which hailed a much more prominent theme in Jefferson's thought: the sovereignty of the people.[82] This elision presages Nock's later *Our Enemy, the State,* which is not a Jeffersonian tract, as many imagine it to be, but rather, as one astute reader put it, a "repudiation of Jefferson's faith in the potential ability of the average man to govern himself."[83]

Bowers, in contrast, assumed that all history was about resistance of the people to the economic uses of the state in the service of particular—essentially aristocratic—ends. But where Roosevelt and Bowers differentiated a Democratic Party that sought "primarily the good of the average citizen" from a Republican Party that favored "a mere moneyed prosperity of the nation through the control of government by a self-appointed aristocracy of wealth and of social and economic power," Nock saw nothing but cant.[84] There never was such a party in all of American history, Nock argued, and there was simply no way to have a politics that could tran-scend the interest of a particular class and serve the "nation" as Bowers and Roosevelt (and Jefferson) assumed; the state itself rendered such a dream elusive. If Herbert Hoover and the Republicans were Philistines, servants of the business community, and if the business community's platitudes about individualism and laissez faire were "imposter-terms" to disguise their lust for manipulating state power, Nock had no illusions about Roosevelt as the servant of the people. No one could even become president unless he had already proven himself subservient to Wall Street.[85] For Nock, the "essential difference" between Republicans and Democrats was "merely that one was in office and wished to stay in, and the other was out and wished to get in." It boiled down to this: you could put a "Sunday-school superintendent or a Y.M.C.A. secretary" in charge of a brothel, and he just might "trim off some of the coarser fringes of the job." But the place would be a whorehouse still.[86]

Bowers and Nock are little read today, and whatever remains salient about their writing on Jefferson weighs little, it would seem, against what that work reveals about their own ideological presuppositions. How quickly the secondary literature becomes primary (let all historians take note). Bowers and Nock, neither one a professional historian pledged to contemporary dis-ciplinary standards of a quasi-scientific objectivity, are perhaps particularly egregious examples of unwarranted use of the founders for contemporary and idiosyncratic ends. Yet both, it should also be noted, believed they were describing the real Thomas Jefferson and not merely projecting onto him their own ideals and commitments. Neither was shy about the depth of admiration he revealed for his subject nor was either cynical about what now reads, in retrospect, like something of a caricature (however well they each may have captured certain aspects of Jefferson's character and career in both sweep and detail). It may be that Bowers and Nock confirm better than most Richard Hofstadter's trenchant observation that the Founding Fathers are not "timeless oracles" to be "consulted for wisdom on perplexing current problems."[87] As one perceptive contemporary reader of Nock and Bowers noted in the 1927 *Sewanee Review,* "the story of the life and times of Jefferson that would leave ourselves out remains yet to be written."[88] But perhaps the ironic stance of this volume, which obliquely admits that we can learn less about history from historians than we might hope, is simply the other side of its most deeply sincere insight: Americans continue to write about Jefferson because something about Jefferson transcends time and place—his as well as ours—and will speak to future generations as it did to past ones. If we want to understand what that is, then we are compelled, in yet another twist, to continue to consider carefully what others have understood about him, even as we recognize that whatever insight *we* glean will one day bear the marks of our time, just as theirs does. No wonder Jefferson liked "the dreams of the future better than the history of the past."[89]

Notes

Portions of this chapter first appeared in an article with a somewhat different focus: "Thinking with Jefferson in the Age of Gatsby: Narratives of the Founding in American Political Discourse," *Amerikastudien* 61 (2016): 69–94.

1. TJ to William Johnson, 4 March 1823, in Ford, 10:247.

2. The Anas, in Ford, 1:155.

3. TJ to William Johnson, 12 June 1823, *TJW,* 1471.

4. See TJ to Joel Barlow, 3 May 1802, *TJP,* 37:400–401; TJ to John Taylor, 4 June 1798, ibid., 30:389.

5. See Peter J. Sehlinger and Holman Hamilton, *Spokesman for Democracy: Claude G. Bowers, 1878–1958* (Indianapolis, 2000), 26–29; Claude Bowers, *My Life: The Memoirs* (New York, 1962), 39.

6. Claude Bowers, "What Is Republicanism?" *The Jeffersonian Democrat* 2 (January 1900): 549–62, and "Republicanism vs. the People," ibid., 2 (March 1900): 710–20, quoted in Sehlinger and Hamilton, *Spokesman for Democracy,* 31–32, 74, 108, 36.

7. See Sehlinger and Hamilton, *Spokesman for Democracy,* 272.

8. See David E. Kyvig, "History as Present Politics: Claude Bowers' *The Tragic Era,*" *Indiana Magazine of History* 73 (March 1977): 20.

9. Bowers, *My Life,* 179–80.

10. See David J. Goldberg, *Discontented America: The United States in the 1920s* (Baltimore, 1999), 176–79.

11. Quoted in Bowers, *My Life,* 179–80.

12. Claude Bowers, *Jefferson and Hamilton: The Struggle for Democracy in America* (New York, 1925), v, vii. Also see Merrill D. Peterson, "Bowers, Roosevelt, and the 'New Jefferson,'" *Virginia Quarterly Review* 34 (1958): 530–43.

13. Claude Bowers, *Jefferson in Power: The Death Struggle of the Federalists* (Boston, 1936), v–vi.

14. Bowers, *Jefferson and Hamilton,* vi, 37, 65; Bowers, *My Life,* 126, 139.

15. Bowers, *My Life,* 126; Bowers, *Jefferson and Hamilton,* 28–29.

16. Bowers, *Jefferson and Hamilton,* 43, 45.

17. However, see ibid., 59, 64.

18. Ibid., 94–97.

19. Ibid., 97.

20. Claude Bowers, *The Young Jefferson, 1743–1789* (Boston, 1945), vii.

21. Ibid., 141–42.

22. Ibid., 142.

23. Bowers, *Jefferson and Hamilton*, 108, 111. Also see Claude Bowers, "Jefferson, Master Politician," *Virginia Quarterly Review* 2 (1926): 321–33.

24. Bowers, *Jefferson and Hamilton*, 107–15.

25. Ibid., 444.

26. Ibid., viii.

27. Ibid., 395.

28. Claude Bowers, "History's Warning Finger," *Indiana Magazine of History* 50 (March 1954): 1–10.

29. Bowers, *Jefferson in Power*, 258.

30. Bowers, *Jefferson and Hamilton*, 511. For praise of Bowers's book, see A. N. Holcombe in *American Political Science Review* 20 (1926): 215–17 ("a masterly study"); H. C. Nixon in *Annals of the American Academy of Political and Social Science* 126 (July 1926): 164–65 ("a close acquaintance with the historical sources and the capacity for a vivid and lively style"); Samuel Flagg Bemis in the *American Historical Review* 31 (1926): 543–45 ("those who complain that American history is not made interesting enough must be satisfied with this engrossing volume . . . the most interesting and the most readable which we have on the subject"); J. D. Woodruff in *Journal of the Royal Institute of International Affairs* 5 (1926): 250–52 ("brilliantly painted"). J. Fred Rippy, writing in *the Mississippi Valley Historical Review* 13 (1926): 426–27, was more ambivalent about the "over-dramatized" aspects of what he nevertheless admits is a "great book." H. Hale Bellot, writing in the *English Historical Review* 42 (1927): 447–49, was sharply critical, though more of the "shallowness of interpretation than of the dramatic style."

31. Franklin Delano Roosevelt, "Is There a Jefferson on the Horizon?" *American Mercury* 61 (September 1945): 281, originally published in the *New York Evening World*, 3 December 1925.

32. Bowers, "History's Warning Finger," 1; Michael Bordelon, "Claude G. Bowers," in *Dictionary of Literary Biography*, vol. 17, *Twentieth-Century American Historians*, ed. Clyde N. Wilson (Detroit, 1983), 92.

33. FDR to D. C. Martin, 9 December 1925, and FDR radio address to "Thirty Luncheons in Honor of Thomas Jefferson," 12 April 1930, quoted in Graham J. White, *FDR and the Press* (Chicago, 1979), 148. On political and economic conditions in the 1920s, see Lynn Dumenil, *Modern Temper: American Culture and Society in the 1920s* (New York, 1995), 15–55; William E. Leuchtenburg, *The Perils of Prosperity, 1914–32* (Chicago, 1958), 96–103.

34. Quoted in Peterson, "Bowers, Roosevelt, and the 'New Jefferson,'" 536.

35. "Democratic Revival Is Party Hope," *St. Petersburg Times,* 9 March 1925, 2.

36. "Text of Claude G. Bowers' Keynote Speech," *Washington Post,* 27 June 1928, 4.

37. Note Nock's contrast between journalism and serious analysis in *Our Enemy, the State* (1935; repr., Caldwell, Idaho, 1950), 21.

38. Albert Jay Nock, "Historical Portraits," *Saturday Review of Literature,* 6 March 1926, 607.

39. Claude Bowers, review of Albert Jay Nock, *Jefferson,* "The Heart of Jefferson," *Bookman* 64 (1926): 100–101.

40. Dumas Malone, review of Albert Jay Nock, *Jefferson, American Political Science Review* 20 (1926): 908.

41. Quoted in Robert M. Crunden, *The Mind and Art of Albert Jay Nock* (Chicago, 1964), 102.

42. Michael Wrezin, *The Superfluous Anarchist: Albert Jay Nock* (Providence, R.I., 1971), 73. On Nock's thought and trajectory, see also Crunden, *Mind and Art of Albert Jay Nock*; Michael Wrezin, "Albert Jay Nock and the Anarchist Elitist Tradition in America," *American Quarterly* 21 (Summer 1969): 165–89.

43. Albert Jay Nock, "Peace, the Aristocrat," *Atlantic Monthly* (May 1915), reprinted in Albert Jay Nock, *The State of the Union: Essays in Social Criticism,* ed. Charles H. Hamilton (Indianapolis, 1991), 67–75.

44. Albert Jay Nock, "What We All Stand For: The Significance of the Behavior of a Community toward Its Citizens Who Burned a Man Alive," *American Magazine* 75 (February 1913): 57.

45. Although see Albert Jay Nock, "Prohibition and Civilization," *North American Review* (September 1916), reprinted in Hamilton, *State of the Union,* 149–53. On George, see Christopher Lasch, "Henry George," in *A Companion to American Thought,* ed. Richard Wightman Fox and James T. Kloppenberg (Malden, Mass., 1995), 276–77; and John L. Thomas, *Alternative America: Henry George, Edward Bellamy, Henry Demarest Lloyd and the Adversary Tradition* (Cambridge, Mass., 1983), esp. 115–25.

46. Albert Jay Nock, "Isaiah's Job," *Atlantic Monthly* (June 1936), reprinted in Hamilton, *State of the Union,* 124–35.

47. See Albert Jay Nock, *A Journal of These Days, June 1932–December 1933* (New York, 1934), 43–44; Albert Jay Nock, *Memoirs of a Superfluous Man* (New York, 1943), 127–28, 136–40, 214–15; Albert Jay Nock, "Are All Men Human?" *Harper's* 166 (January 1933): 241–44. Nock denied that his stance was misanthropic: one could hate human beings; but it was impossible, Nock wrote, to "hate sub-human creatures or be contemptuous of them, wish them ill, regard them unkindly" (*Memoirs,* 138).

48. Claude Bowers, *Jefferson in Power: The Death Struggle of the Federalists* (Boston, 1936); Albert Jay Nock, "A Study in Manners," in *On Doing the Right Thing: And Other Essays* (New York, 1928), 191–92.

49. Bowers, *Jefferson and Hamilton,* 94–97; Albert Jay Nock, *Jefferson (1926; repr., New York, 1960),* 5, 3, 15, 23, 45–46, 70, 81, 94.

50. Nock, *Jefferson,* 104. See TJ to Francis Hopkinson, 13 March 1789, *TJP,* 14:650.

51. Nock, *Jefferson,* 107, 116, 163, 120.

52. Ibid., 118–21; Nock, "Historical Portraits," 607. See TJ, *Notes on the State of Virginia,* ed. William Peden (1787; repr., Chapel Hill, N.C., 1954), 144.

53. Nock, *Jefferson,* 123.

54. Ibid., 219; Albert Jay Nock, "An Autobiographical Sketch," [1944,] in Hamilton, *State of the Union*, 33.

55. Nock, *Jefferson*, 132–33.

56. Ibid., 166.

57. Bowers, *My Life*, 126; Albert Jay Nock, "Mr. Thomas Jefferson," *Saturday Review of Literature* 6 (11 January 1930): 631.

58. In Peterson's judgment, Nock's was "the most captivating single volume in the Jefferson literature." See Peterson's 1960 introduction in a reprint of Nock, *Jefferson* (New York, 1963), vii. In a contemporary review, Samuel Eliot Morison called Nock's book "the most sparkling study of Jefferson yet written." See Samuel Eliot Morison, "Thomas Jefferson Still Lives," *New Republic* 49 (15 December 1926): 115. Note that neither suggests that Nock's is the most well-rounded portrait or the most accurate; the superlatives in these reviews are reserved for imagination and style, the very categories Nock himself valued over strict accuracy (see his evaluation of James Parton's work in the bibliographical note in *Jefferson*, 203). Richard Hofstadter's later appreciation is more eager to embrace the entire portrait. See Richard Hofstadter, *The American Political Tradition and the Men Who Made It* (1948; repr., New York, 1973), 467: "Mr. Nock understands Jefferson so well that one despairs of going beyond him." Jefferson had been "overdramatized" by writers like Bowers, Hofstadter noted in his classic essay on Jefferson, "The Aristocrat as Democrat," ibid., 22. Hofstadter appreciated Nock, one surmises, because Nock's analysis paralleled Beard's. See Richard Hofstadter, *The Progressive Historians: Turner, Beard, Parrington* (New York, 1968), 292–98, where Hofstadter contrasts Beard's "superior" work with "the effusions of wholly partisan historians like Claude Bowers" (295). The final chapter of Beard's *Economic Origins of Jeffersonian Democracy* (New York, 1915), which wrestles with Jefferson himself, is an obvious inspiration for Nock. For Nock's acknowledgment of Beard's influence, see *Jefferson*, 204.

59. See Peterson, "Bowers, Roosevelt, and the 'New Jefferson,'" 534–35, which informs this and the following three paragraphs.

60. Franklin D. Roosevelt: "Address at Jefferson Day Dinner in St. Paul, Minnesota," 18 April 1932, in Gerhard Peters and John T. Woolley, The American Presidency Project, http://www.presidency.ucsb.edu/ws/?pid=88409.

61. For a description of this shift and the impact it had on Bowers himself, see Thomas T. Spencer, "'Old Democrats and New Deal Politics: Claude G. Bowers, James A. Farley, and the Changing Democratic Party, 1933–1940," *Indiana Magazine of History* 92 (March 1996): 26–45.

62. Roosevelt to Edward M. House, 10 March 1934, in *F.D.R.: His Personal Letters, 1928–1945*, ed. Elliott Roosevelt (New York, 1950), 394.

63. Sehlinger and Hamilton, *Spokesman for Democracy*, 176–77, 168.

64. Mencken quoted in Sheldon Richman, "New Deal Nemesis: The 'Old Right' Jeffersonians," *Independent Review* 1 (Fall 1996): 204.

65. See ibid., and George H. Nash, *The Conservative Intellectual Movement in America since 1945* (New York, 1976), esp. chap. 1.

66. Nock, "Life, Liberty, and . . . ," in *Snoring as a Fine Art and Twelve Other Essays* (Freeport, N.Y., 1971), 16–28, originally published in *Scribner's Magazine,* March 1935. This standard description of the state's role as either negative or positive in orientation—"freedom *to*" versus "freedom *from*"—is informed by Isaiah Berlin's classic essay "Two Concepts of Liberty," in Isaiah Berlin, *The Proper Study of Mankind: An Anthology of Essays,* ed. Henry Hardy and Roger Hausheer (New York, 1997), 190–242. For an important critique of this way of dividing up things in such tidy fashion (and with which I am in greater sympathy), see Quentin Skinner, *Liberty Before Liberalism* (New York, 1998), esp. chap. 3. Another way of thinking about this issue is in terms of procedural versus substantive liberty and equality.

67. See "Anarchist's Progress" and "On Doing the Right Thing," both in Nock, *On Doing the Right Thing,* 123–78.

68. See Nock, *Our Enemy, the State,* 14.

69. Quoted in Sehlinger and Hamilton, *Spokesman for Democracy,* 113.

70. Nock, *Jefferson,* 62 (where Nock attributes this line to Voltaire); Nock, "Anarchist's Progress," 138.

71. Nock, *Our Enemy, the State,* 47, 57. Contrast this with Nock's earlier appreciation of Jefferson's sense that republicanism mitigated the exploitation of "producers" by the "monopolists" precisely because it at least "gave the producer some kind of voice in the direction of affairs" (*Jefferson,* 67).

72. Nock, *Our Enemy, the State,* 45, 14; Nock, *Memoirs,* 175.

73. Nock, *Jefferson,* 48; Russell Kirk, introduction to 1983 reprint of Nock's *Jefferson* (Delavan, Wis., 1983), xix.

74. Nock, *Our Enemy, the State,* 21. Also see Nock, *Memoirs,* 175; Albert Jay Nock, "Progress Toward Collectivism," *American Mercury* 37 (February 1936): 168–74.

75. Nock, *Jefferson,* 163.

76. Nock, *Memoirs,* 175.

77. Including, Nock notes, "Mr. Jefferson" himself. Ibid., 136–38.

78. Nock, *Jefferson,* 190–91.

79. Nock, *Memoirs,* 86, 275.

80. See esp. "The Decline of Conversation," in Nock, *On Doing the Right Thing,* 25–47. Also see Nock, *Jefferson,* 172.

81. Nock, *Memoirs,* 146.

82. See Wrezin, *Superfluous Anarchist,* 3. Also see Nock, *Our Enemy, the State,* 57.

83. Wrezin, *Superfluous Anarchist,* 134–35. Note, however, that there is little, if any, of this in the (in my view) superior summary of Nock's thinking in "Liberalism, Properly So Called" (1943 or 1944), in Hamilton, *State of the Union,* 276–84, just as the disdain for the masses seen in "The Decline of Conversation," "On Making Low People Interesting," and "A Cultural Forecast" is absent in the really beautiful and compelling essay "The Path to the River" (1932), which merely notes that the cultivation of that which is worth immortality is rare and precious. For the former essays, see Nock, *On Doing the Right Thing,* 25–96. For the latter, see Hamilton, *State of the Union,* 52–63.

84. "Democratic Revival Is Party Hope."

85. See Nock, "Anarchist's Progress," 133. Also see Wrezin, *Superfluous Anarchist,* 126–28.

86. Nock, "Anarchist's Progress," 147, 152–53.

87. Hofstadter, *Progressive Historians,* 5–6.

88. E. M. K., in *Sewanee Review* 35 (1927): 114–19.

89. TJ to John Adams, 1 August 1816, in *The Adams-Jefferson Letters: The Complete Correspondence between Thomas Jefferson and Abigail and John Adams,* ed. Lester J. Cappon (Chapel Hill, N.C., 1959), 485.

9   The Cosmopolitan and the Curator

Gilbert Chinard, Marie Kimball, and Jefferson Biography
in the Mid-Twentieth Century

HERBERT SLOAN

Gilbert Chinard and Marie Goebel Kimball represent what is a now neglected slice of Jefferson biography from the 1930s and 1940s. Neither was trained as a historian, and each came to the study of Jefferson by a fairly oblique path. Both embraced older traditions of scholarship that from the standpoint of the twenty-first century seem to have something of the amateur about them. Of the two, Chinard's work is the more enduring, if only because at the time of Kimball's death she had not managed to take Jefferson's life beyond 1789. Chinard, on the other hand, made lasting contributions through editorial work on the Jefferson manuscripts. And, if Merrill Peterson was right, the questions Chinard asked and the themes he explored helped to set the course for Jefferson biography in the decades to come.[1] Kimball, to be sure, was ahead of her time—at least as far as academic historical scholarship was concerned—in emphasizing Jefferson within the context of social history, but her initiatives bore little fruit in the decades after her death, a period marked by the ascendancy of the political and the intellectual in Jefferson studies.

If this seems like a mixed verdict on these two students of Jefferson, both pioneers in different ways, it is worth remembering that, as Robert Merton put it, there is a long tradition of regarding scholars as standing on the shoulders of giants—and on the shoulders of those of lesser stature, a point Merton failed to make.[2] Unlike some of the literature on Jefferson in the first half of the twentieth century, Chinard's and Kimball's contributions were serious and, in Chinard's case, permanent additions to the body of work on Jefferson.

Re-reading their books, one has to remind oneself how much expected standards of scholarship have changed in the last eighty years. And therein lies the problem when we deal with authors whose works appeared before most reading this essay were born. Measuring by the standards of how they contributed to Jefferson's changing image, to evoke Peterson's classic study, produces one sort of evaluation; measuring by how useful they are to modern efforts to understand Jefferson is likely to produce a very different result.[3] A broad assessment of these two interesting if neglected biographers will inevitably point in more than one direction.

Gilbert Chinard was a short (5'6") and very Gallic looking man.[4] Born in 1881 in Châtellerault in the heart of Poitou, he was a son of the French provinces. Locally educated, he acquired his basic degrees not far from the town of his birth (first from the University of Poitiers in 1899 and a Licence ès lettres from the same institution in 1902). Although he seems to have contemplated writing a thesis at the Sorbonne, that never happened, in large part because those who would have supervised it rejected his proposal for a dissertation on "Le Sentiment de la nature dans la littérature américaine," on the grounds, as he recalled many years later, that "there was neither a *sentiment de la nature* nor a literature in America."[5] Unlike most of his contemporaries with degrees in French literature from French institutions, he spent the bulk of his adult life teaching at American universities. He began at the City College of New York in 1907–8, moved briefly to Brown from 1908 to 1912, and then went to Berkeley, where he stayed until 1919, his tenure there interrupted by service in World War I (he returned to France and was then sent back to the United States as a member of a French mission).[6]

In 1919, Chinard took up a new position, at Johns Hopkins. This was a critical shift of location, for it meant that he was in easy commuting distance of the Library of Congress. Before the days when the Jefferson papers would be microfilmed, let alone digitized, in the 1920s archival research still meant research in the archives. He began to exploit the library's collection of Jefferson manuscripts, and in particular Jefferson's correspondence with various French men and women. As he later explained, he hoped "to determine more exactly than had heretofore been done the contribution of the French thinkers to the political thought of Thomas Jefferson."[7]

Once he began to explore the Jefferson manuscripts, the discoveries and publications came fast and furiously. He was the first to pay serious attention to Jefferson's commonplace books, producing an edition in 1926 of the legal commonplace book that is still our only published version of this extremely important text.[8] Beyond that, there were editions—typically published in an American version by Johns Hopkins and a French version in Paris—of Jefferson's correspondence with Lafayette, with the ideologues, with Volney, with Du Pont de Nemours, and with Mme d'Houdetot, Mme de Tesé, Mme de Corny, and Mme de Bréhan.[9] Some of these—in particular, the correspondence with Lafayette and the correspondence with the ideologues—have yet to be replaced in full by *The Papers of Thomas Jefferson* and *The Papers of Thomas Jefferson: Retirement Series*. Chinard's editions of Jeffersoniana were the works of one trained philologically, and very much in the French tradition of publishing celebrated writers' *correspondence inedite*. They suggest that he began by seeing Jefferson first and foremost as an author.

In 1929, building on his work in the Library of Congress manuscripts, Chinard published the book that, more than any other, keeps his reputation alive today, at least among American historians. This was his *Thomas Jefferson: The Apostle of Americanism*.[10] Handsomely turned out in a striking green binding, it calls to mind the days when the appearance of books mattered and houses like Chinard's publisher (Little, Brown) paid attention to the details. Long the best one-volume study of Jefferson, it was, clearly, an interpretation and had no pretentions to being the exhaustive life-and-times account of the sort that Kimball would plan to write or that Dumas Malone would eventually produce.[11]

In its early chapters, Chinard's biography drew heavily on his preparatory work with the literary commonplace book, which had familiarized him with the sources Jefferson absorbed as his political thought took shape in the decade or so before he composed the Declaration of Independence. To be sure, Chinard missed points that seem fundamental today, for while Chinard placed a good deal of emphasis on the classical origins of Jefferson's thought (Chinard's education would have made him familiar with the Greek and Latin authors Jefferson knew so well), he had relatively little to say about the sorts of themes explored by Caroline Robbins, Bernard Bailyn, and other scholars who have opened up the mental world of late eighteenth-century Anglo-America.[12] But compared to what American authors other than Henry Adams had produced on Jefferson—one thinks of Claude Bowers, whose volumes were appearing during the years when Chinard was at work—this was a remarkably serious, sophisticated, and solid piece of scholarship.[13] For

Chinard was a scholar, first and foremost, indeed a textual scholar, and it was the scholar's habits of mind that he brought to his work on Jefferson.

Readers who revisit the introduction to the first edition of *Thomas Jefferson: The Apostle of Americanism* will be struck by how quickly Chinard moved through the available bibliography. He noted the nineteenth-century biography by Henry S. Randall, the twentieth-century biographies by Claude Bowers and Francis Hirst, Carl Becker's *The Declaration of Independence,* Charles Beard's *The Economic Origins of Jeffersonian Democracy,* and the recent work of Albert J. Nock, which he had not been able to consult. And that, along with mentions of the Jefferson papers housed at the Massachusetts Historical Society and in the Library of Congress, together with the inadequate editions published by Lipscomb and Bergh and Paul Leicester Ford, was it. If anything highlights what has changed in the last eighty years, it is the minimalist nature of those brief bibliographical acknowledgments.[14]

It was ironic, to say the least—the point is emphasized by Peterson—that Chinard's Jefferson was above all an American. Unlike others in the 1910s and 1920s, Chinard did not see Jefferson's thought as influenced by European—and especially by French—sources. Remember that Chinard was a Frenchman and a professor of French literature, and his position becomes all the more intriguing. He had very little use for Vernon Parrington's account in *Main Currents in American Thought,* which cast Jefferson as the exponent of "French romantic thought" and as a transatlantic disciple of Rousseau. Nor, as Peterson argues, was he particularly taken by Henry Adams's account of Jefferson the democrat.[15] For Chinard, Jefferson was, first, last, and always, American: his political thought—which more than anything else commanded Chinard's interest—was "distinctly an American doctrine; one cannot imagine it to have originated in any European country, for what would have been a Utopian and chimerical dream in the Old World was within reach of man in America." Chinard's Jefferson, in short, was the prophet of American exceptionalism. Louis Hartz was just over the horizon.[16]

No doubt the fact that Chinard was French helped him to view Jefferson as distinctly American. But even before studying Jefferson, he had been exploring the notion of Americanism. In 1919, he had published a short book in French on the idea of Americanism from the Puritans to Woodrow Wilson that was intended to explain the concept to his no doubt perplexed countrymen.[17]

If there is a fault in *Thomas Jefferson: The Apostle of Americanism,* it is one common enough to single-volume biographies of major figures. The proportions seem skewed. By the time he reached the presidency (surely not the least important part of the story but perhaps for someone like Chinard not the most interesting), he had used up some 375 pages out of a total of 532 of text. And fewer than seventy pages were devoted to the rich years of the retirement. Did Chinard begin to flag as he made his way through Jefferson's last quarter century? Did the prospect of all that politics, all that diplomacy, all that *stuff,* in short, begin to seem overwhelming?

In contrast to *Thomas Jefferson: The Apostle of Americanism,* his other major contribution to the history of the early republic, *Honest John Adams,* his life of the second president, has fared less well.[18] Adams's French connections were, of course, much thinner than Jefferson's, and, in addition, when Chinard was writing his life in the 1930s, most of the manuscript sources were still locked away by the family.[19] Thus Adams the loveable curmudgeon, portrayed in not one but two miniseries (PBS's *The Adams Chronicles* of 1976 and HBO's *John Adams* of 2008), had yet to become a familiar figure. And while the story of the romance of Abigail and John had been available since Charles Francis Adams began publishing his grandparents' letters, equal time for founding mothers as well as founding fathers was not part of Chinard's agenda. "Remember the Ladies" does not get quoted in *Honest John Adams,* and so the work may seem dated in ways that *Thomas Jefferson: The Apostle of Americanism* does not (admittedly, Chinard had nothing to say about either Maria Cosway or Sally Hemings).[20]

But could one write on Adams without invoking Jefferson? For Chinard, this was evidently impossible. As he explained in the introduction to the second edition to *Thomas Jefferson: The Apostle of Americanism,* his work on Adams had strengthened his understanding of Jefferson, who stood in contrast to "John Adams, the New England champion of tradition somewhat out of place in the younger American world."[21] Indeed, as he explained in *Honest John Adams,* making the implicit comparison with Jefferson, it was Adams who "was more conscious than any of his contemporaries of the cultural bonds which connected America with Europe, and of her intellectual and moral kinship with the nations of the Old World."[22]

Having established himself as an expert not simply in French literature but on Jefferson as well, Chinard made his next academic moves. Johns Hopkins was having difficulty weathering the Depression, and it seems from press accounts that Chinard was asked to teach undergraduates. This was apparently too much for the distinguished professor, and he began to cast about for more congenial environments. A year's return to Berkeley (1936–37) was followed by his transition to Princeton, where the trustees appointed him the first Meredith Howland Pyne Professor of French, and he took up his new duties in 1937. His salary was a princely $10,000 (about $171,000 in today's values), and his teaching responsibilities do not seem to have been onerous.[23]

Apart from Princeton's failure to increase his salary (eaten away by wartime inflation, in 1945 it was worth only $7,980 in 1937 dollars), he seems to have been reasonably content throughout his years there.[24] During the Second World War, he was active in propaganda activities on behalf of the Free French, and his son, a doctor, served in the American military.[25] He took part in the celebrations of Jefferson's 200th birthday in 1943—he was, after all, the foremost academic expert on Jefferson, unless one wants to assign that role to Carl Becker on the strength of *The Declaration of Independence*. At the time of the bicentennial, *Thomas Jefferson: The Apostle of Americanism* was still without peer as *the* interpretive biography.[26]

At least as important for us today, Chinard had long been urging the need for an up-to-date edition of Jefferson's papers; he feared they might not survive as manuscripts. Some of his worries seem to have been caused by the condition of the press copies, which he, like others, probably had considerable trouble reading. He had made his views on this subject public on more than one occasion.[27] Readers will note his plea in the introduction to *Thomas Jefferson: The Apostle of Americanism* for a comprehensive edition of Jefferson's papers. Monticello, he remarked, had become a national shrine, thanks to its purchase in 1923 by the Thomas Jefferson Memorial Foundation; it was therefore time to move on and make sure that the corpus of Jefferson's manuscripts—that other invaluable (and no doubt to Chinard more important) part of his legacy—survived as well.[28]

At the end of 1943 came the announcement that the *New York Times* had underwritten a project (to be completed in twenty years) that would publish Jefferson's works in some sixty volumes.[29] Chinard, appropriately enough, was on the advisory committee assembled to help oversee the project, and his name regularly appeared when the *New York Times* reported on the progress of the edition, including its account of the presentation of the first volume to President Harry S. Truman.[30]

In 1950, Chinard retired from Princeton, and there are suggestions that both he and his wife experienced a good deal of medical difficulty in the later 1950s and 1960s, or at least a good deal of anxiety about how they would manage to cope with medical bills. Chinard outlived his wife, celebrating his ninetieth birthday to considerable acclaim in 1971. He died not long thereafter in early 1972.[31]

Marie Goebel Kimball, the second of the biographers to be considered in this essay, was born in 1889. Hers was an academic family. Her father, Julius Goebel, a German immigrant with a Ph.D. from Tübingen, had a peripatetic career that took him from Johns Hopkins to the newly founded Leland Stanford Junior University in the wilds of California, where he remained until forced out by Stanford's president, David Starr Jordan. He then decamped, first to Harvard and next to Champaign-Urbana, where for many years he was professor of German at the University of Illinois and prominent in German American cultural affairs.[32] Among Marie Goebel's six siblings, her younger brother Julius Goebel Jr. would go on to a distinguished career at the Columbia Law School, where he taught legal history for many years and was responsible, with his colleague Joseph Smith, for the editing of *The Law Practice of Alexander Hamilton*.[33] Another younger brother, Walther Frederick Goebel, was an important organic chemist at Rockefeller University.[34] Marie Goebel thus had her formation in an academic environment, one she never really left.

Following two years at Radcliffe, she finished her B.A. at Illinois in 1911. It was in Champaign-Urbana that she met a dashing young architectural historian, the mustachioed Fiske Kimball—"a cross between a Renaissance *putto* and a Bulgarian cavalry officer," someone once said.[35] They were married in 1913. He was the first to explore in depth Jefferson's architectural drawings, then recently deposited in the Coolidge collection of Jefferson materials at the Massachusetts Historical Society. In the course of that work he did what so many other male academics then and since have done and turned his wife into his research assistant. The publication in 1916 of the work that resulted from the Kimballs' labors, *Thomas Jefferson, Architect*, made Fiske Kimball's career.[36] In rapid-fire order, he moved from the art history department at Michigan, his base since 1913, to the University of Virginia in 1919, and then in 1923 to New York University, where he helped to establish the Department of Fine Arts. In 1925, he became the director of the Philadelphia Museum of Art, which he headed until 1955. Kimball, it is safe to say, bestrode the field of eighteenth-century American architectural history like a colossus. His hand, it seemed, was everywhere—including the Rockefeller-sponsored reconstruction of Colonial Williamsburg and the early renovations at Monticello. Importantly for this story and Marie Kimball's future career, he served as the head of the Thomas Jefferson Memorial Foundation's restoration committee from 1924 to 1955, and on the board of the foundation itself from 1939 to 1955.[37]

Where Fiske Kimball went, his wife followed. Since they never had children, Marie Kimball turned her mind and her energies to the furtherance of her husband's scholarly career.[38] (We know little about the other part of her duties as a faculty wife—her role as her husband's social aide—although there must have been a fair amount of that, given his need to cultivate patrons and trustees.[39]) The Kimball connection with Jefferson and Monticello led her to begin publishing on Jefferson and material culture, as we would now call it. The 1920s and 1930s saw articles on Monticello's furnishings, on the liaison with Maria Cosway, and on William Short.[40] But they also saw money-making ventures in the form of popular culinary history—*Thomas Jefferson's Cook Book* (1938) and *The Martha Washington Cook Book* (1940).[41]

Marie Kimball then undertook to write a multivolume life of Jefferson. The 1943 bicentennial was on the horizon, and there was no detailed, life-and-times modern biography on the market. To be sure, Chinard's *Thomas Jefferson: The Apostle of Americanism* had been reissued in a slightly revised form in 1939, but it was not the full-scale study that readers arguably needed and that was increasingly becoming fashionable. Other Virginia worthies were receiving that treatment. Irving Brant, a journalist at the *St. Louis Star-Times*, was busy with his life of James Madison, publishing its first volume in 1940.[42] Douglas Southall Freeman, like Brant a newspaperman—he was the editor of the *Richmond Times-Dispatch*—had completed a four-volume account of Robert E. Lee, as well as a three-volume study of Lee's subordinates, and would soon be starting work on what was to be a seven-volume life of George Washington.[43] Surely Jefferson deserved as much.

Kimball sat down to produce a large-scale biography that would do justice not simply to the man's ideas (in truth, she seems not to have been much interested in them) but also to the full range of his activities. The first volume appeared in time for the bicentennial birthday in 1943. *Jefferson: The Road to Glory, 1743 to 1776* was a strange book. Kimball had mined the archives for all they were worth, but her use of the material she found seems questionable. The book is replete with lists; no detail, it seems, had failed to make its way into the text. Nor did she skimp on quotations, which sometimes went on for pages.[44] For an author whose title claimed to leave Jefferson in 1776, Kimball had real difficulty staying within her self-imposed limits. She offered pages on Jefferson's later religious opinions, on his reaction to Martha Jefferson's death in 1782, on the Walker affair in 1805–6, on the revisal of Virginia's laws, and on the "Manual of Parliamentary Practice."[45] It is as though she could not decide how to organize her material; every note card ended up finding its way into the finished manuscript.

Nothing better illustrates Kimball's obsession with detail than her discussion of dating the entries in Jefferson's literary commonplace book. She provided an elaborate examination of watermarks and of changes in his early handwriting, backing up her analysis with a photograph illustrating those developments.[46] Julian Boyd, founding editor of *The Papers of Thomas Jefferson*, singled this discussion out for special praise in his review of *Jefferson: The Path to Glory* for *the New York Times*; one may wonder what other readers made of it.[47]

And then there is the question, unavoidable, of how Kimball dealt with slavery, an issue that today seems central to understanding Jefferson. But it was not so for Kimball, in whose biography the enslaved African Americans at Monticello are almost invisible. The index has three references to "slavery" (none of them to Jefferson's metaphorical uses of the term), and the attentive reader will find but a handful of other mentions in the text. Thus there is a reference to "servants" and another to "field hands." And, in the context of Kimball's discussion of the Walker affair, there is mention of "a certain Black Sally" (along with an aside insisting that "the scurrilous charge of miscegenation . . . has never found any respectable support").[48]

Kimball, in short, had offered her readers something most of them lacked and apparently wanted—reams and reams of information about Jefferson, much of it new. Data collection was her forte; critical interpretations and big themes seemed not to matter. While her research advanced our understanding of the Jefferson family's social position, it was not clear what else her book accomplished. Thus she provided no new explanation of the Revolution—indeed, she simply accepted it as a given, and of course the Americans were right. Beyond lists of Jefferson's reading and book purchases, she offered little to trace the development of his thought. As might be expected, she had expert words about the creation of Monticello, but nothing to say about the political culture from which its builder sprang. Above all, and the contrast with Chinard is unmistakable, she did not try to explain what Jefferson means.

Nonetheless, contemporary reviewers were generally favorable. Writing in the *Mississippi Valley Historical Review,* Verner Crane, the historian of the southern colonial frontier, found much to praise in the first volume, as did Carl Becker in the *American Historical Review,* calling it "admirable" and saying Kimball "has taken the trouble to find out all there is to find out about young Thomas Jefferson."[49] In the *New York Times,* Boyd's glowing assessment appeared just in time for Jefferson's 200th birthday.[50] Given that Boyd had good reason to be grateful to Fiske Kimball, who was instrumental in having him appointed to the Jefferson Bicentennial Commission, one might surmise that Marie Kimball was guaranteed a favorable review.[51] But hers was the Jefferson life (albeit incomplete) for the bicentennial, and Boyd did his best to play it up. Still, as Dumas Malone began to work on his biography, it would have been clear to many that his was likely to dominate the field—a prospect that led Fiske Kimball to try to dissuade Malone from his undertaking.[52]

In 1944, following the warm reception of volume 1 of her biography, Marie Kimball was named the first curator of Monticello, a post she held until her death in 1955. It is hard to avoid the suspicion that the fine Italian hand of her husband had more than a little to do with the appointment, which solidified the Kimball influence on the mountaintop. Her role at Monticello has been expertly and sympathetically described in an essay by Megan Stubbendeck entitled "A Woman's Touch," which alerts us to the ways in which Marie Kimball tried to escape the limitations her gender imposed in the male-dominated historical world of the day.[53]

In due course, volumes 2 (*Jefferson: War and Peace, 1776 to 1784* [1947]) and 3 (*Jefferson: The Scene of Europe, 1785 to 1789* [1950]) would appear. Just as volume 1 had failed to add much to what was known about Jefferson's activity in the early stages of the Revolution, so volumes 2 and 3 did relatively little to advance the state of knowledge about the periods they covered. *Jefferson: War and Peace* recycled material from volume 1's premature discussions of Jefferson's revisal of Virginia's laws, the death of Martha Jefferson, and other topics. The years it deals with have never been seen as the high point of Jefferson's life, and it is always difficult to make them come alive. Interestingly, at 362 pages of text, volume 2 is somewhat longer than volume 1's 306 pages of text. One might conclude from this that Kimball was driven by her material; the more of it there was, the longer her story became, with each bit of Jeffersoniana treated as though it were of equal weight with every other bit.[54]

It goes almost without saying that Kimball defended Jefferson's wartime governorship against any and every criticism. Some found this unconvincing; thus Margaret Macmillan, who knew something about the Revolutionary governors, described Kimball's "general conception of his governorship" as "unduly favorable" in her review for the *William and Mary Quarterly*.[55] This and other negative assessments no doubt rankled, for Kimball was increasingly possessive when it came to Jefferson. In 1945, in the pages of the *American Historical Review*, she would describe Claude Bowers's *The Young Jefferson* as a "negligible" "contribution to knowledge," and its author as "someone to whom the most recent, and some not so recent, contributions to the vast literature on Jefferson are not familiar."[56] Her day would come.

In volume 3, where Jefferson's activity in Europe might have provided a focus for Kimball's interests, again there is little evidence of new thinking or unexplored pathways. Comparison of volume 3 with Howard Rice's *Thomas Jefferson's Paris* (1976) suggests how much more there was to learn about Jefferson's time abroad, just as Howard Adams's catalog for the 1976 exhibit *The Eye of Thomas Jefferson* suggests what could be done on a similar if wider scale.[57] Kimball disposes of Jefferson's diplomatic work in three brisk chapters occupying some 54 pages (about one-sixth of the 310 pages of text). Rather more space is devoted to his travels in England, in Provence and Italy, and in the Rhineland, which take up seventy-four pages. Kimball pays very little attention to the growing sense Jefferson's correspondents were giving him that the United States was in big trouble, or to the development of Jefferson's relations with Madison. That Kimball never so much as mentions Jefferson's comments on Shays's Rebellion or his September 6, 1789, letter to Madison insisting "*that the earth belongs in usufruct to the living*" generation only strengthens the impression that she had no interest in the political side of things.[58]

Given the position Kimball had already taken on Sally Hemings in volume 1, one would hardly expect her to have anything to say on that subject. But it does strike one as odd that for all intents and purposes Jefferson's daughters are relegated to a brief mention in the final chapter, almost as though Kimball had suddenly remembered that they had been living in Paris with their father for some years.[59]

Before she died in 1955, Kimball had begun work on the fourth volume of her biography, but it had not progressed beyond initial notes and drafts.[60] It did not take long for her work to fade. Dumas Malone published his first volume in 1948; the second volume, taking Jefferson through 1792, appeared in 1951. Kimball's third volume, taking Jefferson to 1789, had come out in 1950. Thus, by the beginning of the new decade, Malone had overtaken and passed her. In 1960, five years after her death, Peterson was prepared to dismiss Kimball's work as largely irrelevant. He did note the contribution Kimball had made by refuting the notion that Jefferson was a product of the frontier; otherwise, her work struck him as essentially antiquarian. "Mrs. Kimball," as he called the author in the gendered language of the day, had little to offer the serious student.[61]

Yet it was not simply the appearance of Malone's *Jefferson and His Time* that rendered Kimball superfluous. The decade after the Second World War saw important new work in the history of the Revolution and the early republic, work that both deepened and recast our understanding of those periods. One could now—and this is a list that can be expanded at will— write about late colonial Virginia using Charles Sydnor's *Gentlemen Freeholders* (1952), understand Madison's political thought through the essays of Douglass Adair, better appreciate the significance of the exchanges between Jefferson and Madison thanks to Adrienne Koch's *Jefferson and Madison: The Great Collaboration* (1950), investigate with Daniel Boorstin *The Lost World of Thomas Jefferson* (1948), explore Jefferson's books in E. Millicent Sowerby's magnificent five-volume *Catalogue of the Library of Thomas Jefferson* (1952–59), ponder Joseph Charles's three 1955 articles in the *William and Mary Quarterly* on the origins of American party politics, consult Louis Gottschalk's *Lafayette between the American and the French Revolution* (1950), and, of course, take advantage of the opening volumes of *The Papers of Thomas Jefferson*, which by 1955 had reached volume 12 and the end of March 1788. Inaugurated in 1944, the third series of the *William and Mary Quarterly* was providing an essential forum for the new scholarship.[62] Against the background of these scholarly developments, Kimball's volumes could only appear dated. Indeed, as early as 1952 it was fairly clear that Kimball was falling out of the running. A sample of American historians asked to rate "preferred American biographies" from a selected list of thirty published between 1920 and 1950 ranked Malone's *Jefferson* (1948) fifth, Claude Bowers's *Hamilton and Jefferson* (1925) twenty-seventh, and Chinard's *Jefferson* (1929) twenty-eighth. Marie Kimball received a handful of write-in votes.[63] The end had arrived.

Marie Kimball still has fans, as one learns by visiting the Monticello website, where a note by Anna Berkes discusses "The Cult of Marie Kimball."[64] But by and large they are not among professional historians. Unfinished, her biography of Jefferson is not much read these days, and one suspects that, had she lived to carry the story forward, it would not have been a success in her hands. (What would she have done with the presidency, one wonders?) To be sure, her work at Monticello was important and deserves to be remembered.[65] But Marie Kimball's biographical project petered out. Given her intellectual resources, given the moment of its creation, it was probably too ambitious an undertaking.

Chinard, on the other hand, remains a figure of some significance to historians, if unknown to the general public. Peterson's assessment of Chinard's impact on Jefferson studies—that he established an agenda for Jefferson biographies that followed—was quite an accomplishment for a boy from the French provinces. But then Chinard had the advantages that Kimball lacked—he was male in a scholarly world that privileged men, he held advanced academic degrees and important academic appointments, and, perhaps most of all, he did not bite off more than he could chew.

Notes

1. *Jefferson Image,* 417.
2. Robert K. Merton, *On the Shoulders of Giants: A Shandean Postscript* (New York, 1965).
3. For a sense of developments in the half-century following the bicentennial of Jefferson's birth, see Peter S. Onuf, "The Scholars' Jefferson," *WMQ* 50 (1993): 671–99. The two decades since the appearance of Onuf's article have seen substantial additions to the corpus he describes.
4. For his height, see Gilbert Chinard to Alexander Leitch, 19 May 1959, Chinard faculty file, Princeton University Archives, Mudd Library, Princeton. The file has a picture of him dating from his retirement, wearing a beret and smoking a pipe, making him look stereotypically French. Apparently taken in his home in Princeton, it portrays

him against a background of shelves stuffed with paperbound French volumes. His residence at 93 Mercer St. was a few doors away from Albert Einstein's at 112 Mercer St. For biographical information and the details of his academic career, see Chinard faculty file. Useful obituaries include those in the *New York Times,* 10 February 1972, 46, and the *Proceedings of the American Philosophical Society* 82 (1972): 15–17.

5. On Chinard's failure to complete a doctorate, see Howard C. Rice Jr., "Man and Nature in the New World: A Check-List of the Writings of Gilbert Chinard," *Princeton University Library Chronicle* 26 (1965): 148. He would later receive honorary doctorates from Princeton and St. John's. For a sense of what it meant to study literature in France at the dawn of the twentieth century, see Antoine Compagnon, *Connaissez-vous Brunetière? Enquête sur un antidreyfusard et ses amis* (Paris, 1997).

6. For Chinard as an academic agent of French propaganda in the United States, see Robert J. Young, *Marketing Marianne: French Propaganda in America, 1900–1940* (New Brunswick, N.J., 2004), 55, 87, 105, 144.

7. Gilbert Chinard, *Thomas Jefferson: The Apostle of Americanism* (Boston, 1929), v.

8. Gilbert Chinard, ed., *The Commonplace Book of Thomas Jefferson: A Repertory of His Ideas on Government* (Baltimore, 1926); Gilbert Chinard, ed., *The Literary Bible of Thomas Jefferson: His Commonplace Book of Philosophers and Poets* (Baltimore, 1928). Douglas Wilson has criticized Chinard's editorial practice, at least in the case of the literary commonplace book: "This edition," he says, "was very carelessly transcribed and proves to be strewn with errors." Douglas L. Wilson, "Thomas Jefferson's Early Notebooks," *WMQ* 42 (1985): 438.

9. For details of Chinard's publications, see Rice, "Man and Nature," 150–96. Those just noted can be found on 160–63. Reviewing a group of documentary collections he edited, Marie Kimball referred to him as "the diligent M. Chinard." Marie G. Kimball, "Footnotes to History," *Virginia Quarterly Review* 5 (1929): 632. But Kimball also insisted on priority: "The contemporary interest in Jefferson's personal papers began in 1916," she wrote, "with the publication, by this writer, of the correspondence between Jefferson and Madame de Staël. . . . It was subsequently observed that many interesting documents . . . still lay hidden in the manuscript collections of the Library of Congress. . . . A few years later Chinard published" the editions mentioned above. Marie G. Kimball, "Three Friends of Jefferson," *Virginia Quarterly Review* 4 (1928): 625. For the publication Kimball refers to, see Marie G. Kimball, "Unpublished Correspondence of Mme. de Staël with Thomas Jefferson," *North American Review* 208 (July 1918): 63–71, which contains all of three letters.

10. A second, revised edition of Chinard's *Thomas Jefferson: Apostle of Americanism,* also from Little, Brown, appeared in 1939. It contained a new "Introduction" but few substantive changes to the text. Both "Introductions"—that of 1929 and that of 1939—should be read by anyone looking for a sense of what Chinard thought he was up to. The 1939 edition—without the revised "Introduction"—was later republished in paperback by the University of Michigan Press; this is probably the version to which most readers will have had access.

11. Admittedly, it is not a best seller; Amazon ranks it (27 May 2012) at 2,736,920

in books. For comparative purposes, it may be useful to know that Herbert E. Sloan, *Principle and Interest: Thomas Jefferson and the Problem of Debt* (New York, 1995) comes in at 422,583, and Andrew Burstein and Nancy Isenberg, *Madison and Jefferson* (New York, 2010), at 365,702.

12. Caroline Robbins, *The Eighteenth-Century Commonwealthman* (Cambridge, Mass., 1959); Bernard Bailyn, *Ideological Origins of the American Revolution* (Cambridge, Mass., 1967).

13. Bowers's Jeffersonian trilogy includes *Jefferson and Hamilton: The Struggle for Democracy in America* (Boston, 1925); *Jefferson in Power: The Death Struggle of the Federalists* (Boston, 1936); and *The Young Jefferson, 1743–1789* (Boston, 1945).

14. Chinard, *Thomas Jefferson,* xiv–xv. Chinard does allow that he read "too many books to list them all," but the brevity of his list says something. This is certainly not in keeping with current academic fashions when it comes to citation. Nor is his actual citation practice, which generally involves only his primary sources.

15. *Jefferson Image,* 414–17.

16. Chinard, *Thomas Jefferson,* xiii (Chinard hastens to add, "Whether it corresponds to present conditions is still another question."). For Hartz, see *The Liberal Tradition in America: An Interpretation of American Political Thought since the Revolution* (New York, 1955). As Nancy Isenberg has suggested to me, some of these themes featured prominently in J. Hector St. John de Crèvecouer's *Letters from an American Farmer* (1782), a work with which Chinard was undoubtedly familiar.

17. Gilbert Chinard, *La doctrine de l'américanisme des Puritains au président Wilson* (Paris, 1919).

18. Gilbert Chinard, *Honest John Adams* (Boston, 1933). For an appreciation of *Honest John Adams,* see Douglass Adair, "Gilbert Chinard's *Honest John Adams*: An Appreciation," *Princeton University Library Chronicle* 26 (1965): 197–99.

19. See Malcolm Freiberg, "The Adams Manuscript Trust, 1905–1955," *Proceedings of the Massachusetts Historical Society,* 3d ser., 106 (1994): 112–27; Freiberg begins his account by referring to the "severe restraints that fourth-generation Adamses imposed on non-Adams access to their inherited family papers" (ibid., 112).

20. Chinard does quote other language from Abigail Adams's famous letter. Chinard, *Honest John Adams,* 91. Note also that Abigail Adams figures as "Adams, Mrs. John (Abigail Smith)" in the index. Ibid., 351.

21. Gilbert Chinard, *Thomas Jefferson: The Apostle of Americanism,* 2d ed. (Boston, 1939), xvi.

22. Chinard, *Honest John Adams,* xii.

23. For Chinard's departure from Johns Hopkins, see "Johns Hopkins Deficit May Cut Faculty," *Baltimore Sun,* 9 February 1936, 18; "Deficit at Johns Hopkins," *New York Times,* 10 February 1936, 12; "Dr. Chinard Gets Post at Princeton," ibid., 9 April 1937, 17. To convert Chinard's 1937 salary into 2017 dollars, see www.measuringworth.com. The calculation used the CPI.

24. Conversion done using the source in the previous note.

25. For propaganda, see articles on Chinard's wartime activities in *the New York*

Times: "French Here Agree with British Views," 26 June 1940, 7; "French Here Laud Roosevelt Stand," 18 May 1941, 11; "Free French Here Assail Riom Trial," 22 April 1942, 8; "Exiles Will Help to Restore France," 2 April 1943, 11; "French Organize Here," 16 May 1943, E13. For his medical son, see Chinard faculty file.

26. See, for example, Gilbert Chinard, "Jefferson and the American Philosophical Society," *Proceedings of the American Philosophical Society* 87 (1943): 263–76.

27. "Jefferson Papers Fading," *New York Times,* 22 January 1930, 18.

28. Chinard, *Thomas Jefferson,* xvi (presciently, Chinard noted that "it would take several lives and a fortune to edit them properly"). In the "Introduction" to the 1939 edition, Chinard again "express[ed] the pious hope that sometime the American powers that be will realize the necessity of giving to the public a complete and correct edition of the Jefferson papers" (Gilbert Chinard, *Thomas Jefferson,* [1939,] xvi). In 1939, however, he omitted his earlier language about the cost in time and money. See *Jefferson Image,* 439–40, for a brief account of the origins of the edition. Peterson suggests (439) that "Chinard, in 1929, first raised the 'pious hope' for a substantially complete and accurate redaction of Jefferson's papers," followed by numerous other pleas on behalf of the project. In fact, in 1929, Chinard "express[ed] the wish" for an edition (Chinard, *Thomas Jefferson,* xvi); "pious hope" was one of the revisions in the second edition. For an account of the project's history as a whole, see Barbara B. Oberg and James P. McClure, "'For Generations to Come': Creating the 'Definitive' Jefferson Edition," in *A Companion to Thomas Jefferson, ed.* Francis D. Cogliano (Oxford, 2012), 491–509.

29. "Jefferson's Full Works to Be Given to the Nation," *New York Times,* 26 December 1943, 1. Note the front-page placement of this piece.

30. "Advisers Discuss Jefferson Papers," *New York Times,* 19 February 1944, 15; "Truman Will Hail Jefferson Papers," ibid., 25 March 1950, 21; "Jefferson Papers to Be Issued Today," ibid., 17 May 1950, 31.

31. For details on the last years and some information on the medical and financial difficulties, see Chinard faculty file.

32. *Johns Hopkins University Circulars* 7, no. 61 (December 1887). On the curious episode at Stanford, related in complicated ways to the poisoning of Jane Lathrop Stanford, see W. B. Carnochan, "The Case of Julius Goebel: Stanford, 1905," *American Scholar* 72 (2003): 95–108.

33. Julius Goebel Jr. and Joseph Smith, eds., *The Law Practice of Alexander Hamilton,* 5 vols. (New York, 1964–81). For a summary of Goebel's career, see Joseph H. Smith, "Julius Goebel, Jr.—A Tribute," *Columbia Law Review* 73 (1973): 1372–82.

34. See Maclyn McCarty's memoir of Walther Goebel, National Academy of Sciences, Biographical Memoirs, http://www.nap.edu/readingroom.php?book=biomems &page=wgoebel.html.

35. There is no academic biography of Fiske Kimball. A sense of the man and his career can be gathered from George Roberts and Mary Roberts, *Triumph on Fairmount: Fiske Kimball and the Philadelphia Museum of Art* (Philadelphia, 1959); and Hugh Howard, *Dr. Kimball and Mr. Jefferson: Rediscovering the Founding Fathers of American Architecture* (New York, 2006). For the quotation about Kimball's appearance, see Walter

Muir Whitehill, review of Fiske Kimball, *Thomas Jefferson, Architect, New England Quarterly* 42 (1969): 278.

36. Fiske Kimball, *Thomas Jefferson, Architect* (Boston, 1916). On this important publication, see Whitehill's informative review of the 1960 reprint, cited in the previous note.

37. For these biographical details, see Monticello.org/site/about/fiske-kimball.

38. One might compare her trajectory with other well-known faculty wives of the period; Mary Ritter Beard (1876–1958) and Helen Merrell Lynd (1896–1982) come to mind. A slightly younger example would be Mary Fieser (1909–1997), wife of the Harvard chemist and inventor of napalm, Louis Fieser. In the 1930s, Mary Fieser's graduate education was blocked by the male chauvinists of the Harvard Chemistry Department; she spent most of her life assisting her husband. For the Fiesers and their joint career, see http://www.chemheritage.org/discover/online-resources/chemistry -in-history/themes/chemical-education-and-public-policy/chemical-education/fiesers .aspx. The Louis and Mary Fieser Laboratory for Undergraduate Organic Chemistry at Harvard helps to perpetuate her memory. My thanks to Robert Neer for alerting me to the Fiesers.

39. Marie Goebel Kimball, "Roughing It in Philadelphia," *Virginia Quarterly Review* 14 (1938): 416–24, suggests some of the challenges she faced as a hostess living in one of the historic houses in Fairmont Park.

40. Marie Goebel Kimball, "Jefferson's Furniture Comes Home to Monticello," *House Beautiful* 66 (August 1929): 164–65, 186–90; Marie Goebel Kimball, "William Short, Jefferson's Only 'Son,'" *North American Review* 223 (1926): 471–86; Marie Goebel Kimball, "Jefferson's Farewell to Romance," *Virginia Quarterly Review* 4 (1928): 402–19.

41. Both of these are still in print. *Thomas Jefferson's Cook Book* is not quite what its title suggests. Most of the recipes come from a collection assembled by Jefferson's granddaughter Virginia Randolph Trist. The most recent serious contribution to our knowledge of Jefferson and food, Damon Lee Fowler, ed., *Dining at Monticello* (Chapel Hill, N.C., 2005), never refers to *Thomas Jefferson's Cook Book*. It does, however, rate brief mention in Dave DeWitt, *The Founding Foodies: How Washington, Jefferson, and Franklin Revolutionized American Cuisine* (Naperville, Ill., 2010), 170, 213–14. For more of Kimball's efforts at culinary history, see "The Epicure of the White House," *Virginia Quarterly Review* 9 (1933): 71–81, and "Some Genial Old Drinking Customs," *WMQ* 2 (1945): 349–58.

42. Irving Brant, *James Madison,* 6 vols. (Indianapolis, 1940–61).

43. Douglas Southall Freeman, *Robert E. Lee: A Biography,* 4 vols. (New York, 1934–35); Douglas Southall Freeman, *Lee's Lieutenants: A Study in Command,* 3 vols. (New York, 1942); Douglas Southall Freeman, *George Washington,* 7 vols. (New York, 1948–57). On Freeman and his *Washington,* see Edward G. Lengel, *Inventing George Washington: America's Founder, in Myth and Memory* (New York, 2011), 169–73. Lengel points out that before becoming a journalist, Freeman earned a Ph.D. in history from Johns Hopkins in 1908 with a 101-page dissertation titled "The Attitude of Political

Parties in Virginia to Slavery and to Secession." Ibid., 169; for the dissertation, see https://catalyst.library.jhu.edu/catalog/bib_2308261.

44. Marie Goebel Kimball, *Jefferson: The Road to Glory, 1743 to 1776* (New York, 1943). For lists, see, e.g., 104–6, 172–73; for quotations, see, e.g., 67–70, 125–27.

45. Ibid., 127–29 (religion), 182–86 (death of Martha Jefferson), 142–46 (Walker affair), 219–28 (revisal), 97–99 (Manual).

46. Ibid., 84–87 (ill. facing 84).

47. Julian P. Boyd, "Armed with Reason, and in Pursuit of Truth," Book Review, *New York Times*, 11 April 1943, 5.

48. Kimball, *Jefferson: The Road to Glory*, 176, 239, 146–47.

49. Verner Crane, review of Marie Kimball, *Jefferson: The Road to Glory, 1743 to 1776, Mississippi Valley Historical Review* 30 (1943): 253–54 (although note that Crane considered Chinard the more reliable guide when it came to the interpretation of the commonplace books); Carl Becker, review of Marie Kimball, *Jefferson: The Road to Glory, 1743 to 1776, AHR* 49 (1943): 111, 110.

50. Two years later, Kimball would in effect return the favor by writing a highly favorable review of Boyd's book on the Declaration of Independence. Kimball, review of Julian P. Boyd, *The Declaration of Independence: The Evolution of the Text as Shown in Facsimiles of Various Drafts by Its Author, Thomas Jefferson, WMQ* 2 (1945): 321–22.

51. On Fiske Kimball and Julian Boyd's career, see *Jefferson Image*, 439.

52. Merrill D. Peterson, "Dumas Malone: An Appreciation," *WMQ* 45 (1988): 241–42. Peterson points out that in 1938, Malone had signed a contract with Little, Brown for a multivolume biography of Jefferson, a project he had long been maturing, and that he felt he had no reason to fear competition from Marie Kimball. R. B. Bernstein discusses the episode in his essay on Malone in this volume.

53. Megan Stubbendeck, "A Woman's Touch: Gender at Monticello," in *Entering the Fray: Gender, Politics, and Culture in the New South*, ed. Jonathan Daniel Wells and Sheila R. Phipps (Columbia, Mo., 2010), 118–35. Stubbendeck argues that Kimball adopted the masculine stereotypes of women as largely unsuited for scholarship and did her best, in effect, to be accepted as one of the boys. Ibid., 128, 130.

54. Thus volume 1 of *The Papers of Thomas Jefferson* ends on 31 December 1776; volumes 2 through 6 cover the period 1 January 1777 through 1 March 1784.

55. Margaret Macmillan, review of Marie Kimball, *Jefferson: War and Peace, WMQ* 5 (1948): 124. Macmillan was the author of *The War Governors in the American Revolution* (New York, 1943). For similar comments, see William H. Gaines Jr.'s review in *VMHB* 56 (1948): 105 ("She has created such a paragon of leadership that the result bears little resemblance to the true Jefferson."). Cf. Christopher Crittenden's conclusion in his review in *AHR* 53 (1948): 557 ("One can't help wondering, however, whether just occasionally he may have made a mistake or have erred in judgment.").

56. Marie Kimball, review of Claude Bowers, *The Young Jefferson, 1743–1789, AHR* 50 (1945): 810.

57. Howard C. Rice Jr., *Thomas Jefferson's Paris* (Princeton, N.J., 1976); William Howard Adams, ed., *The Eye of Thomas Jefferson* (Washington, D.C., 1976).

58. TJ to James Madison, 6 September 1789, *TJP,* 15:392. In comparison, Chinard, *Thomas Jefferson,* 234, does mention the letter to Madison, although he, too, is silent when it comes to Shays's Rebellion.

59. Marie Kimball, *Jefferson: The Scene of Europe, 1784-1789* (New York, 1950), 303–7.

60. These are in the Marie Kimball Papers, Special Collections Library, University of Virginia.

61. *Jefferson Image,* 417–19. For a recent and important study of Jefferson's family background and youth that, broadly speaking, confirms many of Kimball's points, see Susan Kern, *The Jeffersons at Shadwell* (New Haven, Conn., 2010).

62. For an appreciation of the *Quarterly's* first two decades, see Keith B. Berwick, "A Peculiar Monument: The Third Series of the *William and Mary Quarterly,*" *WMQ* 21 (1964): 3–17.

63. John Walton Caughey, "Historian's Choice: Results of a Poll of Recently Published American History and Biography Author(s)," *Mississippi Valley Historical Review* 39 (1952): 301–2.

64. http://www.monticello.org/site/blog-and-community/posts/cult-marie-kimball.

65. Some sense of her role at Monticello can be derived from Francis D. Cogliano, "Preservation and Education: Monticello and the Thomas Jefferson Foundation," in Cogliano, *Companion to Thomas Jefferson,* 713–15.

10   The Perils of Definitiveness

Dumas Malone's *Jefferson and His Time*

R. B. BERNSTEIN

On April 13, 1948, Thomas Jefferson's 205th birthday, Little, Brown published *Jefferson the Virginian,* the first volume of a comprehensive biography by Dumas Malone.[1] *Jefferson the Virginian* won acclaim as the first installment of the definitive life of Jefferson; each succeeding volume evoked similar praise. In 1975, Malone won the Pulitzer Prize for History for his first five volumes, which took Jefferson through the end of his presidency.[2] In 1981, another chorus of encomiums for *The Sage of Monticello* hailed the completion of a monument of scholarship.[3]

Even as Malone was writing, however, scholarly and public assessments of Jefferson entered an increasing state of flux—ending the triumphant third act and beginning a fourth, more ambivalent act of Jefferson's posthumous history. Contrasting with the rapidly evolving state of scholarship on Jefferson and his era, Malone's volumes comprise an elegant case for an earlier interpretation of Jefferson—less critical, more admiring, less sensitive to issues of race and slavery, more partisan in chronicling his political career.[4]

Jefferson and His Time dominates the bookshelves as the Rocky Mountains dominate the American landscape, and it remains a classic of American biography. But is it the kind of classic reputedly mocked by Mark Twain as "a book that everybody praises but nobody reads"? Do we revisit Malone's volumes? Do we need to revisit or consult them? Or, having metaphorically climbed them, can we leave them behind? Nearly forty years after Malone finished his biography and more than thirty years after his death in 1986, *Jefferson and His Time* poses two clusters of questions for scholars, biographers, and readers.

First: the verdict on whether Malone's interpretation of Jefferson stands the test of time is—and must be—mixed. On most factual details of Jefferson's life, on his evolving relations with his (white or legal) family, and on his wide-ranging interests, Malone's work still enlightens us. On other issues central to our time's writing and teaching of American history, Malone's views have encountered serious criticism requiring severe revision or rejection. Chief among these are Jefferson's national political career from 1789 to 1809; the centrality of Jefferson's identity as a politician to our understanding of him; Jefferson's relations with the enslaved Sally Hemings; and the larger issues for which the Jefferson-Hemings controversy is a proxy—the place of slavery and race in Jefferson's life and politics, and Jefferson's identities as conflicted slaveowner and American statesman. Scholarship on these subjects has evolved so rapidly that Malone would not recognize the field that he helped to found.

To be sure, Malone never described his biography as definitive, nor did he voice any ambition to write the definitive life of Jefferson. The label "definitive" was the product of a consensus among his reviewers rather than a goal that he set for himself. Even so, the scope and depth of *Jefferson and His Time* raise inevitable questions about Malone's intentions—although those questions may be beside the point. In *Biography: A Very Short Introduction,* the biographer Hermione Lee observes: "The adjective 'definitive' is often attached to biographies by hopeful publishers or enthusiastic reviewers. There is a lingering idea of biography as the complete, true story of a human being, the last word on a life. But if it is, rather, a mixed, unstable genre, whose rules keep coming undone, then perhaps the only rule that holds good is that there is no such thing as a definitive biography."[5]

This paradoxical situation—our yearning for definitive biography despite its impossibility—raises another set of questions: Does the aspiration to definitiveness—on the part of author, publisher, reviewer, or reader—defeat itself? What consequences does the erosion of the authority of Malone's biography have for biography as a form of historical scholarship, or for the claims of any biography to be definitive?[6] How should we regard *Jefferson and His Time?* Will it remain useful merely as a compilation of biographical data and as a core-sample of past generations' historical and biographical thinking?

Before discussing the biography, we must first consider the biographer.[7] Born in Coldwater, Mississippi, on January 10, 1892, Dumas Malone was raised in rural Georgia. In 1910, he was graduated from Emory College (later Emory

University). He taught high school and junior college before entering Yale Divinity School, where in 1916 he received his Bachelor of Divinity degree. Just after the United States entered the First World War, Malone enlisted in the U.S. Marine Corps. Though he was commissioned a second lieutenant, he never went to Europe, completing his war duty stateside.

After the war's end, Malone returned to Yale for graduate study in history, writing a prize-winning dissertation on Thomas Cooper, a controversial English-born economist and educator whom Jefferson admired and tried to recruit for the University of Virginia; *The Public Life of Thomas Cooper* remains the leading study of its subject. Malone's study of Cooper's public and intellectual career, which highlighted his links to Jefferson, probably led Malone to Jefferson as a congenial biographical subject.[8]

Hired by the University of Virginia's history department, in 1926 Malone arrived in Charlottesville in time for the sesquicentennial of American independence and the centennial of Jefferson's death. It was then that Malone decided "to write a big book about Thomas Jefferson someday."[9] He sought advice from his Yale mentor, Allen Johnson. Although no new political biography was needed, Johnson replied, the field lacked a biography that "could do justice to the many-sided Jefferson." Although Johnson worried that Malone's knowledge might not be wide-ranging enough for the task, Malone decided to go forward.[10]

In 1929, while finishing his edition of Jefferson's correspondence with Pierre Samuel Du Pont de Nemours, Malone received an invitation from Johnson, editor in chief of *The Dictionary of American Biography* (*DAB*), to join him as coeditor, an invitation spurred by Johnson's concern about his own health.[11] If anything happened to him, Johnson promised, Malone would become editor in chief; Malone also would get the coveted assignment to write the *DAB*'s article on Jefferson. Malone accepted and left Charlottesville, joining Johnson as coeditor for the *DAB*'s third volume. In 1931, after Johnson's unexpected death in an automobile accident, Malone succeeded him as editor in chief. Under his leadership the *DAB* published over 13,000 articles by over 2,000 contributors in twenty volumes. Malone finished work on the *DAB* in 1936, only six months after the original deadline.[12]

Malone's 15,000-word essay on Jefferson (one of five articles exceeding the *DAB*'s 10,000-word limit) distills his earliest interpretation of Jefferson. He based his essay on his conception of Jefferson as "the symbol and prophet of a political faith" in constitutional democracy, likening Jefferson's "hostility to

Hamilton" to "that of a religious devotee to an enemy of his faith." Malone highlighted Jefferson's work as a legal reformer in Virginia, his drafting of such pivotal state papers as the Declaration of Independence, and his advocacy of separation of church and state.[13] Malone's admiration did not blind him to Jefferson's shortcomings, however. He offered devastating assessments of Jefferson's governorship of Virginia and of his strict-constructionist constitutional philosophy.[14]

In 1936, again postponing work on Jefferson, Malone became director of the Harvard University Press, turning it into a leading publisher of well-crafted scholarship for a general audience. Yet in July 1943, Malone resigned, returning to his Jefferson project, for which, in 1938, he had signed a contract with Little, Brown to write a four-volume biography.[15]

At the time of Malone's decision in 1926 to write a "big book" on Jefferson, there had been no comprehensive biography since Henry S. Randall's 1858 three-volume authorized life. When in 1943 Malone returned to Jefferson, he regarded his competitors with equanimity. Gilbert Chinard's acclaimed one-volume 1929 biography differed in scale from Malone's plan. The journalist and Democratic activist Claude G. Bowers published the best-selling *Jefferson and Hamilton: The Struggle for Democracy in America* in 1925, but writing the framing volumes of his Jefferson trilogy took him nearly twenty years, by which time the evolution of Jefferson scholarship had left his biography behind.[16]

As Malone was starting work, the architectural historian Fiske Kimball (supervising Monticello's restoration) told him daunting news: his wife, Marie Kimball, about to become Monticello's first curator, was planning her own multivolume Jefferson biography. As Malone told Peterson, he thought that the Kimballs viewed him as "an unwelcome intruder." Conceding their formidable status, he concluded—rightly, in the end—that they would not jeopardize his venture. (Marie Kimball died in 1955; her three volumes took Jefferson only to 1789.[17])

As the 1943 bicentennial of Jefferson's birth showed, a group of Jefferson specialists was coalescing within the historical profession, with Malone standing out as one of its leaders. The growing body of scholarship on Jefferson called for a synthesis to guide future laborers in the field. The ideal form for that synthesis, Malone thought, would be an authoritative biography addressed to historians and to "thinking Americans in the middle of the twentieth century."[18]

In 1944, Malone won a Rockefeller Foundation fellowship that financed his travel to Julian Boyd's project at Princeton University to edit Jefferson's papers and to such storehouses of Jefferson manuscripts as the Library of Congress and the Massachusetts Historical Society. In 1945, Malone joined Columbia University's history faculty, after Allan Nevins resolved conflicts between accepting Columbia's offer and keeping his Rockefeller fellowship.[19]

On April 13, 1948, Little, Brown published *Jefferson the Virginian;* at least one reviewer noted that the volume's publication date was Jefferson's birthday. Malone's first volume appeared between the unveiling in 1943 of the Jefferson Memorial in Washington, D.C., and the publication in 1950 of the first volume of Boyd's *Papers of Thomas Jefferson.* These three events marked the apotheosis of Jefferson that had begun in the 1920s and was peaking in the early years of the Cold War.[20]

Malone opened *Jefferson the Virginian* with an introduction sketching his approach to the subject, defining his view of Jefferson's life, and explaining why he found certain issues, ideas, and events noteworthy. Each later volume included a similar introduction; these essays traced the development of Malone's interpretation of Jefferson, defining his sense of what course Jefferson scholarship should take, what issues it should emphasize, and what matters it should downplay.

Grouping Jefferson, Washington, and Lincoln as the three greatest Americans, Malone insisted that "Jefferson surpassed both of them in the rich diversity of his achievements." Distilling these achievements into a phrase shaped by his experience of two world wars and the Cold War, Malone identified Jefferson "as a major apostle of individual freedom and human dignity [who] has long belonged, not merely to his own compatriots, but to the human race."

Malone defined his objectives and methods: "My major purposes for the work are that it shall be comprehensive, that it shall relate Jefferson's career to his age, and that it shall be true to his own chronology. As a result it will be long, it will be historical (it can hardly be anything else), and it will be primarily a narrative." Declaring *Jefferson the Virginian* the first volume of a comprehensive biography, Malone sketched his plan for the remaining volumes. The second would take Jefferson from his first diplomatic mission in 1784 through his election as president in 1801; the third would cover Jefferson's presidency, from 1801 to 1809; and the last would examine Jefferson's retirement, from 1809 to his death in 1826.

Stressing that Jefferson was a Virginian and an emerging revolutionary, Malone argued that these themes linked the period from 1743 through 1784. Invoking Jefferson's identity as a Virginian as critical to understanding him in this era of his life, Malone defined Jefferson as a reforming liberal, a "philosophical statesman" rather than a grand aristocrat or a fire-breathing revolutionary. Significantly, Malone refused to label Jefferson a politician, by which he meant someone "skilled in partisan maneuver, gifted as an organizer, and a master of the art of winning votes." Rather, Malone argued, he saw Jefferson as Jefferson saw himself: "a personally disinterested public man whose prime concern was the promotion of the public good and who made a special point of avoiding factional quarrels." In this period, Jefferson became "a symbol of ideas which inspired hope among the inarticulate as well as the enlightened."[21] Malone's vision of Jefferson as a symbolic figure dominated *Jefferson and His Time*.

Jefferson and the Rights of Man (1951) began with Jefferson's journey to France in 1784 to begin his work as an American diplomat, but it ended with President Washington's reelection in 1792 rather than with Jefferson's election in 1801. Malone explained that the primary sources' breadth and depth required this revision to his plan. In another revision, Malone included a detailed chronology in this volume and its successors.[22]

Rights of Man linked two subjects—Jefferson as diplomat in Europe and Jefferson as public man in America—by reference to his intellectual interests and commitments. In Europe, Jefferson "never gave clearer proof of his undying belief that men and society can be saved by means of knowledge." Malone juxtaposed Jefferson's response to the French Revolution and his role in establishing the government under the U.S. Constitution, arguing that Jefferson approved both developments "*with qualifications,* and judged them both in terms of human values."

In *Rights of Man,* Malone first came to grips with Alexander Hamilton—as Jefferson's colleague in Washington's cabinet, as advocate of broad interpretation of the Constitution, and as a leading Federalist. Though conceding that some of Hamilton's ideas were sound, Malone insisted that Jefferson was equally sound in his critique of Hamiltonian policy and of Hamilton's methods of making and effectuating policy. Arguing that "Hamilton was clearly the earlier and much the greater offender against official proprieties, though he and his partisans sought to create a very different impression," Malone declared his disappointment that "Hamilton comes out of my investigations worse than I had expected." Malone's view of Hamilton as devious, manipulative, and "lusting for personal as well as national power" defined his place in *Jefferson and His Time.* By contrast, Malone saw Jefferson as "a true and pure symbol of the rights of man because, in his own mind, the cause was greater than himself."[23]

Jefferson and the Ordeal of Liberty (1962) appeared eleven years after *Rights of Man*—a delay caused by Malone's many responsibilities, including his teaching duties, his managing editorship of the *Political Science Quarterly,* his writing commitments, and his return in 1959 to the University of Virginia as the Thomas Jefferson Foundation Professor of History and then, in 1962, as biographer in residence.[24] Another problem for Malone was the stately rate of publication of Boyd's *Papers of Thomas Jefferson.* Having begun work before Boyd's first volume, Malone had hoped to rely on the *Jefferson Papers.* Outpacing Boyd's progress, however, he had to resume digging through manuscript sources.[25]

Malone confessed that *Ordeal of Liberty* "has proved the most difficult [volume] to write." In particular, he noted wryly, "the year 1793, with which the main narrative begins, was an inordinately long one. It may well have been the longest Jefferson ever spent: I thought I should never get him through it." He added, "I must confess that I shared Jefferson's feeling of relief when he completed his arduous tour of duty as secretary of state and retired to the quietude of Monticello. . . . He was for a time a free man."

Ordeal of Liberty completed Malone's emergence not merely as Jefferson's biographer but as his defender against his political and historiographical foes. Noting resonances between the partisanship, intolerance, and persecutions of the late 1790s and "the orgies of suspicious patriotism which accompanied and followed our two world wars," Malone aligned Jefferson with friends of liberty and against avatars of "suspicious patriotism." He noted, "In an age of immoderation and scurrility, Jefferson did not often lapse from his own high standards of propriety, and never consciously in public so far as I know." Yet Malone made a revealing admission: "I must say that after living intimately in spirit with Jefferson in earlier periods of his life, I found him a rather different man in parts of this one. . . . As a party leader he not infrequently seemed out of character."[26]

Coming to terms with Jefferson as a political leader was Malone's greatest difficulty in writing *Ordeal of Liberty*. Perhaps for this reason, in 1962 he gave three lectures at the University of California, Berkeley, in the Jefferson Memorial Lectures series, publishing them in 1963 as *Thomas Jefferson as Political Leader*. Distilling the issues explored at length in *Ordeal of Liberty*, these lectures confirmed Malone's discomfort with Jefferson as a politician. Nonetheless, in his lectures as in *Ordeal of Liberty*, Malone stressed the mendacity and deviousness of Jefferson's foes—specifically Hamilton and Aaron Burr—while insisting on Jefferson's honesty, his distaste for politics, and his longing for retirement.[27]

Jefferson the President: First Term, 1801–1805 (1970) signaled another change of plan—Malone would cover Jefferson's presidency in two volumes. Noting that his "presidency was much the most complicated part of Jefferson's career" and that the "materials bearing on it are considerably more extensive than in any other equivalent period," Malone added that Jefferson's life so entwined with American history that it was hard to disentangle them. As he admitted, the volume was nearly as much a history of Jefferson's administration as a biography of Jefferson, although Malone kept Jefferson at the book's focus.

Both Jefferson's life as president and Jefferson's view of his presidency's significance were central to *First Term,* to American history, and to the history of the human quest for liberty. Malone insisted that Jefferson took seriously the Federalists' threat to liberty and that he meant what he said about the direct relationship between "the revolution of 1800" and the "spirit of 1776." Committed to restoring the balance among the federal government's branches, Jefferson rejected what he saw as Federalist excesses of executive power. For example, he discontinued delivery of presidential State of the Union addresses, instead sending written messages to Congress to be read aloud. In contrast to his friendly relations with Congress, he viewed the nation's courts, dominated by Federalists, with suspicious hostility, fighting a battle "intermittently and indecisively" with John Marshall and the federal bench. Malone also presented a forgiving view of the Republicans' uses of impeachment against Judge John Pickering and Justice Samuel Chase; although identifying Jefferson as initiator of this impeachment campaign, he denied that Jefferson had any direct role in it.[28]

Malone saw the dominant feature of Jefferson's presidency as pragmatism rather than ideological consistency. Deeming Jefferson's constitutional views well-considered, moderate, and suited to the country's condition, he praised Jefferson for reconciling his ideological commitments with his recognitions of things as they were. Thus he praised Jefferson's efforts to acquire the Louisiana Territory and his efforts to uphold what Jefferson called "the illimitable freedom of the human mind." Rejecting Leonard W. Levy's attack on Jefferson's views of liberty of the press, Malone maintained the tone of lofty dismissal pervading his review of Levy's *Jefferson and Civil Liberties: The Darker Side*.[29] Finally, with relief, he acknowledged the differences between Jefferson as partisan leader and Jefferson as president: "Few things about him have impressed me more than his extraordinary ability to hold diverse and even contradictory things in equilibrium. He showed more composure when in the highest office than he had in opposition, and conducted a balanced government as a well-balanced man."[30]

Jefferson's biographers struggle with scandalous charges concerning his private life. The leading controversies focus on his relations with Mrs. John Walker (known as Betsey), the wife of a friend and neighbor, and his relations with Sally Hemings, an enslaved woman who was half-sister to his wife, Martha Wayles Skelton Jefferson. Malone disposed of the Walker affair in an appendix to *Jefferson the Virginian*. He sought to dispose of the Hemings controversy in an appendix to *First Term* because the notorious journalist James Thomson Callender published his allegations about that relationship in 1802. This appendix caused Malone more trouble than anything else he wrote about Jefferson, because the Hemings controversy would not go away.[31]

Jefferson the President: Second Term, 1805–1809 (1974), his longest volume, showed problems of editorial control owing to the profusion of sources and Malone's age, fragile health, and growing blindness. Thanks to his research assistant, Steven H. Hochman, Malone used imaging technology to blow up documents large enough for him to read a word at a time, as well as listening to taped readings of documents. With the aid of Hochman and of Malone's secretary, Katherine Sergeant, Malone finished *Second Term* and its sequel, *The Sage of Monticello* (1981), which he dedicated to them.[32]

In *Second Term*, Malone noted the difficulty of keeping the volume's focus on Jefferson because "his actions were taken to a greater degree in response and reaction to the doings of others." Although Jefferson sought to maintain cordial relations with Congress and to exert indirect control over its legislative agenda, the constitutional purism of such congressional Republicans as John Randolph of Roanoke rendered his dealings with Congress increasingly turbulent. His dealings with the judiciary were even worse than in his first term; Jefferson "was baffled by the problem of reconciling judicial independence with the sovereignty of the people, and his own actions can be interpreted as designed, not to attain dominance over the judiciary, but to prevent it from encroaching on the prerogatives of the executive and obstructing the necessary operations of the government." Trying to set Jefferson's ideas and conduct in domestic and foreign affairs in context, Malone concluded, "It seems to me not far from the truth to say that in the domestic field he was seeking to reconcile the irreconcilable, and in the foreign field to solve the insoluble." It was an "anticlimactic" end to a successful presidency. Like Jefferson, Malone felt "unfeigned joy" to leave the subject and, with Jefferson, to take "the road back to Monticello."[33]

In 1981, Malone published *The Sage of Monticello.* Not only was this last volume the first since *Jefferson the Virginian* to correspond to his original plan, it also covered the most new ground, as no previous scholar had studied Jefferson's retirement with Malone's care and level of detail. Malone explained that, whereas his earlier volumes dealt principally with Jefferson as a public man, *The Sage of Monticello* had a topical structure because it "covers more time than any of the others except the first and has the greatest diversity of them all."

Focusing on Jefferson's intellectual life, Malone stressed his engagement with "the cause of public enlightenment." He lovingly detailed Jefferson's creation of the University of Virginia, his retirement's central project and one of the three achievements that he listed in the epitaph that he composed for himself. Malone also traced, with empathetic sorrow, Jefferson's financial plight, which cast an ominous shadow over his old age. He closed this volume, and his biography, on an elegiac note:

> At the end of this volume it can be said that this man of many
> parts and great generosity offers something of interest to everybody.
> Not only was he an intensely devoted family man; he was a friend
> to mankind. Although rooted in his native soil he never ceased to
> contemplate the universe. No one can sum up his claims to remembrance better than he himself did. As the well-known inscription
> on his tombstone says, he wanted to be remembered as the author
> of the Declaration of American Independence and the statute of
> Virginia for religious freedom, and as father of the University of

Virginia. In these pages he has been viewed in his own time and circumstances. He was limited by these, and he made concessions to the society in which he lived. But he perceived eternal values and supported timeless causes. Thus he became one of the most notable champions of freedom and enlightenment in recorded history.[34]

Fifty-five years after deciding to write "a big book about Thomas Jefferson," Malone had completed his life's work. And yet, in the last year of his life, at Merrill Peterson's request, Malone returned to Jefferson, revising his 1933 *DAB* essay to appear as the first chapter of Peterson's *Thomas Jefferson: A Reference Biography.* The revised essay appeared separately in 1993 as the first Monticello Monograph, with an admiring preface by Peterson.[35]

Reviewing with care, Malone tightened his prose and modified his interpretation. Tellingly, he softened or cut earlier criticisms, deleting most of his strictures on Jefferson's governorship of Virginia and his disapproval of Jefferson's strict-constructionist model of constitutional interpretation. These revisions, Malone told Peterson, corrected his earlier tendency to concede too much to Jefferson's political opponents and historiographical critics. *Thomas Jefferson: A Brief Biography,* a defiant distillation of his six volumes, is the last statement on a large, complicated subject by one of its leading scholars. Malone died at his home in Charlottesville on December 27, 1986, survived by his wife of seven decades, Elisabeth Gifford Malone; by his son, Gifford, and his daughter, Lisa; and by one grandchild.

One might conclude that *Jefferson and His Time* would long stand as an admirable monument to a man worthy of admiration, as well as to the man who created it, and yet the erosion of that monument began even as he was creating it.[36] Malone's critics stress two weaknesses of his view of Jefferson: his treatment of Jefferson as politician, and his views of Jefferson's relationship with slavery and race in general and his dismissal of the Hemings-Jefferson controversy in particular, with reference to Jefferson's contradictory roles as an advocate of human freedom and as a lifelong slaveowner.

Reviews of *Jefferson the Virginian* ranged from generous to enthusiastic, most declaring the book the harbinger of the definitive life of Jefferson.[37] This chorus of praise confirmed for Malone that the time was right to undertake the project, and that his was the right approach. *Rights of Man* also received enthusiastic reviews, but the first notes of criticism appeared.[38]

Though Crane Brinton declared that "the work is destined to be the major life of Jefferson of our time," he questioned Malone's distaste for Hamilton, speculating that, as with biographers of Disraeli and Gladstone, so it might be with biographers of Jefferson and Hamilton, that those who admire one inevitably will dislike the other.[39]

Most reviewers of *Ordeal of Liberty* welcomed Malone's resumption of work on the era's defining life of Jefferson.[40] Some expressed qualms, however. Noble E. Cunningham Jr. disputed Malone's view of Jefferson as a passive political leader, noting Jefferson's use of private correspondence to advance political goals, whereas Keith Berwick questioned the usefulness of a multivolume biography, citing its demands on readers, and concluding that the project's size and duration and Malone's lack of "the polemical instinct" would cost the volumes of *Jefferson and His Time* "the influence they deserve."[41]

One review of *First Term* signaled the emergence of new currents in Jefferson scholarship. Fawn M. Brodie, biographer of Joseph Smith, Sir Richard Burton, and Thaddeus Stevens, published a review essay, "Jefferson Biographers and the Psychology of Canonization," assessing *First Term* and Peterson's *Thomas Jefferson and the New Nation*.[42] Brodie raised unsettling questions about the psychological relationship between biographer and subject, asking whether a biographer is drawn to a subject because of resonances between the biographer's and the subject's lives. In particular, most Jefferson biographers were "extremely protective" of their subject's inner life, "or of his intimate life, which is not quite the same thing." Brodie presented a bold reading of Jefferson's correspondence with the artist Maria Cosway, contrasting with the subject's guarded treatment by Malone and Peterson, and ended with a startling sketch of Jefferson's relations with Sally Hemings, focusing as much on Malone's and Peterson's reactions to the controversy as on Jefferson's relations with Hemings. Three years later, Brodie published *Thomas Jefferson: An Intimate History*, an explosive intervention into Jefferson scholarship drawing national attention.[43]

Although Malone did not answer Brodie, in 1975 he and Steven H. Hochman published "A Note on Evidence: The Personal History of Madison Hemings" in the *Journal of Southern History*.[44] Their controversial article took a standard rhetorical tack—refuting an argument by undermining its principal source. Malone and Hochman argued that the 1873 Ohio newspaper article presenting a memoir by Sally Hemings's son Madison Hemings was actually the work of the editor who interviewed Hemings, the abolitionist S. T. Wetmore, who shaped Hemings's story to suit his critique of slavery in general, slaveholders in particular, and Jefferson above all. (The unexamined assumptions on which Malone and Hochman built their critique did not survive the withering scrutiny of Annette Gordon-Reed.[45]) While trying to appear above the fray, Malone left no doubt that he rejected the Hemings allegations and Brodie's biography; he assisted the journalist Virginius Dabney, who wrote a short book assailing Brodie's interpretation, and he sought to persuade publishers, television networks, and journalists not to pay heed to the Hemings question—although his growing discomfort with any public role in the matter impelled him to distance himself from the controversy.[46]

Other reviewers of *First Term* were kinder than Brodie had been.[47] Often they juxtaposed Malone's work with Henry Adams's *History of the United States during the Administrations of Thomas Jefferson and James Madison*, acknowledging Malone's more favorable assessment of Jefferson's presidency while setting his work on a par with Adams's.[48] Still, some reviewers dissented. As Marshall Smelser wrote, "The author is not uncritical of Jefferson, but all adverse comment is his own; he brings in the censures of other writers only to qualify them."[49] Similarly, Keith Berwick highlighted the gap between "Jefferson's character" and "Malone's idealized conception of it." Noting inconsistencies between Jefferson's constitutional vision of limited government and his willingness to extend federal constitutional power to justify the Louisiana Purchase, Berwick also cited Brodie's view of the Hemings issue, presaging controversies that would swamp the field and plague Malone. He concluded by questioning the definitiveness of Malone's work-in-progress.[50]

Cataclysmic events bedeviled Malone while writing his account of Jefferson's views of executive privilege in *United States v. Burr* (1807), a significant episode in *Second Term*. In 1974, the Watergate scandal engulfed President Richard M. Nixon, who resisted congressional and prosecutorial investigations by pleading executive privilege, in part relying on Jefferson's invocations of that privilege. Malone's analysis, favoring Jefferson's claims of privilege, drew fire from Raoul Berger and Garry Wills, who rejected the privilege's legitimacy.[51] Malone's responses to Berger and Wills exemplified his overall view of Jefferson's presidency; on this as on so much else, he defended Jefferson against all comers.[52]

Reviews of *The Sage of Monticello* were enthusiastic, even celebratory, though criticism was increasingly prominent.[53] For example, Steven M. Stowe questioned Malone's treatment of such questions as Jefferson's financial history and his role as the paterfamilias of Monticello as unique to Jefferson instead of setting them within a larger historical and cultural context.[54] So, too, C. Vann Woodward reproved Malone for being "more indulgent of Jefferson's attitudes and acquiescence toward slavery than able younger scholars have been lately."[55] And Gordon S. Wood noted that the defining features of Malone's biography—"its majesty, . . . its soothing prose, . . . its reasonableness and humane tolerance, and . . . its deeply rooted confidence in things American"—seem "to come from another time and another place." As Wood wrote, the long gestation of Malone's biography rendered it an artifact from a past era.[56]

One key front on which critics took Malone to task was his treatment of Jefferson as a politician. Jefferson was a public man from his first election to the Virginia House of Burgesses in the late 1760s through his retirement from the presidency in 1809; even as a former president he maintained his close interest in American politics, and his retirement's chief project, founding the University of Virginia, immersed him in Virginia legislative politics.[57] Nonetheless, despite the centrality of politics to Jefferson's life, Malone displayed profound discomfort with the subject, as shown starkly in his account of Jefferson's life between his return from France in 1789 and his election as president in 1801. For example, by defining "politician" narrowly as someone "skilled in partisan maneuver, gifted as an organizer, and a master of the art of winning votes," Malone excluded from politics much of Jefferson's most assiduous involvement in politics.[58] As Stephen G. Kurtz and Noble E. Cunningham noted, Malone did not take sufficient account of one of Jefferson's favorite way of practicing politics—using private letters to circulate ideas among like-minded Republicans.[59]

Recent work on Jefferson as a politician studies what he said and did to promote his political goals and to shape the perceptions and actions of fellow citizens and fellow players of the political game. Never giving orders like a Tammany ward boss, Jefferson practiced a deliberately informal, low-key style of politics. His tools were private correspondence and meetings with allies; his approach stressed friendship and collegiality. These methods allowed Jefferson to practice politics in ways suiting his skill with his pen, his distaste for confrontation, and his preference for face-to-face dealings. Insisting that Jefferson stayed out of politics or that he was too passive for political leadership, Malone overlooked precisely the methods of indirect, behind-the-scenes leadership that Jefferson found most congenial.[60] The increasing sophistication of political history illuminates the practice of politics and the grammar of political combat in Jefferson's time. These scholarly innovations supersede the vision of politics embedded in Malone's approach to Jefferson, undermining his constricted view of Jefferson as politician and political leader and undercutting his portrayals of Hamilton, Burr, and Marshall as Jefferson's foils and as villains of the tale.[61]

The most agonizing subjects arising in the reconsideration of Malone's work are slavery and race. From his earliest memory of being carried on a pillow by a slave during his family's move from Shadwell to Tuckahoe when he was two years old to his deathbed request to have his pillow adjusted so that he could lie more comfortably (a request that only his slave Burrell Colbert understood), Jefferson lived his life surrounded and supported by slavery.[62] His struggles with slavery and his discomfort with the clash between his status as a slaveowner and his commitment to principles of liberty and equality form a conflict central to modern Jefferson scholarship. That conflict rarely roils the placid, genial surface of Malone's biography, however. In considering Jefferson's thinking about slavery and about those who were enslaved, Malone took Jefferson at his word, sidestepping conflicts that other scholars have explored. In a more disturbing omission, Malone either failed to consider later scholarship on Jefferson and slavery or dismissed its findings.

To understand Malone's reluctance to engage these matters and his preference for Jefferson's views of them, we must set Malone in context. His upbringing shaped his efforts to understand Jefferson. Like Jefferson, Malone was a man of the American South; like Jefferson, Malone was shaped by his region's cultural and political values, in particular those concerning race, slavery, and the slaveholding culture that reigned for over two centuries before it was shattered by the Civil War and destroyed by Reconstruction. An incident in 1951 at Columbia University illuminates Malone's perspective. Leonard W. Levy was defending his dissertation on Chief Justice Lemuel Shaw of Massachusetts; Malone was one of his examiners. Levy's account of his thesis defense features an unnerving remark by Malone:

> Exposing raw prejudice in the halls of ivy is like fornicating on
> a scared altar. I was shaken, therefore, when Professor Dumas
> Malone, at the defense of my doctoral dissertation in 1951, objected

to my critical assessment of the origins of the "separate but equal"
doctrine by remarking in his pleasant drawl, "When Ah was a
boy in Mississippi we jes' couldn't let a niggra go to a white man's
school." Noel T. Dowling, the Harlan Fiske Stone Professor of
Constitutional Law at Columbia Law School, added, "I associate
myself with the remarks of the distinguished speaker." Henry Steele
Commager, my dissertation supervisor, who sat next to me, kicked
me under the table, a warning to shut up and let the point pass,
while he deftly changed the subject.[63]

This incident raises the question whether a man born in 1892 in the
Deep South could have written a life of Jefferson any different from *Jefferson
and His Time.* Specifically, could Malone have drawn on developments in
the historiography of slavery to deepen his treatment of Jefferson's agonized
struggles with slavery and race? Criticizing Malone for failing to anticipate or
engage with a later generation's perspectives may embody what E. P. Thompson rightly dubbed "the enormous condescension of posterity"—though
other scholars contemporaneous with Malone did make such attempts.[64]

Slaves rarely step out of the background of Malone's portrait of Jefferson. If Malone was capturing Jefferson's view of the enslaved human beings
who ran the plantations that he owned—who harvested the crops, made
the nails, built the house, crafted its furnishings, cooked the meals, and
tended to him, his family members, and his guests—perhaps he pursued
a plausible biographical strategy. And yet by not heeding the limits as well as
the strengths of his hesitant treatment of slavery, Malone obscured a reality
that provoked, in Jefferson and in posterity pondering Jefferson, painful
reflections on the conflicts between his ideas and his daily life, between his
aspirations for Virginia and America and the realities of slavery as an integral
part of life in Virginia and America.

Annette Gordon-Reed demonstrated with devastating results the effects
of unacknowledged assumptions by Malone and other scholars on their
approach to the question of Sally Hemings's relations with Thomas Jefferson.
As Gordon-Reed shows, only assumptions that white people tell the truth
and black people lie, that slaveowners tell the truth and slaves lie, make it
easy to discount the testimony of Madison Hemings and Israel Jefferson and
the oral traditions preserved by the Hemings family—as Malone and other
Jefferson scholars did. By contrast, reversing those assumptions and testing

them against the evidence, including evidence to which the Hemingses had no access, reveals that the evidence fits more accurately these reversed assumptions, requiring reconsideration of Malone's reflexive rejection of the Hemings-Jefferson liaison.

Gordon-Reed focused on Malone's use of Jefferson's character as refutation. Malone held that charges that Jefferson had a sexual relationship with Hemings were "distinctly out of character, being virtually unthinkable in a man of Jefferson's moral standards and habitual conduct."[65] In *Thomas Jefferson and Sally Hemings,* Gordon-Reed painstakingly dismantles Malone's character defense, exposing Malone's limitations and changing scholars' and readers' perceptions of his life's work.

The theme linking these critiques of *Jefferson and His Time* is that Malone failed to grasp that a biographer has not one but two goals—first, to see his subject and his subject's world as he saw himself and his world; and, second, to maintain appropriate scholarly distance from his subject. Malone achieved only the first. By conflating his own perspective with Jefferson's, he succumbed to the greatest danger facing any biographer. Failing to preserve a measured perspective on his subject, he inadvertently reduced his biography to a capacious, eloquent brief for the defense. In light of Malone's failure, Peterson's praise in *The Jefferson Image in the American Mind* can cause eyebrows to skyrocket and jaws to drop. Malone, Peterson concluded, wrote "without acrimony or hyperbole, without one-sidedness or the exaggeration of single-minded interpretations, without concealment of faults or loss of historical perspective, without obtrusive scholarly vendettas, and without the aimless antiquarianism that risked the loss of the subject in the vastness of the record. The work was full, reasonable, and honest. The consistency of Jefferson's life, which had given so much trouble to students who looked for it in the pattern of ideas and politics, became clear in the growing record of the man's experience."[66]

The concepts of definitiveness and masterpiece go hand in hand; reviewers use both terms to compliment a distinguished work of art or scholarship. Masterpiece originally meant a work—of art or scholarship—that a craft's practitioner produced to justify his or her claim to be a master of that craft. Such a masterpiece, however, can be flawed, however great its excellence in craft. In that sense, Malone's *Jefferson and His Time* is a masterpiece. The problem arises when we consider the word's colloquial meaning, denoting not just a great but a perfect work. That is when the term "masterpiece" can obscure understanding.

In 1995, Frank Shuffelton published a meditation on the definitiveness of *Jefferson and His Time* as admiring as (but more nuanced and reflective than) Peterson's comments in *The Jefferson Image in the American Mind.*[67] Marveling at Malone's heroic achievement despite debilities of age and illness, Shuffelton juxtaposed his biography with previous claimants to definitiveness—the earlier biographies by George Tucker and Henry S. Randall—while pondering what definitiveness means for any historical biography.[68]

Definitiveness, Shuffelton observed, carries the implication that the work need never be done again—although, as he noted, Malone's volumes have not dissuaded later authors from writing Jefferson biographies. Rejecting that conventional understanding, Shuffelton argued instead that a definitive work is so authoritative and comprehensive that it always will be indispensable for future scholars and readers, even if later works match or exceed its achievement. (Shuffelton's understanding of a definitive work may be applied with equal force to the idea of a masterpiece.)

Shuffelton cited four factors justifying a biography's claims to definitiveness: its status as a major advance beyond the historiographical context giving rise to it; its author's authority to undertake such a work; the degree to which the biography meets the needs of its cultural-historical moment of publication; and the author's industry in research not only in published sources and scholarship but also in otherwise-inaccessible manuscript sources. On all four counts, Shuffelton declared, *Jefferson and His Time* deserves the label "definitive."

Shuffelton accepted Malone's achievement at face value, assuming that his six volumes constituted a biography rather than a biographical defense. That said, the biographer's tendency to conflate his or her perspective with that of his or her subject can prove nearly inescapable, especially after the devotion of nearly forty years of close study to one person's life.[69] It may be impossible for a biographer to go from seeking to understand to wanting to defend, or (as Gordon S. Wood wrote in 1981) "deadening the criticism of Jefferson by enclosing it within [Malone's] scholarly synthesis."[70] Even so, if Malone's experience in writing *Jefferson and His Time* teaches anything, it is that it is impossible to deaden criticism of Jefferson, no matter how well-written, scholarly, and formidable the scholarly synthesis may be.

The aspiration to definitiveness carries various perils. Some are obvious—definitiveness all too easily can become obsolescence, given changes wrought by the passing of time on cultural and political values, and given innovative scholarship increasingly difficult to assimilate within a biographical synthesis conceived years or decades earlier. Some are more subtle, such as the shift in readers' tastes from large, even monumental, works to shorter, distilled studies, whether concise biographies or thematic lives. Definitiveness, nonetheless, is an appealing goal. It is the scholar's way to achieve the enduring fame that is "the ruling passion of the noblest minds," as Hamilton wrote in *The Federalist No. 77*. But, as the case of Dumas Malone shows, definitiveness has its perils.

The only works that may deserve the accolade of definitiveness, even using Shuffelton's precise and thoughtful definition, are such documentary-editing projects as the *Papers of Thomas Jefferson,* the *Papers of Benjamin Franklin,* the *Adams Papers,* and the *Documentary History of the Ratification of the Constitution.* Enriching the lives and work of generations of scholars and readers, these projects will nurture historical and biographical scholarship long after their editors have gone to their rewards. It is in creating such works as these that definitiveness loses its perils. The rest of us stand and fall by the work that we do, and we assume the risk that future scholars will find our work wanting. Those are the rules of the game, whether for historians or biographers, especially in dealing with Thomas Jefferson.

Notes

I am grateful to New York University Law School's Golieb Research Colloquium—William E. Nelson, John Phillip Reid, William P. LaPiana, Norma Basch, Bernard Freamon, Daniel Ernst, Frank Henderson Stewart, Harold Forsythe, Veronica Hendrick, Jessica Lowe, Ada-Maria Kuskowski, and Kaius Touri—for a valuable session discussing a draft of this essay; to Michael D. Hattem and Michael Blaakman of Yale University, for their close and attentive reading, and to their mentor, Joanne B. Freeman of Yale University, for her sage counsel, careful reading, and years of collegial friendship; to Maeva Marcus, Director of the Institute for Constitutional History at the New-York Historical Society and George Washington University, and Charles L. Zelden of Nova Southeastern University, Pauline Maier of MIT, Edward A. Purcell Jr. of New York Law School, David Thomas Konig of Washington University–St. Louis, and Peter Charles Hoffer of the University of Georgia at Athens for reading over my shoulder and providing encouragement and illuminating criticism; to George and Margaret Billias, for many reasons; and to my friend and law school classmate Maureen K. Phillips for catching two vital points that everyone else missed.

1. Dumas Malone, *Jefferson the Virginian* (Boston, 1948).

2. See http://www.pulitzer.org/awards/1975.

3. See sources cited in note 53.

4. Compare Merrill D. Peterson, *The Jefferson Image in the American Mind* (New York, 1960; reprint with new introduction, Charlottesville, Va., 1998), with Francis D. Cogliano, *Thomas Jefferson: Reputation and Legacy* (Edinburgh, 2006; Charlottesville, Va., 2006), 6–9 and *passim*. See also R. B. Bernstein, *Thomas Jefferson* (New York, 2003), 191–98.

5. Hermione Lee, *Biography: A Very Short Introduction* (New York, 2009), 18.

6. For the usefulness and drawbacks of biography as a genre of historical scholarship, see Trevor Burnard, "Review Essay: The Founding Fathers in Early American Historiography: A View from Abroad," *WMQ* 62 (2005): 745–64. On the disputed place of heroes in American culture, see Peter H. Gibbon, *A Call to Heroism: Renewing America's Vision of Greatness* (New York, 2002).

7. This essay draws on Merrill D. Peterson, "Dumas Malone: An Appreciation," *WMQ* 45 (1988): 237–52 (hereafter cited as Peterson, "Appreciation"); Merrill Peterson, "Dumas Malone: The Completion of a Monument," *VQR* 58 (1982): 26–31, http://www.vqronline.org/articles/1982/winter/peterson-dumas-malone/ (hereafter cited as Peterson, "Completion"); Merrill D. Peterson, "Preface" to Dumas Malone, *Thomas Jefferson: A Brief Biography* (Charlottesville, Va., 1993), 7–9; Eric Pace, "Dumas Malone, Expert on Jefferson, Is Dead at 94," *New York Times*, 28 December 1986, http://www.nytimes.com/1986/12/28/obituaries/dumas-malone-expert-on-jefferson-is-dead-at-94.html; and G. Allen Giannini, "Dumas Malone," in *American National Biography*, ed. John A. Garraty and Mark C. Carnes, 24 vols. (New York, 1999), 14:384–85. *American National Biography* is the successor to the *Dictionary of American Biography*—for which see text at notes 11–15. Since writing this essay, I have read William G. Hyland Jr., *Long Journey with Mr. Jefferson: The Life of Dumas Malone* (Washington, D.C., 2013), with skeptical disappointment. An exercise in hagiography rather than biography, it is a companion to Hyland's disputatious *In Defense of Thomas Jefferson: The Sally Hemings Sex Scandal* (New York, 2009).

8. Peterson, "Appreciation," 238–39.

9. Ibid., 239; Malone, *Jefferson the Virginian*, vii.

10. Dumas Malone, "My Long Journey with Mister Jefferson," quoted in Peterson, "Appreciation," 239–40. Johnson's advice that there was no need for a political biography may have been prompted by Claude G. Bowers, *Jefferson and Hamilton: The Struggle for Democracy in America* (Boston, 1925). On Bowers, see Brian Steele's essay in this volume.

11. Dumas Malone, ed., and Linwood Lehman, trans., *Correspondence Between Thomas Jefferson and Pierre Samuel Du Pont de Nemours, 1798–1817* (Boston, 1930); Gilbert Chinard, ed., *The Correspondence of Jefferson and Du Pont de Nemours* (Baltimore, 1931); Gilbert Chinard, *Thomas Jefferson: The Apostle of Americanism* (Boston, 1929). Da Capo Press reprinted Malone's edition in 1970, with a supplement by Chinard. For a comparative review, see T. J. Wertenbaker, Book Review, *AHR* 37 (1932): 357–59.

Allen Johnson, Dumas Malone, et al., eds., *The Dictionary of American Biography*, 20 vols. (New York, 1927–36) (hereafter cited as *DAB*).

12. Dumas Malone, "Who Are the American Immortals?," *Harper's Monthly Magazine* 174 (1937): 544–48.

13. *DAB*, s.v. "Jefferson, Thomas," 10:17–35, esp. 26 ("symbol and prophet"), 22 ("civic faith"), 25 ("hostility to Hamilton").

14. *DAB*, s.v. "Jefferson, Thomas," 20, 24.

15. Dumas Malone, "The Scholar and the Public," *Proceedings of the American Philosophical Society* 80 (1939): 25–36; Peterson, "Appreciation," 241–42.

16. Henry Stephens Randall, *The Life of Thomas Jefferson*, 3 vols. (New York, 1858; Philadelphia, 1865) (see Andrew Burstein's essay in this volume); Chinard, *Jefferson: Apostle of Americanism* (see Herbert Sloan's essay in this volume); Bowers, *Jefferson and Hamilton*; Claude G. Bowers, *Jefferson in Power: The Death Struggle of the Federalists* (Boston, 1936); Claude G. Bowers, *The Young Jefferson, 1743–1789* (Boston, 1945) (see Brian Steele's essay in this volume).

17. Peterson, "Appreciation," 242; Marie Kimball, *Jefferson: The Road to Glory, 1743 to 1776* (New York, 1943); Marie Kimball, *Jefferson: War and Peace, 1776 to 1784* (New York, 1947); Marie Kimball, *Jefferson: The Scene of Europe, 1784 to 1789* (New York, 1950). On Kimball, see Herbert Sloan's essay in this volume; the biographical article from "The Thomas Jefferson Encyclopedia," http://www.monticello.org/site/about /marie-kimball; and Anna Berkes's excellent appreciation, "The Cult of Marie Kimball," http://www.monticello.org/site/blog-and-community/posts/cult-marie-kimball.

18. Peterson, "Appreciation," 243. For a pioneering review essay, see Douglass Adair, "The New Thomas Jefferson," *WMQ* 3 (1946): 123–33, reprinted in Trevor Colbourn, ed., *Fame and the Founding Fathers: Essays of Douglass Adair* (1974; repr., Indianapolis, 1998), 335–49.

19. Peterson, "Appreciation," 243–44, 244, 245.

20. Adrienne Koch, "'A Predominantly Good Man': Jefferson, Our Philosopher-Statesman, in a New, Rich, and Spirited Biography," *New York Times Book Review*, 11 April 1948, 1, 28. See also *Jefferson Image*, 432–58; Cogliano, *Thomas Jefferson*, 5–6, 9, 262; Bernstein, *Thomas Jefferson*, 192–94; Adair, "New Thomas Jefferson."

21. Malone, *Jefferson the Virginian*, viii, x, xii, x, xv–xvi.

22. Dumas Malone, *Jefferson and the Rights of Man* (Boston, 1951), xiii (explanation of revision). For a sampling of reviews, see Crane Brinton, *WMQ* 9 (1952): 265–67; George Harmon Knoles, *JSH* 18 (1952): 225–29 (noting improvement in style); and Christopher Crittenden, *AHR* 57 (1952): 690–91. For the chronology, see Malone, *Jefferson and the Rights of Man*, xxv–xxix. For praise of this feature, see Peterson, "Appreciation," 247.

23. Malone, *Rights of Man*, xv, xvi (emphasis in original), xx, xxi–xxii, xxiii–xxiv.

24. Dumas Malone, *Jefferson and the Ordeal of Liberty* (Boston, 1962), xiii; Peterson, "Appreciation," 244; Pace, "Dumas Malone."

25. Peterson, "Appreciation," 244–45.

26. Malone, *Ordeal of Liberty*, xiii, xiv, xvi, xviii, xix–xx.

27. Dumas Malone, *Thomas Jefferson as Political Leader* (Berkeley, Calif., 1963).

28. Dumas Malone, *Jefferson the President: First Term, 1801–1805* (Boston, 1970), xiii, xvii–xix (hereafter cited as Malone, *First Term*).

29. Ibid., 228n13, xxi; Leonard W. Levy, *Legacy of Suppression: Freedom of Speech and Press in Early American History* (Cambridge, Mass., 1960); Leonard W. Levy, *Jefferson and Civil Liberties: The Darker Side* (Cambridge, Mass., 1963; reprint, with new introduction, Chicago, 1972); Dumas Malone, "Book Review," *AHR* 69 (1964): 787–89.

30. Malone, *First Term*, xxiii, and see generally xxi–xxiii.

31. Malone, *Jefferson the Virginian*, 447–51; Malone, *First Term*, 494–98. On Callender, see Michael Durey, *"With the Hammer of Truth": James Thomson Callender and America's National Heroes* (Charlottesville, Va., 1990). On Hemings, see Winthrop D. Jordan, *White Over Black: American Attitudes towards the Negro, 1550–1812* (Chapel Hill, N.C., 1968), 461–89; Fawn Brodie, *Thomas Jefferson: An Intimate History* (New York, 1974); Annette Gordon-Reed, *Thomas Jefferson and Sally Hemings: An American Controversy* (Charlottesville, Va., 1997); Jan Ellen Lewis and Peter S. Onuf, eds., *Sally Hemings and Thomas Jefferson: History, Memory, Civic Culture* (Charlottesville, Va., 1999); Annette Gordon-Reed, *The Hemingses of Monticello: An American Family* (New York, 2008). See Gordon-Reed's essay on Brodie in this volume.

32. Dumas Malone, *Jefferson the President: Second Term, 1805–1809* (Boston, 1974). On Malone's struggles with his increasing debility, see Peterson, "Appreciation," 245–46. On Hochman, see http://www.cartercenter.org/news/experts/steven_hochman.html.

33. Malone, *Second Term*, xi, xv–xvi, xix–xx, xxi, xxiii, 668.

34. Dumas Malone, *The Sage of Monticello* (Boston, 1981), xii, xvii, xviii, xvii, 498–99.

35. Peterson, "Preface," 8; Merrill D. Peterson, ed., *Thomas Jefferson: A Reference Biography* (New York, 1986); for Malone's essay, "The Life of Thomas Jefferson," see ibid., 1–24; Dumas Malone, *Thomas Jefferson: A Brief Biography* (Charlottesville, Va., 1993).

36. [Garry Wills,] "An Un-American Politician?," *New York Review of Books* 21, no. 8 (16 May 1974), http://www.nybooks.com/articles/archives/1974/may/16/an-un-american-politician/.

37. Claude G. Bowers, review in *Annals of the American Academy of Political and Social Sciences* 261 (1949): 192. For other reviews, see, e.g., Adrienne Koch, "'A Predominantly Good Man': Jefferson, Our Philosopher-Statesman, in a New, Rich, and Spirited Biography," *New York Times Book Review*, 11 April 1948, 1, 28; Daniel J. Boorstin, *WMQ* 6 (1949): 26–30; William Peden, *American Literature* 21 (1949): 120–21 (arguing that Malone combines the virtues of Bowers and Kimball without the drawbacks of either); George Harmon Knoles, *JSH* 14 (1948): 409–12 (a rare critical note about Malone's style at 412); Benjamin F. Wright, *American Political Science Review* 42 (1948): 1213–14 (criticizing insufficient analysis of Jefferson's political thought and actions); G. H. Guttridge, *English Historical Review* 66 (1951): 113–15.

38. For reviews, see, e.g., Crane Brinton, *WMQ* 9 (1952): 265–67; Christopher Crittenden, *AHR* 57 (1952):690–91; George Harmon Knoles, *JSH* 18 (1952): 225–29.

39. Brinton, "Book Review of *Rights of Man*," 265, 267. See Joanne B. Freeman's essay in this volume.

40. For reviews, see, e.g., Noble E. Cunningham Jr., *JSH* 29 (1963): 258–60; Wendell Holmes Stephenson, *Mississippi Valley Historical Review* 50 (1963): 299–301; Raymond Walters Jr., *AHR* 69 (1964): 476–77; Keith Berwick, *WMQ* 24 (1967): 146–48.

41. Cunningham, "Book Review of *Ordeal of Liberty*," 259; see also Stephen G. Kurtz, *WMQ* 21 (1964): 465–66 (reviewing *Thomas Jefferson as Political Leader*); Berwick, "Book Review of *Ordeal of Liberty*," 148.

42. Fawn M. Brodie, "Jefferson Biographers and the Psychology of Canonization," *Journal of Interdisciplinary History* 2 (1971): 155–71 (quote at 161); Merrill D. Peterson, *Thomas Jefferson and the New Nation* (New York, 1970). On Peterson, see Francis D. Cogliano's essay in this volume.

43. Brodie, *Thomas Jefferson*. On Brodie, see Annette Gordon-Reed's essay in this volume.

44. Dumas Malone and Steven H. Hochman, "A Note on Evidence: The Personal History of Madison Hemings," *JSH* 41 (1975): 423–28.

45. Gordon-Reed, *Thomas Jefferson and Sally Hemings*, 8–16.

46. Scot A. French and Edward L. Ayers, "The Strange Career of Thomas Jefferson: Race and Slavery in American Memory, 1943–1993," in *Jeffersonian Legacies*, ed. Peter S. Onuf (Charlottesville, Va., 1993), 418–56 (esp. 428–34, 435, 436–39, 440–44); Cogliano, *Thomas Jefferson*, 172–74, 177, 187, 188. Virginius Dabney, *The Jefferson Scandals: A Rebuttal* (New York, 1981), appeared at the same time as *The Sage of Monticello*; they often were reviewed together.

47. Other reviews include Adrienne Koch, *New York Times Book Review*, 15 February 1970, 1, 51; Eric L. McKitrick, "The View from Jefferson's Camp," *New York Review of Books* 15, no. 11 (15 December 1970), http://www.nybooks.com/articles/archives/1970/dec/17/the-view-from-jeffersons-camp/?pagination=false; William E. Kelly, *The History Teacher* 4 (1971): 78–79; Morton Borden, *JSH* 36 (1970): 433–35; Richard P. McCormick, *AHR* 75 (1970): 1782–83; Marshall Smelser, *JAH* 57 (1970): 704–5; Keith Berwick, *WMQ* 28 (1971): 653–55.

48. Henry Adams, *History of the United States during the Administrations of Thomas Jefferson and James Madison*, 9 vols. (1889–93; reprint ed., 2 vols., New York, 1986). On Adams, see Richard Samuelson's essay in this volume.

49. Smelser, "Book Review of *First Term*," 704.

50. Berwick, "Book Review of *First Term*," 654, 655.

51. Raoul Berger, "Jefferson v. Marshall in the Burr Case," *American Bar Association Journal* 60 (1974): 702–6; Raoul Berger, "The President, Congress, and the Courts," *Yale Law Journal* 83 (1974): 1111–55; Garry Wills, "The Strange Case of Jefferson's Subpoena," *New York Review of Books* 21, no. 7 (2 May 1974), http://www.nybooks.com/articles/archives/1974/may/02/the-strange-case-of-jeffersons-subpoena/ (reviewing

Malone, *Second Term*, focusing on issues of executive privilege). Malone answered Wills's second essay, noting wryly that he had become a victim of Watergate, and Wills replied: "Exchange: Jefferson & Burr & Nixon & Ehrlichman," *New York Review of Books* 21, no. 12 (18 July 1974), http://www.nybooks.com/articles/archives/1974/jul/18/executive-privilege-jefferson-burr-nixon-ehrlichma/. This was the second of Wills's three 1974 reviews of Jefferson scholarship for the *New York Review of Books*: Garry Wills, "Uncle Thomas's Cabin," *New York Review of Books* 21, no. 6 (18 April 1974), http://www.nybooks.com/articles/archives/1974/apr/18/uncle-thomass-cabin/ (reviewing Brodie, *Thomas Jefferson*); and [Wills,] "An Un-American Politician?," http://www.nybooks.com/articles/archives/1974/may/16/an-un-american-politician/. (The online version omits the author's byline, but the issue's cover reports that it includes an article by Wills, and this is the only article in that issue that qualifies, especially as it is labeled as the third of a series of three articles on recent books about Jefferson.)

52. For other reviews, see Noble E. Cunningham Jr., *JAH* 61 (1974): 774–75; Morton Borden, *JSH* 41 (1975): 109–10; James Roger Sharp, *AHR* 81 (1976): 445–46; Bradford Perkins, *WMQ* 32 (1975): 130–33.

53. For example, C. Vann Woodward, "The Hero of Independence," *New York Times Book Review,* 5 July 1981, http://www.nytimes.com/1981/07/05/books/the-hero-of-independence.html?ref=bookreviews&pagewanted=all; Herbert Mitgang, "Books of the Times," *New York Times*, 11 August 1981, http://www.nytimes.com/1981/08/11/books/books-of-the-times-228099.html?ref=bookreviews&pagewanted=all ; Gordon S. Wood, "The Disappointments of Jefferson," *New York Review of Books* 28, no. 13 (13 August 1981), http://www.nybooks.com/articles/archives/1981/aug/13/the-disappointments-of-jefferson/; Peterson, "Completion"; Edwin M. Yoder Jr., "The Sage at Sunset," *VQR* (1982): 32–37, http://www.vqronline.org/articles/1982/winter/yoder-sage-sunset/ ; Noble E. Cunningham, *AHR* 87 (1982): 534–36; Robert McColley, *JAH* 69 (1982): 144; Morton Borden, *JSH* 48 (1982): 282–83; Steven M. Stowe, "Review Essay: Private Emotions and a Public Man in Early Nineteenth-Century Virginia," *History of Education Quarterly* 27 (1987): 75–81, esp. 75–78.

54. Stowe, "Review Essay," 78–79.

55. Woodward, "Hero of Independence."

56. Wood, "Disappointments of Jefferson."

57. On Jefferson's role in the invention of the ex-president, see R. B. Bernstein, "Book Review, *The Papers of Thomas Jefferson; Retirement Series,* Volume 1," *JER* 26, no. 4 (Winter 2006): 682–97.

58. Malone, *Jefferson the Virginian*, xvi; see discussion preceding note 21 and at notes 26–27.

59. Kurtz, "Review of *Ordeal of Liberty,*" 465–66; Cunningham, "Review of *Ordeal of Liberty,*" 259.

60. For a masterly examination of Jefferson as politician, see Joanne B. Freeman, *Affairs of Honor: National Politics in the New Republic* (New Haven, Conn., 2001), 62–104. See also R. B. Bernstein, *The Founding Fathers Reconsidered* (New York, 2009), 76–89, and sources cited.

61. For contrasting views of these figures, in addition to the works by Freeman (who coined the phrase "the grammar of political combat") and Bernstein cited in note 60, see Lynton K. Caldwell, *The Administrative Theories of Hamilton and Jefferson*, rev. ed. (New York, 1987); James F. Simon, *What Kind of Nation? Thomas Jefferson, John Marshall, and the Epic Struggle to Create the United States* (New York, 2002); Nancy Isenberg, *Fallen Founder: The Life of Aaron Burr* (New York, 2007); Stephen Knott, *Alexander Hamilton and the Persistence of Myth* (Lawrence, Kans., 2002). See also the essays by Joanne B. Freeman and Nancy Isenberg in this volume.

62. Bernstein, *Thomas Jefferson*, 1, 189.

63. Leonard W. Levy, *Ranters Run Amok: And Other Adventures in the History of the Law* (Chicago, 2000), 51. The dissertation was published as Leonard W. Levy, *The Law of the Commonwealth and Chief Justice Shaw* (Cambridge, Mass., 1957).

64. For example, John Chester Miller, *The Wolf by the Ears: Thomas Jefferson and Slavery* (New York, 1977), and Jordan, *White Over Black*, 461–89. The quoted phrase is from E. P. Thompson, *The Making of the English Working Class* (New York, 1963), 12. See also John Herbert Roper, *C Vann Woodward: A Southern Historian and His Critics* (Athens, Ga., 1997).

65. Gordon-Reed, *Thomas Jefferson and Sally Hemings*, 107–8, 156–57 (quoting at 107 Malone, *First Term*, 214).

66. *Jefferson Image*, 454–55.

67. Frank Shuffelton, "Being Definitive: Jefferson Biography Under the Shadow of Dumas Malone," *Biography* 18, no. 4 (Fall 1995): 291–304.

68. On Tucker, see Christine Coalwell McDonald and Robert M. S. McDonald's essay in this volume; on Randall, see Andrew Burstein's essay in this volume.

69. For a counterexample, see Charles McGrath, "Robert Caro's Big Dig," *New York Times Magazine*, 12 April 2012, http://www.nytimes.com/2012/04/15/magazine/robert -caros-big-dig.html?pagewanted=all (discussing Robert A. Caro's ongoing biography of Lyndon B. Johnson).

70. Wood, "Disappointments of Jefferson."

11

Merrill D. Peterson and
the Apostle of Freedom
Thomas Jefferson and the New Nation

FRANCIS D. COGLIANO

Although he wrote widely on Jefferson in particular and American history
more generally over the course of a lengthy academic career, Merrill D. Peterson's most notable contribution to Jefferson studies came in the form of three
main publications. In 1960, he published his first book, *The Jefferson Image
in the American Mind*—the foremost examination of Jefferson's reputation
in the century after his death. He followed *The Jefferson Image* a decade later
with a single-volume biography, *Thomas Jefferson and the New Nation*. In
1984, the Library of America published a 1,600-page collection of Jefferson's
writings edited by Peterson (itself based on a 600-page collection he did in
1975 as *The Portable Thomas Jefferson*). While aimed at a general audience, this
collection has also proved to be extremely valuable to scholars awaiting the
scheduled completion of the Princeton edition of Jefferson's papers in 2026.
Taken together, Peterson's three works interpret the meaning of Jefferson's
legacy, present an interpretation of Jefferson's life and times, and provide the
raw material for subsequent generations to take the measure of the person
who Peterson conceded was "an impenetrable man." To have been the author
or editor of any one of these works would be a remarkable scholarly achievement. To have published all three, each a masterpiece in its own way, guaranteed Peterson a place alongside Dumas Malone and Julian P. Boyd as one
of the leading Jefferson scholars of the middle and late twentieth century.[1]
    There have been four distinct periods in the history of Jefferson's rep-
utation. The first, extending from Jefferson's death in 1826 until the end
of the Civil War in 1865, saw Jefferson's image and legacy contested by the

proponents and opponents of slavery, nullification, states' rights, and secession. After the war, during its second stage, Jefferson's reputation went into
decline. In the aftermath of the bloody sectional conflict that cost the lives of
hundreds of thousands of men, Jefferson was viewed as an advocate of nullification and a defender of secession and slavery—indirectly he was blamed
for the war. Moreover, in an age of industrialization and a more centralized
national government, Jefferson's beliefs in the virtues of state sovereignty,
small government, and rural agriculture seemed increasingly inappropriate.
The excesses of the 1920s, followed by the onset of the Great Depression, saw
the beginnings of a recovery for Jefferson's reputation, marking the beginning
of the third stage in its history. With the onset of World War II Jefferson
was rehabilitated as a national hero. No longer a divisive figure, he came to
be seen as a symbol of the nation and the embodiment of its founding principles. This image persisted during the early Cold War. Not until the early
1960s did the revisionist fourth stage in the history of Jefferson's reputation
commence. Against a backdrop of the civil rights movement, the war in
Vietnam, and the Watergate scandal, American historians, like Americans
more generally, became more critical of their nation's rulers and institutions.
For many historians, increasingly concerned with questions of class, gender,
and, especially where Jefferson was concerned, race, his limitations seemed
more important than his achievements. While the Jefferson of the 1940s and
1950s stood as the embodiment of American values for many historians, since
the 1960s he has come to represent the limits of the American Revolution
and has emerged as the patron saint of American hypocrisy.[2]

Peterson came of age during the third stage of Jefferson's posthumous
evolution. On April 13, 1943, the bicentenary of Jefferson's birth, President
Franklin D. Roosevelt paid homage to his predecessor when he dedicated
the Jefferson Memorial in Washington, D.C. "To Thomas Jefferson," the
president intoned, "Apostle of Freedom, we are paying a debt long overdue."
For Roosevelt, Jefferson epitomized the ideals for which Americans fought
in 1943. "His cause," he said, "was a cause to which we are committed, not
by our words alone but by our sacrifice." Roosevelt invoked his predecessor's
language, carved on four panels mounted on the inside of the memorial,
to close his address: "I have sworn upon the altar of God eternal hostility
against every form of tyranny over the mind of man."[3] The image of Jefferson
as Apostle of Freedom infused Peterson's scholarship. In *The Jefferson Image
in the American Mind*, Peterson declared that the building and dedication of

the Jefferson Memorial was "the most important thing to happen to Jefferson since July Fourth 1826." By 1943, Jefferson had emerged as the symbol of the principles for which the nation fought. Peterson wrote:

> On the two hundredth anniversary of his birth the nation was locked in a desperate world struggle for the rights he had declared inalienable. The nation, the world, were so distressingly different from anything Jefferson had envisioned; yet, fundamentally, his faith was the American faith, reaching out now to the world from which he had reluctantly withdrawn. . . . Viewed as a patriotic rite, the Bicentennial marks Jefferson's passage into the American pantheon.

No longer an object of partisan squabbling, by 1943 Jefferson had come to embody America itself. Peterson concluded his study by speculating that Jefferson "may yet go on vindicating his power in the national life as the heroic voice of imperishable freedoms. It is this Jefferson who stands at the radiant center of his own history, and who makes for the present a symbol that unites the nation's birth with its inexorable ideal."[4]

Peterson's view of Jefferson reflected his own intellectual and political development. Although written during the 1960s, the Jefferson who emerges from the pages of *Thomas Jefferson and the New Nation* is very much a third-stage Jefferson, the nonpartisan epitome of American values. This view was the product not only of Peterson's reading of the sources—he achieved a mastery of the Jefferson corpus rivaled only by Boyd and Malone—but also by Peterson's journey as an earnest and thoughtful observer of politics and history. During his formative years, Peterson immersed himself in liberal politics—supporting the New Deal at home and the fight against totalitarianism abroad. He came to the study of American history through political science and the study of "American civilization," the forerunner to the postwar American Studies movement. His liberal outlook, in terms of his politics and his scholarship, influenced his interpretation of Jefferson, who emerges from the pages of *Thomas Jefferson and the New Nation* as an exponent of democratic values at home and abroad. Yet Peterson's focus on Jefferson as an exponent of American principles in a turbulent world led him to misread a crucial aspect of Jefferson's personal life—his relationship with Sally Hemings. This misreading, in turn, has obscured Peterson's critique of

Jefferson on one of the most vexing moral issues of his and our time—the vexed tangle of race and slavery.

Merrill Daniel Peterson was born in Manhattan, Kansas, "where the prairie meets the plains," on March 31, 1921. His father—"old enough to have been my grandfather," Peterson later recalled—"was an ordained Baptist minister, sans pulpit, who had a hard time making a living." His parents divorced when he was in elementary school, and Peterson's mother supported her three sons, of whom he was the youngest, by running a boardinghouse for students at the Kansas State Agricultural College (now Kansas State University). According to Peterson, his mother "calculated, quite accurately, that her sons would have a better chance of getting college degrees if we lived in a college town." In high school, Peterson was exposed to the wider world by the students who resided at his mother's boardinghouse and by his social studies teacher, William Purkaple, who shared such journals and magazines with his students as the *Nation,* the *New Republic,* and the *Atlantic Monthly.* Peterson, who worked as a soda jerk at the local drugstore, spent some of his savings on a subscription to the *New Republic,* which became his "guide and preceptor" throughout the 1940s. Indeed, late in life, when he wrote a memoir focusing on his early intellectual development, he called it *Coming of Age with the New Republic.* Influenced in large part by the *New Republic,* Peterson embraced New Deal liberalism. He differed from the magazine's stance during the early days of World War II, urging that Roosevelt adopt a more interventionist foreign policy than the magazine's editors were willing to countenance.[5] When in April 1940 the radical social critic Lewis Mumford published an essay, "The Corruption of Liberalism," in the *New Republic* that was critical of the journal's isolationism, Peterson wrote a letter to the editor in support of Mumford, declaring that as a college student he had no desire to die on a foreign battlefield but also that "I have the courage to believe in the principles of democracy, and the realization of the unalterable fact that those very principles—of freedom, justice, and the supremacy of the individual over the state—are at stake in Europe today."[6]

Peterson began college at Kansas State, a block and a half from his mother's boardinghouse, in 1939. He undertook his academic career with the intention of becoming a doctor. However, Peterson soon found himself drawn to politics and international affairs. In 1941, he transferred to the University of Kansas. As he recalled, "Its faculty and curriculum ran more to liberal arts than Kansas State's, and it boasted a department of political science, that esoteric branch of learning I wished to pursue." At Kansas, Peterson worked his way through the political science curriculum. His major influence was Hilden Gibson, an expert on Marxism. Under Gibson's tutelage Peterson "became a budding Marxist." His flirtation with Marxism was relatively brief, but, he remembered, "It introduced me to a fascinating intellectual system, one that gave me a critical vantage point on the society I knew, together with a sense of history that appealed to my hopes for a better world." Gibson also introduced Peterson to the study of American history, including Vernon Parrington's *Main Currents in American Thought,* "which offered a liberal Jeffersonian interpretation of the nation's literary tradition." According to Peterson, *Main Currents in American Thought* was "the primary piece of intellectual furniture I brought to graduate school." After the Japanese attack on Pearl Harbor Peterson accelerated his studies so that he could enter the navy. He completed the requirements for his bachelor's degree ahead of schedule in January 1943.[7]

After completing his undergraduate degree, Peterson headed east. His mother's boardinghouse in Kansas had failed in 1941, and she had moved to North Adams, Massachusetts, to stay with her sister. She found work in a fraternity house at Williams College. While awaiting his naval training, Peterson visited his mother and attended political science classes at Williams. In the spring of 1943, Peterson received orders to report for naval training in Chicago. He learned about a program that provided seamen with the opportunity to study at Harvard Business School to train them for service in the navy supply corps. Peterson was accepted to the program. After a year studying at Harvard, he received his commission as an ensign in May 1944. He served aboard the supply ship USS *Parle* in the Atlantic, Mediterranean, and Pacific. Peterson was discharged in January 1946.

While he was training at Harvard Business School, Peterson learned about Harvard's new Ph.D. program in American civilization. "The course of my education had enforced the conviction that the democratic future in America depended, in some part, upon a better understanding and appropriation of the nation's past," he recalled. Peterson spoke to the program's director and applied with the intention of starting soon after his discharge. Peterson returned to Harvard and discovered that the strength of the program lay in literature. Perry Miller, a professor of English with a proclivity for intellectual history, became his adviser. When it came time to choose

a dissertation topic, Peterson was inspired by a course on American roman-
ticism that he had taken with Miller. He wrote:

> I thought it would be interesting to pursue the way Americans
> had thought and written about Jefferson through time—a sort of
> myth and symbol study—and I had the wit to seize upon the word
> *image,* which was entering the vocabulary to describe the historical
> phenomenon. And so, after passing my general examination for
> the degree early in 1948, I submitted to Miller the prospectus for
> a dissertation entitled "The Jefferson Image in the American Mind."
> Miller laid no claim to authority on Jefferson, but he immediately
> grasped the idea. Not only had I come to regard him as a mentor,
> but he was easily the best American intellectual historian around.

Peterson submitted his dissertation in 1950. At two volumes and a thousand
pages, it considered Jefferson's posthumous reputation from 1826 until 1861.
"Looking back, I am amazed by how innocent I was about things academic,
beginning with the potential significance of the doctoral dissertation for
one's career," Peterson recalled. The significance of his choice soon became
clear: "It proved to be the turning point in my career."[8]

While finishing his Ph.D. dissertation in 1949, Peterson accepted his
first teaching job at Brandeis University. Brandeis had opened in 1948 to
provide an educational alternative for Jewish students denied places at Ivy
League universities, where anti-Semitic quotas limited their number. Peterson was hired to serve as a teaching assistant to Max Lerner on such courses
as "Contemporary American Civilization" and "Introduction to Politics."
Peterson had long admired Lerner, a prolific contributor to the *New Republic*
and other periodicals, and a prominent social critic and sociologist. Lerner
was a fervent supporter of the New Deal and civil rights. Before entering
the navy, Peterson had attended Lerner's seminars on contemporary American politics at Williams.[9] On completing his Harvard doctorate in 1950,
Brandeis elevated him to an assistant professorship. In 1955, he was offered
a three-year assistant professorship at Princeton, including a year's research
leave that allowed him to complete his manuscript. He extended his analysis
down to the dedication of the Jefferson Memorial in 1943. After returning
to Brandeis in 1958, *The Jefferson Image in the American Mind* was published
in 1960 and won the Bancroft Prize. "Not long after," Peterson wrote, "I was

offered a contract by Oxford to write a substantial one-volume biography of Jefferson."[10] *The Jefferson Image in the American Mind* had established Peterson's reputation as one of the leading Jefferson scholars alongside Boyd and Malone. In 1962, the University of Virginia recognized Peterson's pre-eminence when it invited him to succeed Malone as its Thomas Jefferson Memorial Foundation Professor of History.

Peterson's interpretation of Jefferson and his time was shaped by his own experiences. "Each American generation has had its own perspective on the founding and the founding fathers," wrote Peterson in the preface to *Thomas Jefferson and the New Nation.* "In the case of my generation, which came of age in the Second World War," he continued, "and has witnessed shattering global upheaval for a quarter-century, the experience throws into sharp relief the nation's beginnings in another age of revolution." For Peterson, Jefferson "embodied the nation's aspirations for freedom and enlightenment" and "was intellectually and politically engaged not only in American affairs but in the affairs of a world unhinged by war and revolution"—a world not unlike that in which Peterson matured in the 1930s and 1940s.[11] On its face, this may seem unremarkable. It is a truism that historians and biographers are shaped by their times. What is notable, perhaps, is that Peterson's Jefferson, a product of the third-stage Apostle-of-Freedom era of Jefferson studies, appeared at a time when that interpretation was in retreat. As such, his scholarship stands out for its admiration of its subject, to the point of misinterpreting one key aspect of Jefferson's life—his relationship with Sally Hemings. Its failure to take account of the Hemings-Jefferson relationship obscures, however, the book's critique of Jefferson's positions on race and slavery. This, too, was a product of Peterson's liberal, midcentury sensibility.

Peterson spent nearly a decade writing *Thomas Jefferson and the New Nation.* He explained that, whereas his first book, *The Jefferson Image in the American Mind,* had been concerned not with the history that Jefferson made but what history made of Jefferson, *Thomas Jefferson and the New Nation* focused on the historical Jefferson. As such, it could be viewed "as a biographical companion to the former work." At the outset, Peterson conceded that certain obstacles confront all Jefferson biographers. The first of these was that "Jefferson became so much a part of the nation's ongoing search for itself, so deeply implicated in the whole epic of American democracy, that succeeding generations were unable to see him clearly and objectively in his own life and time." At the time of writing, Peterson felt that this tendency might be diminishing and that it might be possible at last for Americans in the second half of the twentieth century to appreciate the historical Jefferson. Nonetheless, Peterson conceded, "Even now, however, the student of Jefferson cannot be truly detached and disinterested. I have not been, though I have sought that 'disciplined subjectivity' someone has defined as the essence of the historian's craft."[12]

The second major obstacle confronting the biographer, according to Peterson, is Jefferson himself. He posed a challenge on two levels. First, as a historical figure, Jefferson's contributions to the era of the American Revolution were so multifaceted that there is a danger that the biographer will lose him amid the welter of events: "He was so closely identified with the first half-century of the nation's history that the human figure fades into the events massed around it." Perhaps more acute is the challenge that Jefferson's personality poses for his biographers. "Although he left to posterity a vast corpus of papers, private and public," Peterson noted, "his personality remains elusive. Of all his great contemporaries Jefferson is perhaps the least self-revealing and the hardest to sound to the depths of his being. It is a mortifying confession, but he remains for me, finally, an impenetrable man." This was a remarkable confession from a man who had spent more than two decades studying Jefferson. Peterson modestly directed readers who sought "the *real* Jefferson" to Malone's multivolume *Jefferson and His Time* and Julian Boyd's edition of *The Papers of Thomas Jefferson*. If Peterson could not penetrate Jefferson's facade and understand the man within, however, one could reasonably doubt whether Malone and Boyd would be any more successful.[13]

Faced with these challenges, Peterson eschewed attempting to offer "a definitive life of the man" in favor of what he termed "a basic narrative of Jefferson's life"—a modest description for a thousand-page volume—"formed by my own understanding of its place, its problems, and its importance in the history of the United States as the first revolutionary new nation." Peterson elected to focus on Jefferson's public career. He did so in part because of Jefferson's impenetrability, but also because this approach suited Peterson's main theme. Peterson sought to present Jefferson as the apotheosis of the values of the American Revolution, values that were globally significant. Such an analysis, sitting comfortably at the center of the third stage of Jefferson studies, required a focus on Jefferson as a public man and, in Peterson's view, did not require the biographer to consider Jefferson's inner life.[14]

To make sense of Jefferson's lengthy and multifaceted career, Peterson guided his interpretation of Jefferson's public life by reference to three main themes: democracy, nationality, and enlightenment. He intended these not as rigid categories but as "symbols for whole clusters of principles and actions and passions, not altogether coherently arranged." For Peterson, Jefferson embodied American values, but instead of being narrow and parochial these values were universally important, speaking to the larger concerns of the Enlightenment and the Age of Revolution. In the late eighteenth century, the United States led the world by example in promoting principles of democracy and republican government. The same principles were relevant in the twentieth century, although the global situation had changed greatly. "The United States holds a very different position in today's world—the lamb has become the lion," Peterson wrote. But "its early history may help yet to recall Americans to a spirit and a purpose still valuable and, one trusts, not without relevance to old and new nations alike in our time." Jefferson, a provincial Virginian, had helped to create a new nation through his commitment to his country, democracy, and enlightenment. By heeding the lessons of Jefferson's life, the United States might continue to promote the values and principles of democracy and republican government in the twentieth century.[15]

As a study of Jefferson's public life, *Thomas Jefferson and the New Nation* presents a generally sympathetic, detailed, political narrative. As befits a third-stage Jefferson, Peterson presents Jefferson as upholding liberty at home and abroad in the face of dangerous foes. Domestically these were Federalists, particularly Alexander Hamilton and John Marshall. On the international stage, the young United States was buffeted and threatened by various European empires, particularly Britain, France, and Spain. Peterson provided a chronological narrative of Jefferson's life in eleven lengthy chapters that focused on his various public roles. (The 270 pages dedicated to Jefferson's two terms as president are a monographic study within the biography and constitute one of the most important scholarly treatments of the subject—arguably superior to Malone's two volumes on Jefferson's presidency.) Owing to his focus on Jefferson's public service, Peterson devoted relatively little space to Jefferson's early life—he dedicates a mere twenty-eight pages to Jefferson's first thirty years. In this brief portrait, Peterson suggested that "certain dominant traits of mind and character had formed a personal style destined to have profound public effects." These traits, which Peterson described as the "controlling features" of Jefferson's personality, included intellectuality, emotional control, fussiness, high seriousness, industry, orderliness, a hatred of idleness, fondness for detail and record-keeping, and optimism. Taken together, these traits guided Jefferson throughout his public life. "His whole tendency," Peterson wrote, "was to combat the chaos of experience and submit it to the dictates of reason, which, of course, he identified with the laws of nature."[16] When combined with the main motifs of Jefferson's life—democracy, nationality, and enlightenment—these character traits, Peterson concluded, explained the course of Jefferson's lengthy public career. Whether this portrait is accurate or not (leaving aside whether readers found it attractive), it suggests that Peterson may have found Jefferson more penetrable than his earlier disclaimer suggests.

Of course Jefferson's papers were Peterson's main source for *Thomas Jefferson and the New Nation.* For the period down to 1790, Peterson drew on the first seventeen volumes of Boyd's edition of the papers published by Princeton. For the period after 1790, Peterson relied on previous, less reliable editions of Jefferson's papers as well as the manuscript originals and microfilms at the Library of Congress, the Massachusetts Historical Society, and the University of Virginia. Contemporary scholars, who benefit from no fewer than forty-five volumes in three series of *The Papers of Thomas Jefferson,* as well as searchable online editions and databases, can only marvel at the mastery of the sources demonstrated by Peterson (and Malone), who wrote substantial biographies without such advantages. Undoubtedly Peterson could compile and edit a single-volume edition of Jefferson's writings for the Library of America in part because of the expertise in the source materials that he developed writing *Thomas Jefferson and the New Nation.*[17]

"After considerable agonizing," Peterson made a decision to omit footnotes or any form of citation. He explained:

In a work of synthesis and interpretation, addressed more to readers than to scholars, making no pretensions to definitive treatment, and on a subject so much researched and written about as Jefferson, it seemed to me that footnotes would place an unnecessary burden on the text. Complete notation would be very burdensome indeed to the general reader and partial notation merely an annoyance to the interested scholar. So I have allowed the book to stand free of the scaffolding.

This decision was lamented by reviewers, who otherwise admired *Thomas Jefferson and the New Nation* but felt that the absence of citations was an error. As Jackson Turner Main wrote in the *American Historical Review*, "Historians if not the general reader will resent the absence of footnotes. This is no popular biography, no brief sketch, but over a thousand solid pages of scholarship. Granted that detailed citations would burden most readers, yet the serious student deserves to know the sources for important statements and controversial interpretations, while scholars will miss historiographical comments. Footnotes of an explanatory nature would not greatly increase the length of the book and would exceed in value much of the detail."[18] Peterson did supply a thorough, thirty-six-page "select bibliography." One consequence of this decision is that it is difficult for scholars to use *Thomas Jefferson and the New Nation* as a reference work. By contrast, Malone's six-volume biography, which has copious footnotes, continues to serve as a near-encyclopedic guide to its subject. Another consequence is that Peterson, while rendering judgments on controversial aspects of Jefferson's life, did not engage in specific historiographical debates. As such, the book reads as Peterson's personal rumination on Jefferson's life and times; it is unencumbered by historiographical debates that become dated over time. Among the controversies that Peterson addressed, albeit briefly, was whether Jefferson had a sexual relationship with one of his slaves, Sally Hemings.[19]

Peterson first addressed the controversy over Jefferson's relationship with Hemings in *The Jefferson Image in the American Mind*. He ascribed the persistence of what he termed "the miscegenation legend" to three factors: politics, slavery, and "the personal habits and history of Jefferson himself." According to Peterson, Jefferson's Federalist political enemies fostered the legend during his lifetime, and it persisted after his death among those opposed to the principles that Jefferson stood for and embodied—particularly British critics of American democracy. With respect to slavery, Peterson claimed that the legend operated on several levels. It appealed to "the Negroes' pathetic wish for a little pride and their subtle ways of confounding the white folks." It also appealed to slave traders and auctioneers "who might expect a better price for a Jefferson than for a Jones." Finally, abolitionists were attracted to the tale as a means of demonstrating the moral degradation caused by slave-holding. Peterson concluded that "the overwhelming evidence of Jefferson's domestic life refuted the legend." But for the hatred of the Federalists who fostered the legend and abolitionists and British critics who kept it alive, he concluded, the story would have been forgotten.[20] Whereas he was concerned primarily with tracing the pedigree of the "miscegenation legend" in *Jefferson Image,* Peterson made clear his belief that the claim that Jefferson fathered children by Sally Hemings had little or no merit.

Given his existing skepticism about the Hemings relationship, Peterson did not devote much attention to it in *Thomas Jefferson and the New Nation.* He addressed the topic in his chapter on Jefferson's first term as president, introducing the subject in the context of the political attacks that Jefferson endured during his first term. Of the relationship he wrote:

> Sally Hemings was apparently the mulatto offspring of John Wayles and Elizabeth Hemings, his concubine, and hence the half-sister of Jefferson's departed wife. Sally it was who had accompanied Polly to Paris in 1787. After her return she had a number of children, all light skinned, whose paternity some wanton men ascribed to Jefferson. Like most legends, this one was not created out of whole cloth. The evidence, highly circumstantial, is far from conclusive, however, and unless Jefferson was capable of slipping badly out of character in hidden moments at Monticello, it is difficult to imagine him caught up in a miscegenous relationship. Such a mixture of the races, such ruthless exploitation of the master-slave relationship, revolted his whole being.[21]

Peterson articulated what has come to be known as the "character defense" of Jefferson. Essentially, he took the view that it was impossible for Jefferson to have had a sexual relationship with Hemings because it would have been out of character for Jefferson to engage in behavior that he deemed immoral. This view is premised on the assumption that its advocates know and understand Jefferson's character to the extent that they can understand his most intimate actions, urges, and thoughts. This assumption, however, seems to fly in the face of Peterson's assertion that he found Jefferson impenetrable.[22]

Peterson was fundamentally wrong with regard to the relationship between Hemings and Jefferson. His judgment failed him with respect to both the relationship itself and its significance for Jefferson's legacy. He concluded his discussion of the matter in *The Jefferson Image* by asserting that, "when there was little but Jefferson's own history and the memories of a few Negroes to sustain it, it faded into the obscure recesses of the Jefferson image."[23] Since the appearance of *Thomas Jefferson and the New Nation* in 1970, the Hemings-Jefferson relationship emerged as a central concern in Jefferson scholarship thanks to the efforts of scholars such as Fawn Brodie and Annette Gordon-Reed. Brodie's best-selling 1974 biography asserted that there was a sexual relationship between Hemings and Jefferson. Gordon-Reed's 1997 study, *Thomas Jefferson and Sally Hemings: An American Controversy*, examined all the extant evidence on the controversy (evidence available to Peterson) and demonstrated that previous scholars, including Peterson, had not treated oral evidence from African American sources in the same way that they had testimony from white witnesses. The result was an imbalance in the scholarship.[24] In 1998, a DNA study published in the scientific journal *Nature* confirmed that a male Jefferson was the father of one of Hemings's children. Two years later, after surveying the evidence, new and old, the Thomas Jefferson Foundation formally acknowledged that Jefferson was the father of Hemings's last child and likely the father of all of her children.[25] Peterson was not persuaded by the weight of new scholarship on the question. In 1998 (before the publication of the results of the DNA study), he wrote a new introduction to a reprint edition of *The Jefferson Image in the American Mind*. Peterson wrote:

> No book of the last quarter century has left a more indelible mark on the Jefferson image than Fawn M. Brodie's *Thomas Jefferson: An Intimate History* (1974). She caused many readers to accept as true the slander of a vindictive journalist, James T. Callender, in 1802 that Jefferson fathered a number of children by a Monticello slave, Sally Hemings. (The conception of the first of the brood would be tantalizingly portrayed in the film *Jefferson in Paris*.) In my book the story is placed in its political context and its survival treated as a legend, neither verifiable nor credible.[26]

Peterson believed that the allegation that Hemings and Jefferson had a sexual relationship was a "legend" fostered by Jefferson's enemies. This "slander," he insisted, left an "indelible mark" on Jefferson's reputation. He based this conclusion on his knowledge of Jefferson's character, which he had accrued over five decades of studying Jefferson's life and times. Despite his conclusion that the relationship was "neither verifiable nor credible," the evidence suggests that on this matter Peterson was incorrect and that he had misread Jefferson's character. Peterson's error with respect to the relationship between Hemings and Jefferson is explicable, in part, by how he positioned himself in the literature. The third-stage, Apostle-of-Freedom Jefferson who appears in *Thomas Jefferson and the New Nation* does not lend himself easily to analysis of intimate matters. Rather Peterson's emphasis is on Jefferson as a public figure, a revolutionary, a politician, and a thinker who articulated and advanced the principles of the American Revolution that became the mission statement for the American republic. Given his focus on Jefferson as an apotheosis of American values, there is little room in Peterson's portrait for Jefferson's inner life, nor did Peterson consider it suitable or relevant.[27]

Does it matter that Peterson was incorrect on one, albeit significant, matter in Jefferson's long life? Annette Gordon-Reed, who did more than any single scholar to change our understanding of the Hemings-Jefferson relationship, has urged caution with respect to her scholarly predecessors. "It is my belief," writes Gordon-Reed, "that those who are considered Jefferson scholars have never made a serious and objective attempt to get to the truth of this matter. This is not a criticism of their work on any other aspects of Thomas Jefferson's life or any other subject about which they have written."[28] Peterson's two major books on Jefferson, *The Jefferson Image in the American Mind* and *Thomas Jefferson and the New Nation,* are 548 pages and 1,072 pages in length, respectively. Of more than 1,600 pages combined, only 6 pages concern Sally Hemings. Where Peterson is concerned, it is important to exercise the caution and the generosity of scholarly spirit expressed by Gordon-Reed. Sadly, Peterson's defense of Jefferson against the "slander" that he fathered children by Hemings based on his knowledge of Jefferson's character has obscured his forceful criticism of Jefferson regarding race and slavery.

There is a clear tension between the Jefferson as author of the Declaration of Independence and the man who held 600 persons as slaves during the course of his long life. As a slaveholder who also was the embodiment of the principles of the American Revolution and the articulator of its core creedal statement, Jefferson becomes the personification of the fundamental dilemma posed by the persistence of slavery in a republic premised on liberty and equality. As a consequence, a core tenet of the third-stage interpretation is that Jefferson opposed slavery. In *Thomas Jefferson and the New Nation*, Peterson depicted Jefferson as an ardent opponent of unfree labor. "All of Jefferson's values and goals dictated the extermination of slavery," he wrote. "This was as self-evident as the principles of 1776 themselves." Elsewhere he wrote, "Basically his position was a moral one, founded in the immutable principles of human liberty. No abolitionist of later time ever cried out more prophetically against slavery."[29] According to this view, Jefferson not only opposed slavery but also was aware of the moral and political danger that the institution posed to the American republic. Although Jefferson did not succeed in promoting abolition in his lifetime, his opposition to slavery laid the foundation for its subsequent demise. This view is central to the third-stage interpretation of Jefferson, for it allows him to remain the premier American exponent of democratic values while addressing the challenge that slavery poses to his legacy (and, by implication, to the United States).

Whereas Peterson presented Jefferson as an opponent of slavery, he was very critical of the Virginian's racial attitudes. Peterson discussed Jefferson's proposed plan for emancipation in the *Notes on Virginia*, noting that, for Jefferson, the consequence of emancipation was "not amalgamation but expulsion." He attributed Jefferson's colonization plan to his racial attitudes, "opinions that seriously embarrassed his philosophy." Peterson reflected that Jefferson's claims for African inferiority "came with ill grace from the man who demolished [the Abbé] Raynal for employing the same line of argument against the American whites!" Peterson described Jefferson's racial views as "a product of frivolous and tortuous reasoning, of preconception, prejudice, ignorance, contradiction, and bewildering confusion of principles. . . . The discussion of the comparative beauty of the two races betrayed an insensibility to standards other than his own. Many of his observations, paraded as scientific, were but thinly disguised statements of folk beliefs about Negroes." Although Peterson praised Jefferson for his opposition to slavery, which he felt was sincere, he condemned him for his racism, which he attributed to his "observation from the post of a Virginia planter."[30]

Peterson wrote *Thomas Jefferson and the New Nation* during the transition from the third to the fourth, more critical, stage in the history of Jefferson's reputation. This stage coincided with the civil rights revolution. In such a context, it is not surprising that Jefferson's racial views were found wanting. Peterson's own views on the matter, as with his interpretation of Jefferson more generally, have their roots in his intellectual and political development during the 1930s and 1940s. Early in his life he developed sympathy for persecuted minorities. In his memoir, he recalled that he first encountered Jewish students in his mother's boardinghouse. They had come to Kansas State Agricultural College to study veterinary medicine because they had been barred from admission to Cornell by quotas: "My acquaintance with Jews, Jewishness, and anti-Semitism began with the transients in my mom's boardinghouse, and the rapport I felt then stayed with me always." An ardent New Dealer, Peterson came to realize that "the social and economic reforms legislated by the Roosevelt Coalition exacted the price of acquiescence in the South's peculiar arrangements for the Negro. The same Democratic votes that helped enact the New Deal measures, including those leading to war, also blocked antilynching and anti–poll tax legislation and sustained the reign of Jim Crow. The price of liberal reform, in some sense, was paid by black Americans." Peterson recalled reading Gunnar Myrdal's 1944 study of race in the United States, *An American Dilemma,* after reading a favorable review in the *New Republic,* and declared that "its postulates entered deeply into everything I thought and wrote about America."[31]

When he entered graduate school at Harvard, the program in American civilization appealed to Peterson because of its interdisciplinarity and because he hoped it would allow him to understand and shape the course of American history. He recalled, "Having started in 1941 to study political science, I found myself on the track of something quite different, something interdisciplinary, something I later learned had a name, 'the search for a usable past' in American history and letters."[32] Jefferson gave him an entrée into what was usable in the American past. Although Peterson was aware of Jefferson's racial views, which he found abhorrent, he believed that Jefferson still should be used as an exemplar of American values. He demonstrated this belief soon after he arrived in Charlottesville to take up the Thomas Jefferson Memorial Foundation chair.

On March 17, 1965, a "Sympathy for Selma" ceremony was held at the University of Virginia's Rotunda to mark the murders of civil rights activists during the previous weeks' demonstrations in Selma, Alabama, and to express support for the Voting Rights Act. The demonstration included students, staff, faculty, family members, and Charlottesville residents. Paul Gaston, an associate professor of history and the Charlottesville coordinator for the Selma movement, was an organizer of the event. He recalled, "As I leaf through the letters, documents, and news clips from that era, I am reminded how nervous and defensive both the university and the Charlottesville white community were about the black freedom movement. I think they feared both the freedom and the movement to secure it. Political and business leaders kept their distance. White ministers told their congregations to steer clear of us." When Gaston wrote a letter to his colleagues inviting them to participate in the ceremony, he received a "mild reprimand" for implying that the university endorsed the event and urging him to be more discreet in the future. When a Virginia student, Tom Gardner, demonstrated at Selma with a sign that read, "All eyes are opening to the rights of man. UVA," he was called into the dean's office and told that "the university's good name should not be put into public debate on controversial issues."[33]

Speaking before the north front of the Rotunda, facing the statue of Jefferson, Peterson was the demonstration's featured speaker. It is worth considering his remarks in full:

> This University, dedicated by its father to the illimitable freedom of the human spirit, bears a high responsibility to the cause of free men everywhere—in Europe, in Asia, above all in the Selma of our own beloved country. The University is not a sanctuary—not for the students, not for the professors—from the actions and passions of the time. The University is, or ought to be, an intellectual ganglion at the nerve center of our society. Its mission is incomplete unless it cultivates in its young men and women the sense of responsibility to the values imparted by instruction. And this can hardly be done within the artificial walled-in atmosphere of an academic grove. In the words of a great alumnus, Woodrow Wilson, "So long as instruction and life do not merge in our universities, so long as what students *do* and what they are *taught* occupy two separate, air-tight compartments in their consciousness, so long will the university be ineffectual."
>
> We are concerned with what is happening in Selma because the struggle *there* involves what is taught *here:* truth, honesty, justice, compassion, the rights and freedom of all men in a democratic society. Today Selma is a vital link in the heritage of American liberty. No University—in America or in the world—has a clearer title to speak for that heritage in the present crisis than the University of

Virginia. And it is high time (long past time) we were heard from! Selma is a symbol, but as President Johnson told us the other night, it has become a turning point, like Lexington and Concord and Appomattox, of America's unending search for freedom.

Thomas Jefferson was the leading architect and champion of American liberty. He was no respecter of venerable authority, nor would he ask us to respect his. It was from the folly, not the wisdom, of ancestors that he learned. And could this statue but speak, his best advice to us would be "the earth belongs to the living," not the dead, and the present sovereign generation should declare the law of direction. Let us not be misled by those who would substitute Jeffersonian means, which were transcient for the enduring Jeffersonian ends of freedom. Let us come out from the dark Jeffersonian shadow of *state* rights in the bright Jeffersonian day of *human* rights. Let us take our testament from the eternally democratic spirit of Mr. Jefferson.

"I hold," he said, "that a little rebellion, now and then, is a good thing, and as necessary in the political world as storms in the physical."

He said: "And can the liberties of a nation be thought secure when we have removed their only firm basis, a conviction in the minds of the people that these liberties are a gift of God?"

He said: ". . . that the laws and institutions must go hand in hand with the progress of the human mind."

And he said: "Nothing then is unchangeable but the inherent and inalienable rights of man."

And so, in honoring those men and women who have worked, suffered, bled and died in Selma, we also renew our faith in the enduring values of the founder and spiritual head of this University.[34]

Peterson's words at the Rotunda echo those of Franklin Roosevelt a generation earlier at the dedication of the Jefferson Memorial. Where Roosevelt invoked Jefferson's spirit in support of a global struggle against fascist totalitarianism, Peterson did so to defend democracy closer to home. Peterson eloquently appealed to Jefferson in support of the cause of racial justice and equality in the United States. From his early reading of the *New Republic* with William Purkaple, through his desire as an undergraduate to read "history that appealed to my hopes for a better world," to his search for a usable past at Harvard and his teaching of American Civilization at Brandeis with Max Lerner, Peterson sought to write history with a political purpose.

Peterson wrote of Roosevelt's remarks in 1943, "nearly every celebrant saluted Jefferson's livingness." He continued, "What was living was, in general, the idea of the rights of man. The world might still need instruction in this idea; but among Americans it was generally accepted as the definition of national character and purpose."[35] Peterson sought to summon Jefferson's livingness during his remarks at the Rotunda in 1965. And the living Jefferson, conceived as an exponent of the rights of man, suffuses *Thomas Jefferson and the New Nation*.

Notes

1. Merrill D. Peterson, *Thomas Jefferson and the New Nation: A Biography* (New York, 1970), viii; *Jefferson Image*; Merrill D. Peterson, ed., *Thomas Jefferson: Writings* (New York, 1984); Merrill D. Peterson, ed., *The Portable Thomas Jefferson* (New York, 1975).

2. Francis D. Cogliano, *Thomas Jefferson: Reputation and Legacy* (Charlottesville, Va., 2006), 4–9, 261–62; R. B. Bernstein, *Thomas Jefferson* (New York, 2003), 191–93. Also see Gordon S. Wood, "The Trials and Tribulations of Thomas Jefferson," in *Jeffersonian Legacies*, ed. Peter S. Onuf (Charlottesville, Va., 1993), 395–417. Arguably we are in the fifth stage of Jefferson's reputation. This phase can be said to have begun with the "Jeffersonian Legacies" conference convened by Peter Onuf—Merrill Peterson's successor at Virginia—in Charlottesville in October 1992. The resulting volume, Onuf's own scholarship on Jefferson, and that of his numerous graduate students have presented a nuanced reassessment of Jefferson that has moved beyond the attack/defense paradigm.

3. Franklin D. Roosevelt, "Address at the Dedication of the Thomas Jefferson Memorial. Washington D.C., April 13, 1943," in *The Public Papers and Addresses of Franklin D. Roosevelt*, ed. Samuel I. Rosenman and William D. Hassett, 13 vols. (New York, 1938–50), 12:162–64. Also see *Jefferson Image*, 377–78, 420–32.

4. *Jefferson Image*, 379, 457.

5. Merrill D. Peterson, *Coming of Age with the New Republic, 1938–1950* (Columbia, Mo., 1999), 2, 5; Bruce Weber, "Merrill D. Peterson, Jefferson Scholar, Dies at 88," *New York Times*, 2 October 2009, www.nytimes.com; Andrew Burstein, "Merrill D. Peterson and the Pursuit of 'An Impenetrable Man,'" *Uncommon Sense* 128 (Summer 2010), http://oieahc.wm.edu/uncommon/128/peterson.cfm.

6. This letter marks the first time that Peterson's name appeared in print. Peterson, *Coming of Age with the New Republic*, 21; Lewis Mumford, "The Corruption

of Liberalism," *New Republic*, 29 April 1940, 568–73; Letters, *New Republic*, 3 June 1940, 762.

7. Peterson, *Coming of Age*, 36, 38, 39, 80.

8. Ibid., 67, 72, 73; Merrill Daniel Peterson, "The Jefferson Image in the American Mind, 1826–1861," 2 vols. (Ph.D. diss, Harvard University, 1950).

9. Peterson identified Lerner, with Vernon Parrington and Lewis Mumford, as the writers whose books did the most to shape his mind. Peterson, *Coming of Age,* chap. 5. The manuscript of what would be Lerner's most famous book, *America as a Civilization: Life and Thought in the United States Today* (New York, 1957), served as the main text for a course on contemporary America that Lerner and Peterson taught together. The course was compulsory for all sophomores at Brandeis. See also Dennis H. Wrong, "The United States in Comparative Perspective: Max Lerner's *America as a Civilization*," *American Journal of Sociology* 65 (1960): 499–504.

10. Peterson, *Coming of Age*, 129.

11. Peterson, *Thomas Jefferson and the New Nation*, ix.

12. Ibid., vii.

13. Ibid., viii.

14. Ibid., ix. For a critique of Peterson's approach, see Fawn Brodie, "Jefferson Biographers and the Psychology of Canonization," *Journal of Interdisciplinary History* 2 (1971): 155–71.

15. Peterson, *Thomas Jefferson and the New Nation*, ix. It's worth noting that Peterson was not a hawk in his approach to the Cold War. He supported Henry Wallace's Progressive Party candidacy for president in 1948 in part because of Truman's hard-line view of the Soviet Union. Peterson favored negotiation with the Soviet Union over nuclear arms rather than confrontation. He believed that the main contest between the Soviet Union and the United States during the early Cold War was ideological and that the United States should promote and protect its Jeffersonian values. See Peterson, *Coming of Age*, 98–99.

16. Peterson, *Thomas Jefferson and the New Nation*, 28–31.

17. For the various editions of Jefferson's papers, see Cogliano, *Thomas Jefferson*, chap. 3. For the Princeton edition, see Barbara B. Oberg and James P. McClure, "'For Generations to Come': Creating the 'Definitive' Jefferson Edition," in *A Companion to Thomas Jefferson*, ed. Francis D. Cogliano (Oxford, 2012), 491–509.

18. Jackson Turner Main, review of Merrill D. Peterson, *Thomas Jefferson and the New Nation: A Biography, AHR* 76 (1971): 549. Stephen G. Kurtz wrote of "the unfortunate decision to omit footnotes for the sake of what may be a largely mythical body of general readers" (*JAH* 57 [1971]: 909); see also the reviews by James Z. Rabun, *JSH* 37 (1971): 288–90; Harry Ammon, *WMQ* 28 (1971): 487–89; and Aubrey C. Land, *New England Quarterly* 44 (1971): 149–51.

19. This deficiency has been mitigated significantly by the emergence of digital editions of Jefferson's papers.

20. *Jefferson Image*, 186–87.

21. Peterson, *Thomas Jefferson and the New Nation*, 707.

22. For other examples of the "character defense," see Douglass Adair, "The Jefferson Scandals," in *Fame and the Founding Fathers: Essays by Douglass Adair,* ed. Trevor Colbourn (New York, 1974; repr., Indianapolis, 1998), 227–73; Dumas Malone, *Jefferson the President: First Term, 1801–1805* (Boston, 1970), 494–98.

23. *Jefferson Image,* 187.

24. Fawn M. Brodie, *Thomas Jefferson: An Intimate History* (New York, 1974); Annette Gordon-Reed, *Thomas Jefferson and Sally Hemings: An American Controversy* (Charlottesville, Va., 1997). The scholarly revision of the Hemings question began with Winthrop Jordan's study *White Over Black: American Attitudes toward the Negro, 1550–1812* (Chapel Hill, N.C., 1968).

25. Eugene Foster et al., "Jefferson Fathered Slave's Last Child," *Nature* 396 (5 November 1998), 27–28; Report of the Research Committee on Thomas Jefferson and Sally Hemings, Thomas Jefferson Memorial Foundation, January 2000. The report is available at www.monticello.org. For an overview of the controversy, see Cogliano, *Thomas Jefferson,* chap. 6.

26. Merrill D. Peterson, "Introduction to the Virginia Edition," in *The Jefferson Image in the American Mind* (1960; repr., Charlottesville, Va., 1998), ix.

27. Peterson also dismissed the possibility of a sexual relationship between Jefferson and Maria Cosway. He wrote: "Jefferson's feelings towards Maria, while no doubt sexual in origin, had an airy quality that leaves no suggestion for ardent desire. They were gay and light-hearted with each other, affectionate in a pleasant way, flirting at love with neither choosing to embrace it" (*Thomas Jefferson and the New Nation,* 348). The absence of serious consideration of Jefferson's inner emotional life is Fawn Brodie's main criticism of *Thomas Jefferson and the New Nation* (Brodie, "Jefferson Biographers"). Jefferson's inner life was the main focus of Brodie's own biography of Jefferson.

28. Gordon-Reed, *Thomas Jefferson and Sally Hemings,* 224.

29. Peterson, *Thomas Jefferson and the New Nation,* 998, 260.

30. Ibid., 259, 260, 262.

31. Peterson, *Coming of Age,* 4, 46, 48.

32. Ibid., 67.

33. Paul Gaston, "When We Marched for Selma—and Freedom," *The Hook* (Charlottesville, Va.), 410 (10 March 2005), http://www.readthehook.com/files/old/stories/2005/03/10/essayWhenWeMarchedForSelma.html.

34. Merrill D. Peterson, "Remarks by Merrill D. Peterson, Thomas Jefferson Professor of History, at the Rotunda, March 17, 1965 as part of the 'Sympathy for Selma' Ceremony," typescript in the possession of Nini Almy. I am grateful to Almy for sharing a copy of these remarks with me.

35. *Jefferson Image,* 378.

12

"That Woman"

Fawn Brodie and Thomas Jefferson's Intimate History

ANNETTE GORDON-REED

When Fawn Brodie published *Thomas Jefferson: An Intimate History*, it attracted much attention—bad and good—from both the scholarly world and the public at large. The 1974 book, which has never been out of print, forever changed the way historians and others write about the personal life of Jefferson. Indeed, one could say that Brodie's work marked the beginning of all really serious attempts to bring the private Jefferson into considered view. What does "considered" mean in the context of Jefferson biography? It is not as if no one had written about the personal side of Jefferson before Brodie's book appeared. Certainly, Henry Randall, in his three-volume biography, made his version of an "intimate" look at Jefferson a major selling point of his work. In preparation for his project, he spent time at Monticello talking with, among others, members of Jefferson's family. His portrait of Jefferson, Randall wrote, was enriched by the anecdotes told by the Jefferson grandchildren who had heard "from the lips of their parents" stories about Jefferson as "the son and the husband." Their own recollections of him added even more substance to the picture because "they had ample opportunities for observing him in nearly every relation of private life—as the father, the master, the neighbor, the friend, the companion under all circumstances, the farmer, the business man." Furthermore, their memories were unquestionably creditable because they were "rendered precise and minute by the intense interest with which, from infancy, they regarded everything connected with one revered as few men were ever revered in their families."[1]

Randall accomplished at least three important things with the above-quoted passages. First, he demonstrated that his biography was unique because of his unprecedented access to members of Jefferson's family who were, for the first time, willing to share their memories of their famous relative, along with some of the family correspondence. Second, he established the "legal-family-as-expert" and "legal-family-as-owner" views of Jefferson biography, which privilege the perspectives of officially recognized relatives over so-called outsiders who, if they said any thing remotely critical of Jefferson, were deemed to be his "enemies." The language Randall employed suggests that Jefferson's family was ever-present, subjecting him to near continuous scrutiny. He could not do anything they did not know about, and had he done anything untoward or disturbing under their watchful gaze, that would have diminished their reverence for him. That they revered him "as few men were ever revered" in their family was proof that he could not have done anything to betray that feeling. If outsiders could not possibly know certain things because they were not present "in the family," neither could they have a form of what could be called a property interest in the family. They could no more pronounce on what happened at Monticello than they could, without the family's permission, build a cabin on Jefferson's mountain.

The practice of relying on family members to give the true and accurate story about their relative and treating them as the owners of the family history is wildly out of synch with current understandings that tend to value independent, outside views over those from inside the family that is under study. It is a safe bet that historians in the future will not likely treat the Bush family, the Clintons, and the Obamas as the final, and most reliable, authorities on matters involving their families, particularly not on matters that might cause those families embarrassment or discomfort. Taking the "legal-family-as-expert/owner" route does something else that has distorted views about what we might call the private Jefferson. It encouraged readers to see him through the eyes of his grandchildren, a very tricky proposition that ignores the important stages of what was a very long life, more than half of which was lived before his grandchildren were even born—even more years before they were old enough to have a true understanding of their surroundings.

Third, Randall—with the aid of Jefferson's family—presented a compelling, but uncomplicated, portrait of "the sage" at home on his farm surrounded by his loving daughters and gaggle of grandchildren. Even the enslaved made appearances in Randall's depiction of Jefferson's private realm as a sort of antebellum slavery apologist's dream world in which African

Americans lived happily under the regimes of benevolent masters, of whom Jefferson was said to have been an exemplar. What is striking about Randall's passages is the undercurrent of defensiveness that runs through them about Jefferson the family man and Jefferson the slaveholder. Both the family and the enslaved were offered up as if they were character witnesses. Without knowing anything about Jefferson as a slaveholder, one could understand why Randall, who wanted to sell books in the South, too, would be anxious to find witnesses to certify that Jefferson was a "good" master. We know now what was stake in the depiction of life at Monticello, but it is quite telling that Randall felt so strongly that witnesses to Jefferson's character as a family man were, in fact, needed.

With all of this, Randall's book set the template for descriptions of family life at Monticello for decades to come, a presentation that fostered the view of the Jefferson/Randolph clan as an uncomplicated bunch bound together by their endless affection for the beloved patriarch—Jefferson. One of the few discordant notes, sounded in works that followed Randall's, was the recognition of the troubles of Jefferson's son-in-law Thomas Mann Randolph Jr.[2] The major biographers after Randall—Dumas Malone most notably—did their part to further the picture of a generally harmonious domestic situation—interspersing their telling of the story of Jefferson's more boisterous and contentious political life with family letters and anecdotes that supported the image Randall put so firmly in place back in the 1850s.

While Leonard Levy, with his book *Jefferson and Civil Liberties: The Darker Side* (1963), is often credited with delivering the first full modern challenge to the more heroic version of Jefferson advanced by writers such as Randall and Malone, Brodie's biography of Jefferson can be considered the first modern—and major—reworking of Jefferson the man in full.[3] She accomplished this, in large measure, through her startling reconfiguration of domestic life on the mountain. Brodie traveled straight to the heart of the world that Randall created and complicated in substantial ways—this is understatement, of course—his narrative. She disregarded and, in doing so, demolished the "legal-family-as-expert/owner" template, casting the domestic arrangements at Monticello in a wholly new light. Love most assuredly remained at the center of the Jefferson household as Brodie reconstituted it. But Brodie knew, and was willing to acknowledge and work with, the truth that the great soul singer Reverend Al Green pronounced long ago: "Love will make you do right. Love will make you do wrong."[4]

It was, in part, her willingness to explore the second part of that formulation—the way that love can make people do less than admirable things, including quite surprising and seemingly uncharacteristic things—or just make them "do wrong"—that lifts *Thomas Jefferson: An Intimate History* to the status of a masterpiece. It is not that her book is without flaws or that she gets everything exactly right (although Brodie got Thomas Jefferson *the man* almost exactly right). The most pedestrian of works can be perfectly accurate when nothing daring or especially useful is attempted. Instead, what makes her book a masterpiece is that it is the product of a courageous, first-rate, creative, and disciplined mind. It reflects Brodie's curious intellect, her large and wise soul—asking the right questions, grappling with them, answering most of them in the right way, in a sincere attempt to get as close to the historical truth as possible within the limits of human imagination and capacity. Masterpieces completely change the nature of the conversation. Brodie's *Thomas Jefferson* meets all these criteria.[5]

How did Brodie go about her attempt to discover the intimate Thomas Jefferson? A good Freudian, Brodie saw Jefferson's early family experiences shaping his personality and setting the course of his progress through life. Although not much is known about Jefferson's early years with his parents and siblings—the fire that destroyed their family home, Shadwell, was an incalculable loss to historians—her chapters "The Parents" and "A Sense of Family" pulled together as much as could be learned, seeking to move beyond the recitation of genealogy and vital statistics to try to capture the events and situations in the young Jefferson's life that would have indelibly marked his character. She discusses the high points—Peter Jefferson's accomplishments, the importance of Jane Randolph Jefferson's forebears—but she noticed potential conflicts in the picture. How does a young boy who adores his father, and loses him just when approaching manhood, deal with that father's larger-than-life persona? What did it mean to Jefferson, an eldest son, to have spent his formative years not at Shadwell, but with his nuclear family at his Randolph cousins' Tuckahoe, which his father superintended after the death of his mother's prominent kinsman? What did it mean to Jefferson that the house was not really his, and that it already had its own scion, his cousin, Thomas Mann Randolph, who was only a year older, and—in later years— the father of his son-in-law? What about Jefferson's parents and the small, but likely still significant, class difference between them? Peter Jefferson was a prosperous but self-made man who did not come from an illustrious and old Virginia family. Jefferson's mother, however, was a member of the Randolph family, which had a long history in Virginia.[6] Brodie's intuition that Jefferson's mother influenced him far more than Jefferson scholars let on—Merrill Peterson wrote that Jane Jefferson was "a zero quantity in his life"—has been borne out since Brodie's writing by the creative work of Susan Kern in her interpretation of archaeological discoveries at Shadwell and early written family records. In addition, the historian Virginia Scharff's intrepid searching out of Jane Jefferson's origins and life as mother to the future president and his siblings suggests that she was, in fact, very much *something* to her eldest son.[7]

Brodie followed the same pattern in writing about Jefferson's wife, Martha Wayles Skelton Jefferson. Again, there is scant information about Martha. Almost nothing of substance written by her survives. That has not prevented historians from drawing a picture of the Jefferson marriage by filling in the blanks with visions that were not always rooted in the eighteenth-century understanding of what upper-class marriages between white people were like, and what they were about. Brodie echoes the sentiment that the Jeffersons' union was a true love match. She did not, however, accept at face value Jefferson's characterization of his marriage, in his late-in-life attempt at autobiography, as "ten years in unchequered happiness." Martha suffered through many difficult pregnancies and postbirth illnesses. The couple lost three of their children, and Martha may have suffered a miscarriage during that ten-year period. It could not have been a continuously happy situation for the pair.[8]

Brodie also knew that love could not have been enough to stamp out all potential conflict. Referencing comments that Jefferson made about marriage in letters to his daughters, she persuasively suggested some points of conflict that may have existed in the Jeffersons' union. She also highlighted more specific instances when husband and wife did not seem to be on the same page—for example, Martha's initial refusal to accompany her husband to Williamsburg when he became governor of Virginia. He wanted her to come. She did not want to go and, for a time, stayed home. Jefferson could not always make his wife do what he wanted her to do.[9]

In the chapter entitled "The Two Marthas" and in other sections of the book, Brodie highlighted Jefferson's relationships with the daughters of his marriage, Martha and Maria. With determined and observant close reading

of the letters that passed between the three, she revealed the tensions, competing interests, and insecurities, along with the deep love, that existed between
father and daughters. Relationships that had been presented before in almost
treacly fashion came alive as dynamic, flesh-and-blood connections, with
all the messiness and uncertainty close connections can generate. What did
Jefferson's daughter Martha's intense devotion to him mean for her marriage
to Thomas Mann Randolph Jr.? What did it mean for her younger sister,
Maria, who seemed to have understood that her sister was her father's favorite? Brodie handled this latter question beautifully, describing an exchange of
letters between Jefferson and Maria not long after the election of 1800. Maria
plaintively noted the "distance which Nature [had] placed" between her and
Martha, saying that she rejoiced that in Martha her father had "a source of
comfort and one who is in every way worthy of you." Maria went on to say
that, despite Martha's advantages, she yielded "to no one" in her love for her
father. Brodie wrote in a way that allows the reader to almost see Jefferson,
the father, at first dimly aware, and then finally getting the message, and
with great tenderness and care, answering his younger daughter's obvious
plea for reassurance. The situation is made all the more poignant because
Maria would be dead within three years, and, as Lucia Stanton has noted
and Brodie also sets out with great feeling, her father would be shattered by
her death.[10] Love is rendered deep and complex; feelings fragile, hearts were
easily broken and, often, quickly healed. The Jefferson family became more
real and human in Brodie's hands than it had ever seemed before.

After Brodie, everyone who wrote seriously about Jefferson's family
noticed and noted the tensions she observed, as well as the love that most
assuredly existed. Since the publication of *Thomas Jefferson: An Intimate
History*, a plethora of books, articles, and essays have appeared discussing
Jefferson's relations with his family and, in particular, with the women in
his life. Brodie's work made it clear that, in order to understand him, one
had to do more than use the people in his life as props—as human versions
of scenery—to highlight the spectacle of Jefferson. Taking the people who
surrounded him seriously as human beings in their own right (to see them
as he knew them in their day-to-day interactions with him) brings Jefferson
himself into clearer view.

It was not, however, Brodie's more nuanced and sophisticated view of
Jefferson's relationships with his parents, wife, and daughters that drew the
intense interest in her biography and created a permanent space for her in

the field of Jefferson studies. It was, of course, her no-holds-barred expansion of Jefferson's family to include six half-siblings to his wife, including Sally Hemings, who became his mistress, and the seven children he had with her. This caused a firestorm of controversy that propelled the book to the best-sellers list and Brodie to a great degree of notoriety.

Brodie did not discover Sally Hemings. Hemings had been linked to Jefferson since the 1790s, but entered the larger public consciousness in 1802 when the notorious journalist and former Jefferson partisan James Callender published an exposé of Jefferson's private life. Callender's dealings with Jefferson have been recounted often.[11] Until Brodie, no Jefferson biographer had accepted that Hemings was Jefferson's mistress. Each insisted instead that Callender and his sources were lying about Jefferson—Callender in pique because Jefferson had denied him a government position after he had worked on behalf of Jefferson's election to the presidency; his neighbors out of partisan animus, jealously, or both. Randall handled the matter obliquely, mentioning Hemings (although not by name) in a footnote describing, and disputing, an item that had appeared in the Federalist press about Jefferson's daughters "weeping to see a *negress* installed in the place of their mother."[12] He spent far more time addressing Jefferson's payments to Callender and whether they were for the purpose of attacking John Adams. Given the mores of the day and, no doubt, his concern for the sensibilities of Jefferson's legal white family, it is understandable why Randall, in effect, buried the one Callender story that has lived through the ages. It would simply not do to talk too much about a sex scandal (and an interracial one at that) involving a founding father. Randall knew it was important, however, because he actually spoke with Thomas Jefferson Randolph about the matter when he was working on his *Life of Jefferson*. In that conversation, Randolph apparently convinced him that the story was untrue. He famously reported his conversation to a later Jefferson biographer, James Parton, who queried him on the subject.[13]

In the years that followed, Malone and other Jefferson scholars were more vigorous in denying that Jefferson and Hemings were involved in a long-term liaison. Brodie's biography incensed them and many others. Brodie's open acceptance of the paternity of Elizabeth Hemings's children by John Wayles, Jefferson's father-in-law, together with the incorporation of Sally Hemings into Jefferson's biography as his enslaved mistress, sent the Jefferson establishment reeling. Her open employment of Freudian psychology to assess Jefferson's personality constituted another irritant.[14] Virginius Dabney, a Jefferson descendant and former editor of the *Richmond Times-Dispatch,* wrote an entire book rebutting not only Brodie's biography (and Barbara Chase-Riboud's similarly themed historical novel) but also casting doubt on the Hemings relationship.[15] Julian Boyd, the first editor of *The Papers of Thomas Jefferson,* referred to Brodie as "that woman" and at least once directed an assistant not to give her information when she asked for it. Her book was subjected to scathing reviews by, among others, David Herbert Donald and Garry Wills. It is hard to imagine now the level of vituperation employed to discredit a work that has, in the fullness of time, turned out to have been remarkably on target about a major issue in Jefferson's personal life.[16]

Few would now deny the fevered reaction to Brodie's Jefferson biography—the sexual and racial panic that undergirded many of the often hysterical (that is, both irrational *and* humorous) responses to it—and the challenge to notions of authority the book represented. But, at base, adding a long-term enslaved African American mistress and seven children to Jefferson's domestic arrangements immediately and fundamentally disrupted Randall's foundational narrative of Monticello as a paradise of domestic white family felicity. It is one thing to point out that the many letters expressing undying devotion and love that passed between family members tended to obscure deeper passions, conflicts, and uncertainties among them. It was quite another to add *a whole new family* to the mix—a family who lived, not at some distant plantation, but at Monticello among Jefferson's daughters and the beloved grandchildren who had helped create the vision of Monticello as a near paradise with themselves as the rightful objects of historical attention for anyone writing about Jefferson's private life. Every line written about the way that family operated would, at least, have to be reconsidered. That notion discomfited many.

"How could he have done something like that when he loved us so?" Ellen Coolidge essentially asked in an 1858 letter to her husband. She denied that her grandfather had children with Hemings and claimed that his nephew Samuel Carr had fathered all of her children. "There are such things . . . as moral impossibilities," she wrote; for Jefferson to have kept a mistress, in full view of his grandchildren, was among them. As Randall did—in part under her direction—she offered Jefferson's happy family as a bulwark against the

stories about his private life. In Coolidge's formulation, love could only make her grandfather do what she, in her nineteenth-century upper-class southern slaveholding white woman way, would think was "right." And right was most assuredly not keeping a mixed-raced woman as a mistress and fathering children with her when he had other people, herself included, to love. Her grandfather could not "do wrong" in this fashion.[17]

Brodie destroyed this line of thinking by offering, with great daring, a different story of love. Jefferson, while a middle-age man serving as minister to France, fell in love with his deceased wife's teenage half-sister who, by complete chance, had been sent to live with him in Paris in 1787. This was well before Ellen Coolidge was even thought of—before, indeed, Ellen's mother and father had even courted and married. The home that she and her siblings conjured in opposition to the Hemings story did not even exist. She offered the world of 1813 to answer what had happened in Paris between 1787 and 1789. That should have been obvious to all. Apparently, it was not.

Here was another instance where Brodie's narrative about the Hemings story invites us to reconsider the way Jefferson scholarship works in general. There has long been a problem with the concept of chronology. In descriptions of domestic life at Monticello, it is always somewhere between 1813 and 1826. Jefferson is always in his seventies or eighties, and he is always surrounded by numerous and ever-present grandchildren. Hosts of visitors are constantly ascending Monticello mountain to visit the great man. The tyranny of the grandchildren's recollections, and the family letters they wrote when they were old enough to write, takes the period they lived at Monticello and stretches it back to, often, the very beginning of Jefferson's time at the place. Letters from the 1820s are used to make arguments about unrelated things that happened in the 1780s or 1790s. Brodie's placement of the origins of Jefferson's relationship with Hemings chronologically in the story of his life—not in 1802 when Callender first wrote about the affair, while most Jefferson biographies raised it when they discussed Jefferson's presidency—required thinking about Jefferson in that time and place. When he was in Paris, he was not the kindly grandfather of Ellen's memory. Instead, he was a man in the prime of his life whose senses had been reawakened in a new setting after the devastating loss of his wife and the professional pain he suffered due to his disappointing tenure as governor of Virginia. Jefferson's grandchildren did not know this man and, therefore, could not speak of him with authority.

Brodie's acceptance of the Hemings story was bad enough. Her talk of love, which exasperated many who wrote about Jefferson, actually drove some to utter distraction. And here the issues of gender and the writing of history come very much into play. When reading the many comments and reviews of Brodie's work, it becomes apparent that at least some of the male historians found her talk about love to be icky "girl stuff," not worthy of a serious consideration of a statesman's life. Those all too common putdowns of the work of women writers in all genres, "romantic" and "romance," cropped up often to describe Brodie's work on this subject. These words, then and now, are not so subtle code for "girl stuff," and we know what that is worth—certainly not as much as "guy stuff" or "manly stuff."

See Jefferson wheel and deal with Hamilton for the placement of the nation's capital. See him sink Federalism into the abyss. See him agonize over the Missouri crisis because it threatens to destroy the Union and the country he had helped to create. Wheeling and dealing, sinking, creating—this putative "guy stuff" involved the building and shaping of the country. Because such things are about the country, "our" country, they are ultimately about what Jefferson did, or did not do, for us. *See Jefferson in distress at the thought that the young woman he desires might decide that freedom in France was better than living in slavery with him at Monticello. See Jefferson try to figure out how to handle his "shadow family" and get his children into freedom and whiteness while maintaining his relations with his legal white family.* The latter two actions were more immediately about the demands of his inner life, not the country. As important as those things may have been to him, what do they have to do with us?

Getting beyond Jefferson's responsibilities to us, and how to hold him to our standards and scold him when he does not meet them, was precisely what Brodie attempted with her *Intimate History.* What mattered to him that did not relate to his role as a statesman? The tendency to render life in the home as "soft" and unimportant is not unique to Jefferson biography and, of course, can be seen as sexist. The public things an important man did were the things that mattered the most. Jefferson believed that himself. It does not take much imagination to know why he would not have been so keen on having too much attention paid to the true circumstances of his life. But as almost always happens, at the end of the day, the private world looms the largest for the individual. When Jefferson was facing death and financial ruin, the country he helped establish and served for years, like the state for which he had devoted so much time and energy dreaming, fretting, and planning, did little to come to his rescue. In 1824, just two years before Jefferson died, to honor Lafayette on his triumphant tour of the United States, a tour that brought him to Monticello, the U.S. Congress voted to give the French patriot $120,000 and grants of land. There was nothing for Jefferson. The state lottery that he hoped would help save him from going under did not materialize. Virginia simply could not be bothered. Instead, there he was in 1826, a frail man attended in his final days by his white family and the enslaved people who included members of his extralegal family. Neither the country nor the state of Virginia was there to help ease his passage out of this world. It was this man, and all that had gone into making him, that Brodie wanted us to know.[18]

Brodie did, in fact, deal with public side of Jefferson and tried, with some success, to show how the inner Jefferson—to borrow a characterization from Andrew Burstein—shaped his public persona and actions.[19] She drew a connection between the personal and the political. Passion and sentiment were parts of his life in the public realm as well as the private. It was Jefferson, the man himself, who interested Brodie. One of the oddest charges against her was that she was out to destroy Jefferson, when it is so clear to anyone who reads her work with an open mind that she loved him as much as Malone did, if not more, for it was not a love born of her personal needs. She loved him while being able to see and talk openly about his faults. In fact, a weakness of the book is her tendency at too many points to strain to excuse his behavior.

Brodie's incorporation of the Hemings story into Jefferson's biography accomplished another important thing that opened the door to a new way of thinking about life at Monticello. It may well have been her most transformative contribution. In directly challenging the "legal-family-as-expert" notion that had held sway in more traditional Jefferson biography, and accepting the Hemings story, she explicitly rejected the words of Jefferson's grandchildren, Thomas Jefferson Randolph and Ellen Randolph Coolidge, who denied that Jefferson fathered Hemings's children. Randolph reportedly named Jefferson's nephew Peter Carr as the father and, as noted earlier, Coolidge named Samuel Carr. Instead, Brodie relied on the words of Madison Hemings, a former enslaved man at Monticello, who said that he was the son of Thomas Jefferson and Sally Hemings, as well as Israel (Gillette) Jefferson, who had also been enslaved on the mountain, who corroborated Hemings's account.

To establish the equality of the men for purposes of writing history, she placed their recollections in an appendix along with Henry Randall's letter to James Parton, which contained Thomas Jefferson Randolph's statements about the Hemings matter. At the time her book was published, the Coolidge family would not allow Ellen Coolidge's letter to be printed in its entirety, although they allowed Brodie to view it. She described what was in it. This was enormously important because Brodie put the words of people who had been enslaved on par with the people who had enslaved them. Instead of the normal picking and choosing of the words of those enslaved at Monticello—printing the "good" things they said while leaving out, or failing to analyze, anything "bad"—she invited readers to take the men seriously, as if their words actually mattered. That she was willing to argue that these men, former enslaved African Americans, were telling the truth while the upper-class white Randolphs were lying was enormously significant and groundbreaking given Jefferson's stature. These men were defining who he was in opposition to what his white family and generations of scholars had said. It was a courageous thing for her to do, because more than "the truth" was at issue.

There is a wonderful and instructive scene in Stanley Kubrick's classic film *Paths of Glory,* an antiwar movie about soldiers who are made to pay the ultimate price for the blunders of their superiors. When a corporal calls out a lieutenant for cowardice, drunkenness, and the reckless killing of one of his own men, the lieutenant reminds him of the way their very hierarchical world worked: "Have you ever tried to bring charges against an officer? It's my word against yours. Whose word do you think they are going to believe? *Or let me put it another way. Whose word do you think they are going to accept?*"[20]

Whose word are they going to accept? Later in the film, the corporal and two others are made scapegoats to shield a general from blame for a failed offensive. It was not about what everyone knew to be true. Everyone knew that the general had screwed up, and that innocent men were going to be sacrificed to maintain his status. Truth was immaterial. To uphold the world as they knew it and valued it, truths had to be submerged or ignored—even if that meant slaughtering the innocent. The hierarchy could not stand if every person was given the dignity of being heard. Only certain people were eligible to construct the truth, and when push came to shove, the elect were supposed to stand together. Until Brodie, at least in mainstream histories,

Madison Hemings and Israel Gillette Jefferson were outside of the magic circle for purposes of telling the truth about life on the mountain.

In bringing these men into "the circle," Brodie forcefully introduced the idea that people outside of Jefferson's legal family could shape our understanding of his domestic life, even about things that were of critical importance. The enslaved on the mountain had legitimate stories to tell—and not just about the Hemings matter—and those stories could be accepted into the narrative of Jefferson's life, even when they did not reflect well upon him and his family. This was light years away from Randall's use of the words of enslaved people, which he deployed in service of bolstering the image of Jefferson as a man and as a slaveholder.

To be sure, much had happened between the time of Randall and the time of Brodie. By 1974, the historiography of slavery, which did not exist when Randall wrote, had embraced the notion that the words of enslaved people should help inform our understanding of the world of American slavery. Seeing that world through the eyes of the slaves, long a practice among African American historians, became a part of the mainstream academy in the 1950s with the publication of Kenneth Stampp's *The Peculiar Institution*.[21] Brodie was not doing anything completely new when she inserted enslaved people into the narrative of life at Monticello. It was new, however, for scholarship on the American founders and their relationship to slavery. It was one thing to allow slaves to shape our understandings of slaveholders in general, or even men and women who held no special position in the hearts and minds of most Americans. It was something altogether different to allow the slaves of the founding fathers to shape, in ways perhaps not always flattering, the historical view of these revered figures. Witness the parade of hapless alternative fathers to Sally Hemings's children: Peter Carr, Samuel Carr, Randolph Jefferson, and Randolph Jefferson's sons. These men mean nothing to most Americans, so assertions about them appear to require less substantiation.[22]

Brodie's intervention was not without weaknesses. Her detractors pounced upon factual errors such as her confusing Light Horse Harry Lee with Richard Henry Lee.[23] She worked far too hard to prove that Jefferson and Hemings had a son named Tom, who was sent away from Monticello after the Callender articles appeared. In that instance, she disregarded Madison Hemings's statement that the child his mother bore upon her return from France died as an infant. And even if one thinks there is something to

Sigmund Freud's pronouncements, there is good reason to question Brodie's use of his theories at particular points—there is the much-maligned association of the moldboard plow with sexuality and comparing the number of times Jefferson used the word "mulatto" before Sally Hemings arrived in Paris with the number of times he used it after. (By the way, there was a huge increase.)[24] But other historians have written far sillier things than that in the course of producing, sometimes, even great work. The immense tragedy of all this is that Brodie, who died in 1981, did not live long enough to see her daring vindicated. Fortunately, her book, with all its flaws and important truths, is still with us.

Notes

1. Henry S. Randall, *The Life of Thomas Jefferson*, 3 vols. (New York, 1858), 1:vii.

2. See, for example, Dumas Malone, *Jefferson and His Time*, 6 vols. (Boston, 1948–81), 5:665–66, 6:157, 303, 449, 452–56, 459, 460, 472, 481, 488.

3. Leonard W. Levy, *Jefferson and Civil Liberties: The Darker Side* (Cambridge, Mass., 1963).

4. "Love and Happiness," Al Green, 1975, http://www.youtube.com/watch?v=pSTwdYmT7Pw.

5. Annette Gordon-Reed, "Introduction," in Fawn M. Brodie, *Thomas Jefferson: An Intimate History* (repr., New York, 2010), xvii–xviii.

6. Fawn M. Brodie, *Thomas Jefferson: An Intimate History* (New York, 1974), chaps. 2 and 3.

7. Merrill D. Peterson, *Thomas Jefferson and the New Nation* (New York, 1970), 9; Susan Kern, *The Jeffersons at Shadwell* (New Haven, Conn., 2010); Virginia Scharff, *The Women Jefferson Loved* (New York, 2010).

8. Brodie, *Thomas Jefferson*, 86, 109, 117, 125–27, 131–32, 140–41, 144–45; TJ, "Autobiography," 6 January 1821, *TJW*, 46.

9. Brodie, *Thomas Jefferson*, 27, 109, 117, 125–27, 131, 140, 144.

10. Ibid., 328–29, 377–81.

11. For one of the most thorough accounts, see Michael Durey, *With the Hammer of Truth: James Thomson Callender and America's Early National Heroes* (Charlottesville, Va., 1990), esp. 104–6, 110–13, 119–20, 145, 157–60.

12. Randall, *Life of Thomas Jefferson*, 3:19.

13. Annette Gordon-Reed, *Thomas Jefferson and Sally Hemings: An American Controversy* (Charlottesville, Va., 1997), 80–81.

14. Ibid., 3–4, 111–12, 182–83, 205–6; Francis D. Cogliano, *Thomas Jefferson: Reputation and Legacy* (Charlottesville, Va., 2006), 173–75; Scot A. French and Edward L. Ayers, "The Strange Career of Thomas Jefferson: Race and Slavery in American

Memory, 1943–1993," in *Jeffersonian Legacies,* ed. Peter S. Onuf (Charlottesville, Va., 1993), 427–34.

15. Virginius Dabney, *The Jefferson Scandals: A Rebuttal* (New York, 1981). On Dabney's life and career, see Marie Morris Nitschke, "Virginius Dabney (1901–1995)," in *Encyclopedia Virginia,* http://www.encyclopediavirginia.org/Dabney_Virginius_1901–1995.

16. Virginia Scharff, "What's Love Got to Do with It? A New Turner Thesis," *Western Historical Quarterly* 40 (2009): 16; David Herbert Donald, "By Sex Obsessed," *Commentary* 58, no. 1 (1 July 1974): 96–98; Garry Wills, "Uncle Thomas's Cabin," *New York Review of Books* 21 (18 April 1974): 26.

17. Ellen Randolph Coolidge to Joseph Coolidge, 24 October 1858, Coolidge Family Papers, Special Collections, University of Virginia Library.

18. Annette Gordon-Reed, *The Hemingses of Monticello: An American Family* (New York, 2008), 646–47, 650–51, 658–59.

19. Andrew Burstein, *The Inner Jefferson: Portrait of a Grieving Optimist* (Charlottesville, Va., 1995).

20. Stanley Kubrick, *Paths of Glory,* 1957. Emphasis added.

21. Kenneth M. Stampp, *The Peculiar Institution: Slavery in the Ante-Bellum South* (New York, 1956).

22. See Dabney, *Jefferson Scandals;* Robert F. Turner, ed., *The Jefferson-Hemings Controversy: Report of the Scholars Commission* (Durham, N.C., 2011).

23. Brodie, *Thomas Jefferson,* 125, 444; Holman Hamilton, review of Fawn M. Brodie, *Thomas Jefferson: An Intimate History, Journal of Southern History* 41 (1975): 108.

24. Brodie, *Thomas Jefferson,* 229–30, 298, 358–59, 439–40, 531–32.

Afterword

A Tribute to Peter Onuf

GORDON S. WOOD

Thomas Jefferson's Lives, dedicated to the scholarly career of Peter Onuf, is very different from most such tributes, which contain a wide variety of subjects that have little or no relation to one another. By contrast, the scholarly contributions in this volume written by Peter's friends and students have an extraordinary thematic unity. All these sophisticated pieces written by these Jefferson scholars have a common purpose—to describe and analyze the writings by many important biographers and historians of Thomas Jefferson, beginning with Jefferson's own effort at autobiography, followed by the lives of Jefferson composed by George Tucker and Henry Stephens Randall in antebellum America up through the Jefferson biographies written in the last half of the twentieth century. It is fitting that Peter be included in this volume.

Peter was the third holder of the University of Virginia's Thomas Jefferson Foundation Professorship, and over the course of two decades or so he more than ably filled that eminent post. Over that time he produced not only a large number of graduate students interested in the era of Jefferson but also an enormous body of work on Jefferson. But that work is different from that of the other biographers and historians of Jefferson included in this volume. His interpretations of Jefferson in many respects are superior to most, if not all, of the previous interpretations. Unlike many of his predecessors, he has never written a full, traditional biography of Jefferson, although in 2016 he authored with Annette Gordon-Reed *"Most Blessed of the Patriarchs,"* an intellectual biography of the man. Peter has also written a series of influential studies on various aspects of Jefferson's life and on Jefferson's relationship to the new nation. He has also edited numerous books, sometimes collaborating with other scholars, dealing with Jefferson and a variety of subjects in the early republic.

In all of his writings Peter has always demonstrated an acute sensitivity to the contingent and problematical nature of events in the era of the Revolution and early republic. People in the past, including Jefferson, did not know their future any more than we know ours, and they scarcely understood the implications of what they were doing. Things turning out differently from what the participants in the past expected makes for ironic developments everywhere, to which Peter, with his very ironic sensibility, naturally responds. Indeed, his acute sense of irony is perhaps the principal source of his infectious humor. He generally takes an ironic stance toward Jefferson: what else could he do with the slaveholding aristocrat who has become the nation's supreme spokesman for democracy? His ironic sensibility also tells him that history, as he recently put it, "is largely a chronicle of frustrated intentions and unintended consequences." This is probably the most important insight that the study of history offers us.

Peter is also acutely sensitive to the gap between then and now. He has always been aware that the past, especially the past of 200 years ago, is a foreign country where they do things differently. "The Revolutionaries," he writes in a typical statement, "could not have had our idea of what a 'nation' is, or of how it might be situated in the 'world.'" Indeed, for Peter words such as "empire, "nation," and "people" should not be taken for granted. They are not timeless in meaning, and they are always slippery. Such terms possessed, as he likes to say, a "protean" character for people in the past; and he has spent a considerable amount of time in his career spelling out the fluid meanings they had for Jefferson and his fellow Americans. He has always been fascinated with language and has urged us to pay attention to the indeterminacy of these kinds of terms and to set them in their proper context. Indeed, the subtitle of one of his important books is *The Language of American Nationhood.*

Moreover, he has always understood the difference between mythology and reality, between memory or "invented traditions" and critical history, and he has always written sensibly about these distinctions. He knows better than most the many distorted ways Americans have used Jefferson over the past two centuries.

Peter has tended to be much more involved in the age of Jefferson, in the larger arena of Jefferson's life, than nearly all of his previous biographers and historians. He has constantly tried to set Jefferson and the new United States in the broadest and most cosmopolitan context possible. Indeed, I believe he has always sought to place Jefferson and the new nation in an international setting, to see Jefferson and the new nation as part of the greater Atlantic world, in ways that previous historians of Jefferson never did.

In an important article in the journal *Diplomatic History* in 1998, Peter set forth a fresh reading of the Declaration of Independence, something not easy to do with that much-studied document. In his new interpretation he contended that we have been too fascinated with the second paragraph of the document and thus have ignored the diplomatic significance of the first paragraph. "For Jefferson," Peter said, "the great, self-enacting claim of the Declaration is to be found in its opening sentence, where Jefferson claimed that the Americans constituted 'one people.'" This was an assertion of nationhood, said Peter. Once the old "political bands" with Britain had been dissolved, this new nation of "one people" was entitled by the law of nations "to assume among the powers of the earth, the separate and equal station" to which it was entitled. Instead of "leaving the separate states in an anarchic condition with respect of one another," Peter contended, the Declaration "drew them into a new and unprecedented 'union,' a union that could in turn forge further alliances—or unions—across the Atlantic." In other words, Jefferson saw his Declaration, as he insisted in 1825, as "the fundamental act of union of these States." Jefferson never saw the federal Constitution of 1787 creating a "more perfect union," but in fact he believed, as Peter pointed out, that it "*jeopardized* union by consolidating too much power in the new national government." Our preoccupation with "the inherent and inalienable rights" emphasized in the second paragraph of the document, wrote Peter, has deflected attention away from Jefferson's "bold claim to nationhood." All the Lockean talk of natural rights in the second paragraph "may have been pregnant with profound implications for later generations of democrats and libertarians, but it is Jefferson's *first* paragraph that changed the world."

"'Union,'" said Peter, "was not the belated outcome of the Revolution, but rather its central and defining problem from the very outset." And although this union was a weak one, it was backed up by the strong republican sentiments and durable ties of affection among the American people themselves. Contrary to the fears of the Federalists, who had little confidence in the people and saw the possibility of disunion everywhere, Jefferson claimed in his inaugural address that the United States was "the strongest Government on earth."

The Americans' union was connected to the world, or at least to the European states, which is how the revolutionaries conceived of the world. The Revolution became "an epochal moment in international history"; it promised a "new order for the ages." By declaring independence the Americans were claiming membership in the international community of the European sovereigns. But not just membership, they wanted to change the world. They aimed to use commerce and enlightened diplomacy to create a world union that would work to eliminate the causes and pretexts for war. The Articles of Confederation—this treaty or constitution among thirteen states ("the terms 'treaty' and 'constitution' were used interchangeably")—was a model that might be extended throughout the Atlantic world. Hence, Peter concluded, "the American Revolution was first and foremost an episode in the history of the European states-system."

This article was a tour de force of scholarship. With it not only did Peter revitalize the importance of the American Revolution for historians of diplomacy, but he made new sense of the Americans' Model Treaty of 1776 and its significance for the enlightened world of the late eighteenth century. In subsequent works Peter has gone on to extend his argument and to make the importance of the Revolution for federalism and for the international community of states the signature theme of his scholarship.

Another example of the many insightful and original contributions that Peter has made to our understanding of the era of the early republic is his essay on Jefferson and slavery. To say anything new about this much written about subject was no small achievement, and the fact that Peter has done so is a tribute to the brilliance of his scholarship, to his ability to extract new meaning from what was there all along—in this case, Jefferson's well-known statements in his *Notes on the State of Virginia*. In his essay, which was Peter's 1997 presidential address to the Society for Historians of the Early American Republic, he called our attention to Jefferson's conception of the African American slaves as a separate and distinct nation. As far as I know, no previous historian had ever made this point in the way Peter did, even though Peter was working with the same material that countless scholars had read and used. "Virginia slaves," Peter wrote, "were a people without a country, a captive nation forcibly restrained from vindicating their rights against their white oppressors." Hence the slaves could have no patriotism, no love of country. "The blacks and whites of Virginia," said Peter, drawing out the implications of Jefferson's writings in a manner that no one else had quite done, "were two distinct nations whose natural relationship was one of war, and the only arbiter between nations at war was a 'just God.'" By "defining slavery as a state of war," Peter went on, "Jefferson could only conceive of its abolition in terms of a peace that would secure the independence and integrity of two distinct nations, each with its own 'country.'" From this logic flowed Jefferson's solution to the problem of slavery: "The captive nation must be liberated, 'colonized' in some new country that they could claim as their own, and thus be declared and recognized as 'a free and independent people.'" "Jefferson therefore concluded," said Peter, "that the only humane and prudent policy was expatriation—from a country that blacks could not claim as their own without violence—and colonization in new land." We all knew that Jefferson favored colonization of the freed slaves, but, as far as I know, never before Peter's paper had the logic of Jefferson's thinking been laid out so clearly. That is the measure of a keen mind and a very perceptive historian.

There are many such original studies of Jefferson in Peter's remarkable body of scholarship, a body of scholarship that has fundamentally enriched and expanded our understanding of Jefferson and his era beyond anything his predecessors have done.

Although Peter has nearly always sought to place Jefferson in the broadest possible context, he never loses sight of the man himself. And his Jefferson always turns out to be a much more complicated figure than he was for previous historians and biographers of the man. As Peter often says, he is "conflicted" about Jefferson. Consequently, he has a different relationship to this overarching historical figure than his predecessors. He has always seemed to me to be much more impartial about Jefferson than most of the previous biographers. Peter has a detachment they never had. He has no deep-rooted emotional need either to celebrate or to bash Jefferson. As he repeatedly told his classes at the University of Virginia, he would never be considered as an apologist for Jefferson. At the same time, however, he never seeks to blame Jefferson for the ills of America.

In his course on the Age of Jefferson he always made Jefferson the central figure. Peter says that he has "always found great pedagogical value in the sharp focus on Jefferson, because it allows us to talk about everything." Peter delights in exploiting the fact that Jefferson was a polymath involved in everything. He doesn't treat Jefferson with awe and reverence, but neither does he focus on Jefferson's obvious hypocrisy, which would be so easy to do. He sees Jefferson as a frustrating subject to study. "I get very impatient with him as a person," he has been quoted as saying. Nevertheless, he writes that Jefferson "rewards close study." "This is partly," he says, "because there are so many important tensions or contradictions that we need to attend to that he illustrates." Despite Peter's acute sense of the difference between the past and present, he manages to bring Jefferson alive for his audiences and to make him part of our own time. He uses Jefferson, he says, "as an individual to get into those problems" of our time. Indeed, he points out that "practically anything you can think of, you can approach in Jefferson and see what look to us to be conflicting imperatives and tensions."

Peter's detachment toward Jefferson is remarkable, especially when you consider that he taught for over two decades at Mr. Jefferson's university, where, as Merrill Peterson once pointed out, "one could scarcely turn a corner or open a door without expecting to encounter the founder."

Although Peter quotes Jefferson endlessly, his impartiality has allowed him to weave his way through the political minefields that litter our historical profession—something not easy to do, given the sensitive subject matter about which he writes. He has avoided being cast as either a progressive or a conservative in his take on Jefferson and the founding period of American history, and, consequently, he is courted and honored by all political sides.

Although he usually maintains some distance from Jefferson, sometimes he can be passionate about the man and his ideals, especially in his public lectures. Many of his students have noted his passion, and they call him an exciting lecturer. I have seen him lecturing in various venues throughout the world, and it is a sight to behold. He lectures without notes and with great emotion, and his tie is never tightly knotted.

In October 2011, Andrew Jackson O'Shaughnessy, on behalf of the Robert H. Smith International Center for Jefferson Studies of which he is director, brought a number of scholars to Moscow in order to spread knowledge of Jefferson and his values to the scholarly world in Russia. In Moscow, Peter's lecture on Jefferson and freedom to a group of Russian academics attained a new height of evangelical passion. All those Americans who were there will attest to this. Some of us like to think that it was his lecture that brought the Russian dissidents into the streets of Moscow within weeks of our visit. Peter has courage. I believe that he is Andrew O'Shaughnessy's most important weapon in furthering the aim of the International Center for Jefferson Studies of bringing Jeffersonian ideals to the world.

In 2012, many wondered why Peter retired from his academic position. After all, he still rides his bike vigorously and is still very youthful in spirit. It turned out that he had to make room for another career. As many readers might know, in 2008 Peter helped launch a three-person *BackStory with the American History Guys* radio talk show program helping to educate the American people about their history.

He and two colleagues, Edward L. Ayers of the University of Richmond and Brian Balogh of the University of Virginia, started with a single station in 2008 and then went national with a weekly show on National Public Radio. The National Endowment for the Humanities gave the show a $350,000 production grant that allowed it to become a weekly program, now more simply called *BackStory.* It has grown rapidly and is carried on 173 stations; episodes have been downloaded as podcasts more than 7.8 million times. In 2017, Yale's Joanne Freeman, who earned her Ph.D. under Peter, and Nathan Connolly of Johns Hopkins joined the show as regular hosts, allowing Peter to step back and contribute on occasion as a guest host.

The emergence of the show was not easy. As the show's producer said, the challenge for these academics was "to find their voices as radio professionals instead of as professors." At first, these professors thought the idea of a radio show dedicated to history was crazy. Peter was quoted as saying that he doesn't think "history is funny." But those who know Peter know he makes it funny. He says that what he loves most about the show are the times "when we surprise each other with something weird, off-the-wall, some weird angle." When books finally disappear from our lives, we can be happy knowing that history will be kept alive by his and his colleagues' radio talk show.

It is not just his books, his lectures, and his radio show that have mattered in the way he has spread historical knowledge. An equally important contribution to history has been his mentoring of numerous students and fellow historians. He has directed the dissertations of twenty-eight students, including some of the most prominent members of the profession.

But that figure of twenty-eight does not do justice to his influence, his outreach, to students around the world. He has always been free with his time for young scholars seeking help and advice. And if the number of people he thanks in the acknowledgments sections of his books is any indication, they reciprocate in kind. Peter has acted as a midwife to a spate of books on Jefferson and on various issues concerning the early republic, from the subject of nationhood to the issue of time and history. He has helped foreign students get their books published even when he has no official connection with them. No wonder they call him "the paterfamilias of Jefferson's intellectual family."

I believe he has more friends in the American historical profession than any person I know. How could he not have so many friends, given his amiable personality and his willingness to joke and laugh about everything? He is known and admired by everyone in the profession. And the profession has recognized the role he has played in the lives of so many students and fellow historians. At the American Historical Association (AHA) convention in 2013 Peter was presented with the Nancy Lyman Roelker Mentorship Award—a fitting tribute to his extraordinary generosity. "Dr. Onuf," the announcement in the newsmagazine of the AHA reported, "established an environment of trust, openness, and respect and a model of mentoring that is valued by all who interacted with him."

Peter continues to be a teacher and mentor to all those who constitute his intellectual family. So dedicating this volume to him is our way of congratulating him for a career well done. And may it long continue in articles and books and even on the airwaves.

Contributors

R. B. Bernstein is Lecturer in Law and Politics at the City College of New York; he is also Distinguished Adjunct Professor of Law at New York Law School, where he has taught since 1991. Born and raised in New York City, he was educated at Amherst College, the Harvard Law School, and New York University. His books include *The Founding Fathers: A Very Short Introduction* (2015); *The Founding Fathers Reconsidered* (2009), a finalist for the 2010 George Washington Book Prize; and *Thomas Jefferson* (2003). He also is coeditor, with Barbara Wilcie Kern and the late Bernard Schwartz, of *Thomas Jefferson and Bolling v. Bolling: Law and the Legal Profession in Pre-Revolutionary America* (1997). He is now completing *The Education of John Adams* (forthcoming 2020), *Hamilton: A Very Short Introduction* (expected 2020), and *Jefferson: A Very Short Introduction* (expected 2020).

Andrew Burstein is the Charles P. Manship Professor of History at Louisiana State University and the author of five books about Thomas Jefferson: *The Inner Jefferson* (1995), *Letters from the Head and Heart: Writings of Thomas Jefferson* (2002), *Jefferson's Secrets: Death and Desire at Monticello (2005)*, *Democracy's Muse: How Thomas Jefferson Became an FDR Liberal, a Reagan Republican, and a Tea Party Fanatic, All the While Being Dead* (2015); and, with Nancy Isenberg, the *New York Times* ebook bestseller *Madison and Jefferson* (2010). With Isenberg, he has most recently coauthored *The Problem of Democracy: The Presidents Adams Confront the Cult of Personality* (2019). Among his other books are *The Passions of Andrew Jackson* (2003), a main selection of the History Book Club; *The Original Knickerbocker* (2007), the first full-length biography of Washington Irving by a professional historian; and *Lincoln Dreamt He Died: The Midnight Visions of Remarkable Americans from Colonial Times to Freud* (2013). He has also published journal articles and contributed book chapters to several edited volumes on Jefferson's life and times. He earned his Ph.D. from the University of Virginia.

FRANCIS D. COGLIANO is Professor of American History at the University of Edinburgh where he also serves as Dean International for North America. He specializes in the history of the American Revolution and the early national United States. He is the author of *Emperor of Liberty: Thomas Jefferson's Foreign Policy* (2014) and *Thomas Jefferson: Reputation and Legacy* (2006). Presently he is writing a book on the relationship between Jefferson and George Washington.

JOANNE B. FREEMAN is Professor of History and American Studies at Yale University, specializing in the politics and political culture of early national America. She is the author of the award-winning *Affairs of Honor: National Politics in the New Republic* (2001) and the editor of *Alexander Hamilton: Writings* (2001) and *The Essential Hamilton* (2017). She is a cohost of the American history podcast *BackStory* and a frequent commentator on PBS, NPR, CNN, and MSNBC. Her Yale online course, *The American Revolution,* has been viewed by hundreds of thousands of people around the world. Her most recent book, *The Field of Blood: Congressional Violence and Road to Civil War* (2018), explores physical violence in the U.S. Congress in the decades before the Civil War.

ANNETTE GORDON-REED is Charles Warren Professor of American Legal History at Harvard Law School and Professor of History in Harvard's Faculty of Arts and Sciences. Gordon-Reed won the 2009 Pulitzer Prize in History and the 2008 National Book Award for Non-Fiction, along with twelve other awards, for *The Hemingses of Monticello: An American Family* (2008). She was awarded a 2009 National Humanities Medal by President Barack Obama, and was named a MacArthur "Genius" Fellow in 2010. Among her other honors are a Guggenheim Fellowship in the Humanities (2009) and a fellowship from the Dorothy and Lewis B. Cullman Center for Scholars and Writers at the New York Public Library (2010–11). In 2011, she was elected to membership in the American Academy of Arts and Sciences. Gordon-Reed's other published works include *Thomas Jefferson and Sally Hemings: An American Controversy*

(1997); *Vernon Can Read: A Memoir* (2001), which she cowrote with the famed civil rights leader, lawyer, and presidential adviser Vernon E. Jordan Jr.; *Race on Trial: Law and Justice in American History* (2002), a collection of scholarly essays she edited examining the role and impact of race in significant American legal cases over the last 200 years; and *Andrew Johnson* (2011), a short biography of America's seventeenth president. In 2016, Gordon-Reed published with coauthor Peter S. Onuf *"Most Blessed of the Patriarchs": Thomas Jefferson and the Empire of the Imagination.* Gordon-Reed is a 1984 graduate of Harvard Law School and a 1981 graduate of Dartmouth College.

NANCY ISENBERG is the T. Harry Williams Professor of American History at Louisiana State University. She is author of the New York Times best seller *White Trash: The 400-Year Untold History of Class in America* (2016). She is also author of *Fallen Founder: The Life of Aaron Burr* (2007), which was a finalist for the *Los Angeles Times* book prize in biography. *White Trash* was a finalist for the *Los Angeles Times* book prize in history, the Anthony Lukas Book Prize for nonfiction from the Columbia School of Journalism, and the John Kenneth Galbraith Award from PEN America. She was #4 on *Politico Magazine*'s 2016 list of the "50 Most important thinkers." With Andrew Burstein, she has written *Madison and Jefferson* (2010), a Kirkus "Best Book of the Year." Their next coauthored book is *The Problem of Democracy: The Presidents Adams Confront the Cult of Personality* (forthcoming in 2019). *Sex and Citizenship in Antebellum America (1998),* her first book, received the best book award from the Society for Historians of the Early American Republic in 1999. She has published in the *New York Review of Books, Washington Post, American Scholar, Chronicle of Higher Education, Journal of American History, American Quarterly,* and *Hedgehog Review.* She received her Ph.D. in history from the University of Wisconsin–Madison.

JAN ELLEN LEWIS was Dean of Faculty and Professor of History at Rutgers University, Newark, where she taught American history since 1977. She taught in the history Ph.D. program at Rutgers, New Brunswick, as well, and served as a Visiting Professor at Princeton University. She received her A.B. from Bryn Mawr College; A.M.s in both American culture and history from the University of Michigan; and the Ph.D. in history from the University of Michigan. A specialist in colonial and early national history, with a particular interest in gender, race, and politics, she was the author of *The*

Pursuit of Happiness: Family and Values in Jefferson's Virginia (1983). She was the coeditor (with Peter N. Stearns) of *An Emotional History of the United States* (1998); (with Peter S. Onuf) *Sally Hemings and Thomas Jefferson: History, Memory, and Civic Culture* (1999); and (with James Horn and Peter S. Onuf) *The Revolution of 1800: Democracy, Race, & the New Republic* (2002). She reviewed history and fiction for the Phi Beta Kappa *Key Reporter.* She coauthored a college-level American history textbook, *Of the People* (2010). Lewis held fellowships from the National Endowment for the Humanities, the Philadelphia Center for Early American Studies, the Center for the History of Freedom at Washington University, and the International Center for Jefferson Studies. She chaired the New Jersey Historical Commission and the American Historical Association's Committee on Women Historians; she also served on many boards, including the Advisory Board of the International Center for Jefferson Studies, and the editorial board of the *American Historical Review.* She was an elected member of the American Antiquarian Society and a Fellow of the Society of American Historians.

J. JEFFERSON LOONEY is the Daniel P. Jordan Editor of The Papers of Thomas Jefferson at Monticello. He is the founding editor and project director of the Jefferson Papers Retirement Series. Sponsored by the Thomas Jefferson Foundation, Inc., Charlottesville, Virginia, fifteen volumes of this definitive edition of Jefferson's writings and correspondence between 1809 and 1826 have been published, and a sixteenth is in press. Looney was formerly editor and project director of the *Dictionary of Virginia Biography,* and he is the author or editor of several works on the history of Princeton University. He did his doctoral research in British history under Lawrence Stone at Princeton.

CHRISTINE COALWELL McDONALD teaches history at Westchester Community College. Former Research Associate at Monticello's Robert H. Smith International Center for Jefferson Studies, she is a graduate of the American University and St. John's College. She has published several articles and essays on Jefferson, his family, and education in the early republic

ROBERT M. S. McDONALD is Professor of History at the United States Military Academy. He is author of *Confounding Father: Thomas Jefferson's Image in His Own Time* (2016) and editor of *The American Revolution: Core Documents* (2019), *Sons of the Father: George Washington and His Protégés* (2013), *Light and Liberty: Thomas Jefferson and the Power of Knowledge* (2011), and *Thomas Jefferson's Military Academy: Founding West Point* (2004).

JON MEACHAM is a presidential historian, contributing writer for *The New York Times Book Review,* contributing editor at TIME, and Pulitzer Prize–winning author whose books include *The Soul of America: The Battle for Our Better Angels* (2018), *Destiny and Power: The American Odyssey of George Herbert Walker Bush* (2015), *Thomas Jefferson: The Art of Power* (2012), *American Lion: Andrew Jackson in the White House* (2008), *American Gospel: God, the Founding Fathers, and the Making of a Nation* (2006), and *Franklin and Winston: An Intimate Portrait of an Epic Friendship* (2003). A regular guest on "Morning Joe" and other broadcasts, he is a distinguished visiting professor at Vanderbilt University.

BARBARA OBERG is a Senior Historian Emerita in the Department of History at Princeton University, where she served as the General Editor of the Papers of Thomas Jefferson for fourteen years. She is a graduate of Wellesley College and received her Ph.D. from the University of California, Santa Barbara. Before coming to Princeton she was the Editor of the Papers of Benjamin Franklin at Yale University. In 2008–9, she held the R. Stanton Avery Distinguished Fellowship at the Huntington Library and has also held fellowships from the International Center for Jefferson Studies at Monticello and the American Philosophical Society. She has coedited two books, *Federalists Reconsidered* (with Doron Ben-Atar, 1998) and *Benjamin Franklin, Jonathan Edwards, and the Representation of American Culture* (with Harry S. Stout, 1993). She has served as President of the Society for Historians of the Early American Republic, the Association for Documentary Editing, and the Society for Textual Scholarship. She chairs the Board of the Omohundro Institute for Early American History and Culture at the College of William and Mary and serves on the Council of the American Philosophical Society. Her latest edited volume, *Women in the American Revolution: Politics, Gender and the Domestic World,* appeared in 2019.

RICHARD SAMUELSON is Associate Professor of History at California State University, San Bernardino. He is the editor of *The Collected Political Writings of James Otis* (2015). He received his Ph.D. in American history from the University of Virginia and has held fellowships or teaching positions at

Princeton University; Claremont McKenna College; the National University of Ireland, Galway; and the University of Glasgow.

HERBERT SLOAN is Professor Emeritus of History and Senior Scholar at Barnard College, Columbia University. The author of *Principle and Interest: Thomas Jefferson and the Problem of Debt* (1995), he is at work on a study tentatively titled "Disappointed Founders," on those who came to see the Constitution as a mistake.

BRIAN STEELE is Associate Professor of History at the University of Alabama at Birmingham. He is the author of *Thomas Jefferson and American Nationhood* (2012). More recent work has appeared in *Variaciones Borges* and the *Journal of American Studies*.

GORDON S. WOOD is Alva O. Way University Professor Emeritus at Brown University. He received his B.A. degree from Tufts University and his Ph.D. from Harvard University. He taught at Harvard University and the University of Michigan before joining the faculty at Brown in 1969. He is the author of many works, including *The Creation of the American Republic, 1776–1787* (1969), which won the Bancroft Prize and the John H. Dunning Prize in 1970, and *The Radicalism of the American Revolution* (1992), which won the Pulitzer Prize for History and the Ralph Waldo Emerson Prize in 1993. *The Americanization of Benjamin Franklin* (2004) was awarded the Julia Ward Howe Prize by the Boston Authors Club in 2005. His book *Revolutionary Characters: What Made the Founders Different* was published in 2006, and *The Purpose of the Past: Reflections on the Uses of History* was published in 2008. His volume in the Oxford History of the United States, entitled *Empire of Liberty: A History of the Early Republic, 1789–1815* (2009), was given the Association of American Publishers Award for History and Biography in 2009, the American History Book Prize by the New York Historical Society for 2010, and the Society of the Cincinnati History Prize in 2010. In 2011, he was awarded a National Humanities Medal by President Obama and the Churchill Bell by Colonial Williamsburg. In 2011, he also received the Arthur M. Schlesinger Jr. Award from the Society of American Historians. His most recent book is *Friends Divided: John Adams and Thomas Jefferson* (2017). He is a fellow of the American Academy of Arts and Sciences and the American Philosophical Society.

Index

The abbreviations TJ, *History,* and *Papers* stand for Thomas Jefferson, *History of the United States of America during the Administrations of Thomas Jefferson and James Madison,* and *The Papers of Thomas Jefferson,* respectively.

Harding, Warren G., 158, 162
Harrison, Gessner, 50
Hartz, Louis, 203
Harvard University, 15, 206, 216n38,
   248–49, 259, 262
Harvard University Press, 222
Hawks, Francis, 57–58, 61n24
Hawks, Frank Lister, 168n9
Hay, George, 136
Hemings, Elizabeth, 255, 271
Hemings, Madison, 230–31, 234–35,
   275–77
Hemings, Robert, 104n40
Hemings, Sally: about the TJ relationship
   with, xvii, 220, 227, 246; addressed
   by Brodie, 256, 265–78; addressed by
   Gordon-Reed, 256–57; addressed by
   M. G. Kimball, 208–10; addressed by
   Peterson, 254–57; addressed by S. N.
   Randolph, 83–101, 101n3; addressed
   in Hamilton biographies, 165, 174n82;
   addressed in other TJ biographies, 5–7,
   204, 271–72; biographers' dismissal of
   TJ relationship with, xx, xx–xxi, 14,
   76, 95, 229–31, 234–35, 254–56, 271–73;
   Callender allegations of TJ relationship
   with, 5–6, 37, 53–55, 227, 256, 271,
   273, 277; children of, xvii, 76, 95, 100,
   255–57, 271–78; descendants of, DNA
   testing, xxi, 256; Paris, presence in, 92,
   255, 273, 278; portrayal in Vidal novel,
   142; presence at TJ's death, 105n45
Henrietta Golden (fictional character), 142
Henry, Patrick, 6, 67, 69, 78–79, 127
Herrick, Myron, 172n60
Hirst, Francis, 203
"History and Memory" (field of study), xiv
History of the Life and Times of James Madi-
   son (Rives; 1859–68), 153
History of the Republic of the United States
   (J. C. Hamilton; 1857–64), 152–55, 162
History of the Republic of the United States
   of America, as Traced in the Writings of
   Alexander Hamilton and of his Contem-
   poraries (J. C. Hamilton), 168n7

History of the United States of America
   during the Administrations of Thomas
   Jefferson and James Madison (Henry
   Adams), xix, 10, 106–21
History of the United States of America
   during the First Administration of
   Thomas Jefferson (Henry Adams), 168n2
Hitler, Adolph, 182, 191
Hochman, Steven H., 227, 230–31
Hofstadter, Richard, 14, 193, 197n58
Home Journal, 77
Honest John Adams (Chinard), 204
Hopkinson, Joseph, 168n9
Howells, William Dean, 77
Hyland, William G., Jr., 238n7

inalienable rights, 246, 261, 283. See also
   equality/equal rights, democracy and
   the concept of
In Defense of Thomas Jefferson: The Sally
   Hemings Sex Scandal (Hyland), 238n7
Inquiry into the Origin and Course of
   Political Parties in the United States (Van
   Buren), 62
Inventing George Washington: America's
   Founder in Myth and Memory (Lengel),
   216n43
Ireland, 158
Irving, Washington, 63
Isenberg, Nancy, 8–9, 214n11, 214n16
It's a Wonderful Life (film), xv–xvi

Jackson, Andrew, ix, 11, 62, 76, 79, 179
James (TJ slave), 100
Janson, H. W., 122n6, 122n8
Jefferson, George, 102n15
Jefferson, Israel Gillette, 277
Jefferson, Jane Randolph, 5, 65, 78, 268–69
Jefferson, Martha. See Randolph, Martha
   Jefferson
Jefferson, Martha Wayles Skelton, 69, 227
Jefferson, Peter, 5, 64–65, 78, 250, 252, 254,
   268–69
Jefferson, Polly (nee Mary/Maria). See
   Eppes, Mary Jefferson (aka Polly, Maria)

of papers of, 43n27; as source of TJ
biographical material, 2–3, 4, 51–52,
57–58, 68; TJ description, 29; TJ relationship, 18, 34, 70–72, 98, 133–34
Madison and Jefferson (Burstein and Isenberg), 214n11
Main, Jackson Turner, 254
Main Currents in American Thought (Parrington), 203, 248
Malcolm, William, 140
Malone, Dumas: characterization of TJ,
185, 267; death of, 229; denial of TJ-
Hemings relationship, 271; examining
the TJ autobiography, 28–29; Peterson
comparison to, 244, 246, 250–52;
published biographies by, 219–37; as
TJ biographer, x, xx, 4, 14–16, 41; 2012
conference discussion on, 2; on University of Virginia faculty, 221, 225; writing
Second Term, 231, 240n32, 242n51; writ-
ing TJ biographies, 202, 209, 211–12,
217n52. See also *Jefferson and His Time*
(Malone; six-volume biography)
Malone, Elisabeth Gifford, 229
Malone, Gifford, 229
Malone, Lisa, 229
Marshall, John: about the Washington
biography, 2–3; challenging the Wash-
ington biography, 34, 36, 39; damage
done to TJ's reputation by, 68–69; TJ
portrayal by, 177–78; TJ's relationship
with, 49, 136, 138, 226
Martha Washington Cook Book, The (M. G.
Kimball), 207
Marxism, 248
Mason, John M., 168n9
Massachusetts Historical Society, 203, 206,
223, 253
Mayo, Bernard, 41, 83
Mazzei, Philip, 79
McClure, James P., xi
McDonald, Christine Coalwell, 4–5
McDonald, Forrest, 164–65, 173n72,
174n81, 174n86

McDonald, Robert M. S., 4–5
McDougall, Alexander, 140
McKitrick, Eric, 127, 143–44n1
McManus, Jane, 145n10
Meacham, Jon, 17–18
Melinda (TJ slave), 100
*Memoir, Correspondence, and Miscellanies
from the Papers of Thomas Jefferson* (ed.
T. J. Randolph), 44n35, 50, 61n24, 90,
145n5, 147n35, 153
Memoir of the Life of Aaron Burr (Knapp),
8–9
Memoir of Theophilus Parsons (Parsons),
168n2
Memoirs of Aaron Burr (Davis; 1836–37),
8–9, 128–29
"Memory Studies" (field in history), xiv
Mencken, H. L., 190
Merry, Anthony, 172n56
Merton, Robert K., 200
Mexico, 82n18
Michaux, André, 37
Miller, John C., 163
Miller, Perry, 15, 248–49
Mind of Thomas Jefferson, The (Onuf),
xxii
Miranda, Francisco de, 81n18
Mississippi Valley Historical Review, 209
Mitchell, Broadus, 163–65, 174n81
Model Treaty (1776), 284
monarchy/monarchists, 33–34, 119, 138,
142, 149, 154, 177–78, 180, 188
Monroe, James, 54, 70, 119–20
Monticello: design and building of, 18;
desperate finances and sale of, 39, 95;
deterioration and vandalism, 85; M. G.
Kimball as curator, 209, 212, 222; pur-
chase and restoration of, 205, 207
Monticello Monograph (series), 229
Moore, Thomas, 145n11
"more perfect union." *See* union, concept
of
Morris, Gouverneur, 18, 72, 149, 167–68
Morse, John Torrey, 9–10, 156–57, 170n30

Randolph, Carolina Jefferson, 50, 94, 97, 104n35
Randolph, Edmund, xiii, 29, 33
Randolph, John, 122n16, 227
Randolph, Martha Jefferson, 44n35, 71–72, 85, 88, 90–91, 93–94, 96–97, 99, 208–9, 269–70
Randolph, Mary, 50
Randolph, Sarah N., xix, 4, 7–8, 16–17, 80, 83–101, 101n3, 103n19
Randolph, Thomas Jefferson ("T.J."), 4, 6–8, 29, 34, 39, 50, 54, 64, 70, 76, 77, 85, 90, 98–99, 101, 109, 128, 131, 153, 271, 275–76
Randolph, Thomas Mann, Jr., 7, 77, 84, 93–94, 267–68, 270
Rayner, B. L., 47
R. E. Lee: A Biography (D. S. Freeman), 207
religion: about TJ's views on, xvii, 3, 58, 73, 75; criticism of TJ's views on, xiii, 3, 56–57, 61n24, 111; disestablishment of Episcopal Church, 29; and political philosophy, 109–11; TJ's belief in God, 7, 61n24, 112; TJ's personal expression, 40, 58
Remus (TJ slave), 100
Repository of the Lives and Portraits of Distinguished Americans (Delaplaine), 26
Republic (Plato), 120
republicanism, 32–33, 63, 115, 119, 123n37, 178, 191, 198n71
Republican Party, 34, 53, 127–28, 130, 143, 184, 192–93
Reviews in American History, 144n1
Reynolds, Maria, 37, 79
Rice, Howard, 210
Richmond Recorder, 53–54
Richmond Times-Dispatch (newspaper), 207, 272
"rights of man," TJ and, 120, 224–25, 229, 260–62
Rippy, J. Fred, 195n30
Rives, George, 50
Rives, William Cabell, 153–55

Robbins, Carolyn, 202
Robert H. Smith International Center for Jefferson Studies, ix, xxii, xxiii, xxv, 2, 286–87, 292–93
Roberts, George, 215n35
Roberts, Mary, 215n35
Robertson, Andrew W., 144n1
Robinson, James Harvey, 12
Rochefoucauld-Liancourt, François Alexandre Frédéric, 100, 122n17
Rockefeller Foundation, 223
Roosevelt, Franklin D., ix, xi, 13–15, 20n32, 163, 183–84, 186–87, 189–90, 192–93, 245, 247, 261–63
Roosevelt, Theodore, xi, 158–59
Roosevelt Coalition, 259
Rosenblum, Robert, 122n6, 122n8
rules of evidence, biography and, 144n1
Rush, Benjamin, 188
Russia, TJ studies in, 286–87

Sage of Monticello, The (Malone). See under *Jefferson and His Time* (Malone; six-volume biography)
Samuelson, Richard, 10
Sawvel, Franklin B., 35
Schachner, Nathan, 138–39, 147nn34–35
Scharff, Virginia, 269
Schlesinger, Arthur, Jr., xii, 1, 10
science/scientific method, TJ and, 18, 27, 52, 65–66, 73, 107, 110–12, 116–21, 123n17, 185, 187
secession, 116, 180, 245
Selma, Ala., 259–62
Sergeant, Katherine, 227
Seurat, Georges-Pierre, 107, 122n6, 122n8
Sewanee Review, 193
Shadwell, Va., 40, 233, 268–69
Shakespeare, William, 134–35
Shaw, Lemuel, 233
Shays's Rebellion, 210, 218n58
Sheridan, Eugene R., 44n39
Sherman, Stuart, 192
Short, William, 207
Shuffelton, Frank, 32, 38, 43n24, 236–37

Recent Books in the JEFFERSONIAN AMERICA SERIES

Era of Experimentation: American Political Practices in the Early Republic, Daniel Peart

Collegiate Republic: Cultivating an Ideal Society in Early America, Margaret Sumner

Amelioration and Empire: Progress and Slavery in the Plantation Americas, Christa Dierksheide

Becoming Men of Some Consequence: Youth and Military Service in the Revolutionary War, John A. Ruddiman

Patriotism and Piety: Federalist Politics and Religious Struggle in the New American Nation, Jonathan J. Den Hartog

Between Sovereignty and Anarchy: The Politics of Violence in the American Revolutionary Era, Patrick Griffin, Robert G. Ingram, Peter S. Onuf, and Brian Schoen, editors

Citizens of a Common Intellectual Homeland: The Transatlantic Origins of American Democracy and Nationhood, Armin Mattes

The Haitian Declaration of Independence: Creation, Context, and Legacy, Julia Gaffield, editor

Confounding Father: Thomas Jefferson's Image in His Own Time, Robert M. S. McDonald

Blood from the Sky: Miracles and Politics in the Early American Republic, Adam Jortner

Pulpit and Nation: Clergymen and the Politics of Revolutionary America, Spencer W. McBride

Jefferson's Body: A Corporeal Biography, Maurizio Valsania

Jefferson on Display: Attire, Etiquette, and the Art of Presentation, G. S. Wilson

Jeffersonians in Power: The Rhetoric of Opposition Meets the Realities of Governing, Joanne B. Freeman and Johann N. Neem, editors

Thomas Jefferson's Lives: Biographers and the Battle for History, Robert M. S. McDonald, editor